CHILD ABUSE
AND THE
LEGAL SYSTEM

CHILD ABUSE AND THE LEGAL SYSTEM

Inger J. Sagatun

San Jose State University

Leonard P. Edwards

Santa Clara County Juvenile Court

Nelson-Hall Publishers
Chicago

Project Editor: Dorothy J. Anderson
Typesetter: E. T. Lowe
Printer: Capital City Press
Cover Painting: "Our Children" by Bayo Iribhogbe

Library of Congress Cataloging-in-Publication Data

Sagatun, Inger J.
     Child abuse and the legal system / Inger J. Sagatun and Leonard P.
Edwards.
         p. cm.
     Includes bibliographical references and index.
     ISBN 0-8304-1207-7.--ISBN 0-8304-1420-7 (pbk.)
     1. Child abuse—Law and legislation—United States. I. Edwards
Leonard P. II. Title.
KF9323.S24 1995
344.73'03276—dc20
[347.3043276]   94-28672
                                                                           CIP

Manufactured in the United States of America

10   9   8   7   6   5   4   3   2   1

 ™ The paper used in this book meets the minimum requirements of American National Standard for Information Sciences—Permanence of Paper for Printed Library Materials, ANSI Z39.48-1984.

To Erik and Don

CONTENTS

PART 3

CHILDREN IN COURT   155

PART 4

EMERGING ISSUES IN CHILD ABUSE   229

ACKNOWLEDGMENTS

The authors wish to thank H. Ted Rubin and Michael Agopian for their helpful suggestions on an early draft of this book. We reserve our greatest thanks to Martha McNeely for her invaluable help in typing and editing the manuscript. Her tireless devotion to the numerous drafts enabled us to complete this project.

INTRODUCTION

A dramatic increase in child abuse and neglect reporting in the past ten years has had a remarkable impact upon our legal system. Never before have our courts had to process so many different claims of child maltreatment in so many different legal settings.

The increase has also significantly affected the entire justice system. Law enforcement professionals have had to develop expertise in child abuse investigation and child interviewing techniques. Social workers and probation officers have had to develop expertise in child abuse and neglect investigations and have had to appear in court to testify in highly charged cases. Medical professionals have had to develop expertise in the detection of child abuse and neglect. Their investigative findings are also tested regularly in court proceedings. In addition, attorneys and guardians *ad litem* have had to learn how to represent children in several different types of court proceedings.

One concern with the increased legal activity surrounding child abuse and neglect has been the impact upon the child. The legal system was not designed for children. In fact, the investigative and legal response to child maltreatment may have a traumatic effect upon the child. Courts and legislatures have responded to this issue with new procedures and laws in an effort to make the legal system more sensitive to the child's needs.

Many of these changes have been tested in the court system. The tension between the court's desire to be sensitive to the needs of the child and the due process rights of the accused is faced daily in different court proceedings. Issues such as special exceptions to the hearsay rule, testimony out of sight of the accused, videotaping of testimony, closed-circuit television, and expert testimony relating to the issues of child maltreatment are innovations which may not survive legal challenges. Professionals working in the justice system need to understand these issues, since they may have an impact on their work.

To add to the complexity, these issues may arise in several different legal settings. The claim of abuse may arise in a domestic relations court, it may be the reason for a child protection action, it may be the focus of a criminal prosecution, or it may be the reason for a civil suit by a child against an alleged abuser. Each of these legal settings has its own set of rules and procedures. Each operates under different policies and assumptions about the participants. A claim of child abuse may be found true in one setting and not in another.

This book addresses the principal issues raised by the increase in child abuse and neglect reporting and the response of the legal system. Each chapter presents materials which highlight the most controversial issues in a particular setting. The materials also explain the differences between the various courts and how these differences may lead to conflicting results arising from the same factual setting.

While the majority of the material is legal in nature, the text is not written primarily for law students. It would be best used by college students, graduate students, and professionals who may be interested in careers relating to children's services, social work, probation, mental health, family counseling, or law enforcement.

This text deals with one of the most explosive and important issues facing our society: child abuse and neglect. The reader will be able to appreciate the complexities surrounding child abuse allegations and their treatment by the various parts of the legal system.

PART 1

CHILD ABUSE IN AMERICA

Part One examines the parameters of child abuse and the legal system in America. We begin with a discussion of the scope of the problem of child abuse in the United States. We learn that while child abuse has always been present, our country has only recently begun to intervene on behalf of abused children. In chapter 1 we present a historical overview of child abuse. We turn to an examination of the types of child abuse and neglect in chapter 2. Child abuse includes physical, sexual, and emotional abuse, as well as physical, medical, and emotional neglect. For each type of child abuse we present case examples from different types of court proceedings. We also discuss the indicators that suggest whether abuse has occurred.

Chapter 3 begins with a description of the mandatory reporting laws that trigger the investigation in most child abuse cases. Key professionals who work in the systems that detect, investigate, and process child abuse cases are introduced. The discussion outlines the roles of child protective services and social services workers, law enforcement personnel, attorneys, guardians *ad litem*, judges, and other professionals who are involved with child abuse and neglect cases.

In chapter 4, we discuss the most important person in all of these proceedings, the child. Advocacy for children is a new phenomenon, and in the legal system there is still much confusion about who speaks for the child. In chapter 4 we review each type of legal proceeding in which child abuse may arise and examine who, if anyone, appears on behalf of the child and the role of that person.

CHAPTER 1

Scope and Historical Overview

SCOPE

Child abuse is not a new problem. Children have always been abused and neglected. They are weaker beings, often defenseless and without resources. They are easy to harm. American history is full of recorded cases of child abuse and neglect (Aries, 1962, Radbill, 1987, deMause, 1988). There is consensus among all these authors and others that child maltreatment has existed throughout history. According to deMause: "The history of childhood is a nightmare from which we have only begun to awaken" (deMause, 1988, 1).

Child abuse includes both abuse and neglect. Abuse, in turn, includes physical, sexual, and/or emotional abuse, while neglect may constitute physical neglect, medical neglect, and emotional neglect.

Such child abuse is no longer an ignored phenomenon. Today we are making the most serious effort ever to detect, report, investigate, protect against, and treat harm to children. The detailing of America's legal response to child abuse is the focus of this book.

How Widespread Is Child Abuse?

It is impossible to say precisely how many children are abused and neglected. Clearly, many cases are never detected or reported. Some statistical sources rely on random interview data to estimate incidents, while others rely on reported cases of abuse and neglect, which may include both substantiated and unsubstantiated cases. From these various sources it is possible to glean some understanding of the volume of child abuse cases, but variations in definitions and measurements suggest that great caution must be exercised in interpreting these data.

Perhaps the most realistic estimates of child abuse cases come from random studies which solicit information via telephone and household surveys of the general population. Such incidence studies try to estimate the actual number of children who have been maltreated and whether or not they have been reported to the authorities. The first incidence studies were conducted in the late 1960s and early 1970s. Studies by Gil (1969, 1970, 1971) using national random samples indicated that between 2.53 and 4.07 million individuals had personal knowledge of a child-abusing family. In 1977 Gelles interviewed a random sample of 1,146 families with children between the ages of three and seventeen. Based on this study, Gelles estimated that between 1.2 and 1.7 million children had been physically abused during their childhood (Gelles, 1977). The National Crime Survey (NCS) shows that in 1987 children in the twelve-to-fifteen age group suffered a rate of victimization exceeded only by that of people aged sixteen to twenty-four (Whitcomb, 1992). The National Family Violence Survey, conducted in 1985, found that 1.5 million children suffered very severe physical violence by their parents each year, and that children who were hit by a stick or belt included 6.9 million per year (Strauss and Gelles, 1986). The National Incidence Study reported that in 1986 155,300 children were endangered by sexual abuse committed by parents or caretakers (National Center on Child Abuse and Neglect, 1988). A Gallup poll conducted in 1989 estimated that 25 million Americans, or 15 percent of the adult population, knew children they suspected of being physically or sexually maltreated, while other estimates suggest that over 250,000 children per year are sexually molested (Lloyd, 1991). Finally, according to a 1990 Annual Fifty-State Survey conducted by the National Committee for Prevention of Child Abuse, almost a million children are victims of child abuse and neglect (National Institute of Justice, 1992). Again, the wide variations in estimates may be due to differences in the way *childhood*, *abuse*, and *neglect* were defined and differences in response groups.

Another way to measure child abuse is through the number of cases reported to public authorities. Since 1973, many professionals working with children have been required to report any reasonable suspicions of child abuse to child protective services or law enforcement. The mandatory reporting laws immediately led to a great increase in the number of reports of child abuse. In 1974, there were about 60,000 cases reported, a number that rose to 1.1 million in 1980 and more than doubled during the 1980s (The U.S. Advisory Board on Child Abuse and Neglect, 1990). The American Society for Protecting Children noted a 158 percent increase in abused children from 1976 to 1984 (Daro, 1988). In the authorization for a recent Act of Congress, the Victims of Child Abuse Act of 1990, Congress estimated that over 2 million reports of suspected child abuse and neglect are made each year.[1] According to a recent estimate from the National Resource Center on Child Sexual Abuse (Lloyd, 1991), the latest data indicate that of the children reported to child protective services agencies annually, between 132,000 and 155,900 children have been sexually molested by someone in a caretaking role. This excludes children sexually molested by a noncaretaker.

The FBI's Uniform Crime Reports (UCR) publishes crime statistics reported by nearly 16,000 law enforcement agencies covering 97 percent of the American population. Unfortunately, the UCR provides almost no information on crimes against children, and their statistics are typically not reported by victim age, except for murder victims. It is clear from the UCR data, however, that children also are at high risk for murder and other serious crimes. In 1988, 1,698 children under the age of fifteen were victims of murder, according to the UCR (Federal Bureau of Investigation, 1989). Similarly, in 1988 the National Committee for Prevention of Child Abuse estimated that there were 1,225 reported child abuse fatalities in the U.S. (Whitcomb, 1992). In 1989, at least 1,200 and perhaps as many as 5,000 children died as a result of maltreatment and over 160,000 children were seriously harmed (Daro and Mitchell, 1990). The FBI's 1990 Uniform Crime Report found 4,280 juveniles arrested for forcible rapes. For

1. Victims of Child Abuse Act of 1990, § 201:3266.

other sex offense categories, 16 percent of the offenders were under eighteen years of age. Quite possibly, their victims were equally young (Federal Bureau of Investigation, 1991).

Once a report of child abuse has been reported, investigated, and found likely to be a case meriting further involvement, it may be petitioned to juvenile court if parents or other guardians are involved, or referred to other legal authorities, such as the District Attorney's Office and the criminal courts. In recent years, there has been an increase in such interventions as well. According to Daro (1988), the percentage of reported cases requiring child protective services intervention increased from 30 percent in 1979 to 36 percent in 1980 and to 49 percent in 1983. According to the Victims of Child Abuse Act of 1990, there were 270,000 cases of child abuse and neglect in juvenile and family courts in 1988 (Victims of Child Abuse Act, 1990).

Recent studies show that the average age of the sexually abused child has been on a downward trend since the late 1970s (Lloyd, 1991). Evidence of sexual abuse is found in preschool-aged children much more frequently than twenty years ago. Now it appears that sexual abuse may occur as frequently in children between the ages of five and twelve as it does in adolescents. Studies from the National Resource Center on Child Sexual Abuse note that boys are abused much more frequently than previously thought. As many as 25 percent of the sexual abuse victims may be male. Similarly, more of the abusers are female than was commonly believed. Some clinicians believe that the percentage of female abusers may be as high as 15 percent. One reason for this surprisingly high number may be that sexual abuse of children by adolescents is higher than earlier studies indicated (Lloyd, 1991).

Not all child abuse is reported, and some child abuse and neglect reports are false. Child sexual abuse, in particular, is hard to prove, and many reported cases may remain unsubstantiated. In recent years, we have also seen a steady increase of false accusations of child abuse (see chapter 3 for a further explanation of the mandatory reporting law and the roles of the various professionals and agencies involved, and chapter 6 for a discussion about the problem of false accusations).

Has Child Abuse Always Been This Pervasive?

The question is often raised whether the large numbers of children who have been abused is a recent phenomenon or whether it is a recent discovery of a perennial problem. Is there actually more child abuse or are we simply better at detecting it? We will never know for sure, because of the lack of reliable knowledge in the past. As the historical review indicates, child abuse has always existed. Through our heightened awareness of such problems, many more cases are now being reported. At the same time, there may in fact also be more child abuse because of changing social conditions. Increasing violence in our society, the lack of family stability, the high divorce rate, lack of family and community ties, increased drug and alcohol problems may all have contributed to an increase of child abuse.

In recent years the media have focused much more on the problem of child abuse, raising our awareness of the issue. Spectacular cases such as the famous *McMartin* preschool case out of Manhattan Beach, California, in the early 1990s have focused our attention on the issues surrounding the investigation of child abuse (*People vs. Peggy McMartin Buckey and Ray Buckey*, 1990). At the same time, more social, legal, and community programs have been developed to respond to the problem. These include educational awareness programs for children in the elementary schools, self-help groups for abusive families, and a host of legally mandated programs. As a nation we are more committed to the problem of child abuse than ever before.

HISTORY

Until recently our legal system provided little protection for children. American law is based to a large extent on English common law. In 1601, in England, the Elizabethan Poor Law authorized the wealthy householders of each parish to apprentice children of parents whom they thought were not able to "keep or maintain their children" (Pumphrey and Pumphrey, 1961). The first American settlers brought with them the English attitudes toward children. Apprenticeships were common, and children were subject to the whims of their masters. The law held parents responsible for their children and in turn gave parents the authority to punish harshly. "Spare the rod and spoil the child" was an important standard. Parents did not hesitate to utilize corporal punishment. Parents were generally considered immune from criminal prosecution, except when children suffered permanent injury or when parents inflicted manifestly unfair punishment. Civil law provided even less protection.

The Nineteenth Century

In the first half of the nineteenth century, the larger cities in the eastern United States experienced unprecedented growth in industrialization and the accompanying urban phenomena of crime, child labor, and slums. Immigrants flocked to the cities. As the Industrial Revolution gathered momentum, so did urban slums with gangs of "street urchins" and neglected children. The reform movements of the first half of the nineteenth century brought with them a concern for the welfare of these neglected children (Page, 1982). Two significant child welfare reform movements, the Refuge Movement and the Child Saver Movement, developed during the nineteenth century as a response to the conditions of children in the cities.

The Refuge Movement

Begun in the 1820s, the Refuge Movement sought to remove children from the almshouses for adults and to place them in institutions for children, so-called houses of refuge (deMause, 1988). The first "Refuge statute" was passed in New York State in 1882, and it permitted the incarceration of "neglected and dependent" children in a house of refuge (Pfohl, 1977). The house of refuge statutes were soon copied by many other states.

Not everyone approved of these statutes, charging that children were incarcerated under terrible conditions in the refuge houses. In fact, many children were "housed" in these refuge houses simply because they were poor or orphans, as well as abused, neglected, or delinquent. During this period of early reform, child welfare policies did not focus too much on saving children from cruel or abusive parents; rather, the emphasis was on saving society from future delinquents (Pfohl, 1977). Often, children were removed from their homes based on their poverty status rather than the fact that they were abused or neglected. Not infrequently these children became indentured to factory owners, large farms, or other establishments that needed cheap labor.

In 1838, a Pennsylvania court applied the doctrine of *parens patriae* to a public custody case in *Ex Parge Crouse* which placed a child in a house of refuge on the mother's petition and over the father's objections (Flicker, 1987). *Parens patriae* describes the power of the state to act in the parents' place for the purpose of protecting a child and his or her property. In essence, the doctrine gave the state the authority to serve as a substitute parent and ultimate protector of the child. The nineteenth century American courts did not distinguish between public and private custody disputes in applying the *parens patriae* doctrine to justify state intervention in child abuse cases.

Child protection policies of the early and middle nineteenth century tended to punish children rather than parents. Prior to the 1870s there was

no movement to reduce child victimization. Only after a domestic child abuse case, the so-called "Mary Ellen case," captured the public's attention was the first child protection agency founded in 1874 in New York by Elbridge T. Gerry, an attorney (Dorne, 1989). The Mary Ellen case was first reported to the American Society for the Prevention of Cruelty to Animals, since at the time there were no laws to protect children. The case was brought into court on the argument that Mary Ellen, as a member of the animal kingdom, was entitled to the same protection as abused animals. Apparently, a neighbor had noticed that Mary Ellen had been brutally beaten by her stepmother and had reported the case to the Society for the Prevention of Cruelty to Animals (Nelson, 1984). As a result of the Mary Ellen case, which received wide publicity in the newspapers, Gerry founded the New York Society for the Prevention of Cruelty to Children. With the help of the Society, the stepmother was prosecuted for assault and battery and sentenced to one year of hard labor in the state penitentiary.

In 1881, the New York Society for the Prevention of Cruelty to Children was authorized by statute to place agents in magistrate's courts, to make investigations, and to recommend placements for children coming before the court. This was the first child protection agency in the country. The statute also made it a misdemeanor to interfere with the society's work. The ideology of the society was twofold: to detect and rescue neglected children and to bring the parents to justice. At the same time, similar societies in Boston and Philadelphia rejected the punitive approach advocated by the New York society and emphasized a protective service approach which would allow the child to stay in the family home (Page, 1982).

The Child Saver Movement

The second large reform movement in the nineteenth century was the Child Saver Movement (Kelling, 1987, Platt, 1969). Dominated by middle- and upper-class women, the Child Saver Movement had several different goals. These included protection of children from abuse, restriction and regulation of child labor, supervision of children, and efficient law enforcement. The movement culminated with the passage of the Illinois Juvenile Court Act of 1899. Among other reforms, the act established a separate juvenile court for children, which was based on the well-established concept of *parens patriae*.

The juvenile court became society's legal and social institution for holding children and families accountable for their behavior. Cases came before the court when children were delinquent or ungovernable or parents were abusive or neglectful of their children. Based upon the *parens patriae* doctrine, the juvenile court was mandated and empowered to give these children the care and control that should have been provided by their parents.

The juvenile court was both a legal and a social institution. Relying upon the expertise of sociologists, psychologists, and other experts in human behavior, and utilizing programs and placements intended to rehabilitate and care for children, the juvenile court was a uniquely American experiment in the control of family behavior.

The juvenile court was based in part on the belief that problem children and abused and neglected children resulted from special conditions. It was believed that urban environment, poverty, lack of education, and other social needs often caused delinquency and child maltreatment. The juvenile court's mandate was to save these children. The strategies included a separate court with no contact for the children with hardened adult criminals, a confidential process which would protect the identity of the child and family before the court, and the powers to order services for the children and families needing court intervention and, if necessary, to remove the child from the care and control of the family.

The creators of the juvenile court established procedures emphasizing individualized attention to each case, informal proceedings, and a focus upon the best interests of the child. Since the juvenile court ostensibly acted on the child's behalf, the normal legal rights attached to criminal proceedings were deemed unnecessary. The right to notice, the right to have an attorney, the right to a jury trial, the right to confront and cross-examine witnesses, the privilege against self-incrimination, and related rights were not afforded children who appeared before the juvenile court.

The Twentieth Century

The Juvenile Court

The juvenile court movement swept the country. By 1920, all but three states had created juvenile courts. The new court encompassed a number of unique characteristics:

1. The juvenile court was a special court created for delinquent, neglected, dependent, and ungovernable children.
2. The purpose of the juvenile court was to rehabilitate rather than punish children.
3. No stigma would be attached to children from a court appearance because all records and proceedings were to be confidential.
4. Juveniles were to be separated from adults when incarcerated and placed in special institutions for juveniles.
5. Juvenile court proceedings were to be informal and were to be based more on a social work model rather than a legal model.
6. The use of juvenile probation officers to help the court carry out its purposes. (Wadlington, Whitebread, and Davis, 1987)

From the early 1900s until the 1960s, the juvenile courts functioned more or less unchanged. The courts operated without legal oversight or monitoring. There were hardly any lawyers or legal proceedings, since the juvenile court movement had specifically rejected formal legal process as necessary for the rehabilitation of children.

Although the original reason for the informal and individualized treatment in juvenile court had been to allow for better rehabilitation of minors, over time it became increasingly clear that many minors suffered greatly as a result. Juveniles often received longer "sentences" than adults for the same offense in the name of "treatment," and there were no safeguards built in to protect their constitutional rights. National studies reported practices that failed to provide adequate protection for juveniles and their families from excessive state intervention. Most of the attention was focused on the plight of juvenile delinquents.

The juvenile court system was significantly changed with the rulings by the United States Supreme Court cases in *Kent v. United States* (1966) and *In re Gault* (1967). Both of these cases emphasized the juvenile's rights to due process in a delinquency setting before any state intervention. In the *Kent* case a minor had been transferred to adult criminal court without an adequate hearing. The Supreme Court noted that the minor was receiving the "worst of both worlds," as he received inadequate due process and inadequate care and treatment. In the *Gault* case, a minor had been summarily placed by the juvenile court in a training facility for possibly five years (until age of majority) for a crime for which an adult would have received only a few months in jail. In *Gault* the Supreme Court found that the state had assumed jurisdiction of Gerry Gault without affording him certain constitutional rights. The court ruled that before the state could intervene in an accused delinquent's life, it must provide him with due process, including

1. the right to an attorney;
2. the right to notice of charges;
3. the right to confront and cross-examine witnesses; and
4. the privilege against self-incrimination (the right to remain silent).

Kent and *Gault* were delinquency cases. It took still more time for the law to address the plight of abused and neglected children. Child abuse and neglect issues remained largely unrecognized until the 1970s.

A Major Breakthrough

In the early sixties, national attention towards child abuse issues was greatly increased. The use of radiology made it possible to detect injuries that were not visible to the naked eye. Pediatricians began to suspect that a much larger number of children had been abused than they had previously thought. Dr. Henry Kempe, Professor in the Pediatrics Department, University of Colorado School of Medicine, was the most influential of a team of medical doctors who studied the extent of physical abuse in children. In 1962 Dr. Kempe and his colleagues introduced the term "battered child syndrome" in an important article which successfully brought national attention to the problem of child maltreatment (Kempe, et al., 1962). The "battered child syndrome" has since become a recognized medical diagnosis describing a child who has suffered physical injuries by nonaccidental means (see chapter 13 for more detail).

The work by Dr. Kempe and his coauthors encouraged further research in the field and prompted state and federal governments to design new policies related to child abuse and neglect. More importantly, Dr. Kempe and his colleagues were instrumental in the development of laws requiring physicians and health workers to report suspected cases of child abuse. In 1963 the Children's Bureau of the Department of Health, Education and Welfare issued a model child abuse reporting statute. By 1967 all fifty states had enacted child abuse reporting laws (see chapter 3). Today, the important Kempe Center at the University of Colorado in Denver continues to carry on important research on child abuse.

Federal Legislation

The movement to save children had also reached the federal political arena. In 1909 President Theodore Roosevelt had called for the first White House Conference on Children, with the purpose of making child welfare a major social objective (Proceedings of the White House Conference, 1909). As a result of this conference, the United

States Children's Bureau was created through Congressional legislation in 1912 (Fredericksen and Mulligan, 1972). In 1921, after another White House conference, the Shappard-Towner Act, which was intended to promote maternal-infant health and establish the Children's Bureaus at the state level, was passed (Grotberg, 1977). In 1946 Aid to Dependent Children became part of the Social Security Act. Additional White House Conferences on Children were held in 1950 and 1970, each leading to reorganizations in the federal response to child maltreatment. These acts and conferences were the forerunners of today's child protection agencies and of modern legislation.

In 1974, after sensational media coverage on child abuse and congressional hearings on the subject, the U.S. Congress passed landmark legislation, the first Federal Child Abuse Prevention and Treatment Act (Public Law 93-247; CAPTA).[2] This act established a National Center on Child Abuse and Neglect (NCAN) to serve as a clearing-house of information concerning child protection research and programs. The act also provided states with grant money to investigate and prevent child maltreatment. Only states that had passed mandatory child abuse reporting laws which incorporated several important requirements were eligible for such funding. These requirements involved the immunity of reporters, confidentiality of records, and the appointment of guardians *ad litem* for all abused or neglected children before the juvenile court (Hardin, 1988). (See chapter 4.) Soon most states had amended their laws to include the federal requirements.

Since 1974, reporting laws have been expanded to include all types of child maltreatment and mandatory reporting by many professionals working with children in addition to physicians, such as other health care workers, teachers, and child health care providers (Besharov, 1983). (Chapter 3 describes the duties and regulations under the law in more detail.) Under current statutes all persons

working with children in a professional capacity must report suspected cases. Failure to report is a misdemeanor in most states. Typically, child abuse reporting laws require all suspected cases of child maltreatment to be investigated immediately by a child protection agency or by the police. There is no civil liability for mistaken reports of child abuse and neglect.

In the federal law the National Center on Child Abuse and Neglect (NCAN) was also directed to do the following:

1. compile, analyze, and publish research results on child abuse and neglect;
2. develop and maintain an information clearing-house;
3. compile and publish training materials;
4. provide technical assistance to agencies to develop and execute programs related to prevention and treatment; and
5. conduct research regarding causes and pre-vention.

As a result of the legislation, several regional centers were created to disseminate research and information and to provide technical assistance to states within each region (Page, 1982). The bill authorized $85 million to be spent from 1974 to 1978. In 1978 an "Adoption Reform Act" was added to the Child Abuse Prevention and Treatment Act (Nelson, 1984). Funding was extended through 1982 and 1983. The Act was amended again in 1984 to include assistance to medically disabled infants and the reporting of medical neglect as well as maltreatment of children in out-of-home care. The amendments also expanded the definition of reportable child sexual abuse to include sexual exploitation.

Child protective efforts at the federal level were also evident in Title XX of the Social Security Act, which provided for Social Services funding, including funding for child protective programs. The Social Services Block Grant (Title XX) is the major source of federal funds for social services in the states. For example, Aid to Families with

---

2. Child Abuse Prevention and Treatment Act, 42 U.S.C. §§ 5101, *et seq.*

Dependent Children (AFDC) provides cash assistance to needy children and their families.[3] States have discretion in choosing the programs to which they will target their share of funds from the Social Services Block Grant as long as funds are used to meet broad federal goals (Stein, 1991).

States spend approximately one-half of their Title XX allotment on child welfare services. These funds are the major source of money for child protective services; they are used for investigation, management, and treatment of child abuse cases and to support day care, counseling, information and referral services, legal services, homemaker assistance, and other in-home services (Kimmick, 1985). By 1980 federal expenditures for child protective services amounted to over $325 million (Besharov, 1983).

In 1980 Congress passed the Adoption Assistance and Child Welfare Act, which was intended to remedy problems with state foster care systems (P.L. 96–272).[4] The act made federal funding for foster care and child welfare programs dependent on implementation of federally prescribed reform programs. It was also designed to discourage unnecessarily lengthy foster care, and it imposed comprehensive requirements on state foster care systems to accomplish these goals. In addition to various requirements affecting state foster care programs, it specified a number of procedural protections and benefits for individual children in foster care and their families.

In 1983 the Adoption Assistance and Child Welfare Act of 1980 or Public Law 96–272 was amended to include a "reasonable efforts" mandate which has had profound effects on the operations of the child welfare system and the juvenile courts. The "reasonable efforts" mandate included detailed requirements for the provision of preventive services

to a family prior to a child's removal from the home, for the provision of appropriate services to reunify children with their parents, and for decisive action by the court in securing permanent homes for these children. It included specifications for the contents of a case plan, and the regular review of a case.

In adopting this legislation, Congress shifted the emphasis of federally funded programs in the direction of family preservation services for families of neglected and abused children and away from an earlier emphasis on removing the children. Before federal dollars could be spent on foster care, there had to be a judicial determination that reasonable efforts were expended by the social service agency to prevent a child's removal or permit the child to remain or return home.

In adopting the requirements for court reviews, the Congress clearly placed the juvenile courts in the position of monitoring practices of state and local social services agencies. The Act also required that states establish adequate prevention and reunification services in order to receive funds for foster care costs. As an additional incentive, states were permitted to transfer unused federal foster care funds to the Child Welfare Services program to pay for prevention, reunification, and adoption services.

The Adoption Assistance and Child Welfare Act was ambitious and far-reaching legislation. It was designed to assure that abused children were provided with a stable, permanent, and safe home and to prevent children from being needlessly removed from their homes and placed into foster care (Hardin, 1990). At the same time it was designed to assure quality and safety of foster home placements and to induce far-reaching reforms in foster care practice.

According to Hardin (1990), the quality and impact of the courts' implementation of Public Law 96–272 have been uneven. While improvements in judicial proceedings have been an important factor in successful foster care reforms, full judicial implementation has not occurred in many places. Court practice varies widely regarding

---

3. Aid to Families with Dependent Children (AFDC) 42 U.S.C. §§ 601, *et seq.*

4. The Adoption Assistance and Child Welfare Act of 1980, 42 U.S.C. §§ 420 *et seq.*, 470 *et seq.*, as amended by the Omnibus Budget Reconciliation Act of 1987, Public Law 96-272, §§ 913-9133.

reasonable efforts determinations, with some states fulfilling the law only in theory in order to get federal funding. However, overall the law has forced the courts and social welfare agencies to work more closely and to develop a coordinated decision-making process. The National Council of Juvenile and Family Court Judges, with grants from the Edna McConnell Clark Foundation, has developed "model courts" projects which demonstrate appropriate methods to implement reasonable efforts requirements. For example, such projects have been funded in California, Kentucky, Alabama, North Carolina, Michigan, and Iowa.[5]

Other federal civil legislation has also affected maltreated children. In 1986 the Child Abuse Victims' Rights Act of 1986 was passed.[6] This law created a civil cause of action for children who suffer personal injury as the result of being victims of federal sexual exploitation law violations.

In 1991 the U.S. Congress passed the Victims of Child Abuse Act of 1990.[7] This important act included the following:

a. Improving investigation and prosecution of child abuse cases.
b. Court-appointed special advocate program to be available to every victim of child abuse and neglect.
c. Child abuse training programs for judicial personnel and practitioners to improve the judicial system's handling of child abuse and neglect cases.
d. Federal victims' protection and rights, authorizing . . . the use of an adult attendant in court with the child in cases in which the child was testifying, provisions for a child's live testimony by 2-way closed-circuit television, videotaped depositions of the child and procedures for

handling the videotape, and directions on how to conduct competency examinations and direct examination of the child. It also provided for privacy protection through confidentiality of information and addressed the use of multidisciplinary child abuse teams and the appointment of guardians *ad litem* in different types of cases.
e. Child care worker employee background checks.
f. Grants for televised testimony.
g. Treatment for juvenile offenders who are victims of child abuse or neglect.

Additional Child Abuse Developments

In addition to the Victims of Child Abuse Act, Title III of the Crime Control Act of 1990 established a Child Protection and Penalties Enhancement Act of 1990. This act requires updating of the record-keeping requirement for child abuse cases, and it recommends that the United States Sentencing Commission amend the penalties for sexual abuse with the view of strengthening those penalties when necessary.

Laws have also been passed to help child victims of sexual exploitation. Federal as well as state laws prohibit the importation, sale, or distribution of pornographic materials to a person under eighteen, and of materials depicting a person under age eighteen engaging in or simulating sexual conduct. The mandatory reporting laws also prohibit the development, duplication, and exchange of any pornographic materials involving persons under eighteen years of age, and mandate that any film processor or developer must report such materials to the child protective services (e.g., California Penal Code §§ 311.2, 311.3; West's California, 1991).

In the last five years much of the attention nationwide has focused on the plight of the child victim witnesses in court, and the conflict between protecting the child from secondary victimization versus protecting the constitutional rights of the accused. Many states have passed statutes designed to make it easier for the child to testify in court, and to accept "hearsay" statements made out of court. Several landmark U.S. Supreme Court

5. Reasonable Efforts Model Courts Review. Sponsored by the National Council of Juvenile and Family Court Judges and the Edna McConnell Clark Foundation. Michigan: Detroit, 19–20 Oct. 1990.

6. Child Abuse Victims' Rights Act of 1986. U.S.C. §§ 2252-2252.

7. Crime Control Act of 1990, Title II: Victims of Child Abuse Act of 1990, §§ 201:3266.

cases have already been decided on these issues (e.g., *Coy v. Iowa*, 1988). (These topics are discussed in detail in chapters 10, 11, and 12.)

Finally, in the last few years yet another concept of child abuse has emerged. The abuse or maltreatment of the fetus has become an important issue. The most commonly featured type of such fetal abuse is the drug-exposed infant. While the sixties was the decade of the battered child or physical child abuse, the seventies the decade of the sexually abused, the eighties and now the nineties are the decades of fetal abuse. With an estimated 380,000 to 750,000 drug-exposed infants born each year in the United States, the nation is turning to strategies to reduce the impact of substances on fetuses (Gomby and Shiono, 1991). Many states have now included maternal substance abuse with fetal and infant drug exposure under the mandatory reporting law. For example, Minne-

sota requires drug testing of both the mother and the newborn when there are indications of substance abuse, with mandatory reporting of positive toxicology screenings to the child protective services (Marshall, 1991). (These issues are discussed in more depth in chapter 14.)

CONCLUSION

We have described how our society has attempted to protect children through legislation and other legal action. We have shown how the focus has gone from physical abuse to include sexual and emotional abuse. Recently, attention has moved to fetal abuse. It is to the topic of the different types of abuse and neglect that we will now turn.

CHAPTER 2

Types of Child Abuse and Neglect

The problem of child abuse and neglect is of enormous magnitude; it represents a complex interaction of numerous factors which can include poverty, ethnicity, family dysfunction, mental health and personal problems, substance abuse, and children with special needs. Although child abuse occurs in all socioeconomic and cultural groups, its reported incidence is disproportionately large within those groups that are the least powerful and subjected to the most stressors. Although reporting bias may account for some of the relationship between social class and child abuse rates, the evidence is strong that poverty increases the likelihood of child maltreatment (U.S. Advisory Board on Child Abuse and Neglect, 1990). Any definition of child abuse is therefore always suspect to accusations of class and race bias. According to Giovannoni and Bacerra (1980), the issues that surround the definitions of child abuse and neglect include societal values, especially conflicting values. In defining abuse and neglect, society is in essence defining what the limitations of parental authority and the minimum expectations for the care of children are. In order to highlight the problems of determining what is abuse and neglect, they offer examples of cases that cover a broad spectrum of problems:

> A three-year-old in Tennessee was forced by her stepfather to walk for three days and three nights, until she died of exhaustion. A seven-year-old in California was locked in a room and tied to a chair by her parents for her whole life; when she was found she weighed only 59 pounds and was only 33 inches tall and unable to walk. An infant sustained permanent damage from maggots in her ears, maggots that swarmed over the feces-laden rags on which she lay. (Giovannoni and Bacerra, 1980, 1)

Giovannoni and Bacerra note that no one would probably question that these children had been abused and neglected. But what of the following situation that they describe?

> Three children, aged two to ten, were found by the Chicago police at 9:30 P.M. in an apartment to which the officers had been summoned by neighbors' complaints that the children had been left alone. The children, who were barefoot and in their underwear, said that they had not been fed since morning, when their mother had left them in their apartment. The mother arrived at 10:30 P.M. from her job as a cocktail waitress. She angrily protested that she had done nothing wrong; the ten-year-old, she said, was perfectly capable of taking care of the younger children. The police refused to take action. The neighbors were incensed. (Giovannoni and Bacerra, 1980, 1)

This last situation illustrates how difficult it may be to determine what abuse and neglect are; this is particularly true for situations involving neglect and emotional maltreatment. While the situation described above would seem to some to be a clear case of neglect, to others it might seem like a situation where a poor mother is punished for her inability to afford child care.

DEFINITIONS

Child abuse includes both abuse and neglect. The most frequent distinction made between these two terms is between "acts of commission" and "acts of omission" (Kadushin, 1974). Within child abuse we make a distinction between physical abuse, sexual abuse, and emotional abuse. We include child exploitation under the term child abuse. Within child neglect, we make a distinction between physical neglect and emotional neglect or deprivation. Many states use "child endangerment" synonymously with "child neglect." Recognizing the difficulty separating emotional abuse from emotional neglect, we use the term "emotional maltreatment" to include both emotional abuse and emotional neglect. In this text, we will use "child abuse" and "child maltreatment" as

FIGURE 2.1: Child Abuse and Neglect

Child Abuse
  Physical
  Sexual
  Emotional
  Child Exploitation
  Emotional Maltreatment

Child Neglect
  Physical
  Emotional

general terms, which include both abuse and neglect. Our classifications are consistent with those contained in the original Federal Child Abuse Prevention and Treatment Act.[1]

In addition to the classifications discussed above, we use the term "dependent child" to refer to any child who is a ward of the court or under the protection of the court. The part of the juvenile court that handles abuse and neglect cases is often referred to as "dependency court" (see chapter 5).

Definitions of abuse and neglect vary greatly in their specificity. Some states exclude from the coverage of their reporting laws medical situations resulting from the practice of religious beliefs. For example, California law states that if medical care is withheld solely for religious reasons, a child shall not be considered neglected[2]; Colorado law admonishes investigators to take into account cultural differences in child-rearing practices; and some states, such as New York and California, provide for reporting of neglect and abuse of children in out-of-home care (Stein, 1991).

In most states child abuse and neglect are defined separately in both criminal and juvenile

court statutes (see chapters 5 and 7). The criminal statutes define what types of acts constitute abuse and neglect for the purpose of determining criminal responsibility; the juvenile codes define abuse and neglect for the purpose of protection of the child in juvenile dependency proceedings.

In this chapter we define the different types of child abuse, neglect, and emotional maltreatment, give examples of cases that fall under each, and describe how professionals in the field can identify children who fall into each category. We will also discuss some of the class and ethnic biases involved in arriving at definitions of what constitutes child maltreatment, and the advantages and disadvantages of vague as opposed to specific statutory definitions.

PHYSICAL ABUSE

Physical abuse is any act brought about by an outside force which results in a nonaccidental physical injury. Inflicted physical injury most often represents unreasonably severe corporal punishment or unjustifiable punishment. The injury may create a substantial risk of death, disfigurement, impairment of physical health, or loss or impairment of function of any bodily organ (Stein, 1991).

Criminal Court Case Example (*People v. Jackson*, 1971)

Jo Anne B. lived with her boyfriend and had a child by him. One day she left the thirteen-month-old child with him while she went to work, and when she returned in the evening, the child had burns and water blisters on his body. The boyfriend said something like "before you see him . . . don't get shook." Since the child did not

---

1. Federal Child Abuse Prevention and Treatment Act, 1974.
2. Despite this statute, California courts have upheld criminal convictions of Christian Scientists who medically neglected their children.

look too seriously injured to her, she put something on his burns and left for school, returning later in the evening. During the night the burns got worse, and the next day the child was taken to see a doctor, who examined the child but would not treat him for burns, because the child had suffered a previous head injury. The child was then taken to a hospital.

A pediatrician examined the child, found burns on the child's head and upper part of his back, a swollen forearm and distended abdomen, and diagnosed an injury to the liver. He also saw a bruise suggestive of the shape of a thumb and one or two fingers on the child's body; he found that the child had suffered first- and second-degree burns over 23 percent of his body. X-rays revealed two recent fractures in the right forearm, and one recent fracture in the left forearm. There were scratches on his right buttock and left leg. Further X-rays revealed ten broken ribs, five on each side, and the child was "near enough to death where it would not be any surprise if he expired at any time." The child had been admitted to the hospital three months before, when he was diagnosed as having a subdural hematoma, a liquefied blood clot on the brain (*People v. Jackson*, 1971).

Juvenile Court Case Example One (*In re Edward C.*, 1981)

Two children, Eric and Edward, were first placed in protective custody in 1975 because there was no food in the home, the home was in a disheveled condition, and because Eric, then four, had received numerous marks and welts as a result of discipline by the father throughout the night. A juvenile court dependency petition requesting that the boys be adjudged dependents was sustained, and the boys were placed in a foster home. In July 1977, the foster family moved away, and the boys were allowed to return to the parents on a sixty-day trial basis. In March of 1980 the grandmother visited the house and observed several beatings of the children. She contacted the police, and a petition was filed in the juvenile court, alleging that the children were physically abused as described by section 300a of the California Welfare and Institutions Code. The petition was sustained in juvenile court, and the court found that the return of the minors to the physical custody of the parents would be detrimental to the welfare of the minors.

The parents appealed the finding, arguing that their fundamental right of parenting was constitutionally protected, and that the father was simply carrying out the Lord's will in disciplining his children. They contended that the First Amendment to the U.S. Constitution, protecting freedom of religion, severely limits the power of the state to interfere with the parental right to direct the upbringing of their children.

The California Appellate Court upheld the rulings of the lower court, holding that maltreatment of a child is not privileged even if it is imposed in the guise of freedom of religious expression. The court found that there was substantial evidence of actual and imminent physical and psychological harm to support the court's findings that the minors are dependent children who have no parent willing to exercise or capable of exercising proper and effective parental control, and that return of the minors to the physical custody of their parents would be detrimental to their welfare (*In re Edward C.*, 1981).

Juvenile Court Case Example Two (*Dumpson v. Daniel M.*, 1974)

A case example from New York illustrates the problem of cultural differences in determining what constitutes abuse as opposed to proper parental discipline (*Dumpson v. Daniel M.*, 1974). According to the petition, the respondent father had administered excessive corporal punishment to his seven-year-old son, Ekenediliz. It was alleged that on March 7, 1974, the respondent struck the child repeatedly with his hands, a belt, and his feet when summoned to discuss his son's behavior in school. Furthermore, it is alleged that on June 5, 1974, the child suffered a cut lip and bruises because of respondent's use of excessive corporal punishment. The preliminary hearing resulted in a determination that, based upon these allegations, all of the respondent's children should be removed pending further inquiry.

Testimony at the hearing revealed the following: the respondent was a thirty-four-year-old native of Nigeria who settled in the United States in 1968. He drove a taxi part-time and attended Brooklyn College, where he was taking courses to prepare himself for a career in engineering. His wife was thirty-five years old and taught high school chemistry and biology in the New York City school system. The respondent's first wife, from whom he was divorced and who resided in Africa, was the mother of Ekenediliz.

Mr. M. stated to the court that he struck his son because, according to his culture, this type of punishment was necessary and appropriate. In Nigeria, according to the respondent, if a child misbehaves in school and causes shame to the family, the parent has the duty to punish immediately and in any manner he sees fit. On cross-examination, the respondent testified that he was angered also by his son's lack of respect while he was talking with Mrs. G. When asked how the child exhibited a lack of respect during the conversation, the respondent stated "Ekenediliz was looking at Mrs. G.'s face while we were talking about him."

On redirect, Mr. M. briefly discussed Nigerian child-rearing and disciplinary practices, as well as cultural attitudes toward the judicial process. For example, he related that, in his country, if a villager is summoned to court for any reason, he cannot return home until he has purified himself by way of a special cleansing ritual. No matter what the reason, it is a cause for embarrassment and shame if one has to appear in court.

The appellate court reflected that:

> Our society is becoming increasingly mobile. As judges we hear cases involving people from all walks of life and from many different countries. All people have similar problems, but not all of them seek to solve them in the same manner.... While recognizing individual and cultural differences, this court has the obligation to apply the law equally to all men.... The sole issue for determination herein is whether the respondent's conduct constitutes excessive corporal punishment. We think it does. (*Dumpson v. Daniel M.*, 1974)

Discussion

The facts reported in *People v. Jackson* (1971) are an example of the "battered child syndrome" (Kempe, Silverman, Steele, Droegemuller, and Silver, 1962). Kempe, et al., described this condition as "a clinical condition in young children who have received serious physical abuse, generally from a parent or foster care parent" (Kempe, et al., 1962). Both the criminal and juvenile dependency law proscribe physical abuse.

In the *Jackson* case the defendant boyfriend was prosecuted and convicted of committing child abuse, California Penal Code sections 273(a), and child beating, 273(d). According to the California Penal Code, "willful cruelty or unjustifiable punishment of a child" means a situation where any person willfully causes or permits any child to suffer, or inflicts thereon, unjustifiable physical pain or mental suffering, or having the care or custody of any child, willfully causes or permits the person or health of the child to be placed in a situation such that his or her person or health is endangered (section 273a). "Corporal punishment or injury" is a situation in which any person willfully inflicts upon any child any cruel or inhuman corporal punishment or injury resulting in a traumatic condition (section 273d, California Penal Code, 1990).

In the *Edward C.* case, the children were alleged to be dependent children of the court because of the physical abuse of the father. All states have established statutory standards, criteria, and procedures for bringing a child protective proceeding in the juvenile or family court, based on an allegation of abuse by a parent or a caretaker (Bulkley, 1988). Some states refer to both abused and neglected children as "dependent" (as in California), or "in need of care, supervision or assistance" (e.g., Louisiana, Iowa, or Pennsylvania).

The California Welfare and Institutions Code, section 300(a), defines physical child abuse as

> serious physical harm inflicted non-accidentally upon the minor by the minor's parent or guardian. For the purposes of this subdivision, a court may find there is a substantial risk of serious future injury based on the manner in which a less serious injury was inflicted, a history of repeated infliction of injuries on the minor or the minor's siblings, or a combination of these and other actions by the parent or guardian which indicate the child is at risk of serious physical harm. For purposes of this subdivision, "serious physical harm" does not include reasonable and age-appropriate spanking to the buttocks where there is no evidence of serious physical injury. (California Welfare and Institutions Code, 1990)

The last section is clearly an attempt to address the dilemma of the parents' rights to discipline a child. Similarly, the Federal Victims of Child Abuse Act of 1990 says that

> . . . the term "child abuse" does not include discipline administered by a parent or legal guardian to his or her child, provided it is reasonable in manner and moderate in degree and otherwise does not constitute cruelty.

However, the Welfare and Institutions Code also states that abuse of children under five and inflicting cruel acts upon children are considered particularly serious. A child can also be found to be a dependent of the juvenile court if a sibling has been abused and there is substantial risk that the child before the court will be abused as well.

Similarly, the New York State's Social Service Laws define an abused child as a person under the age of eighteen, whose parent or other person legally responsible for his or her care:

> 1) inflicted or allows to be inflicted upon such child physical injury by other than accidental means which causes or creates a substantial risk of death, or serious or protracted disfigurement, or protracted impairment of physical or emotional health, or protracted loss or impairment of the function of any bodily organ; or
> 2) creates or allows to be created a substantial risk of physical injury to such child by other than accidental means which would be likely to cause death or serious or protracted disfigurement, or protracted impairment of physical or emotional health, or protracted loss or impairment of the function of any bodily organ. (New York Social Service Law, section 371 at i, ii)

The *Dumpson v. Daniel M.* case raises the issue of whether different ethnic or cultural groups should be allowed to have their own standards of upbringing and parental discipline, or whether all groups should be held to the same standards. This issue becomes particularly difficult when religious reasons are given for imposing different standards.

In the *People v. Jackson* case, the defendant/ boyfriend was convicted of physically abusing the child, even though the child could not testify and no one saw the defendant do anything. Do you believe there was sufficient evidence to prove him guilty beyond a reasonable doubt?

In the case of Edward and Eric, do you think the state would have considered the father's conduct abusive one hundred years ago? Do you believe that we have a changing definition of physical abuse? Do you believe that the determination of child abuse might be different depending on the state in which the case was heard? The judge before whom the case was tried?

What will the father in the New York case do when he disciplines his child in the future? What should the judge tell him?

Indicators of Physical Abuse

There are a number of indicators of physical abuse. Some indicators, however, may be consistent with accidental injury, and care must be taken not to confuse these with nonaccidental injury (hence the importance of the "battered child syndrome" —which basically describes a series of symptoms that could not have occurred by accidental means). Both physical and behavioral indicators may be used as measures of physical abuse (Child Abuse Manual, 1989). The Victim's Rights Act of 1990 defines the term "physical injury" as including "lacerations, fractured bones, burns, internal injuries, severe bruising, or serious bodily harm."[3] A child who has been physically abused may also exhibit behavioral indicators of abuse. For example, he or she may become overly fearful, compliant, or passive or overly aggressive and violent. The child may also try to hide the injuries by wearing inappropriate clothing and be wary of any physical contact with others.

The explanations and history given can be indicative of abuse. Often parents use inconsistent or incompatible explanations and may delay or fail to seek medical care, and the explanations may be incompatible with the medical evidence at hand. Any statement from the child can be an important indicator that physical abuse has occurred, but of course many abused children are too young to report.

---

3. Victims of Child Abuse Act of 1990, Title II, Subtitle D, § 3509(a)(3); §§ 3266–10.

SEXUAL ABUSE

Sexual abuse is contact with a child where the child is being used for sexual stimulation by the other person. The abuser is older than the child and in a position of authority over the child (*Child Abuse Manual*, 1989). Sexual assault and sexual exploitation are both forms of sexual abuse. Sexual abuse provisions therefore may cover specific acts such as vaginal intercourse and obscene or pornographic photographing of a child engaged in sexual acts, and may include vague terms such as permitting or encouraging a child to engage in offenses against public morality (Stein, 1991).

According to the Victims of Child Abuse Act (1990), the term "sexual abuse" includes the employment, use, persuasion, inducement, enticement, or coercion of a child to engage in, or assist another person to engage in, sexually explicit conduct or the rape, molestation, prostitution, or other form of sexual exploitation of children, or incest with children.[4]

Wald (1975) notes that perhaps the most universally condemned behavior of a parent or other family member toward a child involves sexual conduct with the child. Intercourse, accomplished with or without the use of force or threats, is clearly sexual abuse. But when the activity is less specific than intercourse, definitions become more difficult, and it may be difficult to distinguish between appropriate displays of affection and fondling or other possibly disturbing behavior (Wald, 1975).

Sexual abuse is often particularly difficult to prove because the abuse may not be immediately visible. The damage may be primarily emotional, and the symptoms may not be clear. Many victims may be afraid to talk about what has happened (see chapter 13 for a discussion of the sexual

---

4. Ibid.

abuse accommodation syndrome). Court actions involving sexual abuse allegations may also present many problems regarding child witness testimony and confrontations in the courtroom, especially if the case is pursued in criminal court.

Criminal Court Case Example
(*Gilpin v. McCormick*, 1990)

The following example is from Montana, *Gilpin v. McCormick* (1990). Joel Gilpin and Mary T. worked as nurses at Billings Hospital. Halloween night, 1986, Joel and another friend, Bill Knigge, were at the T. home supervising the T. children, daughters Jamie (eleven) and Jackie (twelve) and son, Jeff, who were dressing up in preparation for going out to trick-or-treat. Jamie testified that she was downstairs alone with Gilpin on a couch. When she leaned forward, he placed his left hand under her buttocks so that when she sat back she sat on his hand. He squeezed her buttocks and then picked her up and placed her on his lap. With one hand on her buttocks, he then rubbed his other hand on her upper thigh about five inches from her vagina. She then stated she heard her doorbell ring and went upstairs.

Gilpin followed her and at the front door grabbed her from behind, placing his hands on her abdomen and raising them toward her breasts. She stepped on his toe, ran away, and returned to preparing her costume downstairs. Gilpin then went into the bathroom where Jackie was putting up her hair. He asked her what she was dressed as, and when she responded that she was a "prostitute or hooker," he said he "wishes he could be my first customer." He then stood behind her, rubbing her breasts and repeating his desire to be her first customer. She wriggled free, he grabbed her arm and pulled her back, but she extricated herself and left the bathroom. The girls then agreed to stay together for the remainder of

the evening. One week later, Jamie left a note in her mother's purse about the incidents, following which her mother contacted the police department. Bill Knigge testified that he was in the kitchen, near the front door, and that he did not hear or see any of this. Neither Jeff nor a friend of his who was visiting saw anything either. Gilpin denied having any sexual contact or any sexual desire involving the girls.

Gilpin was convicted by a state jury of two counts of felony sexual assault and sentenced to two consecutive four-year terms. The Montana Supreme Court affirmed this conviction. Gilpin then filed a petition for a writ of *habeas corpus* in the Federal District Court for the District of Montana.

In the Federal Court Gilpin argued that a psychiatric examination of the two girls was necessary to determine the presence or absence of Rape/Trauma Syndrome, and that the trial court should have ordered such an examination. He contended that the state trial court was required, as a matter of due process, to *order* the victim/witness to undergo psychiatric examination. Children's testimony, he claimed, is inherently incredible and necessitates a psychiatric examination. The Circuit Court of Appeals affirmed the District Court's denial of his request for relief stating in part that the appellant misapprehended the critical issue here.

> Gilpin seems oblivious to the possibility that we may well be *more* concerned with a minor being forced to undergo an examination than an adult. . . . We are fully aware of widespread public concern over child sexual assault and abuse cases and the passions they arouse. Appellant invokes the specter of pliant children being hectored by psychiatrists and social workers into traducing scores of innocent adults with the stain of child abuse. But new constitutional rights cannot be found for every new passion that may drive criminal prosecutions. It is clear that Montana's refusal to compel child sexual assault victims to undergo psychiatric examination does not violate due process.

The court further found that the jury was undoubtedly reasonable in finding that the girls' testimony indicated that sexual contact had occurred, which was arousing or gratifying to the appellant. A rational trier of fact could have found the essential elements of the crime beyond a reasonable doubt. Gilpin insisted that an accusation was not enough, but that in every crime against the person where no physical mark is left, the jury must weigh the testimony of the witnesses with that of the defendant. That this jury believed the girls and not Gilpin was hardly irrational (*Gilpin v. McCormick*, 1990).

Juvenile Court Case Example (*In re Cheryl H.*, 1984)

On December 31, 1981, a petition was filed by the Department of Social Services in the Juvenile Court seeking to subject Cheryl H. to the jurisdiction of the juvenile court. At the time the petition was filed, Cheryl H. was three years old. Her parents, Mr. and Mrs. H., had separated three years earlier after a six-month marriage. The petition alleged that the father had sexually molested Cheryl and that Cheryl was suffering from three hymeneal tears in her vagina as well as other injuries. Both Mr. and Mrs. H. agreed that Cheryl had suffered the injuries alleged, but the father denied that he had caused the injuries and that he had sexually abused Cheryl.

At the jurisdictional hearing (the trial) in juvenile court, Dr. Powell, a psychiatrist appointed by the court, testified on behalf of Mrs. H. Dr. English testified on behalf of Mr. H. Cheryl, the three-year-old subject of the hearing, did not testify.

Dr. Powell's testimony was based on play therapy sessions with Cheryl, involving toys commonly used with very young children and anatomically correct dolls. She testified that Cheryl's behavior during these sessions was consistent with conduct exhibited by other young children who had been sexually abused. This conduct included the following: (1) Cheryl put the male doll on top of the female doll; (2) Cheryl kept the female doll close to her and pushed the male doll away; (3) Cheryl placed the penis of the male doll in her mouth and "glassy-eyed, staring ahead compulsively" sucked on it; (4) when the subject of possible molestation was broached, Cheryl sometimes clung to her mother or hid her face and went into a dissociated state; and (5) when her father was mentioned, Cheryl recoiled.

Dr. Powell also testified that sexually abused children often invent new names for genitalia and that Cheryl told her on several occasions, "Daddy hurt my poopoo" or "Daddy put his poopoo in my mouth." Later Cheryl identified "poopoo" or "booboo" as words describing genitalia. Dr. Powell also testified that based on her knowledge of the development of cognition in children, Cheryl could not have been coached to respond the way she did during play therapy. She concluded that, in her opinion, Mr. H. had sexually molested Cheryl and recommended against any visitation between Cheryl and her father until Mr. H.'s rehabilitation was demonstrated.

Dr. English, testifying on behalf of the father, acknowledged that the injuries were nonaccidental and could have been inflicted during the time that Cheryl visited with her father. At the conclusion of the hearing, the juvenile court sustained the allegations in the petition, and stated that Cheryl's actions with the anatomical dolls met the preponderance of evidence requirements. The court declared Cheryl a dependent of the court. It allowed Cheryl to remain in her mother's home on the conditions that Mr. H. was not allowed to visit Cheryl and that he begin therapy.

Mr. H. filed an appeal arguing that the evidence was insufficient to support the judgment, and that the judgment was based on only hearsay evidence. The appellate court found, however, that the data used by Dr. Powell to derive her opinion that Cheryl had been sexually abused was proper matter on which to base such an opinion, and that expert testimony should be allowed to determine whether vaginal injuries were caused by sexual abuse rather than accident. In the court's view, Cheryl's conduct with anatomical dolls during play therapy was nonassertive conduct and therefore not hearsay. Her play with the dolls was relevant to prove facts at issue in the case. But the Appellate Court also held that Dr. Powell's opinion about who caused Cheryl's sexual injuries was not admissible. Even with this exclusion, the court found that what remained was enough to supply the preponderance of evidence needed to support the court's findings, that Cheryl needed the protection of juvenile court (*In re Cheryl H.*, 1984).

Discussion

In the *Gilpin* case the defendant invoked the specter of pliant children being hectored by psychiatrists and social workers into marking scores of innocent adults with the stain of child abuse. Many people have indeed charged that they have been falsely accused (see discussion in later chapters). Do you think that this defendant should have been prosecuted? If so, do you agree with the conviction, or do you feel that his constitutional rights were violated?

Similarly, in the *Cheryl H.* case should this matter have been brought to juvenile court? Was the evidence sufficient to find that Cheryl had been sexually abused by her father? Did Cheryl need the protection of juvenile court? Should the father have been allowed visitation?

Indicators of Sexual Abuse

The nature of child sexual abuse and the frequent involvement of family members and other persons in a caretaker role may make it extremely difficult for a child to come forward and tell others about the abuse (see the discussion of the sexual abuse accommodation syndrome in chapter 13). Sometimes a child who does come forward may be accused of making up stories and may be punished. Often children who are sexually abused are warned not to tell anyone. The disclosure may be direct or indirect to a friend, a classmate, a teacher, or a trusted adult. It is not unusual for the disclosure to be delayed.

Sexual abuse of a child may surface through a broad range of physical, behavioral, and social symptoms, of both a sexual and nonsexual nature. Sexual abuse symptoms include excessive masturbation, sexual interaction with peers, sexual aggression towards younger or more naive children, sexual accosting of older people or adults, seductive behavior, and promiscuity. Symptoms of a nonsexual nature might include disorders of normal physical functions, emotional problems, behavioral problems, and developmental lags and school problems (Faller, 1990). Medical symptoms include trauma to the genitalia and indicators of sexually transmitted diseases.

It should be noted that many of these behaviors, taken separately, may not be symptomatic of sexual abuse, and that great care should be taken before concluding that sexual abuse has occurred. Masturbation, for example, is developmentally normal for children. Excessive masturbation, on the other hand, is indicated when a child is engaged in compulsive masturbation, such as being unable to stop and causing injury. Children who demonstrate sexual behavior and sexual knowledge and make verbal statements about sexual activities beyond their normal age may have been sexually abused.

Finally, it should be noted that not all children who have been sexually abused manifest overt signs of the trauma. In a study of over three hundred victims of sexual abuse, Conte and Berliner (1988) found that around 20 percent of the children did not show any observable signs of the abuse. In these cases the reactions may be delayed or the child may have been well socialized not to reveal signs of distress (Faller, 1990).

PHYSICAL NEGLECT

Neglect is a difficult concept to define. What is "neglect" to some may be a normal way of life for others. All parents or caretakers neglect their children some of the time. When the neglect is such that the legally responsible caretaker fails to provide adequate minimum physical and emotional care of the child, then the child needs to be protected. What "adequate minimum physical and emotional care" are will be different from community to community and from culture to culture. Legislators and commentators write that neglected children are children without adequate parental or custodial care and control. They are neglected by not being provided with adequate food, clothing, shelter, medical care, supervision, education, and protection necessary to ensure physical and mental health (Metropolitan Court Judges Committee Report, 1986). However, in another sense, a neglected child is one so labeled by the court system; child neglect is what the court decides.

At what point do we decide that a child's care has become so poor that it is neglectful (Polansky, Chalmers, and Bettenwiser, 1981)? Extreme circumstances, like outright abandonment or failure to provide food, are clear enough. But most of the time the situation is not that obvious. According to Polansky, et al., the definitions of neglect will always be culturally relative, and to a large extent the definition of neglect is a matter of agreeing about what standard of care is minimal. Regardless of socioeconomic status, child neglect is difficult to define (Steinbach, 1989).

Child neglect is the most common form of child maltreatment, and can be equally as dan-gerous as physical or sexual abuse. Serious physical and psychological problems may result from neglect. It is a leading cause of death and serious illness in young children. A neglected child may become a delinquent child (Lane and Davis, 1987).

Neglect is often related to the inability of the parents to meet the child's needs. Thus, infants and small children are most affected by neglect. The statistics on neglect are staggering. A recent study prepared by the American Humane Association states that nationwide neglect consistently has accounted for the greatest number of maltreatment reports: in 1988 it represented 63 percent of the approximately 2 million cases of reported incidents of the three predominant forms of child maltreatment—physical abuse, sexual abuse, and neglect (Steinbach, 1989).

Criminal Court Case Example

The following is an account published in the *San Jose Mercury News* (Rogers, 1992, 8B):

> Convicted child abuser Patrick of Santa Cruz, who was arrested last summer after his three young daughters were discovered living amid piles of garbage and unable to speak beyond grunts, was sentenced Tuesday to six months in jail. Santa Cruz County Superior Judge Richard Kessel told Patrick he should have done more to improve living conditions for the girls—ages 2, 5 and 6—after their mother, Ruby, began showing signs of acute mental illness.
>
> The police reported the family's townhouse was covered in mold, piled high with dirty clothes and reeking of rotting food and urine. "It is obvious that the last few weeks in that residence must have been hell for those children," the judge said. Ruby was arrested June 19 after a police officer responding to a noise complaint entered the house. Patrick was arrested several weeks later.
>
> The case gained national attention and sparked sharp criticism from state investigators, who

concluded that Santa Cruz welfare officials knew about Ruby and should have intervened and removed the girls earlier. Ruby was ruled mentally unfit to stand trial. Diagnosed as acutely psychotic and schizophrenic, she remains in a San Bernardino maximum security hospital. Patrick was convicted by a Santa Cruz jury February 20 of three counts of child endangerment—two misdemeanors and a felony. Monday his attorney argued that he was not a criminal, but rather a simple man who did not understand the basics of child-rearing and didn't spend much time at home. "He's been convicted of being a lousy parent," the attorney told the judge. "Yet he didn't know he was a lousy parent." Wright also laid blame on social workers for not stepping in and removing the children. But the judge disagreed. He pointed to a videotape shown during the trial that depicted the girls in a clean house two years ago, playing with toys and speaking simple words. Foster parents who took custody last summer testified that the children growled like animals, defecated on furniture and licked crumbs off the floor. "There was such a regression," said Kessel, "that poor parent or not poor parent, any human being would know something was wrong."

During the hearing, Patrick, 37, wore an orange jumpsuit and leg shackles. He said nothing and showed little emotion. He could have faced three years of jail. Patrick was also placed on five years' probation, which requires him to take parenting classes and undergo psychiatric treatment. Two of his daughters now live in Santa Cruz foster homes. The youngest lives in Southern California with a relative of Ruby's. A juvenile court judge has yet to decide whether Patrick will ever regain custody.

Monday, the criminal court judge advanced a guess. "He might very well be reunified with these children," Kessel said. "It's not going to do them any good to have him shipped off to state prison." Some area children's advocates reacted with anger. "He's just about walking away free," said a woman from Ben Lomond, who adopted one of Ruby's sons a decade ago. "I think our laws for child abuse are way too lenient."

Juvenile Court Case Example

On November 7, 1985, an officer of the San Jose Police Department was working at the Capitol Flea Market in San Jose when he received an anonymous telephone call to the effect that there were some possibly unkempt, transient children at the flea market about whom the caller was concerned. The officer responded to this call and found two children, C. and T., with their parents. The officer noted that the children were unkempt and dirty, were not attending school, and were residing in unclean living conditions. The officer contacted Children's Protective Services, and a social worker responded to the scene.

The social worker also noted the same unclean condition of the children and the unclean, crowded and cluttered condition of the camper in which they were living. The children were therefore placed in protective custody and were transported to the children's shelter because of a possibly unfit home and living conditions. When T. and C. arrived at the children's shelter and were being seen by the clinic staff, the staff decided it was necessary to provide the children with a bath before examining them because of their filthy condition. The nurse later related to the undersigned officer that, after one bath and one shampoo, she did not feel that the children were completely clean and noted that they had ground-in dirt on their bodies which would require several bathings to remove from their skin.

. . . The social worker had learned that the children had a prior referral in that county. . . .

. . . T., after he was initially placed in protective custody, stated that he and his family had been traveling around on a carnival circuit. He said he had not been to school for a long time, and when asked about how he learns, replied that he sometimes reads books and that sometimes he learns from the carnival. . . . Although T. said he enjoyed traveling all the time, he did mention that he would like to be able to have showers and baths more frequently.

. . . The father explained that on the day the children were picked up they had just arrived in town and had not had time to clean the camper. He said he planned to get the camper cleaned the next day and enroll the children in school. He said that although the camper is very small, it will have to do until they are able to get the money together to purchase a trailer, which is what they have been working on recently. In the meantime he feels that the family situation is adequate for the children's care. (Juvenile Court Petition to Santa Clara County Superior Court, 1985)

Based on these facts, the social services department filed petitions in the juvenile court seeking protection for the children. Once a petition was found to be true, the department recommended that before the children could be returned to the parents, the parents had to demonstrate that they had established an adequate living arrangement for the children during the entire school year, whether it be with themselves, friends, or relatives, and present this plan to the court and/or supervising worker for review and approval. Social services recommended that if the children were returned home then in-home long-term supervision of these minors should be ordered to ensure their right to an education.

Discussion

Civil protections for the neglected child are offered in juvenile law statutes and in the common law. In California, the Welfare and Institutions Code describes children as coming within the protection of the court if "the minor has suffered, or there is a substantial risk that the minor will suffer, serious physical harm or illness, as a result of the failure or inability of his or her guardian to adequately supervise or protect the minor or by

the willful or negligent failure of the parent or guardian to provide the minor with adequate food, clothing, shelter, or medical treatment, or by the inability of the parent's or guardian's mental illness, developmental disability, or substance abuse" (Welfare and Institutions Code § 300b).

The issue of cultural, economic, and religious variations in defining what constitutes "neglect" is also addressed in the California statute. With respect to the economic issue, the Code says that no minor shall be found to be a neglected child solely because of the lack of an emergency shelter for the family (Welfare and Institutions Code § 300b).

A minor may also be seen as a neglected child if the following are true:

> The minor has been left without any provision for support; the minor's parent has been incarcerated or institutionalized and cannot arrange for the care of the minor; or a relative or other custodian with whom the child resides or has been left is unwilling or unable to provide care or support for the child; the whereabouts of the parent is unknown, and reasonable efforts to locate the parent have been unsuccessful. (Welfare and Institutions Code § 300g)

In the Santa Cruz case do you think that the sentencing of the father was too lenient or too strict? Should the mother have been prosecuted as well? Do you agree that the laws for child neglect are too lenient? Note that there were two judges in this matter, one in criminal court and one in the juvenile dependency court. What are the responsibilities of each with regard to the family? Should they coordinate their actions?

Should the state intervene in the type of factual situation presented in the flea market case? Should these children have been removed from their home? What alternatives to removal do you suggest? To what extent was this situation a result of poverty rather than neglect? Is parental failure to ensure school attendance in and of itself sufficient to justify removal of children?

Indicators of Physical Neglect

Neglect may be suspected if the following physical indicators are present:

1. Lack of adequate medical or dental care
2. Chronic sleepiness or hunger
3. Poor personal hygiene; dirty clothing; inadequate dress for weather conditions
4. Evidence of poor supervision; child is left alone in the home or unsupervised under circumstances when he or she should have been supervised
5. Conditions in the home constitute a health hazard
6. Home lacks heating or plumbing
7. Fire hazards or other unsafe conditions in the home
8. Inadequate sleeping arrangements
9. Nutritional quality of food in the home is poor
10. Spoiled food in refrigerator or cupboards

It should be noted that many of these conditions may exist at one time or another in a normal home, without being indications of neglect. It is the extreme or persistent presence of these factors that indicates some degree of neglect. Many of these conditions can be remedied with proper education and counseling for the parents, as well as economic and practical assistance. Extreme conditions constitute severe neglect and may justify protective custody and dependency proceedings as well as criminal neglect charges.

When investigating these cases, it is important to look for consistent signs of excessive neglect and to take care not to be biased by different cultural standards for child rearing and cleanliness. Only when the child is suffering from such practices is intervention warranted.

MEDICAL NEGLECT

In the past, court and legislatures long followed a "hands off" policy in the area of ensuring medical care for children (Wadlington, Whitebread, and Davis, 1987). In recent years, however, courts have more frequently intervened in order to ensure that a child is afforded appropriate treatment and medical care. Often the criterion of "life threatening" if medical treatment is not given is used to determine whether court intervention is justified. The problem of defining "medical neglect" is made even more difficult and sensitive because so many parents charged with medical neglect base their behavior on religious beliefs. This in turn invokes the issues of religious freedom and the rights to privacy. For example, the California statute reads:

> Whenever it is alleged that a minor comes within the jurisdiction of the court on the basis of the parent's or guardian's willful failure to provide adequate medical treatment, nontreatment, or spiritual treatment through prayer alone in accordance with the tenets and practices of a recognized church or religious denomination, by an accredited practitioner thereof, and shall not assume jurisdiction unless necessary to protect the minor from suffering serious harm or illness. (Welfare and Institutions Code § 300b)

Case Example (*In re E.G.*, 1989)

The following case example is taken from the Supreme Court of Illinois in *In re E.G.* (1989).

A seventeen-year-old minor contracted acute nonlymphatic leukemia, a malignant disease of the white blood cells. When the minor, E.G., and her mother, R.D., were informed that treatment of the disease would involve blood transfusions, they refused consent to this medical procedure on the basis of their religious beliefs. As Jehovah's Witnesses, both E.G. and her mother desired to observe their religion's prohibition against the "eating" of blood. The mother did authorize any other treatment and signed a waiver absolving the medical providers of liability for failure to administer transfusions.

As a result of their refusal to assent to blood transfusions, the State of Illinois filed a neglect petition in the juvenile court. At that hearing medical testimony revealed that without blood transfusions E.G. would die within a month. Dr. Yachnin testified that transfusions along with chemotherapy would achieve remission of the disease in about 89 percent of all cases, but that the long-term prognosis for survival of patients like E.G. was from 20 to 25 percent.

Dr. Yachnin and others who appeared at the juvenile court hearing testified that E.G. was competent to understand the consequences of accepting or rejecting treatment. The trial court appointed a hospital official temporary guardian and authorized her to consent to transfusions on E.G.'s behalf.

At a further hearing, E.G. testified. She said that her decision to refuse blood transfusions was her own and that she fully understood the nature of her disease and the consequences of her decision. She indicated that her decision was not based on any wish to die, but instead was grounded in her religious convictions. She testified that the court's decision to permit transfusions upset her and that "it seems as if everything that I wanted or believe in was just disregarded."

Other witnesses extolled E.G.'s maturity and the sincerity of her religious beliefs. One witness, Dr. Littner, a psychiatrist with special expertise in evaluating the maturity of and competency of minors, testified that E.G. had the maturity level of an eighteen- to twenty-year-old adult. He further testified that she had the competency to make an informed decision to refuse the blood transfusions, even if this choice was fatal.

At the conclusion of the hearing the trial court ruled that E.G. was medically neglected and appointed a guardian to consent to medical treatment. The trial court stated that this was in

E.G.'s best interests. The court noted that while E.G. was a mature minor and while the court gave great weight to her views, her parents' views, and their religious convictions, the state's interest in the case was greater than either E.G.'s or her mother's interest in refusing to consent to treatment.

The Illinois Supreme Court reversed the trial court, finding that E.G. was a "mature minor" and that if the trial court was satisfied by clear and convincing evidence of her maturity, she should have been able to refuse medical treatment. The Supreme Court also ordered that the finding of neglect entered against E.G.'s mother be expunged.

Discussion

This is an example of the tension between the best interests and the wishes of a minor. The State of Illinois argued that preserving E.G.'s life with blood transfusions was in her best interests. E.G. argued that her wishes should prevail because of her maturity, her religious beliefs, and her mother's desires.

Would there be a different result if E.G. were ten years old? If she were a newborn? There are hundreds of babies born each year with medical problems which require blood transfusions. If the parents refuse blood transfusions, the state consistently files medical neglect petitions and asks the juvenile court to permit medical intervention over the parental objections. Such intervention is routinely authorized by the court system.

These cases all involve life and death choices. Would it make any difference if the medical risk were long-term disability such as loss of hearing or sight or the use of a vital organ? Most state laws use the terms "death or serious physical harm." It would appear that the disabilities mentioned would be covered by the law.

How would the degree of risk in blood transfusions be increased today because of AIDS? Should that affect the court's decision?

Indicators of Medical Neglect

In addition to cases defined as "life threatening," "failure to thrive" children may also be the result of medical neglect. Infants who are smaller than normal or who exhibit other physical problems may suffer because of a failure to meet medical or caretaking standards. Behavioral problems such as developmental lags, infantile behavior, depression or apathy, begging and stealing food, seeking excessive attention, and chronic absence from school may also be indicators of medical neglect.

EMOTIONAL MALTREATMENT

Emotional abuse and neglect can cause severe psychological and behavioral disorders. Examples of emotional maltreatment include excessive verbal assaults such as belittling, screaming, threats, blaming and sarcasm, unpredictable and inconsistent responses, constant family discord and negative feelings. Deprivation of emotional care or emotional neglect can be equally damaging. Children are emotionally neglected when their parents or caretakers do not provide the child with a feeling of being loved and wanted, and with a proper sense of self-esteem. Many of these children are plagued into adulthood by anger, self-loathing, and feelings of helplessness.

Often emotional maltreatment is difficult to detect, and only comes to the attention of authorities in the investigations of other forms of abuse and neglect. While many states have included emotional child maltreatment in the mandatory report laws, many states have not. Such abuse and neglect are the hardest to define and prove in court. According to Daro (1988), there is no single legal standard that determines when the state should intervene.

Family Court Case Example (*Matter of Theresa C.*, 1991)

In this case, the Sullivan Department of Social Services in the state of New York was the appellant and James C., et al., were the respondents.

Respondents are the parents of three children: Theresa (born 1974), Thomas (born 1978) and Joseph (born 1982). Respondents were alleged by petitioner to have neglected the children by impairing or causing the imminent danger of impairment of the children's mental or emotional condition as the result of their failure to exercise a minimum degree of care. Specifically, respondents were charged with continuously engaging in domestic violence against each other in the presence of the children over a ten-year period, resulting in the impairment of the children's mental and emotional health.

At the conclusion of the fact-finding hearing in this proceeding, under Family Court Act Article 10, family court concluded that petitioner failed to meet its burden of proof and dismissed the petition. An appeal by petitioner followed.

From our reading of the record, the evidence adduced by petitioner satisfied the statutory burden of establishing emotional neglect by respondents of their three children, namely, "a state of substantially diminished psychological or intellectual functioning...; provided, however, that such impairment must be clearly attributable to the unwillingness or inability of the respondent(s) to exercise a minimum degree of care toward the children."

The evidence at the hearing included testimony from friends, neighbors, and police officers, who described a pattern of repeated incidents at respondents' residence over a ten-year period, wherein they were observed kicking, beating, and shouting obscenities at each other in front of the children. Following several of these incidents, caseworkers from petitioner and the Onondaga Department of Social Services were called in to assist the children. They testified to the fear and distress the children were experiencing as a result of their exposure to these altercations.

The family was evaluated in 1981 at the Sullivan County Mental Health Clinic in connection with behavioral problems of their oldest child, Theresa, then age six. The mental health professional who assessed the child identified the source of her anxiety as "marital conflict and Theresa's resulting peacemaker role." Among the reasons cited for this conclusion was that Theresa "had been enuretic off and on, and her parents report that her enuresis coincides with family turmoil." Indeed, at that time, both respondents freely admitted that Theresa was affected by "their arguments, which often led to physical attack."

In 1986, the children were seen by an Onondaga County child protective caseworker while temporarily in the care of a maternal aunt in Syracuse after a particularly violent episode. Theresa was rebellious and defiant and still enuretic at age eleven. Her brother Thomas was withdrawn. The caseworker related how the children expressed being upset and depressed by the domestic violence; when the father was interviewed, he again conceded that the family violence was having a deleterious effect on the children.

Subsequently, in 1988, the children were counseled on several occasions by a therapist at the Sullivan County Mental Health Clinic. As to the child Joseph, who was acting out both violently and sexually, the therapist stated that, in her opinion and that of the staff at the clinic, Joseph's behavior was at least partly attributable to the domestic violence in the household, i.e., "discord in the family could have very strongly led to some of the problems he was experiencing." She supported her conclusion by the child's drawings and playing out scenes of domestic violence with dolls during therapy.

The inference of a causal relationship between respondents' conduct and the impaired condition of the children was also supported by the testimony of David Pelcovitz, a clinical psychologist from Long Island, who was a specialist in studying children witnesses of domestic violence. It is true that he testified without ever having examined the children, but the hypothetical question he answered was based upon his reading of the pertinent records and case history of the family. He testified that the emotional and behavioral problems of respondents' children were consistent with his general findings in his studies of the effects upon children of witnessing domestic violence. Although he conceded that other factors could have contributed to the condition of the children, he stated unequivocally that a causal relationship between their problems and witnessing parental violence "is certainly very consistent and very likely."

The appellate court concluded that:

> We believe that the foregoing cumulatively would warrant a finding that the children's serious pathology was at least partially due to their apparently regular and continuous exposure to extremely violent conduct between respondents. This being so, despite the deference generally accorded to Family Court's determinations, this court must weigh the relative probative force of any conflicting testimony and the relative strength of conflicting inferences and, on that basis, may make alternative findings.
>
> We conclude that the weight of the evidence in this record supports a finding of neglect. Despite Family Court's contrary finding, the evidence overwhelmingly demonstrated serious impairment of the children's emotional health. Since respondents chose not to testify at the hearings or otherwise submit proof of any plausible alternative reason for such impairment, we are left only with the previously described credible evidence clearly attributing the children's impaired emotional condition, at least in significant part, to the spousal violence to which they were exposed.

The appellate court adjudicated the children to be neglected and returned the case to the Family Court of Sullivan County for a dispositional hearing.

Discussion

This was a civil case. Emotional maltreatment can also be a criminal offense. For example, in California any person who willfully causes or permits a child to suffer, or inflicts unjustifiable physical pain or mental suffering, or causes a child to be placed in a situation where the child's life is endangered can be punished by imprisonment for up to six years (e.g., California Penal Code 273a.1). Lesser emotional abuse and neglect can be seen as a misdemeanor (CPC 273a.2).

The case of *Theresa C.* presents an interesting connection between spousal violence and emotional neglect. Do you agree that the parents' violence against each other can lead to emotional neglect of the children? Do you agree with the order of the appellate court in this case?

Indicators of Emotional Maltreatment

According to Dean (1979), emotional maltreatment includes persistent verbal attacks and ridicule. Parental coldness and rejection can also be a form of emotional maltreatment (Garbarino and Garbarino, 1986). Parents may place demands on children which are based on unreasonable or impossible expectations. Parents may ignore and threaten their child, and show irrational and bizarre behavior.

Parental emotional abuse may result in depression in the child, apathy, "acting out," self-destructive behavior, or overly compliant behavior. The child may note that he or she is always told that he or she is "bad." Emotional deprivation or neglect may lead to eating disorders, developmental problems, antisocial behavior, and fears. An emotionally deprived child may try to seek out and "pester" other adults for attention and affection.

Home environment problems such as the abuse of drugs and alcohol, psychiatric problems or situational factors such as marital discord may result in emotional abuse or neglect. However, these factors are not in and of themselves reportable unless they lead to willful or unjustifiable maltreatment.

CONCLUSION

Abuse and neglect may take place in the home, in institutions, or in random places by strangers. Child maltreatment occurs in all cultural, ethnic, occupational, and socioeconomic groups but is also strongly correlated with poverty. Child abuse and neglect are seldom the result of any single factor. Rather, a combination of personality factors, family dynamics, and social and economic circumstances may precipitate abuse or neglect.

Physical injuries, severe neglect, and malnutrition are more readily detectable than the subtle and less visible injuries which result from emotional maltreatment. Sexual abuse is also often harder to prove than physical abuse. However, all categories of abuse endanger a child's physical or emotional health and development. A parent or caretaker may begin by inflicting minor injuries, then may cause more serious harm over a period of time. Detecting the initial small injuries may save a child from future permanent injury or death. Early identification, reporting, and intervention are important to protect the child victim, since many abusers are recidivists who may escalate or increase the frequency of abuse over time. Frequently, abusing parents or caretakers have themselves experienced child abuse. Consequently, they often create the same environment for their children. Without intervention, these negative life patterns could continue for generations.

Because of the association between child maltreatment and poverty, the issue of where to draw the lines separating proper parental conduct from neglect becomes an important social policy consideration. In arguing for a presumption of parental autonomy, Wald (1975) suggested that the following criteria should be used to determine when coercive intervention should be statutorily authorized:

1. the harm should be serious and specific; and
2. it must be a type of harm for which, in general, the remedy of coercive intervention will do more good than harm.

In general, Wald concludes that voluntary participation in services is better than coercive intervention.

The views expressed in Wald's article later became the basis for the American Bar Association's Standards Regarding Abuse/Neglect. These positions have in turn been criticized as being too "non-interventionist" (Bourne and Newberger, 1977).

We have to be careful that the definitions of child abuse and neglect described in this chapter do not lead to unwarranted state intervention into private family matters which infringe on parental rights. We must focus upon those children in real danger to ensure that they receive the protection that they need. While statutes in most states speak in terms of "unjustifiable" failure to provide "adequate" or "necessary" or "proper" supervision and care, these terms are ambiguous and are left to the social services and ultimately the judiciary to define.

Such broad definitions are usually defended on the grounds that child protective personnel and courts need discretion in exercising their sound professional judgment in determining whether a particular case should be considered child maltreatment. However, Besharov (1988) agrees with Wald that there is a strong need to narrow the grounds for state intervention in abuse and neglect cases, and that statutes should be drafted in terms of the specific harm that a child must be suffering or is extremely likely to suffer, not in terms of desired parental behavior. His view closely parallels that of Wald.

The importance of giving courts and social agencies preventive jurisdiction explains the sometimes open-ended nature of existing legal definitions. The statutes have been intentionally phrased precisely to authorize intervention before the child has been seriously injured, and even before he has been seriously abused or neglected. Nevertheless, it is important that child protective workers and other professionals be given clear guidance about when state intervention is and is not justified in order to balance the need to protect children with the need to prevent unwarranted state intervention in family life. Vague statutory definitions would not pose a problem if there were clear-cut criteria and standards for interpreting them available to those who must make judgments about specific cases. Often such criteria do not exist (Giovannoni and Bacerra, 1980). The burden of interpretation ultimately falls on the various professionals, who must make decisions about whether individual cases belong under the broader rubrics of neglect and abuse. It is the role and obligations of these professionals that we look at in the next chapter.

CHAPTER 3

Roles of Professionals Involved with Child Abuse and Neglect

The phone rings. A social worker answers. The caller—a first-grade teacher—reports that she suspects a young girl is being sexually abused. She's talked to the girl. The social worker makes a report to law enforcement.

A series of events has just been triggered. The conclusion may come quickly or take years. But the state's obligation is clear. A child may be in danger. Someone must act.

The child will now enter a new world, a world that extends beyond family, friends, and school. She is an alleged victim of child abuse. She may become a crucial witness in complex legal proceedings.

That new world is an adult world. It was not designed for children. Adults do not always remember what it was like to be a child. Many do not understand how a child thinks or remembers or reacts. Many do not understand how a child expresses her view of events involving her.

But the adults have a job to do. The child may need protection. There is an alleged crime. Questions must be asked, legal requirements fulfilled, forms filled out, and above all, appropriate action taken.

In fact, this child may not have entered one world but many. She may be a witness in a criminal investigation and a criminal prosecution. She may also be the subject of a child welfare services investigation and juvenile court dependency proceedings that determine whether she can remain safely in the home. She may be involved in proceedings for dissolution of her parents' marriage, and she may be involved in proceedings arising out of her alleged abuse.

Along the way she may meet and be interviewed by many people. In the criminal proceedings she may be required to tell her story to numerous people, including a patrol officer, a detective, a doctor, a charging deputy district attorney, a deputy district attorney handling the preliminary hearing and one for the trial, and a judge or judges. In the juvenile court proceedings she may be represented by her own attorney. In addition, she may talk to the emergency response worker, a court intake social worker, a family reunification worker, a permanent placement worker, and an adoptions worker. In other proceedings, such as marital dissolution, she may talk to other persons, and the

list goes on. She will have to deal with each of these workers as best she can. Each may interview her. Each will bring to the child his or her sensitivity, professional training, and legal requirements.

She may also have contact with others who are aware of her case and talk to her about it, such as the reporting party, school personnel, emergency shelter care staff, foster parents, the family doctor, a therapist, a child advocate, and her family and friends.

After the interviews, she may be required to testify both in criminal and juvenile court. In criminal court she may be required to testify at the preliminary hearing and trial, both under direct and cross-examination. And she will be asked at these times to recount events and to identify the person who abused her. Every time she testifies she will be required to take an abstract oath. She may be asked complex questions. Attorneys may object to her statements and argue in front of her. The questioning may take hours, days, or weeks. They may expect her to act like an adult.

Time passes. People come and go. They take her to many new places for interviews. They ask her the same questions. They say they want to help her.

This is the story of many boys and girls who are physically and sexually abused, neglected or treated with severe cruelty who then enter the justice system. (California Child Victim Witness Judicial Advisory Committee Final Report, 1988, pp. 2–3)

THE MANDATORY REPORTING LAW

Justice system involvement in child abuse and neglect usually starts with a report. Anyone can report suspected abuse or neglect, but some people are required by law to report. As explained in chapter 1, the Federal Child Abuse Prevention and Treatment Act of 1973 requires states to enact mandatory reporting laws for child abuse in order to be eligible for federal funding for prevention and treatment services. Today, all states have mandatory reporting laws.

It is generally recognized that these laws have led to a large increase in reported cases of child abuse and neglect. Over half of the state laws provide for criminal sanctions ranging from fines to imprisonment for the failure of specified professionals to report. Experts agree that the great bulk of reports now received by child protective agencies would not have been made but for the passage of mandatory reporting laws and the media campaigns that accompanied them (Besharov, 1990).

Most state statutes require professionals coming under the mandate to report when they suspect child abuse and neglect. Almost all states now require any form of suspected child maltreatment to be reported, including physical abuse, sexual abuse and exploitation, physical neglect, and emotional maltreatment (Besharov, 1990).

Who Reports

The professionals required to report under typical mandatory reporting laws include teachers, day care personnel, foster parents, social workers, physicians, dentists, nurses, psychologists, law enforcement, and marriage and family counselors. Some mandatory reporting laws often cover commercial film and photographic print processors.

California is an excellent example of a rigorous mandatory reporting law. The professionals required to report under the California mandatory reporting laws include "child care custodians," "medical practitioners," "nonmedical practitioners," "personnel of child protective agencies," and "commercial film and photographic film processors" (e.g., California Penal Code, §§111654 and 11166).

These categories, in turn, include several different groups that might come into contact with a child as a result of a working or professional relationship. Child care custodians include teachers, school administrators, child care day camp and community services personnel, foster parents, group home or residential personnel, social workers, and probation officers.

Medical practitioners include physicians, psychologists, psychiatrists, dentists, chiropractors, and nurses. Thus, psychiatrists and psychologists must report suspicions of child abuse, an obligation that must override the traditional client-therapist privileged communication. Nonmedical practitioners include marriage and family counselors, a county public health employee and religious practitioners who diagnose, examine, and treat children. Ministers are not exempted from the mandatory reporting law if they are involved with children in a teaching or counseling capacity.

Child protective agency personnel refers to law enforcement officers, probation officers and social workers in county probation and welfare departments. These professionals play a dual role in the processing of child abuse cases, both as sources of reports and as investigative agents. Significantly, lawyers are not mandated reporters under any of these laws.

Commercial film and photographic print processor means any person who develops exposed photographs into negatives, slides, or prints for compensation. If such persons discover pornographic and obscene materials involving children, they are under obligation to report this to the authorities.

These mandated reporters are provided immunity from civil and criminal liability as a result of making required or authorized reports of suspected child abuse when, in fact, no abuse can be proven. However, persons who report are not liable either civilly or criminally unless it can be proven that a false report was made and that the person knew the report was false.

Failure of these mandated reporters to report by telephone immediately or as soon as practically possible is a misdemeanor punishable by confinement in county jail for a term not to exceed six months or by a fine of not more than $1,000 or both. For those required to report who do not do so, there may also be civil liabilities (Attorney General's Commission on the Enforcement of Child Abuse Laws, 1986; *Landeros v. Flood*, 1976). In *Landeros v. Flood*, an attending physician noticed that a child had suffered injuries consistent with physical abuse. He treated these injuries, but did nothing to report the matter to CPS or to the police. The child returned home and thereafter suffered even more serious injuries. The child, through a guardian *ad litem*, sued the doctor for failing to take protective action. The California Supreme Court found that the attending physician and the hospital had a duty to report the child's condition to the authorities, and that the doctor could be civilly liable for injuries suffered by the child thereafter.

These penalties are intended to ensure that all those required to do so will report all suspected incidents of child abuse immediately to a child protective agency. However, according to Besharov (1988), the possibility of civil and criminal liability for not reporting may lead to over-reporting of child abuse cases. Besharov (1990) also notes that there is a problem both with unreported cases that should have been reported and unfounded reports of cases that should not have been reported. He argues that many professionals (and private citizens) do not have a clear idea about the meaning of the terms "child abuse" and "child neglect," and therefore report many minor situations that simply do not amount to child maltreatment. They see an assault on a child, and whether or not it is serious they report it; they see marginal child care, and whether or not the child's basic needs are met, they report it.

Most statutes do not require that the reporter have absolute proof that the maltreatment has taken place, simply that he or she has reason to suspect that abuse or neglect has taken place. Often the standard of "reasonable cause" to suspect is used as the standard of certainty for reporting. Determining exactly what "reasonable cause" means may often be problematic. According to Besharov (1990), the legal injunction to report suspected abuse should not be an open-ended invitation to call in the slightest suspicion. A vague concern over a child's welfare is not a sufficient reason to report. He argues that there must be sufficient objective evidence to justify a report. Such evidence may be either "direct"—firsthand observations or accounts—or "circumstantial"—concrete facts, such

as the indicators of abuse and neglect described in chapter 2.

Other ambiguities in the reporting law involve how direct the information must be and how current the alleged abuse is (Faller, 1990). For example, what if a child discloses that he or she was sexually molested four years ago? Most state laws would require the reporting of such an incident. What if a treating therapist learns that the child victim was abused twice on two separate occasions rather than only once? Again, many reporting laws require a new report to be made.

The reporting provisions in most states provide for keeping the identity of the reporting person confidential. Once a report is made, that information as well as other materials in the protective services record of the reported family is confidential to anyone outside the protective services system.

THE ROLES OF CHILD PROTECTIVE SERVICES AND SOCIAL SERVICES

When a child abuse or neglect report reaches the child protective services (CPS), their staff of intake workers and assessment specialists immediately try to investigate the allegations of abuse or neglect. This response system is legally mandated, and should be open seven days a week, twenty-four hours a day. If the case is serious, the child will immediately be removed from the family and admitted to a shelter care or relative's home. The test for removal is whether a caretaker can ensure the child's safety at home or in the community.

The decision to remove a child from home is one of the most serious in the legal system. In some jurisdictions, the CPS worker may remove the child based upon observation and without further authority. In others a warrant from a judicial officer must be sought. Sometimes the police will be the first to detect a problem, such as when they are arresting a parent for criminal behavior. They may discover a child and then call

CPS to take control of the child by finding a parent or relative or, as a last resort, placing the child in emergency care.

The main goal of the child protective services is to stabilize the family situation so that the child can remain safely in the home. This can often be accomplished by the provision of services directly or by referral. Only in the most serious cases when harm to the child is imminent, and no action by the CPS worker will remove that risk, should the child be removed. Often medical examinations are a necessary part of the investigation, although such examinations usually occur after removal. All CPS agencies have the authority to investigate reports of child abuse and neglect and to make referrals to police, juvenile courts, and the district attorney's office.

Not all cases that reach the CPS hotlines must be investigated. Investigating all reports would immobilize agencies, violate family rights, and invite lawsuits (Besharov, 1990). Reports that should not be investigated include: (1) those that clearly fall outside the agency's definitions of child abuse and neglect as established by state law; (2) reports in which the caller gives no credible reason for suspecting that the child has been abused or neglected; (3) reports whose unfounded or malicious nature is known to CPS; and (4) reports in which insufficient information is given to identify and locate the child (Besharov, 1985).

In making the initial screening decisions the intake workers should rely on three sources of data: information from the reporters, archival data from central registers of case records, and information elicited from collateral service providers and other professionals who have knowledge of the family reported (Stein and Rzepnicki, 1983). Intake social workers should be experienced and highly trained personnel with the ability to understand complex situations and the authority to make decisions. They have a great deal of discretion in making decisions about the validity of a complaint to determine whether it should be investigated (Stein, 1991).

If a case is investigated, most state statutes contain provisions that either mandate or permit a number of important steps. In performing their investigations, the child protective service workers make home visits, interview family members, and contact other professionals who have had some involvement with the family (Faller, 1990).

Child protective services are generally required to begin an investigation within twenty-four hours of receiving any report of abuse or neglect. If it appears that the child is in imminent danger, the investigation must begin immediately. Most state statutes include provisions for home visits, either on a discretionary or mandatory basis. Many statutes authorize home visits without obtaining a warrant or first establishing reasonable cause. The home visit usually begins with the investigator requesting consent to enter the home to interview the child. Even if consent is denied, however, the social service investigator has legal authority to enter and may summon the police or obtain a court order to aid him or her in doing so. If there is reason to believe that a child is in danger, the police may use reasonable force to gain entry (Wald, 1992).

Lower courts have rebuffed challenges to these schemes, finding a warrant requirement inapplicable on the ground that it would seriously impair the state's efforts to protect the child (*Darryl H. v. Coler*, 1984; *Ehret v. New York City Department of Social Services*, 1985; *E.Z., et al., v. Gregory Coler, et al.*, 1985). It should be noted, however, that serious harm can be caused when innocent people are accused of abuse, and that great care should be taken to ensure that an investigation is warranted.

The primary purpose in the initial investigation is to assess the original accusation of maltreatment. The workers must also assess the degree of risk were the child to remain at home. Traditionally, children were removed from home without first considering other alternatives. Based on the Adoption Assistance and Child Welfare Act of 1983, social service departments now must provide services to prevent removal and support family integrity. The "reasonable efforts requirement" of the Adoption Assistance Act (P.L. 96-272; see ch. 1) mandates that efforts be made to prevent removal of children from their own homes and if removed to reunite children with their families. A written judicial determination that social service efforts were reasonable is a contingency for the states to claim reimbursement under Title IV-E of the Social Security Act (Stein and Comstock, 1987).

Social workers have learned techniques to prevent removal and preserve families without endangering the child. Intensive family preservation services have been effectively utilized in many jurisdictions to maintain children in their homes without significant risk of harm. The best-known model, Homebuilders, has been expanded to many jurisdictions across the United States (Barthel, 1992).

In an attempt to direct the discretionary decisions of social workers, standardized protocols for risk assessment are now becoming more and more common in CPS agencies. The use of standardized risk assessment protocols is seen as a protection against a possible liability suit against child care agencies (see chapter 8). According to Stein and Rzepnicki (1983), investigative workers must have a framework for gathering information which directs attention to the data base needed to reach decisions about minimum acceptable standards for parenting. In deciding whether to leave children in their own homes or take them into protective custody, the evaluation of family information is exceedingly important. Properly standardized and validated risk assessment instruments would be valuable tools in assessing past harm to the child and future risk of harm. However, relatively little research has been conducted to ensure that risk assessment instruments currently in use are, in fact, reliable and valid predictors of future risk (Wald and Woolverton, 1990). Another concern is that the requirements of doing a proper risk assessment and providing reasonable services may not be feasible in light of the increased

number of reported cases and reduced services as a result of budgetary cuts.

After assessing the situation, the CPS worker will generally take one of the following courses of action:

1. Do nothing.
2. Provide services and offer future assistance.
3. Leave the child at home, with some safeguards, such as restraining orders or in-home services.
4. Remove the child to a children's shelter or emergency foster home.
5. Remove the alleged offender (sometimes to jail), thus permitting the child to remain.

There need not be a report of child maltreatment for a family to receive social services. A family may voluntarily ask for help in raising their child. In this situation, the family may receive services from the agency voluntarily, or may sign a contract for services. If such voluntary programs fail, other more intrusive steps may be taken. If voluntary services fail or if the risk to the child is too great, a petition may be filed by the social services agency asking for juvenile court protection of the child. All state statutes require that proceedings must be commenced if the child is removed from the parents. A petition may also be instituted even if the child remains at home.

Once a case is in the court system, the court may order the social services agency to continue to maintain contact with the family and provide needed services. In most states the social service agency is mandated to manage the case through to its conclusion. Unless the child abuse is too severe, a social worker will first try to put a case on a voluntary family or a court-ordered family maintenance plan before removal of the child is sought in the juvenile court. If the child has been removed for safety reasons, social service departments are mandated to maintain "family reunification programs" which provide services to reunite the family. These services are provided for up to twelve months with a possible six-month extension by the juvenile court. While the first goal of the child protective services is to protect the child, preserving the family is their second goal. These are the mandates of the Federal Adoption and Foster Care Assistance Act and state laws.

Wald (1988) notes that child welfare laws now are based on the assumption that, whenever possible, protection should be provided in the child's own home, because it is better for the child. He cautions that we may have moved too fast in the direction of home-based services and that we need more data on the impact of interventions on children, in particular the impact of foster care. Other experts argue that home-based services are the best means for effective change within the family while providing protection for the child. Such services have become an integral part of social services to families in many states (Barthel, 1992).

Case Example (*Darryl H., et al., v. Gregory Coler, et al.*, 1984)

The following case example from Illinois illustrates some of the problems involved in investigating allegations of child abuse. The H. family brought a suit for damages against individual members of the Illinois Department of Children and Family Services, and others. The H. family claimed that the defendants violated their constitutional rights during an investigation of a report of alleged child abuse in their home.

The facts reveal that the plaintiffs in this case, the H. family, comprise a family unit of a stepfather, mother, and two children, ages six and seven. On October 25, 1982, Paula Davis, a caseworker for the Illinois Department of Children and Family Services (DCFS), went to the H. family home to investigate a complaint of suspected child abuse received by DCFS from a mandated reporter. Davis, finding the two adults at home when she arrived for her investigation, explained

the purpose of her visit and was allowed into the home to discuss the allegations. Davis interviewed the mother and the stepfather at home and indicated that an interview with the children would be necessary.

The two adult plaintiffs then accompanied Davis to the children's school. At school, the H. children were called into a room near the principal's office. After asking their stepfather, but not their mother, to leave the room, Davis questioned the children about facts pertinent to the allegations. The children indicated that they were spanked infrequently by their mother, bathed daily, and had adequate food. At this point, Davis proceeded to conduct a physical examination of the two children with the help of the mother, but over the mother's objection.

Davis concluded that the report of abuse of the H. children was unfounded. Accordingly, Davis, pursuant to DCFS policy, notified the H. family of the finding and deleted all information identifying the family from the State Central Register.

The H. family thereafter brought suit in the Court alleging deprivation of their constitutional rights under the Fourth, Fifth, Ninth, and Fourteenth Amendments. The plaintiffs claimed that defendants, by searching their home and their children, violated the plaintiffs' right to be free from unwarranted state intrusion into their family privacy and their right to be free from unreasonable or warrantless search of their home and their children. The plaintiffs further sought injunctive relief against the state defendants, which would prohibit future enforcement of DCFS's policy of searching homes and children in suspected child abuse cases without warrants. Finally, the H. family alleged that DCFS violated their right to family privacy by not investigating the complaint of the mandated reporter to determine if it was made in good faith.

With regard to the unreasonable search claim, the court found that a valid exception to the requirement of a warrant under the Fourth Amendment is voluntary consent by the parties, and the Court found that the consent defeated their claim.

The H. family argued that their consent was not voluntary, because they did not know that they had the right to refuse. The Court found that the H. family's consent was voluntary, notwithstanding the fact that they were not informed of their right to deny Davis access to the house.

The H. family also claimed that the state defendants violated their Fourth Amendment rights to be free from unreasonable searches of the children's bodies. According to the facts as stated previously, the search of the children was conducted by the state defendants over the objection of the caretakers, but with the assistance of the mother. The Court held that the examination of the children did not violate the Fourth Amendment for three reasons. First, the mother, by assisting Davis during the examination, consented to the search of the children. Second, even assuming that the mother's participation did not amount to consent, the physical examination did not constitute a "search" within the scope of the Fourth Amendment. Third, even assuming the examination can be considered a "search" under the Fourth Amendment, defendants' conduct did not descend to the level of unreasonableness. Each ground provided an independent basis for granting judgment for the state defendants.

The H. family alleged that the state defendants violated their Fourteenth Amendment right to be free from unwarranted governmental intrusion into their family privacy or autonomy by interfering with their right to raise their children as they see fit. They pointed out that the Supreme Court has recognized that parents have a constitutionally protected right to act with autonomy in their decision-making about their family life. This right has generally been articulated as a right of privacy based on the concept of liberty in the Fourteenth Amendment. The right has been extended to many aspects of family rights.

The Court held, however, that parental autonomy is not absolute. The state, in its role as *parens patriae*, is the ultimate protector of the rights of children, and may act to provide for their health, safety, and welfare when the parents fail to do so. The Court continued that in cases of suspected child abuse, the state has a clear interest in protecting the child from harm by the parents. To protect this interest the state may, if necessary, go as far as to separate the neglectful parents from their children.

Therefore, the state procedure of investigating reports of alleged abuse by going to the family's home within twenty-four hours without first procuring a warrant does not result in an erroneous deprivation of the family's rights. Neither does the state procedure of examining children's bodies in order to determine if the report of abuse is founded create a substantial risk of erroneous deprivation of the children's rights. The examination is not a criminal investigation of the children, but is meant to protect and help them.

In summary, the Court held that the state procedures for investigating a report of alleged child abuse act to protect the private interests involved, with little risk or erroneous deprivation of these rights. It further held that the state defendants had taken care to ensure that the state intrusion into the family's privacy was done in a way that minimized and limited that intrusion and was done with the welfare of the family, especially the children, in mind. For these reasons, the Court found that there was no violation of the H. family's Fourteenth Amendment right to privacy because of the investigation and search of their home and the children.

Discussion

This case addresses a fundamental issue in all child abuse cases, whether society is prepared to sacrifice family autonomy for the goal of child protection. Is the discovery and treatment of child abuse a more important social goal than the right of a family to be free from state intervention?

Based on this case and similar cases throughout the United States, the goal of child protection is of greater social significance.

Due process rights to be free from unreasonable searches and seizures have also given way to child protection. A police officer who hears a child in distress is permitted to enter a house without a warrant and seize contraband which may be discovered inside of the house (*In re Christopher B.*, 1978; *In re Robert P.*, 1976).

One question which the case does not address is how far the child abuse investigators can go to determine whether abuse or neglect has occurred. Sometimes children will not divulge any negative information about their parents if the parents are in the room. Should that fact permit the investigator to insist that an interview of the child take place away from both parents?

The court seems to indicate that the search would have taken place even if the family had tried to resist the investigation to begin with. Do you agree? How would you respond if an investigator asked to interview and inspect your children concerning an allegation of child abuse?

THE ROLE OF LAW ENFORCEMENT AGENCIES

In addition to the child protective services agency, law enforcement agencies also receive reports of suspected abuse and neglect. Since many of these cases may involve criminal behavior, some states require severe cases be cross-reported by CPS to law enforcement immediately by telephone and in written form within a short time (typically thirty-six hours) if at all possible (National Center on Child Abuse and Neglect, 1984). Law enforcement carries a dual role in child abuse and neglect cases: (1) to protect the child and (2) to investigate possible crimes. There are many practical and compelling factors which necessitate the involvement of law enforcement. First, child maltreatment is often criminal behavior which can be punished severely, depending on the facts of the crime. The legal authority of the police to investigate and arrest, along with their perceived authority and status, make it imperative that they assist in the initial investigation. Today, many police officers have received special training in interviewing child victims and in detecting evidence of possible abuse and neglect.

The responding officer, who often goes out to the scene of the alleged abuse, will make several initial decisions: whether to take the child into protective custody, whether to arrest the parents or caretakers or seek the authority to do so, whether to seek criminal charges from the district attorney's office, or whether to take no action.

The immediate and future protection of the child is often dependent on the completeness and accuracy of the initial investigation and report. Sometimes the goal of protecting the child may result in important evidence being lost if the officer must use valuable time placing the child in a shelter facility or in an emergency foster home.

The normal procedure in investigating charges of abuse and neglect is to visit the child's home or the place where the abuse allegedly took place. Investigation usually involves interviewing possible witnesses. Most of the witnesses may be family members, including the alleged victim.

There are several procedures which should be followed when interviewing witnesses. For example, when interviewing any person who is suspected of criminal conduct, the police officers must inform them of their rights pursuant to *Miranda v. Arizona* (1966). If the person interviewed is not a criminal suspect, no such admonitions or warnings need to be given.

While the police can arrest suspects, very few accusations of child abuse result in an immediate arrest. It may take days or weeks to develop enough evidence for an arrest. In many cases, arrest and prosecution may not be in the best interests of anyone, including the victim. The National Center on Child Abuse and Neglect has issued guidelines for arrests in child abuse cases.

The Center's position is that an arrest is justifiable when there is extreme injury to the child, when the child is in immediate danger, when evidence exists that a serious crime has been committed, when there is reason to suspect that the suspect will flee the jurisdiction, or when arrest is necessary to preserve the peace (National Center on Child Abuse and Neglect, 1984).

According to Faller (1990) the central role of the police in trying to identify the suspect may be in conflict with the protective and family reunification functions of the social services agency. However, current police enforcement ideology is similar to that of social services; that is, their main and primary role is also the protection of children.

Whether or not there is an arrest made, the police have the duty to investigate those cases in which a crime may have been committed. This role may be performed by the officer who arrived at the scene or by an investigating officer to whom the case is assigned. If a crime suspect is uncovered, the investigation may lead to a criminal prosecution in the criminal court.

Police agencies have made tremendous progress in working with child abuse and neglect cases through the 1980s and 1990s. Their availability around the clock, their high visibility and authority, their training in collecting evidence, and specialized training in child abuse and neglect make them important partners in the process of protecting children from maltreatment.

THE ROLE OF ATTORNEYS

Juvenile Court Proceedings

If the allegations of abuse or neglect are serious, a petition will usually be filed in the Juvenile Court alleging facts that would bring the child under the protection of the court. The petition may be written by the social services department or by their attorney. Once the petition is filed, the legal process is under way.

There are several different types of attorneys who may participate in the court activities surrounding the legal case. They include the attorney for the petitioner (usually the social services agency), the attorney or attorneys for the parents, and the attorney for the child. Whether any or all of these attorneys will participate in a dependency proceeding will depend on the practices in each jurisdiction.

Attorney for the Petitioner

The agency filing the petition may wish to have counsel to advise them about the petition and then appear on their behalf during the court action. Counsel for the agency most often is part of a public law office, usually a city or county attorney's office.

These lawyers will speak for the social service agency as it attempts to assert court jurisdiction over the child. If there is a contested hearing, the attorney will likely appear on behalf of the agency, produce evidence, and argue the case to the court.

Attorney for the Parents

Parents are entitled to have legal representation in dependency cases. In most states they are entitled to free representation if they are indigent. Counsel for the parents will advise them and appear on their behalf throughout the legal proceedings. In larger jurisdictions, the attorneys who represent parents at state expense are selected from a panel of specialists or from public law offices which have a special division devoted to dependency matters.

Attorneys for the parents may challenge the actions of the social services agency and present evidence to show that state involvement in their family is not necessary or legally permitted. They may also bring to the court's attention the fact that mandated services have not been provided to the parents and that the court should consider making a "no reasonable efforts" finding. Complicating representation of parents is the fact that often parents do not have the same legal position to take the matter before the court. The mother of a child who was allegedly sexually abused by the father has a distinctively different perspective on the case than does the father. These different perspectives may result in the attorney for the parents announcing that he or she cannot legally represent both parents because there is a conflict of interest between them.

For example, in the case of the abusing father and the unknowing mother, the mother may wish to have the court assert its jurisdiction, while the father may resist jurisdiction. One attorney could not represent both interests simultaneously. When such a declaration is made, it is incumbent upon the court to appoint a second attorney to represent one of the parents.

Attorney for the Child

In most jurisdictions someone appears to represent the interests of the child. Since the passage of the Child Abuse and Neglect Prevention and Treatment Act in 1974, states receiving federal funds must ensure that a guardian *ad litem* is appointed to represent the child in maltreatment proceedings. A guardian *ad litem* is an independent advocate for the child. In some states that guardian *ad litem* role is filled by an attorney. In other states there is both a guardian *ad litem* and an attorney to represent the interests of the child. The attorney for the child may be selected from a special panel of attorneys or may come from a public or private law office. They are paid by the state, although parents may be asked to reimburse the state for their services. In most jurisdictions, attorneys are not appointed in every child abuse or neglect case. The frequency and pattern of appointments depend on judicial policy and statutory provisions.

The attorney for the child has different roles depending on the jurisdiction. In almost all jurisdictions, if an attorney is appointed, he or she will take an independent position for the child in the court proceedings. In theory, the attorney for the child could support the parents, the state, or neither.

The effectiveness of the attorney for the child will depend on that person's ability to present an independent perspective to the court. This usually means that the attorney will have to conduct an independent investigation of the case so that it will not be necessary to rely on the facts developed by either the state or the parents. (A more comprehensive discussion of these issues will be presented in chapter 4.)

Other Attorneys

If other interested persons are given legal status to appear in the legal proceedings, they may appear with counsel. Such persons include step-parents, relatives, caretakers, and foster parents. The state will usually not provide free counsel for these persons even if they are indigent.

Volunteer Guardians Ad Litem/CASA

In addition to, or instead of, the attorney for a child, a volunteer guardian *ad litem* may be appointed to appear on behalf of the child. These volunteers are available in all jurisdictions, although their roles and responsibilities may vary from state to state. The use of volunteers to appear on behalf of children in juvenile court child welfare cases is a rapidly expanding movement. The National Court Appointed Special Advocate Program (CASA) was started in 1978. By 1993, it had established more than four hundred programs in all fifty states with more than 40,000 active volunteers. These volunteers may appear on the child's behalf in related proceedings, including domestic relations actions and criminal prosecutions.

Criminal Proceedings

If there are criminal proceedings arising out of the child abuse, the child will encounter another set of professionals. In these proceedings, the child will not ordinarily have an attorney, because the child is a witness and not a party to the proceeding. The prosecuting attorney represents the People of the state and not the child. The only other attorney will be one for the defendant.

On the other hand, in most states the child may have a support person who is assigned to look out for the child's interests. That person may appear with the child, explain the court procedures to him or her, assure that the child's legal rights are brought to the attention of the criminal court judge, and help prepare any victim statement from the child should the court request it. The power and duties of support persons vary from state to state.

Domestic Relations Court Proceedings

If there are domestic relations child custody proceedings involving the family, an attorney may be appointed to represent the interests of the child. Such appointments occur in some jurisdictions, but only in rare cases.

The child's attorney may be selected from a panel of attorneys or may be appointed from a public law office. Payment may be provided by the state or by the parents. The role of the child's attorney is similar to that in dependency matters: to be an independent voice for the child.

THE ROLE OF JUDGES

The role of judges will be different depending on which court the case is in, the structure of the court system, and the relationship between the different divisions of that court.

Juvenile Court Proceedings

If the case of an abused child reaches the juvenile court's dependency division, the judge has several decisions to make. The judge is given the responsibility to determine not only whether the state intervention is justified, but also what the intervention should be. If the judge declares the child to be a dependent of the court, the judge has the legal authority to make all decisions

concerning the custody and control of the child. The judge may have supervision and control over agencies which carry out the orders of the court. The judge may have supervision and control over a court staff. The judge may also have administrative powers over lesser judicial officers, such as referees and commissioners.

The relationship of the juvenile court to the courts of general jurisdiction differs throughout the United States. In most states the juvenile court is one division of the court of general jurisdiction. In some states the juvenile court is part of an inferior trial court.

The responsibility of a juvenile court judge involves much more than making legal rulings in the courtroom. The judge is responsible for ensuring that orders are carried out and that these children are well cared for, physically, medically, psychologically, and educationally—in every way that a parent would ensure that a child is well cared for.

Legislatures throughout the nation have given the juvenile court judge jurisdiction over the temporary and permanent displacement of children from their families. It is therefore important that the juvenile court be led by dedicated and talented judges who are able to work well with all the other agencies involved (Edwards, 1992).

Criminal Court Proceedings

The role of the judge in criminal court proceedings involving child maltreatment allegations is similar to that of the judge in other criminal proceedings. The judge is there to ensure that all legal standards and court procedures are met, and to manage the case. Often, if a case goes to trial, the outcome will be decided by a jury, rather than a judge.

The judge in child abuse cases must, however, be particularly sensitive to the special needs of the child victim witness. In recent years, many new procedures have been created to accommodate the child victim witness (see chapters 10, 11, and 12). At the same time, the rights of the defendant must be protected.

Domestic Relations Court Proceedings

The role of the judge in domestic court proceedings is distinct from the roles of the juvenile and criminal court judges. The parents bring legal actions to the domestic relations court, not the social services agency or the prosecutor. The court system provides a forum for the private ordering of parental rights regarding the child. Nevertheless, in some jurisdictions the court may appoint an attorney or a guardian *ad litem* to represent the child in custody proceedings (Edwards, 1987).

OTHER PROFESSIONALS INVOLVED WITH CHILD ABUSE AND NEGLECT

As stated earlier in this chapter, several other professional groups are mandated to report child abuse and neglect under the mandatory reporting laws. These include health professionals of all kinds, teachers, child care workers, foster parents, and commercial film and photo processors. It is important that each of these groups, particularly health practitioners and teachers, be trained in detecting signs of child maltreatment.

Many child maltreatment cases involve medical assessments or examinations. Doctors and nurses are often the first to report their findings to CPS and law enforcement. Doctors also may perform examinations of children after maltreatment has been reported. These examinations may include X-ray tests and colposcopic tests, as well as general physical examinations. A colposcope is a magnifying device which enables medical doctors to examine vaginal and anal openings for signs of trauma.

The increase in child abuse reports and the need for accurate information in determining whether abuse has occurred have resulted in specialization within the medical field. Detecting signs of sexual or physical abuse may be difficult for the general practitioner. Some hospitals and communities have developed centers where medical expert examinations can take place. Ensuring that suspected abuse is examined by the best medical experts in the community will improve the quality of an investigation and lead to better child protection.

CONCLUSION

A child abuse case can result in several different types of legal proceedings and can bring the child into contact with many different professionals. Each professional has a role as the case progresses.

Whether a case is serious enough to warrant further intervention depends on community standards, CPS practices, attorney standards, and the relevant statutes and local court rules. To some extent, intervention also depends on each professional's interpretation of the above standards. It is therefore important that each of the professionals working within the system receive as much training and experience as possible with child abuse and neglect cases and that they understand the various roles of the different professionals throughout the child protection system.

CHAPTER 4

Who Speaks for the Child?

Child advocacy is a recent phenomenon. Fifty years ago there was little concern about who would speak for children in legal proceedings which affected them. Not until the case of *In re Gault* were children guaranteed the right to an attorney in delinquency proceedings (*In re Gault*, 1967). A few years later, Congress passed the Child Abuse Prevention and Treatment Act (1974), which tied certain federal financial assistance to state child protective services agencies to a requirement that the states enact legislation ensuring that every child involved in a child welfare proceeding have a court-appointed guardian *ad litem*. Representation for children in other legal settings has been even slower in coming.

The dramatic rise in child abuse reports over the past twenty years has led many persons within the legal system to examine the question of representation for children. The assumption that everyone involved in legal proceedings will be looking out for the interests of the child has been discarded. In many situations children have too much at stake to rely upon other litigants to speak for them and ensure that their interests are protected. Moreover, observers appreciate that the legal system was not designed for children and that a child may be traumatized by the very system designed to provide protection (Child Victim Witness Com., 1988).

This chapter addresses the expanding role of child advocates in legal proceedings. We define a child advocate as a person who speaks on behalf of a child in a legal proceeding, whether that person be an attorney, hired staff, or a volunteer. We will discuss the different types of advocates and their roles in legal proceedings. We will then review the role of child advocates in a number of different legal settings, including juvenile, criminal, and domestic relations proceedings. Finally, we will describe some efforts to improve the quality of child advocacy in local communities and across the country.

A VOICE FOR CHILDREN

All children should have someone who speaks for them in any legal proceeding when their interests are at stake. Depending on the type of proceeding and the persons involved, different persons can provide that representation. A parent or relative may accompany a child through court proceedings. The child may be represented by an attorney. A guardian *ad litem* (GAL) may speak for the child.

In this chapter we focus upon the two most widely used types of child advocates in the United States, attorneys and GALs. Attorneys are legally trained professionals who, if qualified, can practice in state and federal courts. GALs are court-appointed individuals who appear on behalf of a child's best interests in legal proceedings. GALs may be attorneys, lay persons, or trained volunteers.

THE ROLE OF THE CHILD ADVOCATE

In the attorney-client relationship the lawyer's principal duty is the representation of the client's legitimate interests. The client's interests are ultimately determined by the client. When the client is a child, a question arises: Should the attorney follow what the child says or what the attorney believes is best for the child? Attorneys representing children have debated this issue for years, and there is still considerable disagreement. The age of the child makes this issue complex. There may be no disagreement if the child is a teenager capable of expressing his or her views. The six- to ten-year-old child will have an opinion, but some would say that this age child has insufficient maturity to make an important decision. The very young child may not be able to express an opinion at all. Even if the attorney were bound to follow the infant's desires, it may be necessary to decide what the infant would want if he or she could express an opinion.

The American Bar Association's House of Delegates approved a set of Juvenile Justice Standards advising court-appointed lawyers for children (Juvenile Justice Standards, 1980). These standards suggest that attorneys exercise their professional responsibility as they would in representing an adult. The standards attempt to ensure that the child's own views concerning the case will be effectively heard in court through the voice of the attorney. Not all attorneys or attorney offices accept the position taken by the Standards.

The role of the GAL is different from that of an attorney. The GAL represents the best interests of the child as determined by the GAL, even if that position is in conflict with the child's desires. The Hawaii Family Court has developed an excellent statement of the duties of a guardian *ad litem* in juvenile dependency cases.

> The guardian *ad litem* is a full participant in the court proceeding and is the only party whose sole duty is to protect the child's needs and interests. The GAL assumes the role of an advocate for the child's interests and in no way represents the petitioner (usually an agency) or the respondents (usually the parents or custodians). A GAL is appointed because of the child's immaturity and lack of judgment. Therefore, the GAL stands in the child's shoes and exercises substitute judgment for the child.
>
> In fulfilling this child-centered role, the GAL performs ten important and interrelated duties. The GAL:

1. Acts as an independent fact finder (or investigator) whose task it is to review all relevant records and interview the child, parents, social workers, teachers, and other persons to ascertain the facts and circumstances of the child's situation.
2. Ascertains the interests of the child, taking into account the child's age, maturity, culture, and ethnicity, including maintaining a trusting, meaningful relationship with the child via face-to-face contact.

3. Seeks cooperative resolutions of the child's situation within the scope of the child's interest and welfare.
4. Provides written reports of findings and recommendations to the court at each hearing to assure that all relevant facts are before the court.
5. Appears at all hearings to represent the child's interest, providing testimony when required.
6. Explains the court proceedings to the child in language and terms that the child can understand.
7. Asks that clear and specific orders are entered for the evaluation, assessment, services, and treatment of the child and the child's family.
8. Monitors implementation of service plans and dispositional orders to determine whether services ordered by the court are actually provided, are provided in a timely manner, and are accomplishing their desired goal.
9. Informs the court promptly in writing or orally if the services are not being made available to the child and/or family, if the family fails to take advantage of such services, or if such services are not achieving their purpose, and brings to the court's attention any violation of orders or new developments or changes.
10. Advocates for the child's best interests in mental health, educational, family court, juvenile justice, criminal justice, and other community systems. (The Duties of a Guardian *Ad Litem*, Family Court, First Circuit, State of Hawaii, 1991)

CHILD'S BEST INTERESTS OR CHILD'S DESIRES?

An attorney and a GAL may take different positions in court when advocating for the same child. Generally, the attorney will advocate for the child's wishes, while the GAL will speak on behalf of the child's best interests. This is an important distinction. For example, in a case in which the parents have severely physically abused a child, the court may have removed the child from parental custody. At a court hearing, if the child wanted to return home, the attorney would argue for that position. The GAL might argue that the child should be maintained in out-of-home placement for the child's safety. These different perspectives have led to situations in which a child is represented both by a GAL and by an attorney.

In the sections that follow, we will review the role of a child advocate in a number of different legal proceedings. It will become clear that the child advocate's role varies greatly depending on the jurisdiction, the age and maturity of the child, and the type of case.

JUVENILE COURT

The role of the child advocate is particularly complex in juvenile court child abuse and neglect cases. The proceedings are brought by the state on behalf of the child and often pit the state against the parents. The state usually appears through a local or state social services agency and asserts that parental behavior has fallen below the minimum level of societal acceptability and that intervention is necessary to protect the child.

The court process begins with the filing of a legal petition, the formal charging document filed by the state alleging parental misconduct or inadequacies. After a petition is filed there are a number of hearings. There may be a shelter or detention hearing in which the temporary placement of the child is decided by the court. The jurisdictional hearing or trial focuses upon the truth of the assertions in the petition, while the dispositional hearing addresses a plan to ensure the child is in a safe environment and that services are provided to the parents to assist them to modify their behavior so that the family can be reunited. The goals of the proceedings are twofold: protect the child and preserve the family.

The dispositional hearing may also specify the social services which will enable the parents to reunify with the child. Review hearings scheduled after the dispositional hearing focus upon whether the child can return to the parents, whether the jurisdiction of court can be terminated, and, if return or dismissal is not possible, what the permanent plan for the child will be. Pursuant to federal law, the permanent plan can be adoption, guardianship, or long-term care.

Representation in Juvenile Court

The Child Abuse Prevention and Treatment Act (P.L. 93-247) of 1974 requires states to appoint a GAL for children involved in juvenile court abuse and neglect proceedings as a condition for receiving federal grant funds authorized by the Act. Since passage of the Act, all states have enacted legislation requiring GAL representation for some or all children involved in legal proceedings arising from child abuse or neglect allegations. States vary greatly, however, in how the representation should be provided, who can serve as a GAL, how that person should be trained, and what role the GAL should play. Some states utilize lawyers as GALs, others have turned to trained volunteers, and others utilize a combination of the two.

States vary in providing GAL representation to children in juvenile court abuse and neglect cases. In eight states the appointment of a GAL is discretionary or required in only some cases. (National Study of Guardian Ad Litem Representation, 1990.) The national study of GAL representation conducted by CSR indicates that not all abused and neglected children are being represented in twenty-six states with only 49 percent in Florida, 32 percent in Nevada, and 22 percent in Delaware. The national study also indicates that most states do not have a sufficient number of trained volunteers or attorneys to be GALs. Inadequate resources and low compensation for attorneys are apparently reasons for the shortage.

Most state courts and legislatures have concluded that the child should have an independent voice in abuse and neglect proceedings. The type and quality of this representation vary from jurisdiction to jurisdiction across the country. In some there is an attorney for the child, in most a guardian *ad litem*, in some a trained volunteer or CASA volunteer, and in others a combination of two or more of these persons. The result is that on occasion there is one voice, sometimes there are several voices of different viewpoints, each expressing a perspective on behalf of the child, and sometimes there is no voice at all.

Case Example (*In re Patricia E.*, 1985)

An appellate court opinion from California illustrates some of the problems involved when the allegedly abused child is not represented by an independent advocate *(In re Patricia E.*, 1985). In August of 1978, the child, Patricia, was made a dependent child of the Kings County Juvenile Court upon a finding that her parental home was unfit. Patricia was born on November 24, 1977. Her home was alleged to be unfit because of neglect and abuse by her parents. She had sustained a skull fracture, two broken wrists, a broken right ankle, contusions, and abrasions. Both she and her brothers were removed from parental custody.

In June 1979, Patricia's status as a dependent child was continued, but she and her brothers were returned to parental custody. In November 1979 Patricia suffered further severe injuries at home, namely, a fractured femur and tibia of her right leg. She was placed in a foster home in Hanford, California. Her brothers were left in the custody of their parents and then placed in the custody of their father upon the dissolution of the parents' marriage. It is unclear from the record what role her father played in inflicting Patricia's injuries.

The case was transferred to Sacramento County, where a review hearing was held in juvenile court in February of 1983. The juvenile court appointed

county counsel to represent both the Sacramento County Welfare Department and the child. The county counsel is the legal representative for the county social services agency.

The child was not present at the hearing, and she appeared only through the deputy county counsel. A social worker testified for the department and recommended continued placement in the foster home. Neither the social worker nor the deputy county counsel spoke with the child prior to the hearing. The father testified in his own behalf and asked that his daughter be returned to his custody. The juvenile court continued the child as a dependent of the court and ordered that she remain in the Hanford foster home. The father filed an appeal of that decision.

On appeal the father contended that it was error to appoint the county counsel to represent both the welfare department and the child. The appellate court reversed the decision of the trial court. It noted that the law had been amended to permit representation for the child by county counsel only if there was no conflict of interest between the county and the child. The court held that even if joint representation could have been permitted, it was error to fail to appoint independent counsel in the absence of an affirmative showing that the child's interests would be adequately represented. It found that the error in not appointing independent counsel may have resulted in a miscarriage of justice.

In its analysis the court first pointed out that the father had the right to raise the issue of his daughter's right to counsel, since their relationship was so interwoven. Noting that Patricia's brothers were safely residing with their father, the court stressed that the parent-child relationship was at stake in the juvenile proceedings.

The court then turned to the question of dual representation. Can the county attorney represent both the social services agency and the child's interests simultaneously? The court found that:

> In this case there are considerations which support "informed speculation" that joint represen-

tation may have led to prejudicial ineffective assistance of counsel. The record contains no indication that the minor's counsel ever spoke to her. The minor was not present in court during the proceedings. The minor's counsel presented evidence of the minor's circumstances by calling as a witness a social worker with the Sacramento County Department of Social Welfare. However, that social worker had not spoken personally with the minor. In short, the record contains no indication the minor's surrogate counsel knew of her concerns or of her view of her situation. Counsel cannot be said to have effectively represented the minor's interests in these circumstances. (*In re Patricia E.*, 174 Cal.App.3d 1, at 9.)

Discussion

Assume that the county counsel had interviewed Patricia and that she had told him she wanted to return to her father. How would the attorney have been able to represent both Patricia and the county? Note that if the attorney believed he was representing Patricia's best interests he might be able to ignore her wishes and tell the court that her best interests required out-of-home placement. However, if he had to provide a voice for her wishes, the county counsel would have to argue two conflicting positions to the court. That is referred to as a conflict of interest. The normal legal remedy for a conflict of interest is to appoint a separate attorney for each party, in this case for the county and for Patricia.

Can you envision circumstances in which the county attorney could have effectively represented both the social services agency and Patricia?

Assume that Patricia was a baby and not able to talk. Are there any circumstances under which she would need to have independent counsel? Would an attorney for the baby be able to decide what her or his client's wishes were? Does a baby always want to return to its mother?

The California statute requires the attorney for the child to conduct an independent investigation to determine any facts necessary adequately to represent the interests of the child. The attorney for the child or GAL has this responsibility in many jurisdictions. Why is this necessary? The statute also requires the attorney to interview any child client who is over four years of age. Is this a good idea?

It is interesting to examine the position of the United Nations Convention on the Rights of the Child, which was written in 1989. With regard to the representation of children in legal or administrative proceedings, article 12 states:

> 1. State Parties shall assure to the child who is capable of forming his or her own views the right to express those views freely in all matters affecting the child, the views of the child being given due weight in accordance with the age and maturity of the child.
>
> 2. For this purpose, the child shall in particular be provided the opportunity to be heard in any judicial and administrative proceedings affecting the child, either directly, or through a representative or an appropriate body, in a manner consistent with the procedural rules of national law.

This article of the Convention guarantees a child the right to representation in all legal and administrative proceedings affecting the child so long as the child is capable of expressing views. When is a child capable of forming his or her own views? Children can be verbal at two and three years old. A baby can be verbal if we understand crying to be a demand for food or comfort. It is unclear who is to determine whether a child is capable of expressing his or her own views. Can the legislature declare that all children under a certain age are incapable of expressing their views? Can the matter be left to judges to decide on a case by case basis?

Under the Convention, the views of the child are entitled to weight in accordance with the age and maturity of the child. This would seem to indicate that a teenager's views would be of greater weight than those of an infant. Yet each has an equal interest in the outcome of the case. Does not this approach seem to give less attention to the younger child? Should there not be a guarantee that someone is speaking on behalf of the child in every proceeding which affects the child? Where the child is incapable of expressing his or her own views, the representative would be similar to a guardian *ad litem*.

Finally, the Convention guarantees the child the right to a representative in any judicial or administrative proceeding affecting him or her. This guarantee would logically extend beyond court proceedings to hearings addressing school expulsion, eligibility for benefits, and medical and mental health decisions. This is a broad range of hearings far greater than what child advocates normally cover in the United States.

The U.N. Convention on the Rights of the Child has been ratified by most countries in the world, but not by the United States of America. Many child advocates have urged the president to refer the Convention to the Senate for confirmation, but thus far, no action has been taken (Cohen and Davidson, 1990).

Case Example *(In re Lisa G.*, 1986)

The state of New Hampshire filed a Child in Need of Supervision Petition before the Concord District Court on behalf of Lisa G, a thirteen-year-old juvenile. Lisa G. had exhibited self-destructive behavior, including drug abuse, and was emotionally handicapped. Lisa's mother was unable to control her daughter, and her father was chronically hospitalized. Lisa's court-appointed attorney determined that neither Lisa nor her parents was able to act in Lisa's best interests and requested the court appoint a GAL for Lisa. The court granted that request, and the county appealed that decision arguing that the court had no authority to make such an appointment.

The Supreme Court of New Hampshire

affirmed the trial court decision. The supreme court wrote that the trial court has an inherent power to appoint a GAL. The question next addressed by the supreme court was whether a GAL was necessary, since Lisa was already represented by counsel. The court noted that when counsel is appointed to represent a juvenile in child protective proceedings and the juvenile is capable of considered judgment on his or her own behalf, determination of the client's interest in the proceeding should remain the client's responsibility. But in the event that counsel believes that the juvenile is unable to act in his or her best interest, counsel should request that the court appoint a GAL. In such a case, the GAL will act as a substitute decision-maker for the juvenile.

The court noted that the role of a GAL in such a proceeding is distinct from the role of defense counsel. In the adjudicatory (trial) stage the GAL may advise the court as to any pertinent information that the prosecuting attorney or defense counsel may choose to ignore. More importantly, at the dispositional phase, the GAL will represent the best interests of the child in recommending appropriate services.

Discussion

The state appealed the decision of the juvenile court judge to appoint a GAL for financial reasons. Court advocates usually cost money, and, since children are always indigent (without funds), the state usually has to pay for these advocates. Do you think that the cost of the child advocate should be a legal consideration?

The resources available for child advocacy remains a serious problem. In some jurisdictions, the caseloads for child advocates are so high that the quality of representation is jeopardized. One child advocate reported:

> This afternoon I am in the midst of a paper mountain, trying to acquire information for the

120-plus children I will represent in over 55 hearings this Friday before my county's Juvenile Court. I have been a lawyer with Child Advocacy for over ten years, have seen caseloads triple and funding decrease, so that my four full-time colleagues and myself have responsibility for more than 1,100 cases each. (Siroky, 1993)

A California appellate court has held that a court policy designed to save money by relieving parties of their attorneys after certain hearings have been completed in juvenile court dependency proceedings is impermissible (*In re Tanya H.*, 1993). The court noted:

> Our conclusion [is] that the juvenile court's fiscal problems cannot justify an interference with a statutory right to counsel. . . .

The struggle to provide adequate child advocacy services in the legal system remains a major challenge to legal communities throughout the country.

Court Appointed Special Advocates (CASA)

The Court Appointed Special Advocate (CASA) program was started in Seattle, Washington, in 1977 by David Soukup, then a juvenile court judge. Recognizing that children needed to have their best interests consistently presented to the court, Judge Soukup asked for volunteers to assist the juvenile court by appearing on behalf of abused and neglected children. The response was immediate and overwhelming. Assisted by the National Council of Juvenile and Family Court Judges, the CASA program has grown dramatically, so that there are chapters in all fifty states and over 40,000 active volunteers today (*History of the CASA Program*, 1987).

CASA programs are known by many different names, including CASA, Guardian *ad litem* programs, Pro-Kids, Child Advocates, Foster Child Advocate Services, and Voices for Children. The volunteers serve different roles in different programs across the country. In some the advocates are appointed to serve as GAL for one child, while in others the advocates represent many dependent children.

One study has concluded that trained volunteers such as CASA volunteers are as effective as trained attorneys in representing their clients and more effective than untrained attorneys (Ramsey, 1983). This is understandable, since trained volunteers may have more time with fewer cases than the professionals representing children. With only one or two cases, the CASA volunteer has the extra time to investigate each child's case. Juvenile court judges have found the work of CASA volunteers to be critical in aiding court efforts to serve abused and neglected children. The National Council of Juvenile and Family Court Judges has supported the use of CASA volunteers.

> Court Appointed Special Advocates (CASAs) should be utilized by the court at the earliest stage of the court process, where necessary, to communicate the best interests of an abused or neglected child. (*Deprived Children: A Judicial Response*, 1986)

Case Example (*In re Christina D.*, 1987)

A foster family filed an adoption petition on behalf of a child who had been relinquished by her parents. The court appointed special advocate (CASA) serving as guardian *ad litem* (GAL) attempted to object to the petition. The CASA wished to show that the foster family had previously had a child removed from their care due to institutional neglect. The Providence, Rhode Island, family court judge held that the CASA did not have standing to object to the petition. The judge held that only the social services agency had a right to appear at such hearing.

On appeal the Supreme Court of Rhode Island held that the CASA/GAL was the independent advocate for the child, and thus had standing to object to the adoption petition. The court stated:

> It is inconceivable that the guardian *ad litem*, appointed to represent the child's interests, would be denied the opportunity to convey those interests to the trial justice in a proceeding in which the ultimate focus is the best interest of the child.

The supreme court further reviewed the facts of the case and determined that inclusion of the evidence sought to be presented by the CASA/GAL would not have changed the outcome of the adoption petition. As a result, it affirmed the granting of the adoption petition.

Discussion

In addition to the type of person who will speak for the child, there is a question regarding in what types of proceedings the advocate will be able to appear. In the *Christina D.* case, the trial court sought to limit the CASA/GAL's role and not permit her to appear at an adoption proceeding. The Supreme Court ruled that the child should have an independent advocate at that hearing.

Several state statutes affirm the duty of the child's representative to investigate the interests of the child beyond the matter in which the advocate appears.

> In addition, counsel (for the minor) shall investigate the interests of the minor beyond the scope of the juvenile proceeding and report to the court other interests of the minor that may need to be protected by the institution of other administrative or judicial proceedings. (California Welfare and Institutions Code, section 317(3), 1993)

The legal status of the child in the proceeding is a matter of some concern. The child may have an advocate, but will the advocate have the same legal rights as the other parties in the proceeding? A party in a legal proceeding is one who has full legal rights, including the right to be heard, to be represented, to be given notice, to call and examine witnesses, and to appeal any decision made by the court. Granting the child party status is an important goal to ensure that the child's voice will be heard.

TERMINATION OF PARENTAL RIGHTS

One possible outcome after a child has been removed from parental custody is the termination of parental rights so that the child can be adopted. Public Law 96-272 designates termination of parental rights and adoption as the preferred plan for a child who cannot be returned home (Adoption Assistance and Child Welfare Act, 1980). It is a more permanent placement than guardianship or long-term foster or institutional care.

The hearing to terminate parental rights usually takes place after a child has been the subject of juvenile court abuse or neglect proceedings. If family reunification has not been successful, a petition to terminate parental rights may be filed in the civil courts of the particular jurisdiction, or it may be held in the juvenile or family court. In that proceeding, the court hears evidence whether the legal ties between the child and the parents should be ended. It is the most serious type of legal proceeding dealing with parents and children.

In many jurisdictions the child is represented by a child advocate. What the role of that advocate should be has been the subject of litigation.

Case Example (*In re J. V. and C. W., Jr.*, 1990)

In the case of *In re J.V. and C.W., Jr.* (1990), a petition to terminate the parental rights of

C.W., Sr., and L.W. was filed. The facts revealed that the children had been removed from the parents because they had been living in a dirty, unsanitary, and hazardous household due to a lack of basic parenting skills and that the children had often been left unattended and, when handled, were cared for improperly. The parents were consistently vague or evasive about the frequency and amount of feeding and medication given to the children. The children were occasionally given sour milk or drank from bottles having mold in them. Both children had numerous medical problems for which the parents failed to obtain medical help. In addition, the children exhibited subnormal growth and delayed development of language and cognitive abilities.

The state provided various daily and weekly services in an attempt to keep the family intact. The record showed repeated examples of parental uncooperativeness and refusals to follow the most basic instructions, even when they pertained to the health of the children.

The trial court found by clear and convincing evidence that the children had been out of parental control for a period of time, that the children could not be returned to parental custody without being exposed to harm and that reasonable efforts had been provided to prevent or eliminate that harm. The trial court terminated parental rights, and the parents appealed.

The appellate court affirmed the termination of parental rights. One issue addressed on appeal was whether the GAL had adequately represented the interests of the children. The parents contended that the GAL failed to act independently and simply adopted the state's position. The facts showed that the GAL appeared at all of the formal proceedings, interviewed the parties, and reviewed the records. He did not, however, visit any of the various homes maintained by the parents, did not interview the parents or service providers, nor introduce any witnesses at trial.

The court of appeal found that the GAL's representation was minimal at best. The court noted that the GAL at a termination proceeding is subject to a high standard of conduct.

> Investigation has to be the cornerstone of the guardian *ad litem*'s representation of a child's best interest. It should go without saying that firsthand knowledge of the parties and the circumstances is, at minimum, helpful and, in the closer cases, necessary.

The appellate court then reflected at some length on the role of the guardian *ad litem* at a termination of parental rights proceeding.

> The guardian *ad litem* is not designed to be the decision-maker and is an advocate for the child, not the parents or the State. It simply is not sufficient for a guardian *ad litem* to sit back, review the record and the arguments, and arrive at a decision. This function is filled ably by the juvenile courts. Neither is it sufficient for a guardian *ad litem* to be a handmaiden to one of the adversary parties. Usually there will be a limited number of options for which to advocate, such as whether or not to terminate the parent-child relationship, and the guardian *ad litem* will often have a position consistent with one of the adverse parties and in opposition to another. This, however, must be solely as an advocate for the interests of the children. Otherwise, the guardian *ad litem* is merely perfunctory, serving only to fulfill arcane, if not empty, requirements of due process.

Discussion

If the GAL had done a substandard job of advocating for the child, would it have been appropriate to reverse the case and send it back for a new trial? Compare this case to *Patricia E.*, in which the appellate court did send the case back to the trial judge for another hearing.

From a judicial perspective, the value of a child advocate is measured in great part by the quality of information the advocate can provide the court. Generally, the court expects to receive information from the state and from the parents. If the court additionally receives an independent perspective from the child advocate, that information will greatly improve the quality of decision the court will make in the case.

Useful information must be based upon an independent investigation. If the child advocate simply reads the reports prepared by the state, he or she will be of little value to the court and will only be able to offer an opinion based upon the same information available to everyone else in the proceeding. If, however, the advocate has conducted an independent investigation, interviewed the child and other parties, consulted experts and made other appropriate inquiries, the court will value the advocate's opinion greatly. After all, the child advocate is speaking for the child.

An independent investigation usually involves time outside of the courtroom. Given the large caseloads in some jurisdictions (up to hundreds of children) and the numerous cases in court every day (as many as five to fifty per attorney), it is clear that some child advocates cannot conduct an independent investigation in every case. Indeed, it is questionable whether some child advocates can even meet with the child client, much less conduct an independent investigation.

In order to provide some degree of quality representation, the child advocate must have a reasonable caseload. This means that there be some days or half-days in which the advocate does not appear in court. It also means that the child advocate must have some access to investigative services. An investigator can do much of the work needed to support the advocate in court, usually more skillfully and for less money.

Lower caseloads and investigative support both cost money. Whether some jurisdictions will be able to support a high-quality child advocacy program remains to be seen. Later in this chapter, we will discuss some efforts to improve the quality of child advocacy in selected jurisdictions.

CRIMINAL COURT

In the criminal courts, the child advocate has a more limited role to play on behalf of the child. Criminal actions are brought by the state against persons accused of violating the criminal law. The child may be a victim of the criminal act or a witness to it, but the child is not a party to the legal action. As a result, the child usually is not represented by an attorney, although in some jurisdictions children may be appointed a support person or GAL to accompany them through the criminal process (Hardin, 1987; Whitcomb, 1988).

Case Example (*State v. Freeman*, 1985)

In *State v. Freeman* (1985), the father was indicted for the murder of his wife. The State made a motion to interview the defendant's three children. The trial court appointed a GAL on behalf of the three children to determine whether such interviews would be in the children's best interests and, if so, the time, place, and manner of such interviews. The father had been acting as the children's GAL and had refused permission for such interviews. The father appealed the trial court's decision.

The appellate court ruled that a GAL should be appointed on behalf of the children. It noted that parents normally make the decision whether to permit children to be interviewed, but that when a parent is a criminal defendant, the parent's interests are in conflict with the best interests of the children. It ruled that

[t]he most advantageous method of balancing the various interests of all concerned is for the courts to appoint a guardian *ad litem* for the children. The court's use of such an appointment has normally been limited to noncriminal matters; however,

where the facts so warrant, there is no good reason why this protective device should not be extended for use in criminal cases.

The court concluded that the role of the GAL in criminal proceedings will be to speak to the children, their teachers, physicians, and other persons they are involved with in order to determine whether an interview by the state would be in the children's best interests. Furthermore, if the GAL determines that such interviews will not have an adverse impact upon the children, he or she shall suggest to the court the appropriate time, place, and conditions for the interviews. Finally, the court added that the GAL is not an investigator relative to the merits of the case against the father and is not to make his or her own determination as to the importance of the children's knowledge of relevant facts.

Discussion

The use of GALs in criminal cases is controversial. Criminal defense attorneys contend that GALs are an unnecessary addition to the criminal process. They fear that the GALs will lend support to the prosecution. Yet it is in the criminal courts that the child is likely to suffer great trauma. The child may be interviewed numerous times by different parties and professionals. Court testimony may be the most traumatic experience of all. The child may have to face the person the child has said inflicted the abuse.

The Supreme Court of North Carolina has developed a special procedure to address the unique needs of the child victims and witnesses who appear in criminal court. It provides for the appointment of a *pro bono* GAL attorney to represent child victims and witnesses in criminal court. The rules further state that if a GAL is appointed to represent a child victim in a criminal court,

any attorney participating in the case will be obligated, as a matter of professional responsibility, to seek the consent of that GAL in order to interview the child. The role of the GAL also includes making certain that the case is progressing through the court process at a speed appropriate to the child's needs, explaining the court process to the child and family as appropriate, recognizing and communicating to the prosecutor any special needs the child may have, and coordinating the civil and criminal cases if there is a related civil juvenile case. The rule makes clear that the GAL is not a party to the case, does not participate in discovery, and cannot actively participate in the trial of the case. A few other states have developed similar protections for children who appear as victims and witnesses in criminal courts. (See chapter 10 and Whitcomb, 1988.)

DOMESTIC RELATIONS COURT

Children are also the subject of litigation in domestic relations proceedings. When parents separate or dissolve their marriage, the care, custody, and control of their children is sometimes contested. Many of these cases end up in the court system for resolution. While all states permit and encourage parents to resolve custody and visitation issues without state involvement, when the parents cannot agree, some states identify an advocate to ensure that the child's interests are protected.

In Wisconsin, for example, the state law requires a GAL be appointed if:

1. The court has reason for special concern as to the welfare of a minor child.
2. The legal custody or physical placement of the child is contested. (Wisc. Stats. Anno. section 767.045, 1993)

Case Example (*Riemer v. Riemer*, 1978)

In a divorce action the husband and wife contested custody of a child born during the marriage and contested the paternity of a child born after the commencement of the divorce proceeding. The trial court appointed a GAL to represent both children. The GAL initially requested that there be blood tests to assist with the paternity determination but did not pursue that request when the husband and wife agreed that the child was not the husband's. The trial court found that the husband was not the father of the second child.

The appellate court reversed the trial court. It held that the GAL could not represent the interests of both minors and that another GAL should have been appointed to represent the interests of the second child. The court noted that the second child had an interest in having the husband declared to be his father. The court held that there was a conflict of interest when one GAL represented two parties with different interests on the paternity issue. In addition, the appellate court noted that it is the duty of the GAL to continue his representation beyond the trial level if an appeal is taken and to represent the interests of the child during the appeal.

Discussion

Some states provide for representation of children in domestic relations custody litigation when there are special circumstances. In Hawaii, the family court has developed factors to be considered in such an appointment. Such factors include:

1. where the level of hostility and conflict between the parents is a substantial impediment to recognition, by either or both, of the needs of the child;
2. where there is an indication the child suffers from serious emotional problems and those problems are not being treated;
3. where there is a serious allegation of child abuse or neglect;
4. where there are complex legal issues involving the child;
5. where a child of sufficient maturity is concerned about the outcome of the case, or expresses an interest in participating in the proceeding;
6. where the custody issues have remained unresolved for a long time and no immediate resolution seems apparent;
7. where there is a juvenile proceeding pending;
8. where there are persons other than a parent requesting custody; and
9. where there is a clinical history of significant psychological or emotional problems with either parent.

The California Standards of Judicial Administration recommended by the Judicial Council, section 20.5, offer similar guidelines for the appointment of counsel for minors when there is a dispute between parents in a domestic relations matter (California Standards of Judicial Administration, 1993).

Do you agree that these factors should be considered? Do you think that children should have their own representation in domestic relations custody litigation? Should such representation be provided only when abuse allegations are involved?

WHAT THE ADVOCATE SHOULD REPORT

In whatever context, in whatever role, the person who speaks for the child should always report to the court what the child wants. Reporting the child's desires may be couched in qualifying terms, but the child's representative must let the decision-maker know what the child's position is regarding the pending matter. Even if the parent has seriously abused the child and it would clearly not be in the child's best interests to return to the parent's custody, the representative must report to the court what the child wants. An example might be as follows:

> Your honor, Johnny wants the court to know that he would like to return home to his mother and father. He has forgiven them for everything they did to him and his sister and believes that everything will be all right now. I, on the other hand, believe that it would be very dangerous for Johnny to return to his parents' home before they have addressed their violence, drug abuse and other problems.

There are several reasons why the person speaking for the child should report the child's desires. First, if the representative does not let the court know what the child wants, no one else will. No other person in the courtroom has the access and legal relationship to the child that the representative does. Second, there will be other voices in the court with different perspectives. The court is in the best position to decide what should happen with the child. In order to make that decision, however, the court needs the highest quality information possible about the case, including what each person's perspective is. Third, if the representative does not distinguish between what the child wants and what the representative's own position is, the court may believe that the representative is relating the child's wishes. Fourth, in some legal proceedings, a different party is reporting to the court what the best interests of the child are. In juvenile dependency matters, that person may be a social worker. Fifth, by giving the court information about the child's desires, the representative is empowering the child. The child will not necessarily be getting what has

been requested, but at least the message will have been given to the court on the child's behalf.

Whatever type of proceeding and whatever the issues, the child's voice must be heard. Unless the representative for the child relates what the child's wishes are, no one will be speaking for the child.

A COMPREHENSIVE APPROACH TO THE REPRESENTATION OF CHILDREN

Children appear as victims, witnesses, or interested parties in various types of legal proceedings. While most commentators agree that their interests should be made known to the court through a representative, in some situations they have no voice in court. That is true for many reasons, including a legal tradition which has not been sensitive to the needs and desires of children, a lack of resources to support representation of children, and a lack of interest in providing such representation.

A number of concerned groups have begun to address the need for children to have adequate representation of their interests in all types of legal and administrative hearings. The American Bar Association has started an ambitious program designed to increase representation for children in legal proceedings. The ABA Section of Litigation's Task Force on Children was created to (1) recruit and assist lawyers to undertake the *pro bono* representation of children, and to match them with children in need, and (2) to support and stimulate the formation and development of *pro bono* children's law programs. The Task Force has collected information about children's legal projects around the country and is offering technical assistance to any community wishing to increase representation for children.

In Santa Clara County, California, a Child Advocacy Coordinating Council has been formed to bring together all attorneys, advocates, and support persons who appear with or on behalf of children in court proceedings. The goal is to ensure that every child who appears in court has a support person or, if necessary, an attorney throughout the legal proceedings. The council has recognized that government does not have the resources to provide representation for every child in every legal setting. The council has been able to identify situations in which children are not adequately represented and, through the use of volunteer advocates and attorneys, has been able to provide that representation (Edwards, 1993).

CONCLUSION

Children need a voice in court when their interests are at stake. Because of their age and legal status, they cannot speak for themselves. It is the responsibility of the legal and volunteer community to ensure that children have representation.

This chapter indicates that the trend is clear. Children are being represented more and more in legal proceedings. In some jurisdictions, the advocates are overwhelmed with high caseloads, and in other jurisdictions there are insufficient resources. Nevertheless, there are more child advocates now than ever. Advocate training is improving, as is the quality of advocacy they provide. As a nation, we have concluded that it is important that children be represented when their interests are concerned. The voice of children will be heard more loudly and clearly in the years to come.

PART 2

Harry and Judy decided to dissolve their fourteen-year marriage. Each hired an attorney and asked for exclusive custody of their two children, five-year-old Sally and three-year-old Bill. Mediation was unsuccessful in resolving their differences, and the family court judge ordered an investigation to assist the court in making a custody order. On a temporary basis the court placed the children with Judy in the family home and permitted liberal visitation with Harry.

Visits seemed to be going well until Judy noticed that Sally was masturbating after her visits with Harry. Judy asked Sally about her behavior, but Sally said very little. Judy persisted with her questioning and tape-recorded her conversations with Sally. After hours of questioning, Sally said, "Daddy and I play a secret game together. Daddy told me I can't talk about it with anyone."

Judy did not know what to do. She called Harry about what Sally had said, and he was furious. He said that Judy was putting ideas into Sally's head. He threatened to take legal action if she pursued the matter or questioned Sally any more.

Judy decided to take Sally to a therapist for counseling. After three visits, the therapist told Judy that she believed Sally had been sexually abused. She said that she was certain that Harry had been having Sally orally copulate him, and he had orally copulated her. The therapist also told Judy that she had reported her suspicions to child protective services pursuant to the mandatory reporting law.

THE LEGAL RESPONSE TO CHILD ABUSE

Judy contacted her attorney and asked if she should file for a change in the temporary custody order so that there would be no further visitation with Harry. Her attorney filed a motion to terminate visitation, and Harry responded with a motion to change custody of both children to him. He indicated in his motion that he would ask each of the children to testify at the custody hearing to report how Judy has been pressuring them to make false statements.

The child protective services worker contacted both Judy and Harry and interviewed both of the children. She is currently considering filing an action in the juvenile court to protect the children. The CPS worker also contacted the police, who are now investigating the case. The investigating police officer has concluded that Sally was molested by Harry and will be taking the case to the district attorney for the filing of charges.

In addition, Judy's attorney suggested that Judy file a civil action against Harry on behalf of Sally, alleging emotional and physical abuse and asking for damages. The attorney is drawing up the necessary legal papers for that action.

In a short period of time, four legal actions are about to commence in our hypothetical case.

Each involves the same family and the same victim, Sally. Each involves the same alleged abuse of Sally. Yet in most court systems in the United States, these actions will not be consolidated or even coordinated. Instead, each will involve different courts, different legal rules, and possibly different judges and attorneys. There is one constant, however. That is Sally and her testimony about the alleged maltreatment.

Part Two offers an overview of the legal system as it deals with child abuse in different legal contexts. The following four chapters examine issues relating to child abuse as they arise in four different legal contexts: juvenile, domestic relations, criminal, and civil. Each chapter outlines the unique aspects of the particular legal proceeding. Then, in chapter 9, we discuss the relationships among these different legal proceedings and the ways in which the legal system can be modified so that it can accommodate the special needs of children and families who must appear in several different court settings.

CHAPTER 5

Juvenile Court: The Child Protective Function

One of the principal tasks of a democratic society is to raise its children to maturity to become productive citizens. In the United States we rely primarily on the family to provide to children most of what they need in order to become citizens. According to the U.S. Supreme Court ruling in *Prince v. Massachusetts* (1941):

> It is cardinal with us that the custody, care, and nurture of the child reside first in the parents, whose primary function and freedom include preparation for obligations the state can neither supply nor hinder.

Other institutions participate in the socialization process, notably schools, churches, and recreational groups, but the fundamental authority for child rearing resides with a child's parents. When the family fails or is unable to raise its child within acceptable norms, society has an interest in intervening for its own goals. A dysfunctional family that is unable to raise its child threatens the viability of the social order.

Our legislatures and courts have recognized the importance of responding to family dysfunctions. Numerous laws detail society's responses to a family that cannot control a child's delinquent behavior, to a family that cannot protect a child from abuse, to a family that cannot adequately provide for a child, or to a family that cannot or refuses to educate its child.

The ultimate authority for the resolution of these problems is the juvenile court. There are many other persons and institutions the child and the family may encounter when and if they reach the court. But if all else fails, the legislatures in the United States have entrusted the authority to address the problems facing dysfunctional families and children to the juvenile court (Edwards, 1992).[1]

---

1. It may be preferable to divert many, if not all, such matters from the juvenile court. There may be better, more lasting resolutions through alternative dispute resolution techniques. Nevertheless, the lack of such alternatives or their failure leads to the ultimate authority, the juvenile court.

THE ORIGIN OF THE JUVENILE COURT

The juvenile court combines legal and social attributes to serve interests relating to children and their families. Established in the late nineteenth century, the juvenile court was for some a humanitarian institution intended to rehabilitate youthful offenders and protect children. It was in part a recognition that children are different from adults and in part a reaction to the treatment of children as adults in the criminal justice system (Sutton, 1988). For others it was an attempt to exert a new form of social control over children (Fox, 1970; Platt, 1977).

The juvenile court was first established in Illinois in 1899 (see chapter 1). The purpose of the court was (1) to assist the parent to raise the child in the parent's home or (2) to remove the child to a better environment. The goal was the same in either case, to ensure that the child was properly raised. The basis for the intervention in juvenile court was *parens patriae*, the state as parent. When the parent fails, the state has the legal power to substitute for that parent and act on behalf of the child.

Implicit in the original Illinois statute was the notion that children are different from adults, that they have developmental needs that they cannot satisfy without assistance, and that care and supervision are critical to their upbringing (Bearrows, Bleich, and Oshima, 1987). If children were no different from adults, the juvenile court would be unnecessary.

The purposes and functions of the juvenile court have evolved significantly since its creation in 1899. In order to understand the juvenile court today, the next section of this chapter examines its various functions and how each has changed over the years.

TYPES OF CASES IN JUVENILE COURT

The juvenile court is a part of the judicial system of all fifty states and the District of Columbia (National Council of Juvenile Court Judges, 1964). Each state's juvenile court has certain unique qualities in the way it is structured, in the powers granted to the juvenile court judge, and in the types of cases it hears (Stapleton, Aday, and Ito, 1988). Nevertheless, there are substantial similarities in the ways in which juvenile courts in all jurisdictions function. These form the core of the juvenile court's responsibilities.

The focus in this book and in this chapter is on child abuse or dependency cases and the role of the juvenile court in protecting abused and neglected children. It is, however, important to recognize that there may well be a strong link between child abuse and delinquency, and between maltreatment and status offenses (National Committee for the Prevention of Child Abuse, 1986). A status offense is an illegal act by a child that is not a criminal offense. Examples include truancy, running away from home, and curfew violations. Retrospective studies have found that juvenile delinquents and status offenders have experienced abuse and neglect at rates much higher than the general population. The links may well be the result of common etiology in disrupted, ineffectual families, or practices that legitimate family violence. We will, therefore, briefly describe each of the different classes of cases in juvenile court.

The three types of cases that are most commonly associated with the work of the juvenile court concern delinquent minors, status offenders, and abused and neglected minors. These three legal classifications are somewhat arbitrary. No clear line separates the factual circumstances that might result in a child or family being in one type of these court proceedings or another. For example, a child may be having an argument with her parents. Tempers flare, and the father strikes the child across the face. The child runs out the door and leaves home for a week, and in leaving she takes the family car. Depending on which part of the story is seen as the most important, this factual situation could result in dependency (parental abuse), delinquency (auto theft) or status offense (runaway) proceedings being instituted in the juvenile court. According to one prominent juvenile court judge, we should abolish the terms "delinquent," "dependent," and "status offender" (Gladstone, 1990). He wonders why we must prolong the fiction that children in need of help may be categorized according to what they have done or what has been done to them in a single moment as opposed to treating them according to the causes and nature of their problems.

Juvenile Delinquency

When a minor commits an act which would be a crime if committed by an adult, he or she may be subject to the delinquency jurisdiction of the juvenile court. Juvenile delinquency law is our society's response to crime committed by children. The creators of the juvenile court envisioned a new social institution and a new law for dealing with delinquents. The role of the court was not simply to determine whether a child was guilty or innocent or to punish, but to answer what would be in the best interests of the child. The concept of individualized justice was the hallmark of the juvenile court. The original role of the juvenile court was to treat and rehabilitate the delinquent minor, utilizing a clinical/medical rather than a justice model (Springer, 1991). Since the state was not punishing the delinquent child, it was unnecessary to utilize the constitutional rights guaranteed to adult criminal defendants. Thus, attorneys rarely appeared in juvenile court, judges were not necessarily trained in the law, and jury trials were not part of the fact-finding process in most states.

Serious criticism of this approach led to significant changes in the juvenile court during the 1960s (see chapter 1). In a series of cases, the United States Supreme Court formalized the adjudicatory stage of delinquency proceedings. Concluding that the child before the juvenile court receives "the worst of both worlds" (*Kent v. United States*, 1966), the Supreme Court ruled that, for the state to take jurisdiction over a delinquent minor, the child must have notice of the charges, the right to an attorney at state expense, the right to confront and cross-examine witnesses called by the state, and the right to remain silent (*In re Gault*, 1967).

Since the *Gault* case, the criminalization of the juvenile courts has continued, and the policies of accountability and punishment have been added to the concepts of rehabilitation and family preservation (Szymanski, 1990). However, the child's due process rights are still not coequal with an adult criminal defendant's due process rights. In most states, the child still does not have the right to bail or to a jury trial. As in each of the types of cases listed above, the juvenile court in delinquency matters is the institution charged with a substitute or *parens patriae* role. The legislature generally charges the juvenile court with preserving and strengthening the family, protecting the public, and correcting and rehabilitating the minor. The juvenile court is advised to remove the minor from his or her parents' care and control only as a last resort, and if the minor is removed, the care, custody, and discipline exercised by the state must be nearly as possible equivalent to that which should have been given by the parents (see, for example, the California Welfare and Institutions Code, section 602).

Status Offenses

Minors also come to the attention of authorities for behavior which is antisocial without being delinquent. Status offenses describe children's behavior society wishes to control. It is the "status" of being a child that is the basis of status offenses. When a minor refuses to go to school or is habitually truant, when a minor runs away from home or is beyond the control of his parents, or when a minor is out in the community after

curfew, he or she has not violated the criminal law, but his or her behavior is of concern (e.g., Welfare and Institutions Code §601). Status offenses can be viewed as addressing duties which our society expects children to follow. Being truant and misbehaving are hardly dangerous or violent actions, but they may have something to do with whether a child is moving in a direction toward responsible citizenship (Bearrows, Bleich, and Oshima, 1987, pp. 84-85).

At its inception the juvenile court did not distinguish between delinquent and status-offending children. Both were labeled delinquent, and each was subject to juvenile court jurisdiction, detention, and incarceration. In the 1960s and 1970s, many critics argued that status-offending children should be removed from the juvenile justice system, or at least be treated significantly differently from delinquents (Teitelbaum and Gough, 1977). They asserted that treatment alternatives and not incarceration should be the juvenile court's response to status offenses. They pointed to large numbers of children incarcerated for long periods of time for merely running away from home or being truant from school. During this time, some states unilaterally began to treat status offenders differently from delinquents, but the most significant change occurred at the federal level with the passage of the Juvenile Justice and Delinquency Prevention Act of 1974 (42 U.S.C.A., sections 5601-5751). In order for a state to be eligible for the receipt of federal funds, it was required to separate juveniles from adults during incarceration, and status offenders were not to be held in secure detention. In 1980 Congress amended the 1974 act and allowed states to detain status offenders if detention occurred for the violation of a valid court order (Public Law, 1980).

Most status offenses never reach the juvenile court. School problems such as truancy and unruly behavior are usually addressed at the school. In addition, many communities have private or court-based agencies, including probation services, which work with families in which children run away or are ungovernable. These agencies provide nonsecure shelter care, counseling, and other services designed to assist children and families and enable them to be reunited (Court-Approved Alternative Dispute Resolution, 1989). In addition, other community agency providers, including churches, recreation departments, and counseling and treatment centers, assist status-offending children and their families.

If these efforts fail, the most serious cases may end up in juvenile court. In that setting the child generally has the same legal and constitutional rights as a delinquent.

Dependency Cases

The juvenile court has been given the legal authority over children who have been abused or neglected. The purpose of the juvenile court law in dependency proceedings is to protect children and preserve families.

> It is the intent of the Legislature in enacting this section to provide maximum protection for children who are currently being physically, sexually, or emotionally abused, being neglected, or being exploited, and to protect children who are at risk of that harm. This protection includes provision of a full array of social and health services to help the child and family and to prevent reabuse of children. That protection shall focus on the preservation of the family whenever possible. (California Welfare and Institutions Code, 1991)

From 1985 to 1990 there was a 31 percent increase in reports of child abuse cases in the United States, reaching a total of 2.5 million reports in 1989-90 (National Committee on the Prevention of Child Abuse, 1990). With this growth came expansion of those agencies and professionals who have to respond to abuse and neglect allegations through reporting laws. Law enforcement, medical personnel, public health workers, child protective officers, social service providers, lawyers, and judges have all had greater demands placed upon them due to the increase in reporting. The work of the juvenile court has

grown so dramatically that most courts now expend equal or greater amounts of time on dependency calendars than they do on delinquency matters (Seymor, 1990).

FUNCTIONS OF THE JUVENILE COURT IN DEPENDENCY CASES

As described in chapter 1, juvenile dependency law in the states is guided by Public Law 96-272, the Adoption Assistance and Child Welfare Act of 1980. This federal legislation was written in response to concerns that the child welfare system in the United States was failing to offer services to children and parents to preserve families and to provide appropriate care and treatment for children in foster care.

The major tenets of this legislation and the state legislation that followed after its passage are as follows:

1. The state must provide services to prevent children's removal from their homes in order to be eligible to receive any federal foster care funds.
2. In order to qualify for federal monies that assist state services, the juvenile court must make "reasonable efforts" findings that the state has in fact provided services to enable children to remain safely at home before they are placed in foster care.
3. The juvenile court must also determine whether the state has made "reasonable efforts" to reunite foster children with their biological parents.
4. The juvenile court must determine that there is a case plan developed to ensure placement in "the least restrictive, most family-like setting available located in close proximity to the parent's home, consistent with the best interests and needs of the child."
5. The juvenile court must ensure that the status

of every foster child is regularly reviewed and that a child is given a timely permanent placement, preferably in an adoptive setting, if return to the biological parent is not possible.

As is the case with juvenile delinquency and status offenses, the majority of dependency cases are resolved without juvenile court intervention. When a potentially abused or neglected child is brought to the attention of the police or child protective services, they will investigate the circumstances surrounding the report. They have the authority to take no action, to issue a warning to the child's parents, or to reach an agreement with the parents that if they change their behavior in specific ways and agree to be under the supervision of a social worker for a limited period of time, no formal legal action will be taken on behalf of the child.

If a petition is filed, the court has a number of legal decisions to make over the life of the case, which often may amount to years:

1. whether the child should be temporarily removed from the care of its parents;
2. whether the petition is true;
3. whether the child should be declared a dependent child of the court;
4. what the dispositional plan should be; and
5. what the permanent plan for the child should be.

If the child is found to be a dependent, the court has the power to return it to its parents on conditions or remove it from its parents. In either case the court has the responsibility to establish the conditions for the care, custody, control, and conduct of the child.

In addition to these decisions, the juvenile court also has the responsibility to monitor the services provided to the family by the social services agency. The court is mandated to determine whether "reasonable efforts" have been provided by the social service agency either to prevent removal of the child from the parents or to facilitate reunifica-

tion after removal (see the discussion of the Adoption Assistance and Child Welfare Act of 1980 in chapter 1). The court or its designee must carry out this responsibility at several stages of the proceedings.

The legislature has left a great deal of discretion to the juvenile judge in determining whether a minor is a dependent child of the court. The statutory language in all states is very general (Besharov, 1988). Whether a child will be a dependent child of the court is determined by the rulings of the court and by community standards.

Whether the juvenile court has supervisory power over a minor who is a dependent child of the court varies from state to state. In virtually all states the child is under the care of the executive branch. Nevertheless, the court must review the status of the case regularly, so that the court can monitor its orders.

At regularly scheduled hearings the court will review parental progress toward reunification with the child or, if the child remains at home, toward dismissal of the case. If the parents are not successful in their reunification efforts, the court must establish a permanent plan for the child. The preferable permanent plan is termination of parental rights followed by adoption, with guardianship and long-term out-of-home care being the other two options.

While most dependency cases are resolved without court action, of those that have reached the juvenile court, more and more have resulted in removal of the child from parents and placements in foster care. From 1984 to 1989 the number of children in foster care rose dramatically from 276,000 to 360,000 (American Public Welfare Assoc., 1990). The most recent estimate is that as of 1990 there were approximately 460,000 children in foster care in the United States.

It appears that some of this increase derives from a weakening family structure, but it is also clear that a major portion of the increase results from an inability of the child welfare system to provide services to families in crisis so that they can continue to raise their children safely. Within this context the juvenile court must determine not only whether a child must be removed from a family or put into permanent placement, but also whether the social services department is adequately fulfilling its responsibilities. Given the enormous increase in foster care placements, the task of the juvenile court takes on an even greater importance for children and states.

DEPENDENCY PROCEEDINGS

Child abuse and neglect cases are classified as dependency cases in juvenile court. To illustrate the processing of such cases through the court, we will use the California Welfare and Institutions Code as a guide.

A dependency case usually starts with a report of suspected child abuse or neglect. A social worker in a county welfare department may take into and maintain temporary custody of a minor who has been declared a dependent child of the juvenile court (section 300) or who the social worker has reasonable cause to believe is a person described as an abused or neglected child. Such temporary custody may be taken without a warrant, and is intended to protect the child from further abuse and neglect. Before taking a minor into custody, a social worker must consider whether there are any reasonable services available to the worker which would eliminate the need to remove the minor from the custody of his or her parent or guardian (section 306[b]).

The social worker may transport the child to either a hospital, temporary shelter care or emergency foster care, or to an approved community program for abused and neglected children with or without parental consent, if abuse is suspected (section 307.5). When a minor is taken into temporary custody, the social worker must take immediate steps to notify the minor's parents, guardians, or responsible relatives and inform them where the minor is, unless it can be shown to the court that such notification would endanger

the child or that the parents are likely to flee with the child (section 308[a]).

Immediately after taking a minor to a place of confinement and, except where physically impossible, no later than one hour after the minor has been taken into custody, the minor has the right to make at least two telephone calls from the place where he or she is being held, one call completed to his or her parent or guardian, and another call completed to an attorney. It is a misdemeanor to deprive a minor of the right to make these telephone calls (section 308[b]).

After putting a minor in temporary protective custody, a probation officer or social worker must immediately investigate the circumstances of the minor and the facts surrounding the minor's being taken into custody and attempt to maintain the minor with the minor's family through the provision of services. A minor held in contemporary custody must be released within forty-eight hours after being taken into custody, excluding nonjudicial days (Saturdays, Sundays, and holidays), unless within that time a petition to declare the minor a dependent child has been filed (section 313[a]).

The law also requires that the court shall appoint an attorney or the district attorney to represent the child (see chapter 4). Counsel appointed by the court must represent the minor at the detention hearing and subsequent hearings. The timing of the California dependency process is outlined in figures 5.1 and 5.2. The statutory schemes of a number of states are shown in figure 5.3.

The Detention Hearing

In juvenile court there are strict time limits for all dependency hearings. The Legislature imposes these limits to ensure that dependency cases will be heard as quickly as possible, because of the importance of these issues (Edwards, 1987). Removal of a child from parents and placement with a nonparent is a serious form of societal intervention and requires fast legal action. As stated earlier, if the child is taken from a parent, a petition must

FIGURE 5.1: Juvenile Dependency Proceedings (Welfare and Institutions Code 300 *et seq.*)

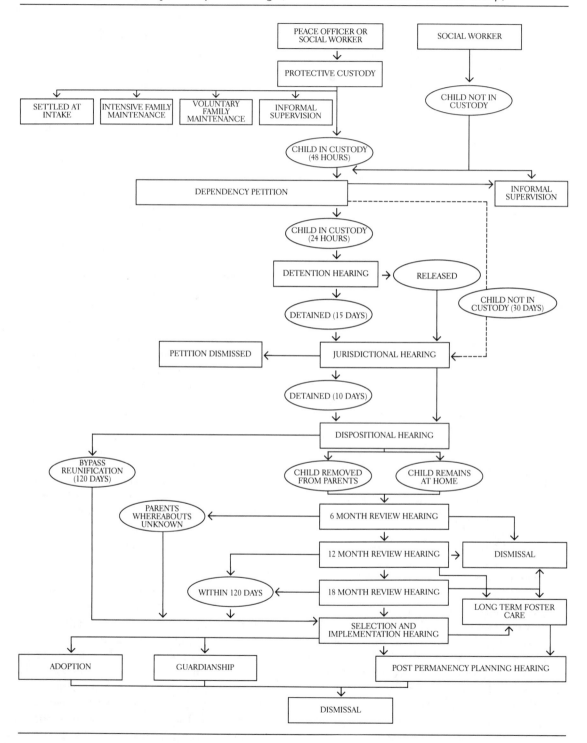

FIGURE 5.2: Time Line for Child Abuse and Neglect Hearings

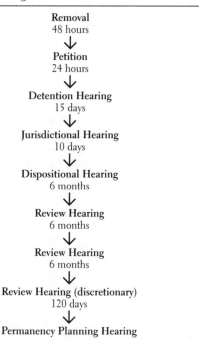

Removal
48 hours
↓
Petition
24 hours
↓
Detention Hearing
15 days
↓
Jurisdictional Hearing
10 days
↓
Dispositional Hearing
6 months
↓
Review Hearing
6 months
↓
Review Hearing
6 months
↓
Review Hearing (discretionary)
120 days
↓
Permanency Planning Hearing

be filed within forty-eight hours (excluding weekends and holidays). A detention hearing must be held within twenty-four hours of filing a petition (section 319). A minor not brought before the court within this period must be released (section 319).

Similar time periods are in place in other states (see figure 5.1). The strict time limits outlined in the chart do not apply when a child is placed with one parent on the condition that the allegedly abusive parent have no contact with the child. If no petition is filed, the parent suspected of abuse may be unable to visit indefinitely, absent a court determination of the truth of the abuse allegation and the necessity of the no-visitation rule (Edwards, 1987).

The petition to initiate juvenile court intervention is usually filed by the county child welfare department. A copy of the petition is speedily provided to the parents, guardian, or other person having care or custody of the child. A dependency petition may also be filed without first taking the child into protective custody. In all cases the social worker who files the petition shall be the guardian *ad litem* to represent the interests of the minor in dependency proceedings, unless the court appoints another adult (see chapter 4 for a description of guardians *ad litem*).

The Jurisdictional or Adjudicatory Hearing

In California a jurisdictional hearing in the juvenile court must be held within fifteen judicial days of the detention hearing, excluding weekends and holidays, or within thirty days of filing the petition if the child is not in custody (California Welfare and Institution Code, section 334). Time limits in other states generally vary from ten to thirty days. The purpose of the jurisdictional hearing is to decide whether the child comes within the description of a dependent child as set forth in Welfare and Institutions Code, section 300.

Upon filing a petition, the clerk of the court must issue a copy of the petition to the minor's parents or guardian, and a notice of when the hearings will take place. In addition to the notice, the juvenile court may also issue a citation directing any parent or guardian concerning whom a petition has been filed to appear at the hearing. In such cases where a citation cannot be served or the person fails to obey it, a warrant of arrest may be issued (section 339).

Pursuant to section 280 of the Welfare and Institutions Code, a social report is prepared for each dependency hearing. California courts have held that this report is admissible as part of the petitioner's evidence at the jurisdictional hearing if the author of the report is present at the cross-examination (*In re Malinda S.*, 1990). Hearsay evidence contained in the report is admissible. In *In re Malinda S.* (1990), the California Supreme Court upheld the rule that the juvenile court could properly rely upon social study which was replete with hearsay in support of its jurisdictional finding that a child was a dependent of the court.

Juvenile court dependency proceedings are designed to protect children. For that reason, traditional evidentiary protections are frequently overridden. If a child is called as a witness at the jurisdictional hearing, both statutory law and case law permit the child to testify outside the presence of the parents (*In re Mary S.*, 1986). Parents can also be called to the witness stand in dependency proceedings. Section 355.7 of the Welfare and Institutions Code provides that any such testimony cannot be used in other legal proceedings. Spousal and marital communication privileges are not available to a parent or guardian in dependency proceedings. Thus, the parent may not resort to evidentiary privileges to avoid testifying, may be called as a witness against a spouse, and may be required to disclose confidential marital communications.

Furthermore, the Welfare and Institutions Code provides that, if certain facts are proven, there is a presumption of abuse or neglect unless the parent produces evidence to rebut the assumption (Edwards, 1987).

The Dispositional Hearing

At a dispositional hearing, the court decides what is to be done as a result of the proven abuse or neglect. The dispositional hearing must be held within ten court days of the jurisdictional hearing (section 358). Other states' limits vary from immediately following the jurisdictional hearing to thirty days later. Continuances are permitted only with very strict guidelines thereafter (section 352[a]). Under no circumstances may the dispositional hearing be held more than six months after the detention hearing (section 352[b]).

If a child is declared to be a dependent of the juvenile court, the court may order the child to remain at home under the supervision of the child welfare services department. Alternatively, the court may take custody from the parents and order the child to be placed in "out-of-home"

care. Removal of the child requires a finding of any of the following:

1. There is a substantial danger to the physical health of the minor and there are no reasonable means to protect the child in the home.
2. The parent or guardian is unwilling to have physical custody of the child.
3. The minor is suffering severe emotional damage and there are no reasonable means to protect the child from further sexual abuse.
4. The minor is under the age of three, and the court makes a finding of severe physical abuse.

The court must state the facts on which the decision to remove the child was based. The standard for removal is "clear and convincing evidence." The court must also inform the parents that their parental rights may be terminated permanently if they do not resume custody within twelve months, or immediately if the court finds that return of a child under three who has been found to be severely physically abused would be detrimental to the minor.

In a case in which a minor is removed from the parents, the court must order the social worker to provide child welfare services to the family for the purpose of facilitating reunification for up to twelve months. Services may be extended for up to an additional six months if it can be shown that the objectives of the service plan can be achieved within the extended period.

Children found to be dependents of the court, who are not reunited with their parents, are usually placed with relatives, in foster homes, group homes, or in other child residential treatment facilities (sections 361.2-362).

Review Hearings

After the dispositional hearing, review hearings must be held within six months of the dispositional hearing or previous review (section 366 [a]). If the child is in out-of-home placement, a permanency planning hearing must be held within one year or eighteen months from the date the child was removed from parental care (section 366.25[a]).

The status of every dependent child in foster care must be reviewed periodically, but no less frequently than once every six months as described above, until the permanency planning hearing is completed (section 366 [a]). Every hearing reviewing the status of a dependent child must be placed on the appearance calendar of the court, and all persons present must be advised of any future hearings and their right to be present (section 366.21).

At the review hearing held six months after the initial dispositional hearing, the court must order the return of the minor to the physical custody of his or her parents or guardians unless, by a preponderance of the evidence, it finds that the return of the child would create a substantial risk of detriment to the physical or emotional well-being of the child. The social services department has the burden of establishing that detriment. The failure of the parent or the guardian to participate regularly in any court-ordered treatment program constitutes *prima facie* evidence that return would be detrimental (section 366.21 [e]).

If the child is not returned to the parent or guardian, the court must determine if reasonable efforts have been provided or offered to the parent which were designed to overcome the problems that led to the initial removal and the continued custody of the minor (section 366.21 [f]).

Similarly, at the twelve-month hearing after the initial dispositional hearing, the court must order the return of the minor to the physical custody of his parents or guardian unless, by a preponderance of the evidence, it finds that a return would create a risk to the child. If the minor is not returned to a parent or guardian, the court must specify the factual basis for its conclusion that return would be detrimental (section 366.21 [f]).

If the minor is not returned to the custody of

the parents or guardian at the twelve-month hearing, the court must do one of the following:

1. Continue the case for up to six months for another review hearing, provided that the hearing occur within eighteen months of the date the child was originally taken from the physical custody of his or her parent or guardian. The court may continue the case only if there is substantial probability that the minor will be returned to the physical custody of his or her parent or guardian within six months or that reasonable services have not been provided to the parent or parents (section 366.21 [1]).
2. Order that the minor remain in long-term foster care, if the court finds by clear and convincing evidence that the minor is not adoptable and has no one willing to accept legal guardianship.
3. Order that a hearing pursuant to section 366.26 be held.

When a case is continued to an eighteen-month hearing and the minor is not returned to the parent, the court must develop a permanent plan for the child. A hearing must be held to determine whether adoption, guardianship, or long-term foster care is the most appropriate plan for the minor. The hearing shall be held no later than 120 days from the date of the eighteen-month hearing. The court must also order termination of reunification services to the parent. The court must continue to permit the parent to visit the minor unless it finds that visitation would be detrimental to the minor (section 366.22 [a]).

At the section 366.26 hearing, the court may take the following actions:

1. permanently sever the parent or parents' rights and order that the child be placed for adoption;
2. without permanently terminating parental rights, identify adoption as the permanent

placement goal and order that efforts be made to locate an appropriate adoptive family;

3. without permanently terminating parental rights, appoint a legal guardian for the minor; and

4. order that the minor be placed in long-term foster care, subject to the periodic review of the juvenile court (section 366.26).

All hearings in the dependency court, from the detention hearing to the termination of parental rights hearing, are closed to the public and are confidential.

CRITICISMS OF THE DEPENDENCY SYSTEM

There are many critics of the dependency system. Some argue that it is out of control and that, in the name of protecting children, our society has unleashed a new system which has resulted in the unnecessary destruction of families (Wexler, 1990). They insist that the child welfare system should provide voluntary services to families and that state coercion is not appropriate or necessary (e.g., Goldstein, Solnit, and Freud, 1980). These critics emphasize the importance of family integrity and the inability of the social services system to provide better homes for abused and neglected children.

Others point out that the dependency system and the juvenile court are "abysmal failures" partly because the juvenile court has not followed the law (*In the Interest of Ashley K.*, 1991). These critics have examined the juvenile dependency courts in operation, particularly in urban centers. They note that the law envisioned an effective juvenile court intervention, one that would protect children, preserve families, and provide permanent placements for children who could not safely be returned to their families.

Several appellate cases indicate the magnitude of the failures of some juvenile court systems. In *La Shawn, A., et al., v. Sharon Pratt Dixon*

(1991), the court found that the dependency system operated as if the federal legislation (the Adoption Assistance Act of 1980) did not exist.

In spite of the criticisms, the juvenile court does have a necessary and important role within the dependency system. In the case of child protection matters, when a child has been abused or neglected and needs protection, the courts provide the most appropriate forum for several reasons. First, parents sometimes do not acknowledge their need for improved performance with respect to caring for their children, and the public must intervene. The courts are a necessary part of this coercive course of action. They explain and provide the due process the law has determined is required in these types of proceedings.

Second, these cases may involve at least temporary transfer of responsibility for the child to a nonparent. The creation and dissolution of legal rights and responsibilities relating to child custody is legal work (*In the Interest of J.R.T.*, 1983). Third, the courts are needed to protect the child's rights, even when the child is a ward of the state. The child's situation in a new setting must be monitored by a responsible authority, and the courts can provide that monitoring. Fourth, through the adjudication process the courts articulate, establish, or reinforce community norms governing the care and protection of children. By ruling in individual cases, the court instructs the community, including the agencies that serve the child welfare system, on the general standards for parenting within the community.

Fifth, there has been intensive public criticism of alleged social worker aggressiveness and overreaching. The juvenile court is society's designated check to insure that children are not improperly removed, that parents are provided due process, and that families are fairly treated. Sixth, some studies indicate that court-ordered services are more likely to be utilized than voluntary services. These studies suggest that voluntary services will simply not result in changed parental behavior (Iruste-Montes and Montes, 1988; Wolfe, Aragona, Kaufman, and Sandler, 1980).

FIGURE 5.3: Statutory Time Limitations for Emergency Protective Proceedings

Alabama

Dependency Petition	Detention Hearing	Adjudicatory Hearing	Dispositional Hearing	Initial Review	12-month Review	18-month Review	Permanency Hearing
Within 72 hours following removal (§12-5-60)	"With all possible speed" 75% of adjudicatory hearings to be held within two months of removal 75% of adjudicatory hearings to be held within one month of adjudication (1990 Guidelines for Timely Case Management)			6 months	Review not less than once every 10 months following the adjudicatory hearing		

Alaska

Dependency Petition	Detention Hearing	Adjudicatory Hearing	Dispositional Hearing	Initial Review	12-month Review	18-month Review	Permanency Hearing
Within 48 hours after removal; Court Rule 6[b]	Within 48 hours of filing a petition	Not more than 90 days from original hearing	"Shall be held without unreasonable delay"	6 months	Annual review		Not specified by statute

Arizona

Dependency Petition	Detention Hearing	Adjudicatory Hearing	Dispositional Hearing	Initial Review	12-month Review	18-month Review	Permanency Hearing
48 hours after removal (§8-546.01 [D])	48 hours after filing of petition (§8-546.01 [c] [7] [6])	21 days from which petition is filed	Time limit not specified by statute	Time limitations not specified by statute			

(continued next page)

FIGURE 5.3: (continued)

Arkansas

Dependency Petition	Detention Hearing	Adjudicatory Hearing	Dispositional Hearing	Initial Review	12-month Review	18-month Review	Permanency Hearing
"Shall be immediately filed" (§45-438)	72 hours after being taken into custody (9-27-326[a])	14 days following detention hearing (9-27-327[b])	Not more than 14 days after adjudication (9-27-329[b])	6 months			

California

Dependency Petition	Detention Hearing	Adjudicatory Hearing	Dispositional Hearing	Initial Review	12-month Review	18-month Review	Permanency Hearing
48 hours after removal	24 hours after petition	15 days after detention hearing	10 days after adjudication	6 months		120 days from 18-month review	

Colorado

Dependency Petition	Detention Hearing	Adjudicatory Hearing	Dispositional Hearing	Initial Review	12-month Review	18-month Review	Permanency Hearing
"Temporary protective custody not to exceed 72 hours" (§19-3-204)	48 hours after petition	"Earliest time possible, but in no instance later than 90 days"	"Not to exceed 45 days after adjudication"	6 months		Time not specific	Not later than 18 months after original placement

Connecticut

Dependency Petition	Detention Hearing	Adjudicatory Hearing	Dispositional Hearing	Initial Review	12-month Review	18-month Review	Permanency Hearing
48 hours after removal (§46[b]-129[d])	Time not specified by statute	10 days following petition (46 [b]-129[b] [2])	Time limit not specified by statute	Time limitations not specified by statute		Upon adjudging minor dependent, maximum of 18 months in custody	

FIGURE 5.3: (continued)

Delaware

Dependency Petition	Detention Hearing	Adjudicatory Hearing	Dispositional Hearing	Initial Review	12-month Review	18-month Review	Permanency Hearing
Within 72 hours, court shall file a petition and set date of adjudicatory hearing (§10-932)	Within 14 days of initial date of detention	Within 30 days from detention hearing	Time limitations not specified by statute				

District of Columbia

Dependency Petition	Detention Hearing	Adjudicatory Hearing	Dispositional Hearing	Initial Review	12-month Review	18-month Review	Permanency Hearing
Detention hearing to be commenced not later than the next day (excluding Sundays) after taken into custody (§16-2312)		Time limitations not specified by statute		6 months (§16-2323[2])			Time limit not specified by statute

Florida

Dependency Petition	Detention Hearing	Adjudicatory Hearing	Dispositional Hearing	Initial Review	12-month Review	18-month Review	Permanency Hearing
24 hours after removal (§39.032)	Within 72 hours of initial detainment	Within 14 days of being taken into custody	Time limit not specified by statute	6 months			Time limit not specified by statute

Georgia

Dependency Petition	Detention Hearing	Adjudicatory Hearing	Dispositional Hearing	Initial Review	12-month Review	18-month Review	Permanency Hearing
"Shall be filed within 72 hours of detention hearing" (§15-11-2[e])	Not later than 72 hours after detainment (§15-11-21 [b] [3])	Not later than 10 days from filing of petition (§15-11-26[a])	Time limit not specified by statute	6 months (§15-11-41 [d])			Time limit not specified by statute

(continued next page)

FIGURE 5.3: (continued)

Hawaii

Dependency Petition	Detention Hearing	Adjudicatory Hearing	Dispositional Hearing	Initial Review	12-month Review	18-month Review	Permanency Hearing
Within 2 working days (§587-21[3])	Within 2 working days of filing of petition (§587-23[a])	Within 10 days (§587-62[b][4])	Within 20 days (§587-62[b][4])	6 months (§587-72[a])			Not later than 1 year after plan ordered by court (§587-73[b][5]) Court shall order within 3 years of when first placed (§587-73[e])

Idaho

Dependency Petition	Detention Hearing	Adjudicatory Hearing	Dispositional Hearing	Initial Review	12-month Review	18-month Review	Permanency Hearing
Within 2 hours (§16–614[d][4])	No later than 15 days after petition	As soon as possible, but not later than 30 days		6 months			Not specified by statute

Illinois

Dependency Petition	Detention Hearing	Adjudicatory Hearing	Dispositional Hearing	Initial Review	12-month Review	18-month Review	Permanency Hearing
Within 48 hours (37:802-9[2])	Within 48 hours (37:802-9[3])	Not later than 14 days after filing petition (37:802-10[d])	Not later than 30 days after adjudication (37:802-21[2])	6 months			Within 18 months of order for shelter care (37:802-28[2])

Indiana

Dependency Petition	Detention Hearing	Adjudicatory Hearing	Dispositional Hearing	Initial Review	12-month Review	18-month Review	Permanency Hearing
Not specified by statute	Within 72 hours of being taken into custody (31-6-4-6[e])	Time limits not specified by statute	To be held immediately after initial hearing (31-6-4-13.6[i])	6 months	Periodic case review at least once every 6 months from removal or disposition, whichever comes first (31-6-4-19[6])		

FIGURE 5.3: (continued)

Iowa

Dependency Petition	Detention Hearing	Adjudicatory Hearing	Dispositional Hearing	Initial Review	12-month Review	18-month Review	Permanency Hearing
Within 3 days after removal (§232.79[4][b])	Time limit not specified by statute		"As soon as practicable" after adjudicatory hearing (§232.99[1])	6 months			Time limitation not specified by statute

Kentucky

Dependency Petition	Detention Hearing	Adjudicatory Hearing	Dispositional Hearing	Initial Review	12-month Review	18-month Review	Permanency Hearing
Petition and hearing shall be held within 72 hours (§620.060[2] and §620.080[1][a])		"Court shall conduct adjudicatory hearing and make disposition within 45 days of removal" (§620.090[5])		6 months			Time limitation not specified by statute

Louisiana

Dependency Petition	Detention Hearing	Adjudicatory Hearing	Dispositional Hearing	Initial Review	12-month Review	18-month Review	Permanency Hearing
Within 72 hours after "entry into custody" (Act 235§624)	Within 10 days (Act 235§618)	Within 45 days of the filing of a petition (Act 235§659)	Within 30 days after adjudicatory hearing (Act 235§678[B])	6 months	Once every six months until the child is permanently placed (Act 235§692)		Time limitation not specified by statute

Maine

Dependency Petition	Detention Hearing	Adjudicatory Hearing	Dispositional Hearing	Initial Review	12-month Review	18-month Review	Permanency Hearing
Within 72 hours (22 §4023[5])	To be set at earliest time practicable (22§4032[3])	Time limitation not specified by statute		Within 18 months of final protection order (22§4308[7][A])			

(continued next page)

FIGURE 5.3: (continued)

Maryland

Dependency Petition	Detention Hearing	Adjudicatory Hearing	Dispositional Hearing	Initial Review	12-month Review	18-month Review	Permanency Hearing
Next day court is sitting (Rule 912[2][i])	Shall be held on the day the petition is filed; may not be continued more than 8 days	Within 30 days from date on which court orders continued detention (Rule 914[b](2))	No later than 30 days after conclusion of adjudicatory hearing (Rule 915(a))	6 months			At 18 months (Rule 915[d])

Massachusetts

Dependency Petition	Detention Hearing	Adjudicatory Hearing	Dispositional Hearing	Initial Review	12-month Review	18-month Review	Permanency Hearing
Must file next day of court (119§51B(3))	Within 72 hours (119§23(G))	Within 10 days (119§27)	Time limitation not specified by statute	6 months	Not more than once every 6 months (119§26(2))		Within 18 months of the original commitment (119§29B)

Michigan

Dependency Petition	Detention Hearing	Adjudicatory Hearing	Dispositional Hearing	Initial Review	12-month Review	18-month Review	Permanency Hearing
May detain until next business day (722.626(1))	Child shall be immediately brought before the court (712.14(2))	If the child remains in protective custody, the cause shall be reheard not more than 182 days after preliminary hearing (712A.19(2))		Rehearing not more than 91 days after disposition, and every 91 days thereafter for the first year following disposition (712A.19(3))			After the first year, every 182 days after permanency plan hearing

FIGURE 5.3: (continued)

New Jersey

Dependency Petition	Detention Hearing	Adjudicatory Hearing	Dispositional Hearing	Initial Review	12-month Review	18-month Review	Permanency Hearing
Protective custody not to exceed 3 court days Complaint to be filed immediately or on first court day after removal (§9:6-8.30(b))	To be held the next court day following complaint (§9:6-8.31(a))	Not more than 30 days after complaint is filed (§9:6-8.35(d))	May commence immediately after required findings are made (§9:6-8.47(a))	Initial placement may be for 18 months and subsequent extended periods of not more than one year each upon hearing (§9:6-8.53)			Time limitation not specified by statute

New York

Dependency Petition	Detention Hearing	Adjudicatory Hearing	Dispositional Hearing	Initial Review	12-month Review	18-month Review	Permanency Hearing
To be filed within 10 days from court's granting order of protective custody (FCA §1029)	Court shall hold a hearing as soon as practicable after filing of petition (FCA §1027)		May commence immediately after required findings are made (FCA §1049)	6 months (FCA §1055)			Time limitation not specified by statute

Rhode Island

Dependency Petition	Detention Hearing	Adjudicatory Hearing	Dispositional Hearing	Initial Review	12-month Review	18-month Review	Permanency Hearing
Detention only until next court day (Rule 8(a))	Seven days from filing of petition (Rule 15(c))	30 days (Rule 8(d))	Time limit not specified by statute	6 months	Periodic reviews not less than once every 6 months upon court approval of placement plan (Rule 17(d))		

(continued next page)

FIGURE 5.3: (continued)

Texas

Dependency Petition	Detention Hearing	Adjudicatory Hearing	Dispositional Hearing	Initial Review	12-month Review	18-month Review	Permanency Hearing
Shall file without unnecessary delay (§17.03(b))	First working day but not later than third working day (§17.03(c))	Full adversary hearing shall be held not later than 14 days after date of removal (§17.03(f))		Review hearing not earlier than 5½ months and not later than 12 months from date of last hearing (§18.01(a))			

Washington

Dependency Petition	Detention Hearing	Adjudicatory Hearing	Dispositional Hearing	Initial Review	12-month Review	18-month Review	Permanency Hearing
Within 24 hours (26 §44.56(1))	Time not specified by statute			6 months	Time not specified by statute		

Wisconsin

Dependency Petition	Detention Hearing	Adjudicatory Hearing	Dispositional Hearing	Initial Review	12-month Review	18-month Review	Permanency Hearing
48 hours only upon showing of cause (§48.21(1)(b))	Within 2 hours of filing of petition (§48.21 (1)(b))	Court may combine filing of petition and hearing		6 months	Court shall review every 6 months from date upon which child was first held in custody or placed outside the home (§48.38(5)(a))		Initial permanency plan within 60 days after child was first held in custody or placed outside the home (§48.38(3))

ALTERNATIVES TO THE JUVENILE COURT

The government's selection of the juvenile court as the institution to fulfill these functions raises an important issue: Is the juvenile court a wise choice? Are there better alternatives than turning to the court system for a resolution of these problems? Have our legislatures chosen wisely in entrusting these types of decisions to the juvenile courts?

These are difficult questions to answer. Moreover, they are beyond the scope of this chapter. For better or for worse, the United States has looked to its court system to resolve many of its most difficult social problems involving children and families. In very few governments around the world does the court system have as much power as in the United States.

The juvenile court serves a number of critical functions for abused and neglected children, functions which could not be as effectively provided on a voluntary basis through social service agencies. Given the great respect and authority the court system enjoys in the United States, it was not irrational to select the court as the institution responsible for addressing the problems presented by delinquent, status, and dependent children.

FULFILLING THE EXPECTATIONS OF THE JUVENILE COURT

In order for the juvenile court to succeed, it must be part of a system, a system which provides appropriate sanctions and services at different junctures, depending on the seriousness of the case. If all cases were to be brought before the juvenile court, the court would sink. The court can be successful only if a balanced view is taken of its capabilities.

To address the needs of children we will have to organize much more than an effective juvenile court system. Law enforcement must be persuaded that they are an important part of the solution and that they can offer effective interventions for many of the cases they encounter, without referral to court. Community-based organizations must also be persuaded that they are part of the solution, and that they must be prepared to work with agencies on behalf of children and their families. Corporations and businesses must be persuaded that they are part of the solution, and that they can offer resources, energy, and expertise to families and children who might otherwise come within the juvenile court jurisdiction. Schools have to be persuaded that they are part of the solution, because there is so much they can offer to these children and their families. No person, no agency, no court can manage these problems alone. The creation of a working coalition of schools, law enforcement, agencies, community-based organizations, corporations and businesses, and the courts can be effective in helping to accomplish the work of the juvenile court.

CONCLUSION

The tasks assigned to the juvenile court by the legislature are enormous. The legislature has determined that the state must investigate the circumstances surrounding children who may have been abused or neglected. If the social service agency wishes to intervene on behalf of those children, the juvenile court has the responsibility to determine whether state intervention is justified and what the intervention should be. The court is further given the responsibility of planning and supervising those children's lives.

The juvenile courts are society's means of holding itself accountable on behalf of its children and families. It is not a question of whether we need the juvenile courts because our society needs them, or a similar institution, to fulfill this task. The issues, instead, are when to turn to the juvenile courts for intervention, how to define the role of the juvenile court as it intervenes, what kinds of resources are necessary for the juvenile courts to be able to complete the tasks assigned to them, and what kinds of judges are necessary for the juvenile courts to succeed. As Mark Harrison Moore has stated,

> The only institution that can reasonably exercise leadership on behalf of the society and the children is the juvenile court. The reason is simply that no other institution can claim to have an equally broad view of all the interests at stake, to have as wide a range of action, or to be able to make decisions that are designed to reflect the values of society as expressed in its laws and Constitution. (Moore, 1987).

CHAPTER 6

Domestic Relations Court

As the hypothetical case that introduces Part Two indicates, child abuse allegations can arise in the context of a marital dissolution. In our case, Judy suspected that Harry was sexually molesting their daughter. Judy returned to the domestic relations court to modify the custody decree in order to protect her daughter.

Child abuse and neglect allegations in a marital dissolution or custody battle raise important and complex issues concerning the well-being of the child involved. Is the domestic relations court adequately equipped to protect the child? Should the maltreatment issue be determined by the domestic relations court or resolved by the juvenile court in a child welfare proceeding? Should the child be appointed an attorney or a guardian *ad litem* in the domestic relations court? Should domestic relations court procedures be modified because of the special problems presented by this type of case?

This chapter first describes how the domestic relations court operates, including the powers of the court, the manner in which cases proceed through the court system, the parties to domestic relations court actions, and a description of the professionals and agencies who may become involved when child abuse allegations are made. Then the chapter outlines how the domestic relations court responds to child maltreatment allegations. It addresses those aspects of the domestic relations court process that make it less appropriate than the juvenile court for the management and trial of child abuse cases. Ways in which the court structure and procedures can be modified to better meet the needs of these complex and difficult cases are discussed.

Next, we discuss the problems of false allegations of child abuse in domestic relations cases. Can the court know when abuse allegations are true or false? And what can the legal system do to protect against false accusations?

Finally, we look at a brief description of parental child abductions. These abductions often take place in the context of a domestic relations

case, sometimes when there has been violence or abuse in the home. The chapter concludes with some recommendations on how to improve the court response to child abuse allegations in domestic relations proceedings.

Case Example (*Moffat v. Moffat*, 1980)

In 1972, in the state of Virginia, Mr. and Mrs. Moffat, parents of two daughters, dissolved their marriage and reached an agreement that Mrs. Moffat would have the primary custody of the children, while Mr. Moffat would have liberal visitation with them. Mr. Moffat agreed to pay child support for the children.

Shortly after the dissolution agreement was signed, the Moffats started fighting over issues of visitation and child support. Mr. Moffat made a motion in court to secure compliance with the property division of the marital decree. Mrs. Moffat moved for a termination of visitation rights, alleging that the father had sexually molested their daughters and lacked control over his "sexual aberrations." The court denied Mrs. Moffat's motion for termination of visitation rights and reinstated Mr. Moffat's visitation rights expressly, finding that none of the child molestation allegations was true. In spite of the court order, the mother refused to let the father visit with the children.

Mr. Moffat brought a *habeas corpus* petition to enforce his six-week summer visitation rights the next year, and the court held Mrs. Moffat in contempt of that order. The judge suspended imposition of sentence and ordered the father excused from support payments until the mother complied with the visitation order.

Mrs. Moffat subsequently moved from Virginia to California and filed an action for collection of unpaid child support. Mr. Moffat responded that he did not have to pay any support, since the judge in Virginia had suspended his child support obligation. The mother responded that the question was only whether the children are entitled to support by one legally liable to support them.

The case was appealed to the California Supreme Court, which wrote an opinion describing the harm done to the children.

> Since that time, Mrs. Moffat has systematically endeavored to circumvent the visitation order through an unrelenting variety of legal proceedings. These include a petition to give up her children and to have them declared wards of the juvenile court, a proceeding in which she reasserted the molestation accusation previously found to be untrue, a motion to terminate the July visitation order, and criminal charges against Mr. Moffat for failure to provide. None of her efforts were successful; in affirming the order dismissing the criminal charges, the appellate department of the Superior Court noted the dismissal rested, in part, on the trial judge's conclusion that the charges were filed for harassment purposes and constituted an abuse of process by Mrs. Moffat.
>
> To this day (eight years after the dissolution), Mrs. Moffat has obdurately refused to comply with the visitation order and has thus denied the children their right to know and be with their father. (Pp. 649-50)

The California Supreme Court agreed with the father. The court held that the previous trial court order relieving Mr. Moffat of his obligation to pay child support was valid and that Mrs. Moffat should have taken legal measures to overturn that order but that she failed to do so. The court then reflected upon the situation as it was presented within these proceedings.

> We believe the children's well-being transcends material considerations. This mother is cruelly inflicting incalculable damage to the children's welfare by arbitrarily denying to them the values inherent in a congenial father-child relationship. Visitation rights are a two-way street: although technically awarded by a court to a parent, the rights belong equally to the children. Thus the

Legislature and our courts alike have declared an abiding parental relationship to be in the best interests of the child.

> While this court has never before ordered a trial court to appoint independent counsel for children in a domestic controversy, this would appear to be an appropriate case for such an appointment. Seldom have we seen such circumstances in which the integral well-being of the children appears to be, at least to some degree, in conflict with the intransigence of both parents. . . . (Pp. 658-59)

Discussion

Parental conflict can have a detrimental effect upon children (Leupnits, 1978; Heatherington, Cox and Cox, 1978; Wallerstein and Kelley, 1980). The Moffat case is an example of parental conduct that had a devastating effect upon the children.

The impact on the children was more than the lost relationship with their father. Apparently, they had received no child support from the father during all of these years. Moreover, the California Supreme Court found that the father need not pay any support, given the prior court orders. The children lost twice, both the relationship with their father and the support he might have provided them.

The Moffat case demonstrates that through the eight years of legal battles, there was little the courts could do. The parents moved from state to state and brought many different legal actions, but they controlled the location and nature of the proceedings. Finally, the California Supreme Court as a last effort suggested that an attorney be appointed to represent the children.

Do you think that the children should have been appointed an attorney? What could the attorney have done for the children? (Recall chapter 4, where we discussed the question of who speaks for the child.)

What other steps, if any, should have been taken by the courts to ensure that there was a good relationship between the father and the children? Are there circumstances in which you would recommend that the court change custody as a response to outrageous behavior by the custodial parent?

What if the mother continued to believe that the father was a child molester? What if she was correct in her belief? Should she permit visitation to take place?

The type of child abuse described in the hypothetical case introducing Part Two can also occur in an intact marriage. If the parents remain together and the nonoffending parent does nothing to protect the child, the matter will never come to the attention of the domestic relations court. It will remain a family secret, unless the child or a sibling reports the abuse to someone outside the family, in which case the child welfare (dependency) system and/or the criminal process may become involved with the family.

FUNCTIONS OF THE DOMESTIC RELATIONS COURT

The domestic relations court provides the forum for the resolution of the legal issues surrounding marriage and the rearing of children. The majority of the court's work focuses upon marital dissolution (divorce), child support, spousal support (alimony), property division, and child custody and visitation. Other issues can include legal separation, nullification of the marriage, paternity, and adoption.

In domestic relations court proceedings, the parents are presumed to be fit and proper adults, fully capable of making decisions to rearrange their lives after they separate or dissolve their marriage. Generally, married persons come to the court with agreements and ask the court to affirm those agreements and make them legally binding.

The domestic relations court offers married persons the opportunity to privately order their relationship. The state has little or no supervision over this process, unless the parties are unable to agree. If that happens, one of the parties may initiate a legal action in the domestic relations court. If neither spouse has sufficient interest, funds, energy, or resourcefulness to bring the matter before the court, the legal action will not be filed and the status quo will remain.

If there are children of the marriage, the law presumes that the parents are fit and proper persons to care for them. The legal process permits parents to determine how they will share the responsibilities of raising their children even after the parents have separated and their marriage is dissolved.

The preference for parental autonomy in the resolution of child custody disputes is based on the assumption that parents know better than anyone else what is in their child's best interests. The state is perceived as unnecessary in making custody and visitation decisions, because the parents will ensure that the child is well cared for. Only when the parents do not agree upon the best plan for the child will the state offer professionals to assist the parents in resolving their differences and, as a last resort, the court process.

The hypothetical case outlines the progress of a child custody determination through the domestic relations court. Once the parents have decided to separate, they can agree between themselves how they will share parenting responsibilities. Judy and Harry agreed that Judy would have primary custody, while Harry would have access to the children at specific times, including weekends, holidays, and a portion of the summer. This agreement was approved by the domestic relations court with minimal, if any, oversight. The court simply made the parents' agreement legally binding by signing their proposed order.

If the parents had been unable to agree on a custody arrangement, the court would have offered them a forum in which they could present their respective positions, so that the court could decide how they would share parenting responsibilities.

At any such hearing, each parent would have the right to be represented by an attorney. If either parent did not have the financial resources to retain an attorney, he or she might appear *in propria persona* (representing him- or herself).

Many states do not permit parents to bring child custody disputes to court without first trying to resolve them by some sort of mediation or counseling. Mediation brings the parents together with a professional to discuss differences, reduce acrimony, and attempt to reach an agreement without resort to the formal court process. It has proven to be a successful means of resolving custody disputes wherever it has been tried. Most parents reach an agreement on child custody issues without turning to the court for dispute resolution (Mnookin, 1975). It should be noted, however, that mediation for families with domestic violence or child maltreatment difficulties may be inappropriate and likely to fail. Studies have shown that mediation does not work well for violent and dysfunctional families (Cauble, Theonnes, Pearson, and Appleford, 1985). Children of such families are particularly at risk, because their parents are often severely limited in their capacity to cooperate and respond appropriately to their children's needs and to provide a consistent, secure environment (Johnston and Campbell, 1988).

If mediation is unsuccessful, a trial can be held in the domestic relations court. The trial may be preceded by social or psychological evaluations, either by private professionals or court staff. As a part of these evaluations, all family members are usually interviewed and a report with recommendations is rendered to the court.

At the trial there may be testimony presented by all family members, by professionals, and by friends of the family. The children of the marriage may be asked to testify, but courts are often reluctant to have children testify in front of their parents. Some domestic relations judges prefer to speak to the children privately, away from their parents. Others prefer to have no testimony from the children, believing that the court process is harmful, because the child is put into the impos-sible situation of choosing between two parents (Edwards, 1987).

There are several different types of hearings at which custody orders can be made by a domestic relations court. At the beginning of the litigation, the court may make a temporary order. After a full hearing or an agreement by the parties, the court will make a permanent custody order. Thereafter, if there is a significant change of circumstances, the court may make a modification order. The custody of children remains a potential issue for the court until the child is eighteen or otherwise emancipated. In our hypothetical case, the permanent order was entered by the court based upon the parents' agreement to share custody of their children. A modification of that order is now being sought by both parents.

PROTECTING THE CHILD

The domestic relations law reflects the emphasis upon parental autonomy and private ordering. The only parties to a marital dissolution action are the husband and wife. The state is not a party and has no representative before the court to take a position contrary to that of the parents. In rare cases, the child may have a representative, but this is still the exception and not the rule. (Refer to chapter 4.)

The issues before the court are defined by the parties. If one of the parties does not ask for relief the court will not be in a position to grant any. This aspect of domestic relations court is very important in child abuse cases. If one parent wishes to prove that the other maltreated the child, it will be up to that parent to prove that the maltreatment occurred. That parent may or may not have an attorney. The parent may or may not have access to an investigator. In the trial, the parent may not know how to prove that abuse occurred. In other words, the proof of any child abuse allegation will be left to the skill and resources of the parent alleging that it happened.

After court orders are made, the domestic relations court is not well equipped to monitor compliance with those orders. Rarely does a domestic relations court have a staff to supervise custody and visitation orders. If a parent does not bring violations of court orders to the attention of the court, it is unlikely that the domestic relations court will learn of them.

Case Example (*Ellibee*, Idaho, 1992)

In an Idaho case (*Ellibee*, Idaho, 1992) the parents ended their divorce with an agreement for joint legal custody of their children, with each parent to share physical custody of the children. The mother noticed that her son had bruises on him after one of the visits with the father. He told her that "Daddy whammed me." The mother petitioned the domestic relations court pursuant to the Idaho Domestic Violence Crime Prevention Act with a request for a temporary order restraining the father from having visits with the children. The court issued a temporary order restraining the father from visiting the children. At a full hearing, the court heard testimony from both the mother and the father, as well as other witnesses. The court found that the father had physically abused his son by giving him a severe spanking resulting in several visible bruises. Based on that finding, the court issued an order that future visits between the children and their father be supervised.

The father appealed that order. He argued that the court had no power to restrict his visitation rights in an action brought under the state Domestic Violence Crime Prevention Act. He claimed that, since he had joint legal custody of his children, the court had no jurisdiction under the Act to deprive him of visitation rights.

The Idaho Supreme Court affirmed the trial court order, finding that the Act empowered the trial judge with wide discretion to consider the best interests of the children. The court found that when the trial judge held that the children were in immediate danger of further domestic violence, it had the power to change temporarily the father's custody rights awarded under the prior decree.

Discussion

This is an example of a case in which a child was abused by a parent during visitation. The other parent was able to take legal steps to protect the child from further abuse. The mother petitioned the trial court with a remedy often utilized by private parties seeking the assistance of the law. Normally these types of actions are heard in domestic relations or family courts. They are brought by a parent or a person wishing to stop abusive conduct by another person.

Note that it was the mother who detected the problem, initiated the action, and followed through by securing the orders from the court. In this case, the mother was a protective parent, one who was looking out for the best interests of her children. If she had not noticed the bruises, had not believed her son, had had no interest in pursuing the matter, or did not have the resources to petition the court, no action would have been taken. Even if the mother had decided to file a petition, she might not have been successful in court.

The mother did not ask for assistance from the state. Unlike Sally in the hypothetical case, she did not call child protective services or the police. Should the court have referred this case to child protective services for further investigation? (In chapter 9, specific cases that involve this issue are discussed.) There are some situations in which a protective parent can prevent the state from taking jurisdiction over the child. If the parent can demonstrate that state action through the child welfare system is unnecessary because the parent has already taken sufficient protective steps, then the court may not permit the social services agency to successfully petition the court for jurisdiction.

In the Idaho case, it appears that the mother took action to protect her child. Was that sufficient to persuade child protective services that a juvenile action was not necessary?

LIMITATIONS OF DOMESTIC RELATIONS COURT

The domestic relations court is not structured to provide protection for abused and neglected children. Because the law presumes parental fitness, the domestic relations court has few of the investigatory, prosecutorial, or supervisorial powers necessary to find out what has happened to the child and ensure that it does not happen again.

In the domestic relations court, the investigation of any child abuse and neglect allegations will usually be left to the parent making the charges and any help that parent can find from law enforcement and other agencies. The domestic relations court will rarely have its own staff trained in child maltreatment investigations or the time to complete them. The only parties in domestic relations court are the parents, which means that the prosecutor of any child abuse allegations will have to be the parent making the assertion. Turning a parent into a prosecutor hardly ensures that the best evidence will be presented in the most effective way to the court. Even if the court finds that some abuse has occurred and makes custody orders to protect the child, it then becomes the duty of the nonabusing parent to monitor the situation. If the child is reabused, the nonabusing parent will be the only party who can return to the court and call the court's attention to the violation. Domestic relations courts rarely have supervisorial staff to assist in the monitoring of court orders.

In many custody cases involving child abuse allegations, an expert may be called in to testify in the case. This expert is often the court-appointed mediator or evaluator. Many judges believe that they can best determine the complex task of who should have custody of the child after being informed by mental health professionals or court mediators who have evaluated the children and parents. This is especially true when there are allegations of abuse. The expert's opinion is not meant to usurp the court's role as trier of fact or assessor of the credibility of the parties involved. However, well-trained and experienced experts can inform and assist the court in determining the costs and benefits associated with potential outcome, regarding how best to allocate parental resources to meet the long-term needs of the children.

The domestic relations court process is often insensitive to the special needs of the child, who may have to be examined by batteries of psychologists and other mental health professionals and then be questioned in court by parents in a contested legal proceeding. Children rarely have their own attorney in domestic relations proceedings, because it is believed to be an unnecessary and costly expense. There are rarely protective orders put in place by the court prohibiting parents from taking the child to mental health or medical professionals for examinations. In hotly contested custody litigation, a child may be examined by five or ten such professionals.

Once in the courtroom, the child may be asked to testify about the allegations while in the presence of both parents (the accuser and the accused). Such a confrontation may be severely traumatic for the child and may be unproductive for the court, which is trying to determine the truth of the allegations. Moreover, the domestic relations court was not created with the special needs of child witnesses in mind. To the extent that children may have to come before the court to testify about allegations of abuse, they may be exposed to insensitive, even harmful, court procedures.

In child custody cases, a child may need to be questioned either as a percipient witness of fact (a person who was there) or to determine the child's needs for custody planning. In the former situation, a child's comments might be sought to prove fitness of a parent. In the latter situation, the purpose of questioning is to determine a plan to reorganize family functioning that best meets the child's needs. In either case, judges are often hesitant to involve a child in this type of courtroom proceeding (*Child Witness Manual*, 1991).

In order to overcome some of these difficulties, judges may sometimes order law proceedings to be closed to the public and press when it considers it necessary in the interests of justice (California Civil Code, section 4360). In family law proceedings, the judge may hear the testimony of children in closed proceedings in chambers (*Marriage of Okum*, 1987). In *Marriage of Okum* (1987), a trial judge who questioned the children in chambers with only the attorneys and court reporter present was upheld on appeal, because the judge was concerned that the "particularly acrimonious" nature of the litigation might have affected the children's later relationship with their parents, particularly if their father were to have questioned them. In another case, a judge who instructed the court reporter not to transcribe notes of chambers proceedings was also upheld (*Marriage of Rosson*, 1986). In fact, many judges will not permit the child witness in a custody proceeding to be examined in open court on the witness stand (Edwards, 1987; Hogobom and King, 1991).

Some judges believe that in child abuse cases it is advisable for the court to conduct its own enquiry on whether and where a child should testify. The court can do this by asking a family court evaluator or mental health expert during his or her testimony to comment on whether it would benefit the court to have the child testify, whether it would be harmful for the child to testify at all, and where and under what conditions any testimony of the child should be taken. This type of questioning builds a record to assist the judge in making the best decision possible regarding the

child's participation in the case and any testimony that might be given by the child.

ACTIONS TAKEN IN DOMESTIC RELATIONS COURT

Custody and visitation battles are among the most difficult tasks for the legal system. This is especially true when allegations of child abuse are raised. The standard most often used to determine custody and visitation is the "best interests of the child" standard. Specific criteria for determining the "best interests" of children have been stated in a number of state statutes. In spite of these criteria, it is usually up to the judge to determine what is in the child's best interests. A typical state statute outlining the factors a judge should consider in making custody orders is as follows:

> The Legislature finds and declares that it is the public policy of this state to assure minor children of frequent and continuing contact with both parents after the parents have separated or dissolved their marriage, and to encourage parents to share the rights and responsibilities of child rearing in order to effect this policy. . . . (California Civil Code section 4600[a])

> In making a determination of the best interests of the child in any proceeding under this title, the court shall, among any other factors it finds relevant, consider all of the following:

> a. The health, safety and welfare of the child;
> b. Any history of abuse against the child. As a prerequisite to the consideration of allegations of abuse, the court may require substantial independent corroboration, including, but not limited to, written reports by law enforcement agencies, child protective services or other social welfare agencies, courts, medical facilities, or other public agencies or private nonprofit

organizations providing services to victims of sexual assault or domestic violence. . . .

c. The nature and amount of contact with both parents. (California Civil Code, section 4608)

Abuse and neglect of a child will often be a determinative factor in custody cases, since it may have direct, harmful impact upon the child (Nicholson, 1988). Physical abuse or sexual abuse by a parent is usually, in and of itself, sufficient to determine that it is not in the best interests of a child to be under the control of that parent (*Seymour v. Walter*, 1982; *In re M. M.*, 1982). For example, the Maryland statutes provide that child abuse is a factor which must be considered in determining custody, and may be the basis for denial of custody and/or visitation. If the court has reasonable grounds to believe a child has been abused, and determines that further abuse or neglect is likely to occur if the custody rights are granted to the party, then the court must deny a custody award to the party (Maryland Family Code, section 9-101, 1985).

In some cases, after reading the investigatory report and hearing all the evidence, the court may decide that the child needs some form of protection from one of the parents. The court may limit contact between the child and one parent by ordering limited visitation, supervised visitation, or no visitation at all between a parent and the child. Supervised visitation is often used in cases involving child maltreatment. Whenever there is a risk of harm to a child resulting from visitation with a noncustodial parent, the court may order the visitation to be supervised. Under such supervised visitation, the noncustodial parent can see his or her child only in the presence of another person who is there to ensure the child's safety. This person might be employed by the court, but is often a relative or a friend of the family. In order to deny a parent access to his child, the court must find that such contact would not be in the child's best interests and would be detrimental to the child.

The court can also issue a protective order directing that there be no contact between that parent and the custodial parent, and the court can prohibit that parent from contacting, annoying, molesting, harassing, or disturbing the peace of the custodial parent and the child (California Civil Code, section 4359, 1991). Additionally, the court can order the noncustodial parent to stay away from designated places which the custodial parent and child might visit. Such orders can be issued only if there is a sufficient showing that the noncustodial parent has harmed or threatened to harm the custodial parent.

Enforcement of such restricted visitation or nonvisitation is generally sought through civil contempt proceedings. Civil contempt is considered to be remedial in nature, primarily to aid the complaining party in coercing the other party to abide by the terms of a court order. Because it is remedial in nature, the punishment for civil contempt may be imposed only for as long as necessary to secure compliance with the court order. The punishment may be a fine, incarceration, or both. However, the punishment must stop as soon as the individual in contempt is ready to abide by the order.

The most famous case in the United States involving the application of civil contempt for failing to comply with a family court visitation order is that of Dr. Elizabeth Morgan from the District of Columbia (*Morgan v. Foretich*, 1988). On August 26, 1987, Dr. Morgan was held in contempt for defying a District of Columbia Superior Court order to deliver her five-year-old daughter Hilary to Dr. Eric Foretich, her ex-husband, for two weeks of unsupervised visitation. Morgan had repeatedly accused Foretich of sexually abusing Hilary. Foretich denied any misconduct. When the case was heard in a domestic relations proceeding in the District of Columbia Family Court, the court found no truth to the abuse allegations and ordered Dr. Morgan to give Dr. Foretich the child for visitation. Morgan refused, believing that there had been abuse. She was supported by several psychologists and pediatricians, who had examined Hilary. Instead of turning her daughter over to her ex-husband, whom she believed to have sexually abused her child, Morgan chose to go to jail, where she stayed for over two years. Had Congress not acted, she might have remained in jail for a much longer period. On September 23, 1989, Congress passed Public Law No. 101-97, which limits imprisonment for civil contempt in child custody cases in the District of Columbia to one year (Public Law No. 101-97, 1989). According to Harmer (1990), the *Morgan* case is a clear example of the misuse of the civil contempt order in child custody cases. He cautions that, since an "indeterminate sentence is ordinarily imposed," a civil contemnor can theoretically remain in jail as long as he or she refuses to promise to behave.

The *Morgan* case was exceptional. In most cases, domestic relations courts have been reluctant to impose such stringent contempt orders on parents, particularly when the custodial parent believes that violating the court order is a means of protecting the child's well-being (Nicholson, 1988).

Child abuse can also be a sufficient basis for modification of prior custody orders. Child abuse has been found to be a significant change of circumstances and harmful enough to the child to be sufficient to modify a previous joint custody order (*Steagall v. Steagall*, 1983).

Charges of child abuse must be proven before a parent loses custody of a child. Mere allegations or unproven allegations made in good faith are not sufficient to change custody of a child (*State in the matter of Williams*). False accusations of abuse can themselves become grounds for removing custody or visitation (*Grein v. Grein*, 1985).

Case Example (*G.S. v. T.S.*, Conn. App., 1990)

Mr. and Mrs. S. married in 1983, and two daughters, H. and N., were born to them. The couple separated in 1988. The separation was not amicable, with both parents asking for custody of the children. In 1988, the court entered a temporary order awarding custody of both children to the mother.

In 1989, the court issued an *ex parte* order changing the custody of H. to Mr. S. That order was based on an affidavit by the father that H. was sexually molested several times by the mother's cousin while H. was in her mother's custody. The affidavit contained statements that both the police and the Department of Children and Youth Services (DCYS) were investigating the allegations and each had suggested that H. not be returned to her mother's custody.

A five-day trial was held over the course of five months. It included testimony from law enforcement, social services, the parents, relatives, and a sexual abuse counselor. Mr. S. asked that the child be made available to testify, but the court indicated that it would not permit a six-year-old child to testify. The father also asked that an attorney be appointed to represent the children, but the court declined to make that appointment. At the conclusion of the trial, the court awarded custody of the children to Mrs. S. Mr. S. appealed that decision.

The Connecticut Court of Appeals reversed the trial court. It discussed child custody cases in general and concluded that the children needed better representation throughout the proceedings.

> The guiding principle applicable to determining the custody of children in a dissolution proceeding is the best interests of the child. Our Supreme Court has stated that 'in search for an appropriate custodial placement, the primary focus of the court is the best interests of the child, the child's interest in sustained growth, development, well-being and in the continuity and stability of its environment.' This standard articulates the right of children in custody cases to be placed in an environment where they are not abused and neglected, but rather they are loved and nurtured.
>
> In determining what is in the best interests of the child, the court is vested with broad discretion.

The court is not privileged to usurp that authority or to substitute its judgment for that of the trial court. A mere difference of opinion or judgment cannot justify our intervention. Nothing short of a conviction that the action of the trial court is one which discloses a clear abuse of discretion can warrant our interference.

General statutes provide that the court may appoint counsel in any case 'when the court finds that the custody, care, education, visitation, or support of a minor child is in actual controversy.' Although the language of the statute leaves such appointments to the discretion of the court, our Supreme Court has stated that 'in the absence of strong countervailing considerations such as physical urgency or financial stringency, the better course is to appoint independent counsel whenever the issue of child custody is seriously contested.'

In this case, where custody is hotly contested, where, prior to trial, the court is made aware of allegations of child abuse and sexual molestation, and where those allegations become abundantly clear during the first day of testimony, it is an abuse of discretion not to appoint counsel for the minor children. When custody is contested and there are allegations of neglect and abuse, children have a unique need to be represented by counsel who will advocate their best interests.

If counsel had been appointed for H. at the time of the *ex parte* order, that counsel most likely would have requested a family relations study and may have requested a hearing on the *ex parte* order to get the court involved in the allegations set forth in the affidavit at the earliest possible date. On the first day of trial, counsel for H. could have pointed out that H. was competent to testify. Counsel could have argued that, because her testimony was pivotal to the determination of her custody and sexual abuse, H. was entitled to testify as of right. Counsel for H. also could have cited (the relevant statute) to highlight the fact that the plaintiff had an interest in the outcome of the dispute and therefore could not waive H.'s privilege of confidentiality with her sexual abuse counselor.

Both the plantiff and the defendant had the benefit of counsel whose advocacy obligations were to their clients. Those obligations do not require that the parents' counsel act in the best interests of the children. Neither parent could be relied on to communicate to the court the children's interests where those interests differed from his or her own. As the United States Supreme Court has recognized,

. . . experience has shown that the question of custody, so vital to a child's happiness and well-being, frequently cannot be left to the discretion of parents. This is perfectly true where, as here, the estrangement of husband and wife beclouds parental judgment with emotion and prejudice.

Finally, the court is not an advocate, but rather is the arbiter of the dispute and of the best interests of the child. It is clear that both H. and N. needed and were entitled to counsel to advocate their best interests. The judgment is reversed as to the award of custody and child support and the state is remanded for a new hearing on those issues; custody of the children and the award of child support shall remain as ordered until further order of the Superior Court. (*G.S. v. T.S.*, 582 A.2d 467 [1990])

Discussion

This case is an example of child abuse allegations being heard in a domestic relations child custody dispute. In this case, the Connecticut appellate court recognized that the domestic relations court offered little protection for the children. While there were child sexual abuse allegations made, the case was heard by the domestic relations trial court and not before the juvenile court. The appellate court determined that the children were not adequately represented in the trial and ordered the trial court to appoint an attorney for the children. The appellate court suggested that the attorney for the child might have ordered a full investigation of the matter through the family services agency. The appellate courts also suggested that the attorney might have made it possible for the child to testify.

If H. were called to testify, by whom would

you suggest that the testimony be taken? Would it be better to have the child testify in chambers without either parent being present? Would it be preferable to have her testify in open court, so that she could understand the importance of telling the truth? What if the parents insisted that they be present during her testimony? Do they have a right to be present?

FALSE ACCUSATIONS

In general, experts agree that the likelihood that an allegation of child sexual abuse will be false has not been accurately calculated (Romer, 1990). An important distinction must be made between fictitious allegations, unsubstantiated suspicions, and insufficient information reports (Jones and McCraw, 1987). A similar distinction is made by Corwin, Berliner, Goodman, Goodwin, and White, 1987. They point out that unsubstantiated reports are not the same as false reports. Terming an accusation unsubstantiated or unfounded does not necessarily imply that it is false. Rather, it means only that one cannot be confident of the allegation due to insufficient or inconsistent evidence. Therefore, one can only have more or less confidence, but not certainty, in the evidence pertaining to whether or not the abuse took place. Corwin, et al., (1987) also applaud Jones and McCraw's use of the term "fictitious" instead of "false," which avoids the pejorative connotation implied in "false accusations."

Some researchers claim that only 8 percent of cases studied are fictitious (Jones and McCraw, 1987). Their study was based on 576 consecutive referrals of sexual abuse to the Denver Department of Social Services. They found that 70 percent of the reports were reliable, and 22 percent were cases of unsubstantiated suspicion. Other studies using all cases reported to social services or medical centers as their data base also report a small percentage of false accusations. Peters (1976) found

that only 6 percent were false. Cantwell (1981) reported 9 percent. Horowitz, Salt, Gomes-Schwarts, and Sauzier (1984) reported less than 5 percent in a sample of 181 cases.

Bulkley (1988) also disputes the claim that there is an increasing number of false allegations of sexual abuse, even in custody cases. Citing the Thoennes and Pearson study (1986), she says that recent surveys of domestic court personnel indicate that sexual abuse allegations are a very small percentage of contested custody cases. While deliberately false allegations occur, they are exceedingly rare and no more likely to be false than allegations in other situations.

However, other studies have reported a larger percentage of false reports. Green (1985) reported on a clinical study in which 35 percent of the eleven allegations of sexual abuse made during custody proceedings were false. Green concluded that some children may be influenced by a vindictive or delusional parent to tell fabricated stories. The Corwin, et al., article, however, takes issue with the findings reported by Green (1985) and argues that his sample was too small to be scientifically valid. Other clinical reports involving very small, nonrandom samples have also found a high percentage of false cases, but the numbers may be too small to make any generalizations (Raskin and Yuille, 1989).

It may well be that allegations made in family court during divorce and custody proceedings are more likely to be false than in any other setting. Most of the studies that reported a low percentage of false accusations based their sample on reports to the social service or medical departments, whereas Green's study is based on allegations made in family court.

Coleman and Clancy (1990) contend that false accusations of child sexual abuse are on the increase as a direct result of the alliance between law enforcement and mental health professionals. They believe that what they call the "current problem" of false accusations of child sexual abuse is due to the incompatibility between the neutrality required of investigators and a series of biases imported into the investigative process from the mental health professionals. They argue that in the 1970s and 1980s investigators came to take the view of therapists and became advocates for children, always believing the child. They cite the results of the *McMartin* case as an example of how the alliance between mental health and law enforcement can lead the prosecution astray (*People v. Peggy McMartin Buckey and Ray Buckey*, 1990). They conclude that not only do false accusations cause psychological damage to the child, they often destroy whole families.

Regardless of the absolute number of false versus true accusations, child sexual abuse cases in the family court are exceedingly difficult and time-consuming. According to Thoennes and Pearson (1986), while the percentage of sexual abuse allegations in their study varied from only 3 percent to 15 percent of all contested cases, these cases took on a disproportionate importance in domestic relations proceedings. They noted that the perception that these cases are far more common may be due to the fact that they are particularly problematic. These cases are among the most troublesome and costly cases in the court. They typically involve an array of agencies, such as the child protective services, juvenile courts, and a host of other professionals. They include dealing with families at a high level of anger and suspicion, and often a host of other problems, such as substance abuse and spousal abuse. To find in the end that all of these problems and extra work are due to false accusations may be particularly vexing.

The issue of false accusations has become an area of contention for mediators and others working in the family court setting. The argument is between those who perceive the court's response to be overly skeptical and those who believe that the court blindly accepts the charge and views the accused parent as guilty until proven innocent. Many believe that such allegations are routinely used by disgruntled parents as a strategy in custody disputes (Gray, 1986). Others argue that the courts are correct in being skeptical of abuse allegations, since many parents use this to gain a strategic

advantage in court (Gordon, 1985). The best view, however, may be that expressed by Corwin (1986), who has suggested that the stress associated with divorce may increase the chances both of real abuse as well as false accusations.

Case Example (*Mullins v. Mullins*, 1986)

The case of *Mullins v. Mullins* (1986) shows how false child abuse allegations in a domestic relations proceeding can result in a change of custody from one parent to the other. In the *Mullins* case, the parents ended their twelve-year marriage and agreed that the mother would have primary custody of the four- and six-year-old children, with the father having liberal visitation rights. Shortly after the dissolution, the mother remarried and attempted to terminate all contact between the father and the children. She tried to have the children change their names to reflect the name of their new stepfather.

The father challenged the mother's actions and filed a legal action to maintain his relationship with his children. The legal actions between the parents stretched out over several years. During the litigation the mother filed a report with the Department of Children and Family Services (DCFS), alleging that the father had sexually abused the children and further petitioned the court to require the father to undergo a psychiatric examination. She also asked the court to terminate or restrict his visitation with the children.

Other legal actions included the father's petition to prevent the mother from moving to Florida with the children, his petition to enforce his visitation rights, and his motion to hold the mother in contempt of court for not permitting him to visit with the children, and for various actions that frustrated his attempts to communicate with his children. The mother filed a second petition alleging sexual abuse by the father and an emergency petition to terminate visitation, alleging that the father had threatened, bribed, attempted to brainwash, and physically assaulted both children.

The litigation stretched over several years and included over a thousand pages of transcript from thirteen days of hearings. Although the trial court at first seemed to believe that there had been some improper behavior by the father, at a later hearing, the trial court concluded that the mother and her new husband had engaged in a self-serving scheme to terminate the father's parental rights and to destroy the children's relationship with him. The court specifically found that the mother had made child sexual abuse reports in bad faith. The trial court awarded custody of the children to the father.

The appellate court affirmed the trial court. It agreed that there was substantial evidence to find that, during the time the children lived with their mother, their environment seriously endangered their physical, mental, moral, or emotional health and that the advantages of transferring custody to the father outweighed the harm to be caused by a change of environment. The appellate court stated:

> In our view, this evidence not only supports the trial court's findings that (mother) deliberately used allegations she knew to be false to denigrate (father)—both publicly and in the eyes of the children—and to destroy his relationship with them, but also that her conduct so harmed them as to result in their need for psychiatric therapy, and that their mental, moral, and emotional health would be further endangered if they were to remain in her custody—grounds which, alone, were sufficient for modification by the trial court of custody under section 610[b] (p. 1389).

Discussion

There are always difficulties when child abuse allegations arise in domestic relations proceedings.

The normal process of dividing parenting responsibilities between the parents is interrupted until the truth of the allegations can be determined. During that truth-finding process, everything seems to be on hold waiting for the determination which, of course, will have a significant bearing upon who cares for the children. A parent who is found to have abused the children may have limited contact or no contact at all with them. As the *Mullins* case indicates, the parent who makes false allegations may lose custody of the children.

A more detailed description of the relationship between the domestic relations court and juvenile dependency proceedings appears in chapter 9.

THE VALIDITY OF ABUSE CLAIMS

Assessing the validity of child abuse claims in domestic relations court can be quite difficult. In all child abuse and neglect cases, the credibility of the child witness is an issue. In domestic relations cases, the credibility of the parents can also be an issue. Efforts towards settlement of the cases can come to a standstill, while accusations and counteraccusations are made. When the child is quite young and there is no physical evidence, it may be very difficult to establish the validity of the accusation.

Typically, expert testimony is sought by one or both parties to corroborate or refute the charges. They might draw on the few studies available (cited above) dealing with false accusations. They might also rely on their own assessment of the truthfulness of each party's statement. If no medical or physical evidence is available, psychological experts are likely to be drawn into the case. The problem is, however, that there are few, if any, scientifically established assessment methods to establish the absolute truthfulness of sexual abuse charges. Child maltreatment is not a disease for which there is a sure diagnosis and treatable symptoms. While there are new techniques, such as having the child play with anatomically correct dolls or participating in a lengthy "diagnostic" investigation, there is no clear profile that separates an abused child from a nonabused child or the abusing parent from the nonabusing parent. (See chapters 10 and 13 for a further elaboration of these issues.)

However, to the extent that false accusations are more likely to arise in domestic relations court proceedings than in any other court, the possibility of false charges is a serious one. While the child's best interests continue to be the guiding standard in determining custody decisions, and accusations of abuse must not be cynically dismissed, the court must also go to great lengths in trying to investigate and determine the validity of the accusations.

PARENTAL CHILD ABDUCTIONS

Sometimes a parent may not be content only to allege that the other parent abused the child; he or she may also abduct the child from the other parent. According to Huntington (1986), parental abductions have become a new form of child abuse. Many of these cases come about as a result of dissatisfaction with family court custody orders. According to the National Incidence Study on Missing, Abducted, Runaway, and Thrown-away Children in America, approximately 354,100 children were abducted by a family member in 1988 (Finkelhor, Hotaling, and Sedlack, 1991). The NISMART study found 41 percent of abductions were prior to the divorce and that males were more likely to abduct their children (73 percent). Similarly, about half of the abductions in one California study occurred before a custody order was in place, and fathers were most commonly the abductors in these instances (Sagatun and Barrett, 1990). It is important to note that the

NISMART study has shown that the risk of family abductions appears to extend over a considerable time during and after the separation and divorce process. Most cases, however, were heavily concentrated in the period of separation prior to the divorce. Rather than being snatched from the other parent, most abducted children were simply kept and not returned after scheduled visitation.

Studies of the effects of parental abduction on the child are sparse. Small, nonrepresentative surveys and clinical case studies of these children often describe serious psychological trauma, especially in more lengthy cases of concealment, which appear to have long-term effects. These symptoms include anxiety and fright, nightmares, sleeping problems, clinging and irritability, and disturbed emotions and behavior (e.g., Sagatun and Barrett, 1990).

Often the desire to avoid domestic violence or child abuse can motivate the other parent. In California, the legislature addressed this possibility in 1986 by enacting a statute that makes it legal for a parent to conceal the child from the other parent if he or she believes the child is in danger of physical or emotional abuse (California Penal Code, section 277, 1991). A parent may legally take the child if he or she has a "reasonable belief" that the abduction or detention was necessary. In 1991, this provision was redefined to include the good faith and reasonable belief of a person with a right to custody of the child who has been the victim of domestic violence by another person with a right of custody, that the child, if left with the other person, will suffer immediate bodily injury or bodily harm. The statute also requires that the parent taking the child must file a report with a law enforcement agency in the jurisdiction where the child has been living, with an explanation of the circumstances that warranted the taking or concealment.

These provisions make it possible for a parent to avoid the criminal charge of child-stealing, if he or she has a reasonable belief that the child is victim of domestic violence or child abuse. However, while these provisions can be seen as being in a child's best interests (i.e., get the child away from the harm of an abusive environment), they can also be seen as encouraging false allegations of abuse. While they help protect the child from abuse, they also make it harder to prosecute abduction cases. Parents who abduct their children are likely to use the provision of the "reasonable belief of harm" and allege abuse by the other parent. When the abuse allegation is untrue, an escalated custody dispute before the family court frequently results. A parent may both be unfairly accused and be deprived of the company of his or her child.

Parental abductions are difficult to prosecute. Many parents abduct their children to another state prior to a custody order being entered, or in violation of a custody order. Relatively few resources have been allocated to locate and retrieve abducted children to the victim parent. It is important to have a uniform response to child abductions, for states to cooperate with each other in the investigation and prosecution of the cases, and for the federal government to assist in the management of these cases.

DOMESTIC RELATIONS COURT VERSUS JUVENILE COURT

Instead of processing child abuse allegations in the domestic relations court, it would be preferable for the child and for the court system to have these allegations heard in the court designed to hear such matters, the juvenile dependency court. After all, child protection is the central purpose of the juvenile dependency court. In the juvenile court the investigatory, prosecutorial, and supervisory resources are available to ensure that the case is fully prepared, presented, and monitored. Moreover, the special needs of the child during all aspects of the process are protected. The child has an attorney

or guardian *ad litem* who appears as a party to the proceedings. There are special evidentiary and procedural rules which reflect the special needs of the child witness.

Despite this reasoning, many child abuse allegations continue to be heard in family court. The reasons for this are several. First, many do not take such allegations seriously. Second, the two court systems are often unwilling to work cooperatively with each other. Reports to child protective services from domestic relations court may not be perceived as "real" child abuse by the dependency system, but some kind of tactical ploy by the accusing parent. Third, the court system, particularly in metropolitan courts, is so large and cumbersome that such cases are unable to move from one setting to another.

Several innovations have made it possible for child abuse cases to be more appropriately handled by the court system. First, there have been efforts, legislative and judicial, to increase the coordination between the two court systems.

Second, in some states the domestic relations court has been empowered to respond more effectively to the needs of the child. Domestic relations courts have been more willing to appoint attorneys for children when child abuse allegations are made. Some appellate courts have been closely monitoring these cases to see that the child's interests are being adequately presented.

Third, some state court systems have been restructured so that domestic relations and juvenile dependency calendars are closely coordinated with one another. Referred to as unified family courts, they are administered with the child's needs in mind and such complex cases become easier to coordinate (Rubin, 1989).

CONCLUSION

The growth of child abuse allegations in domestic relations court proceedings is a cause of grave concern. It is unclear how many of the unprovable allegations are false or simply unsubstantiated. It is clear, however, that the trauma associated with separation and divorce and the often accompanying custody and financial battles provide a fertile ground for child maltreatment, both real and imagined. This chapter has discussed how such allegations are treated in domestic relations court, and suggested ways in which the response might be improved.

CHAPTER 7

Criminal Court and Child Abuse

One of society's most powerful responses to child abuse is the criminal sanction. When an adult harms a child, that behavior can result in criminal prosecution, conviction, and punishment of the offender. The purpose of the criminal response to child abuse is to punish the offender. In addition, the criminal sanction may deter others from committing the same behavior, may result in stopping the abuse, and may provide restitution to the victim. A related but secondary goal of the criminal law is the rehabilitation of the offender so that the conduct is not repeated.

The criminal case starts with the report of a crime. Whether criminal charges will be filed is determined after law enforcement investigation and review by the prosecuting attorney. If the prosecuting attorney concludes that a successful prosecution is likely and that charges should be filed in the interests of justice, the formal charges will be filed or presented to a grand jury for review. In some states the prosecutor can file charges directly with the court, while in others criminal charges must be reviewed by the grand jury before they are filed in the court.

After charges are filed, the defendant is brought before the court. If he or she was arrested, the case is brought before the court quickly. The Constitution guarantees that an incarcerated defendant have a speedy trial, and state statutes require that an arrested accused have speedy procedures throughout the criminal process. In the court the judge will advise the defendant of his or her constitutional rights, including the right to an attorney. Before trial the prosecutor will generally give to the defendant any investigatory information that has been collected. This is referred to as discovery. There may also be pretrial motions and preliminary hearings to test the admissibility and sufficiency of the prosecution's evidence. At the trial the defendant has a number of constitutional and statutory rights, including the right to confront and cross-examine witnesses, to present evidence, and to remain silent.

The consequences of criminal conduct can include loss of liberty and in the most serious cases, death. Because societal intervention can be so serious, there are significant legal protections for those accused of crimes. The defendant in a criminal case has the following constitutional rights:

1. The right to an attorney at all stages of a criminal prosecution. The attorney must be provided by the state at no cost if the defendant is indigent.
2. The right to notice of the charges.
3. The right to confront and cross-examine witnesses who may testify against him or her.
4. The right to remain silent.
5. The right to reasonable bail.
6. The right to a jury trial.
7. The right to appeal decisions made by the jury or court.

The criminal defendant may have other statutory rights in criminal proceedings, depending on the jurisdiction.

As society's most severe response to child maltreatment, the criminal law is also the most complex. Because the criminal sanction may result in deprivation of liberty for the offender, an accused has more statutory and constitutional protections than in any other type of legal proceeding. When compared to the due process afforded parents in family and juvenile dependency cases, the accused in a criminal proceeding receives significantly more rights before being subject to criminal sanctions.

For the purposes of the criminal law, child maltreatment includes sexual and physical abuse of children as well as some types of neglect. There are numerous categories of sexual and physical abuse described by the various criminal codes. These codes include felonies and misdemeanors reflecting more and less serious types of child abuse. Sexual abuse of young children and molestation usually fall in the felony category, while less serious abuse often is charged as a misdemeanor. Some crimes can be charged either as a felony or misdemeanor, depending on the prosecutor's views or the court's decision.

If the criminal charge of child abuse is found to be true, the penal codes often mandate long, severe sentences for the defendant. For example, the Arizona criminal code directs that an adult who stands convicted of a dangerous crime against children involving "sexual assault, taking a child for the purpose of prostitution, child prostitution, or sexual conduct with a minor" shall be sentenced to a presumptive term of imprisonment for twenty years (Arizona Revised Statutes, section 13-604.01[a]). A person who is convicted of a dangerous crime against children involving child molestation, commercial sexual exploitation of a minor, sexual exploitation of a minor, child abuse, or kidnapping shall be sentenced to a term of seventeen years (Arizona Code 13-604.01[b]). In addition to the term of imprisonment, the Arizona code mandates that any person convicted of any dangerous crime against children must be supervised on parole as the court deems appropriate for the rest of the person's life. Similar penalties exist in other states.

Criminal neglect of children is also covered by the penal codes of the various states. It can be charged either as a felony or misdemeanor, depending on the seriousness of the conduct. Emotional abuse of children may also be proscribed by the criminal law, but such cases are rarely prosecuted because of the difficulty of proof.

Case Example (*People v. Superior Court* [Caudle], 1990)

The case of *People v. Superior Court* (Caudle, 1990) presents a question of law relating to criminal charges of child abuse and a defendant's right to due process. The allegations exemplify what is sometimes referred to as a "resident child molester" case. The fact pattern these cases often present is that the defendant has lived in the same residence as the child victim over a long period of time, and is accused of frequent or routine molestation during that period, but the child cannot remember the exact dates and places the molestation occurred. The due process concerns raised by this factual pattern are (1) the sufficiency of the notice of offenses charges, (2) the defendant's ability to assert an alibi defense, and (3) the ability of the jury unanimously to agree on particular acts supporting particular charges.

The defendant was charged with 145 counts of molestation of the minor, N., occurring over the time period from June 1, 1983, until March 3, 1984. During that entire period of time, the defendant and N. lived in the same household. The statutory charge in each count was section 288(a) of the California Penal Code, lewd and lascivious conduct upon a child, except the final count which charged forcible oral copulation. Typical of the charges was count one, which charged that defendant committed an act proscribed by section 288(a) upon N. "on or about and between the 1st day of June, 1983, and the 7th day of June, 1983, in the County of Santa Clara."

The prosecution's evidence consisted largely of the victim's testimony. She was born on March 3, 1970. The defendant was her stepfather. She testified that the family moved to Santa Clara County when she was twelve years old and that the molestations began then. She testified that they were virtually a daily occurrence, a routine which took place nearly every morning. The typical pattern was the defendant would come into her room about 5:45 A.M. before anyone else was awake, awaken her, have her meet him in the family room far away from the bedrooms, take off her underwear, rub her chest and genitals, have intercourse with her and oral copulation. The acts usually happened seven days a week, every day; "it just always happened."

N. testified that the routine stopped some time about November 1986. She said that at that time she became more assertive and angry. She refused to cooperate as she had in the past. She testified that the defendant eventually completely stopped trying.

There were no eyewitnesses to the offenses. The victim's brother and mother did testify as to some circumstantial evidence of sexual conduct between the defendant and N. The mother once surprised the defendant in N.'s bedroom while the girl was disrobing and found his behavior to be inappropriate. The brother came home one day to find the victim locked in a younger sister's bedroom with the defendant. He testified that when his sister emerged, she gave explanations that left him unsatisfied as to what had happened.

N. could not give a specific date for any of the offenses. She testified that these events occurred regularly, except when the defendant was absent from the home on business trips or visiting family members. She had no memory of the dates of his absences.

Upon motion of the defendant, the lower court dismissed all but counts 144 and 145. It held that the charges were not specific as to time, and the defendant was therefore unable to be given fair notice and prepare a defense to the charges. The remaining counts were also not specific as to dates, one charging conduct between February 24, 1984, and March 3, 1984, and the other charged sexual acts on a Friday night between September 1 and December 1, 1984. Nevertheless, the lower court did not dismiss them.

The prosecutor appealed the lower court's dismissal of the first 143 counts. The California Supreme Court reversed the trial court and reinstated all 143 counts. The supreme court noted that cases of this type present tensions between the defendant's due process rights and society's wish to punish the resident molester for his conduct. When the victim cannot pinpoint the dates of the offenses, a dilemma exists: if the law requires specificity, a guilty person may escape accountability; if specificity is not required, the district attorney is free to charge any number of offenses and there is a danger of erroneous conviction or at least overcharging and disproportionate sentencing.

The supreme court found that the victim's testimony was sufficiently specific.

Here, however, we do not believe that the victim's testimony is "generic." Rather, it is specific, in that she has testified to a daily practice of molestation over a defined period of time (namely, from the time of the family's move to Santa Clara until November, 1986). Thus, she has actually accused defendant of having molested her each day of the stated period. This testimony is specific and gives defendant alibis for some or all of the basis of the charges. If he can furnish alibis for some or all of this period, it is incumbent on him to come forward and do so. Alternatively, he can defend by raising a reasonable doubt whether the victim is telling the truth about his routine practice of molestation.

The supreme court concluded that the evidence presented by the victim was sufficiently specific to permit the defendant to be ordered to stand trial. It should be up to the jury to decide whether the charges are true beyond a reasonable doubt.

We hold that it was error to dismiss all but two of the charges for insufficient evidence. . . . We shall issue a writ compelling reinstatement of the charges.

Discussion

The California Supreme Court noted in its opinion that the California state legislature had recently enacted a resident child molester statute (Penal Code Section 288.5). That statute imposes a sentence of six, twelve, or sixteen years for molestation occurring during a three-month period, and requires proof of regular access to the victim and at least three acts of substantial sexual conduct with the child during that period. There need not be unanimous agreement on the particular acts committed, only that three acts did occur. The statute was passed after the Caudle case arose and was not considered by the California Supreme Court in its decision.

Do you believe that it is fair for the prosecutor to charge 145 counts as was done in the Caudle case? Would you suggest that there be a limit on the number of charges that might be filed?

If the defendant had been tried and convicted on all 145 counts, he could have been sentenced to hundreds of years in jail. Is this too severe a sentence?

HOW A CRIMINAL CASE IS PROSECUTED

Report

The progress of a case through the criminal justice system starts with the report of a crime. Several different persons or agencies may respond to the complaining party, but the appearance of law enforcement begins the criminal process. The police make the initial decision to investigate, to record the event, and to present it to the prosecutor for consideration. Depending on the information available from the victim, family members, medical records, and other sources of evidence, the police officer will decide whether there is enough information to take the case further.

Removal of the Child

At the initial contact, the police officer must make a decision about the placement of the child. If the alleged perpetrator is arrested or if other protective measures are taken, such as the issuance of restraining orders, removal of the child may not be necessary. If the family setting is not a safe environment for the child, out-of-home placement may be necessary. In some states the police officer has the power to remove and place the child in a protective setting. In all jurisdictions it is preferable if the police officer and the child protector or social worker coordinate their efforts at this stage.

Investigation

The law enforcement investigation may take hours, days, or months to complete, depending on the availability of witnesses, medical evidence, and other investigative leads. Some cases that seemed promising at the outset may result in a decision not to ask for prosecution. In those cases in which law enforcement decides to seek prosecution, the next stage in the criminal process involves consulting with the prosecutor. The investigating officer will usually meet with the prosecutor and discuss the case, presenting the prosecutor with reports outlining what happened and how the case might be prosecuted.

Prosecuting child abuse cases presents many difficulties. The meeting between the investigator and the prosecutor may include a discussion about the strengths of the case and the likelihood of conviction. The prosecutor may ask for further investigation, believing that more will be necessary for a successful prosecution. The prosecutor may wish to talk with the victim or family members before deciding to prosecute, or he or she may make the decision not to prosecute at all. The decision not to prosecute is often based upon experiences with previous child abuse cases and the difficulty proving these cases in court.

Trauma to the Child Victim in the Investigation

The child victim who allegedly has been abused often must face multiple interviews about the abuse and may undergo medical and psychological tests. These procedures may cause great additional trauma to the child. In some jurisdictions prosecutors, law enforcement, or other community leaders have established child victim centers where all investigatory interviews take place. These centers offer a number of advantages to the children who are the victims of abuse. They are furnished and operated with children in mind. The visiting child encounters a facility sensitive to a child's needs with specially trained persons ready to interview and support the child during the investigatory process. The most famous of these centers is in Huntsville, Alabama, and was established by the local prosecutor, Bud Cramer. The Huntsville project has been a model for communities throughout the country and has become a model for the child-oriented process for investigating child abuse cases (California Child Victim Witness Judicial Advisory Committee, Final Report, 1988).

At these centers all persons with investigative duties meet, so that the child does not have to experience multiple interviews from various persons. The formatting of interviews permits the different potential interviewers the opportunity to gain the information they must have in one interview. The availability of two-way mirrors and videotaping equipment enables others to view the process without intruding on the child. At some centers there is also the availability of a medical specialist who can perform a medical evaluation, including a colposcopic examination. A colposcope is a magnifying device which can reveal injuries to the genitalia of children not visible to the unaided eye.

In some jurisdictions the prosecutor is part of the investigative team. In King County, Washington (Seattle), and Orange County, California, for example, the prosecutor is often present when the child victim is interviewed and in some cases conducts the interview (California Child Victim Witness Judicial Advisory Report, 1988). This early involvement removes the necessity of a separate meeting between law enforcement and the prosecutor, since the prosecutor knows much of the case from the outset. These counties report that there are higher rates of filing charges when the prosecutor observes the interview of the child, probably because a live interview is more persuasive than a written report.

The Court Process

After the prosecutor has reviewed the investigation and the decision to file charges is made,

the process becomes more formal. In some states the prosecutor must take the case before a Grand Jury, which will review the evidence and, if persuaded, will issue an indictment. In other states, the charges are filed in court in the form of an information or complaint. In both systems the defendant is given notice of the charges and must appear in court for arraignment, pleas, and further proceedings. Often the defendant is already in custody, having been arrested at the time of the initial investigation. In these cases the charges must be filed in a short time after the arrest, usually twenty-four to forty-eight hours (excluding weekends), and the defendant must be brought to court during that time period. The criminal justice system places great emphasis on the speedy resolution of criminal charges, particularly when a defendant is in custody. At the arraignment the court must advise the defendant of his constitutional rights and determine whether he qualifies for an attorney at state expense or needs time to hire his own counsel. Usually within a few days an attorney is brought into the case and a plea is entered, and for the in-custody defendant bail is set or the defendant is released on his promise to reappear.

Thereafter, the defendant and his attorney will take steps to discover the reports and other information on which the charges are based. There may be hearings to test the evidence, such as the preliminary hearing or motions to suppress evidence, or to learn more about the prosecutor's case. There will also be efforts by all sides and the court to resolve the case without trial. Most cases resolve short of trial through a plea bargaining process. For example, a defendant charged with three counts of child molestation might be told that if he pleaded guilty to one charge the other two would be dismissed. The benefit for the defendant is that he would be exposed to a lesser sentence, while the benefit to the prosecutor is that he avoids having to try the case. The advantage to the child is that she will not have to testify. However, if the plea bargain is too lenient, the child and those supporting the child may believe that her charges were not taken seriously.

If the case is not resolved, it will be set for trial. Depending on the complexity of the case, the numbers of cases pending in the local court system, and the desires of the court and counsel, the case will be scheduled. The trial will take place within sixty days of the arrest in some jurisdictions, while in others it may be delayed for months or even years.

The trial is like any other criminal trial, except that it involves a child victim. That fact, however, has resulted in a number of significant legal initiatives and numerous legal challenges to those initiatives. Based upon the conclusion that many child victims are revictimized by the very legal process that is designed to assist them, legislators and courts have devised a number of procedures to reduce the trauma to the child victim witness. Almost all of these procedures have been challenged in the court process by those persons accused of abusing the child. The specific issues and their resolution will be discussed in Part Three.

If the jury convicts the defendant or if the defendant has pled guilty to a charge, the court must pass sentence on the judgment. Typically, the court will delay the proceeding until an investigatory report is prepared, usually by a probation department. The report will contain information about the particular charges, the status of the victim, a victim impact statement, the defendant's statements, employment and personal information and any criminal record, and will conclude with a recommended sentence. At the sentencing hearing, the prosecutor and the defense will give the court their comments and recommendations, and the court will make the final determination. The most important factors at the sentencing hearing in child abuse cases include the severity of the abuse or neglect, the attitude of the offender, the relationship of the offender to the child's family, the offender's criminal record, and the needs of the victim. It is possible that the offender will be incarcerated for a substantial period of time. It is also possible that the offender will receive probation and treatment which focuses

upon preventing reoccurrence of the behavior, so that the family can be reunited. The range of sentencing alternatives demonstrates the complexity of the sentencing decision and the need for careful consideration by the court.

If the defendant is placed on probation, he will be expected to follow the terms the court establishes. Typically probation will be set for several years to give the defendant an opportunity to complete conditions ordered by the court. Any failures to follow through will be detected by the probation officer and called to the attention of the court. Violations of probation conditions may result in additional court hearings and in a more severe sentencing by the court. Of course, if the defendant is sentenced to prison, there are typically no conditions of probation. Once the sentence is complete, the defendant is able to return to the community. After release from prison the defendant will have to serve a period of parole before all conditions are lifted. Parole can last from a few months to a few years. In this age of diminishing criminal justice resources, the period of parole and the degree of scrutiny during those periods have both significantly diminished.

EXTENT OF CRIMINAL PROSECUTIONS OF CHILD ABUSE

Criminal prosecutions of child abuse have increased dramatically in the past ten years. Until the mid-1960s the police handled most cases of child abuse and neglect, but only the most severe cases would come to their attention (Martin and Besharov, 1991). What happened in the family was regarded as largely a private matter, and there were no laws requiring reporting. However, with the change in attitude towards child abuse in the early sixties and the passing of the mandatory reporting laws, child abuse evolved into behavior requiring police investigation and potential criminal court intervention.

While cases of criminal child abuse were once rare, today they constitute a substantial percentage of criminal prosecutions. The increase in prosecutions is one of the results of the explosion in child maltreatment reports. In 1963, about 150,000 cases of suspected abuse were reported. By 1987, the number of reports had risen to nearly 2.2 million, an increase of nearly 14 times their earlier number (Martin and Besharov, 1991). According to Martin and Besharov's study on responses to child abuse reports, based on data from fifty-nine urban agencies, it is estimated that police investigate more than 200,000 cases annually (Martin and Besharov, 1991). Of those cases that are closed by the police, nearly 40 percent of the sexual abuse cases and about a quarter of physical abuse and neglect cases result in the arrest of a suspected perpetrator. As noted, this increase is related primarily to the expansion of mandatory reporting laws, the increased public awareness of child abuse, and a commitment to take action on behalf of children.

Today, over forty states have passed legislation requiring child protection agencies to notify either police or local prosecutors of all or certain types of serious cases, with the expectation that these cases will be investigated (Martin and Besharov, 1991). Many of these states also require cross-reporting across agencies, so that if a report should first come to the police, the police must report it to the child protective services and vice versa (Besharov and Asamoah, 1988). According to a study by the American Humane Association in 1988, 13 percent of all reports to child protective agencies were made by police (American Humane Association, 1988).

The system which detects, investigates, prosecutes, and monitors child abuse cases has also grown and become more sophisticated in its operation. Law enforcement, prosecutors, defense lawyers, judges, expert witnesses, treatment programs, and probation departments have developed expertise in dealing with the different aspects of child sexual abuse. There is also a substantial body of law, both statutory and court decisions, describing the rules by which agencies must operate. Today there are more and better training opportunities for criminal justice personnel, including that offered by the National Center for Child Abuse. In many jurisdictions special units in police departments and prosecutors' offices have been created specifically to handle child abuse cases. As a result, child abuse and neglect cases are investigated with greater frequency, and police departments have assumed a larger role in protecting children from abuse.

Barriers to Criminal Prosecution

In spite of the increase in police investigations discussed above, many cases that are filed with police may not result in prosecution for many different reasons. When a criminal act is alleged, other factors may make it difficult to pursue the case. According to Whitcomb (1986), these include inability to establish the crime, insufficient evidence, unwillingness to expose the child to additional trauma, and the belief that child victims are incompetent, unreliable, and not credible as witnesses. The decision not to prosecute may be related to the age of the child, the child's willingness to testify, support from family members, the existence of corroborative evidence, and other factors.

Many of the cases may end up as "unsubstantiated," a term used to describe abuse claims which cannot be proven. Also, reported cases may not be prosecuted because the report does not allege activity that violates a criminal law or does not identify a perpetrator.

Most often a decision is made not to prosecute because there is not enough evidence to meet the criminal standard of proof beyond a reasonable doubt. In a criminal case, the goal of the proceedings is to persuade the court to decide that the defendant abused or neglected the child and impose a sentence that will limit his or her liberty (Faller, 1990). To reach the standard of proof beyond a reasonable doubt, the guilt of the defendant must be established to a greater degree than in any other legal proceeding. However, often there are no witnesses other than the young child victim, and additional proof may be unavailable. If the accused is related to the victim, other family members may all have good reason to hide the truth, especially if they believe that the accused will go away to prison for a long time.

Constitutional requirements such as the protections of the Fourth and the Fifth Amendments may also make it harder to conduct an investigation (Dorne, 1989). The police may be required to obtain a search warrant before they can investigate the family home. This may result in a delay and an opportunity to hide evidence or flee the jurisdiction. The accused may refuse to answer questions during police interrogation.

Many prosecutors are reluctant to prosecute child abuse cases. Compared to other crimes, child abuse cases are difficult to prosecute successfully. Child victims present special problems and corroborative evidence may be minimal. Prosecutors may not want to do the extra work necessary to prosecute these cases. The effect of prosecutors' decisions not to prosecute needs to be examined. Failure to prosecute may discourage all of the persons who have investigated the case and give them the message that such cases will never be prosecuted. If the arrest of a case results in no prosecutions, that decision may impede the willingness of the police to continue to investigate and make arrests in child abuse cases.

The relation between police and child protective services also needs to be further clarified. Law enforcement can protect children through the arrest and criminal prosecution of the offenders, while child protective services can protect children through the provision of services or the removal of the children from their homes. The investigatory processes and goals of both agencies need to be complementary rather than in conflict with each other.

EFFORTS TO OVERCOME PROBLEMS IN PROSECUTION

Even though the standard of proof in criminal court is higher than in civil proceedings, the court decisions in child abuse cases have adopted special guidelines for dealing with such cases. California courts have recognized that, partly because of the limitations of the child witness, child abuse cases often involve difficult, even paradoxical, proof problems (see the *Caudle* case above, where the California Supreme Court noted that a young witness may have difficulty in remembering or even distinguishing specific incidents or dates when there has been repeated, continuous molestation).

Similarly, in *People v. Harlan* (1990) a California appeals court held that even the testimony of a very young witness (under five years old) does not require corroboration and that inability to remember or relate details of the abuse goes to credibility and not to sufficiency of the evidence.

Moreover, in child abuse cases, the condition of the child, such as a physical injury (often testified to by battered child syndrome experts), may be allowed to stand on its own. Nevertheless, it may often be difficult to link the evidence of physical injury to the particular defendant. All that can be established is that the child has been abused, but the evidence is insufficient to determine who committed the abuse. Apparently, this was the general feeling among the jurors in the famous *McMartin* school case in Los Angeles; the jury members believed that the children had been sexually abused, but there was insufficient evidence to convict any of the defendants (*People v. P. McMartin Buckey*, 1990). Of course, if criminal prosecution is not successful, the case may be heard in domestic relations or juvenile court. In each of those courts the standard of proof is lower and more evidence may be admissible (refer to chapters 5 and 6).

SHOULD CHILD ABUSE BE PROSECUTED?

According to Peters, Dinsmore, and Toth (1989), no conflict has caused greater dissension among professionals working on behalf of abused children than the use of criminal prosecution as a response to child abuse. A physician who specializes in child abuse called prosecution of child abusers a cruel alternative to giving people help (Newberger, 1987). A legal scholar wrote that the consequences of increased reliance on prosecution and the adversarial process often outweigh the benefits (Myers, 1985-86). He argued that the belief that the legal system can cope with child abuse is unfounded because reliance on the law ignores the deep social and psychological roots of abuse. According to Myers, the blaming, punitive, and accusatory approach of the criminal justice system can be destructive.

Some argue that child sexual abuse cases should be decriminalized, and that decriminalization would provide better protection for victims and aid the rehabilitation of offenders ("Child Sex Abuse Should be Decriminalized," 1991). According to this viewpoint, punishment of sex offenders just does not work. Doctors are often reluctant to become involved in child abuse cases out of frustration with the present adversarial court system for dealing with such cases. A number of factors are also thought to cause children psychological stress in the courtroom should the case go to trial. Although individual children respond differently to their involvement in the investigative-judicial process, according to Spencer and Flin (1990), the following factors related to the trial process appear stressful for children:

(a) long delays;
(b) child's lack of legal knowledge and preparation, resulting in misunderstandings and fears;
(c) rescheduling of cases;
(d) child's fear of retribution for testifying;

(e) public speaking and revealing intimate personal information in front of strangers;
(f) attempts at character defamation;
(g) intimidating layout of the courtroom;
(h) lack of child friendly waiting areas that ensure no contact with the accused;
(i) confronting the accused, especially if threatened not to tell;
(j) insensitive questioning techniques;
(k) lack of protection during cross-examination;
(l) lack of support from professionals and family.

All of these factors need careful attention in child abuse cases. It is important that children are safeguarded from these sources of stress as much as possible. Children also express fear of being sent to jail if they make a mistake or mishandle a question. If the accused is found not guilty after a trial, the child may suffer the double effects of not being supported by either the parents or the court system.

If the accused is found guilty, the child victim may feel that he or she is responsible for the sentencing of the offender, and suffer guilt and remorse. This is, of course, primarily true if the abuser is a parent, a family member, or a trusted friend. Hostility and anger from the defendant can also be directed at the child, and may make it extremely difficult for them to relate to each other once the offender is released. It may also result in some danger to the child. Rehabilitation programs for child maltreatment offenders, especially for those family members returned to the home, are therefore extremely important.

A few studies dispute the notion that all criminal prosecution is harmful to the child victim. One study found that the overall interviewing and litigation process was not harmful to children, although testifying in court and repeated interviews had higher harmful ratings than other variables (Tedesco and Schnell, 1987). Runyan, Everson, Edelsohn, Hunter, and Coulter (1988) found that children who were not involved in criminal court proceedings evidenced much greater distress, depression, and anxiety. These studies conclude that court testimony may serve to empower the child victims, whose most important need is to regain control over their lives. These studies also concur, however, that protracted criminal cases have a negative effect on children.

Some argue that there should be a different standard for intrafamilial abusers than for those who abuse other people's children (Chapman and Smith, 1987). Once in the system, families may be damaged or destroyed by incarceration and other negative influences. A former director of the National Center on Child Abuse and Neglect wrote that child protective services rarely consider criminal prosecution as an appropriate response to child abuse. These agencies fear that the arrest and possible prosecution of a parent will impair efforts to treat the parent and reunite the family (Besharov, 1987).

The National Center for Prosecution of Child Abuse opposes separate standards for intrafamilial child abuse. It is their position that:

(1) Anyone who physically assaults a child or who sexually molests or rapes a child, regardless of their relationship to the child, has committed a serious crime;

(2) Allegations of physical or sexual abuse must be promptly and thoroughly investigated by well-trained law enforcement officers, and involve social service and medical personnel who are specially trained;

(3) Prosecutors who make decisions about these cases should be specially trained;

(4) If the case is provable, then criminal charges should be filed, irrespective of the familial relationship between the alleged perpetrator and the child; and

(5) Persons found guilty of child abuse crimes should be subject to sanctions, including incarceration and, if the person is amenable, court mandated specialized treatment. (Peters, et al., 1989)

Harshbarger (1987) adds that there is no legal or moral justification for ignoring intrafamilial acts of abuse, while strangers committing similar acts are treated as criminals. Moreover, it is wrong to consider intrafamilial abuse as less serious and assume that these offenders are unlikely to abuse

other children. According to Peters, et al. (1989), a decision to leave the responsibility for an intrafamilial case solely with the department of social services rather than take it to prosecution is typically based on several incorrect assumptions:

(1) that reunification of dysfunctional families is not desirable and possible;

(2) that community interests are best served by not pursuing criminal prosecution;

(3) that juvenile court can adequately protect the children involved;

(4) that proceeding with criminal prosecution would harm children by making them feel responsible and by requiring them to endure humiliation and stressful cross-examination in the presence of the offender;

(5) that criminal prosecution would prevent an abuser from contributing to the support of his or her family;

(6) that the political risks involved in prosecuting an offender who may be a respected community member are unwise and unnecessary; and

(7) that a "record" with the social services will assure community safety.

Using illustrations from an actual case history, Peters, et al. (1989) try to refute each of these assumptions, claiming that they are incorrect. While the federally mandated reunification efforts of the juvenile court may seem to run counter to the prosecution of parents in criminal court, we agree that criminal court intervention is warranted in both intrafamily and stranger abuse. The criminal law is clearly the best way to deal with abusers who are strangers to their young victims. In these cases there is no need to worry about keeping the family together (Dorne, 1989). While such concerns do emerge when a parent or close relative is accused of child abuse, we believe that serious child abuse and neglect should be prosecuted in the criminal courts, perhaps simultaneously with child protective proceedings in the juvenile courts.

The sentence an offender receives, however, should fit the circumstances of the crime. Sexual abuse within the family should be dealt with firmly, but the criminal justice system should recognize that preservation of the family may be a viable goal. Offenders who participate in rehabilitative programs and who attain therapeutic goals should be given lesser sentences than those who continue to deny guilt and are not sensitive to the needs of the abused child. The criminal courts should utilize the criminal sanction to encourage and even force changes in behavior and attitudes in offenders. The court has the authority to mandate treatment programs for the offender, and the ability to mandate strict compliance with treatment conditions and swift consequences when there are deviations.

MANAGING CHILD ABUSE CASES IN CRIMINAL COURT

Case Example (*State v. Johnson* [Ohio App.], 1986)

In a child sexual abuse prosecution in Ohio, the prosecutor asked that the child victim witness be accompanied during testimony by a support person who was a relative of the child. When it appeared that the child would have difficulty testifying without further support, the court permitted the child to sit in the lap of the support person during the giving of testimony.

The defendant was convicted of the sexual abuse crimes and appealed. He claimed that permitting the child to sit in the lap of a relative was prejudicial to the defendant. First, he claimed the child's testimony would not be truthful because of the proximity of the relative. Secondly, he said that the jury would give additional credence to the child's testimony, since it appeared that the relative was supporting the child in what she was saying.

The Ohio Court of Appeals affirmed the conviction and the trial court's decision to permit the child to sit in the lap of the relative during testimony. The Court of Appeals stated:

> . . . the trial judge did what he was not only authorized, but required, to do. He made a decision to exercise reasonable control over the mode of interrogating the infant-witness with a view of making the interrogation and representation effective for the ascertainment of truth while protecting the witness from undue embarrassment. (*State v. Johnson*, Ohio App., 1986)

Discussion

Is the law appropriately responding to the special needs of children who must appear as witnesses in criminal cases? Should the child witness be permitted to sit in the lap of a support person while testifying? What safeguards would you suggest in order to ensure that the accused is not unfairly treated? Would you permit the support person to sit next to the child witness? Would you permit the support person to be in the room?

Do you agree that it is the duty of a judge to insist that questions of children be developmentally appropriate? Should the judge interrupt an examination of a child witness without an attorney first making an objection? Judicial training now stresses the need for judges to be in control of court proceedings to ensure that truthful testimony is elicited. Should that include telling attorneys how to ask questions?

Appellate courts have upheld similar support techniques for children testifying in criminal cases, although the Hawaii Supreme Court has refused to permit such support persons to give similar aid to child victim witnesses (*State v. Suka* [Hawaii], 1989).

These cases indicate the tensions which exist between the due process rights of an accused person and the special needs of a victim witness who must testify in a criminal proceeding.

Prior to the 1980s, the criminal justice system was insensitive to the needs of the child victim throughout the investigative and court processes. Not only were child victim witnesses the subject of numerous interviews and examinations before trial, but once in the courtroom they were treated as though they were adults. The criminal court process made few accommodations for child victims. They were unsupported by friendly adults and were subjected to the full force of the adversarial system. Questions were asked in developmentally inappropriate language. They were also subjected to extensive competency inquiries in which the attorneys were permitted to ask them numerous questions to determine whether they were competent to testify.

The extraordinary rise in the numbers of child maltreatment reports, investigations, and prosecutions has led many to re-examine the criminal justice system and its impact upon child victim witnesses. Many commentators have found the system is insensitive to the special needs of the child victim. Legislators have responded with new procedures designed to accommodate the needs of children while maintaining a defendant's due process rights.

Changes in the investigatory stages have resulted in more child-sensitive procedures. They have led to fewer interviews by fewer people and the creation of child-oriented settings. They have also led to more specialization within law enforcement and prosecutor's offices. It is common in medium-to-large jurisdictions for a police department to have a child abuse investigation unit and for a prosecutor's office to have a team of attorneys who specialize in the prosecution of child abuse cases.

Changes have also been made in courtroom procedures. Because children may be easily intimidated in the courtroom and because their use of language and understanding of concepts is not fully developed, the law has been changed to accommodate some of the needs of child victim witnesses. Judges have been trained in the developmental needs of children who appear as witnesses in their courts. Judges have always had the discretion

to control their courtroom to ensure that witnesses have a full opportunity to give answers to questions asked. Training and legislative initiatives have encouraged judges to consider the special needs of children in court. For example, in California a statute addresses the needs of any witness under the age of fourteen, and instructs the court to

. . . take special care to protect him or her from undue harassment or embarrassment, and to restrict the unnecessary repetition of questions. The court shall also take special care to insure that questions are stated in a form which is appropriate to the age of the witness. The court may in the interests of justice, on the objection of a party, forbid the asking of a question which is in a form that is not reasonably likely to be understood by a person of the age of the witness. (Evidence Code section 765[b], 1993)

Judicial training and legislation have also advised judges that in making decisions about the manner in which the child will be treated in the courtroom, judges should consider the child's age and emotional condition. In many jurisdictions, judges can permit child witnesses to have frequent recesses, have a support person in the courtroom with them, have a special waiting room, and have their testimony extend over a period of several days rather than in one extended session. New laws also address the need for there to be a speedy resolution of cases involving children. Some laws give cases priority if there is a child victim involved. (See California Penal Code, section 1048.) These legislative initiatives recognize that children have the need to complete their testimony in a short period of time after the event.

Ordinarily, attorneys are not appointed for the child in criminal court. However, at least six states have statutes explicitly permitting the appointment of guardians *ad litem* or other independent legal representatives for child victims in criminal proceedings: California, Florida, Iowa, Oklahoma, Pennsylvania, and Wisconsin (Whitcomb, 1988). In addition, court rules in New Hampshire and Vermont authorize the appointment of guardians *ad litem* for child victims in sex-related cases. The Superior Court of New Jersey has also held that alleged child victims have an interest in a criminal proceeding sufficient to justify appointment of a guardian *ad litem* (*State v. Freeman*, 1985). In a recent California criminal prosecution, *People v. Pitts* (1990), an attorney was appointed to help prevent psychological damage to the child.

Legislatures have also recognized that public hearings may be traumatic to a child witness. In some states judges are permitted to restrict public access to criminal hearings in which a child is testifying. For example, in California, during the preliminary hearing (the probable cause hearing), the court may close the courtroom to the public if testimony before the public would be likely to cause serious psychological harm to the child witness. The court can grant the motion to close the courtroom only when there are no alternatives, such as videotaping or use of closed-circuit television, available. However, when public access to the courtroom is restricted, a transcript of the testimony must be made available to the public as soon as possible (see *Richmond Newspaper, Inc. v. Virginia*, 1980).

In California, the court may close the courtroom in any criminal proceeding on the motion of the prosecuting attorney when the defendant has been charged with sex offenses on a child under the age of sixteen years (P.C. section 868.8). Guidelines for judges' consideration in determining whether the hearing should be closed include the age of the child, the nature and seriousness of the offense, and whether there is an overriding public interest in having the trial open. However, to ensure First Amendment rights of the press, closure must be shown to be as narrowly tailored as is necessary to meet the needs of the child victim (*Child Victim Witness Manual*, 1992).

CONCLUSION

In spite of the many problems discussed earlier, criminal prosecution of child abuse cases offers some important advantages. First, the higher standards of proof make it less likely that false accusations will be found true, and thus offer protections to those unfairly accused. Second and more importantly, criminal prosecution of child abuse makes it clear that such behavior constitutes a "real crime" that our society is prepared to take seriously. Sentences that combine mandated counseling and treatment with probation are particularly well suited for the less serious offender. Incarceration of the more serious cases protects children from the danger of re-abuse. At the same time, we must be sensitive to the harm a criminal prosecution can impose on a child, both prior to a trial and during and after the time a verdict has been reached. In all cases it is important that as many resources as possible are available to help the child through the process.

The changes in the criminal justice system in response to the needs of children have not been completed. New procedures are being developed and tested to determine whether they assist children and whether they violate the constitutional rights of defendants. The United States Supreme Court may have the final review of many of these changes.

CHAPTER 8

Civil Court: Recovering Damages and Changing the System

Child abuse issues may arise within the civil courts. There are two principal types of cases in which child maltreatment can arise: tort actions and class actions. In the former, the legal action is directed at recovering damages for the abuse. In the latter, the legal action is intended to change the system so that a particular group of children is treated better by the governmental agency.

In this chapter we address both types of civil action. In the first part of the chapter, we address the civil remedies available to a child who has been abused and we discuss the legal procedures that children must utilize in order to recover damages from those who have abused them. The discussion will include a range of possible persons and entities whom the child might sue, including parents, caretakers, professionals, and the state. Whether insurance coverage is available to pay for abuse claims is also discussed.

In the second part, we address class actions brought on behalf of children to enforce their rights and improve their living environment. Such lawsuits are often called impact litigation, because the intent of the legal action is to have an impact upon all children who are similarly situated and not just one or two. For example, a class action might be brought on behalf of all foster children in a certain jurisdiction. In this part we focus on how such actions are brought and what rights are enforceable under this type of litigation.

RECOVERING DAMAGES

In our hypothetical case, the mother, Judy, was considering bringing a civil action on behalf of Sally against Harry for the alleged abuse he inflicted on Sally. This is a civil remedy. Just as a person injured in an auto accident or because of negligence has the right to bring a lawsuit against the person or entity that caused the injury, the abused child can bring an action for damages against the person or persons who caused the maltreatment.

A tort is any wrong other than a breach of contract for which the law undertakes to give the injured party some appropriate remedy against the wrongdoer (Witkin, 1988, p. 59). A common statute reads as follows:

> Everyone is responsible, not only for the result of his willful acts, but also for an injury occasioned to another by his want of ordinary care or skill in the management of his property or person, except so far as the latter has willfully or by want of ordinary care brought the injury upon himself. (California Civil Code, section 1714, 1991)

Tort actions are generally awarded for the purpose of compensating the plaintiff for injury suffered, thus restoring him as nearly as possible to his former position or giving him some pecuniary equivalent (Witkin, 1988).

When dealing with child abuse, some special considerations arise. Because the injured party is a child and because the defendant is often a parent, caretaker, or a state agency authorized to care for children, there are special problems relating to civil actions brought by or on behalf of children.

Procedural Considerations

Children are not legal persons. Because of their age and lack of maturity, children are not permitted to bring legal actions in the court system by themselves. For a child to file a lawsuit, he or she must act through a guardian *ad litem*, an adult acting on behalf of the child.

A civil lawsuit brought by a guardian *ad litem* on behalf of a child follows the same process that all other civil actions for damages take. The moving papers or complaint are filed with the court and then served upon the defendant, who then has a period of time to file a response. If the defendant fails to respond within the prescribed period, usually thirty or sixty days, the plaintiff can ask the court to enter a default judgment and proceed to trial without the defendant's participation.

If the defendant files a response, the parties,

plaintiff and defendant, usually conduct discovery. Discovery is the investigation that takes place by all parties in preparation for trial. Discovery can include interrogatories (written questions), depositions (sworn testimony by a witness or a party given in a hearing outside the courtroom in response to questions from one of the parties) and *subpoenas duces tecum*, requests for production of relevant written materials. The discovery process can take months or years, depending on the complexity of the issues to be tried.

When the parties have completed discovery, one can ask the court for a trial date. The court system may require the parties to participate in alternative dispute resolution efforts before the case is actually set for trial. Arbitration and mediation are two frequently utilized methods to resolve civil cases before trial. In arbitration, an arbitrator, usually an attorney, will hear the facts of the case and render a decision. If the arbitration is binding, then the parties must abide by the determination by the arbitrator. If the arbitration is not binding, either party may reject the decision and ask that the case go to trial. In mediation, the parties work with a skilled mediator in an effort to reach a settlement of the claim. The mediator does not render a decision. If the parties do not agree, the case can be scheduled for trial.

In addition to arbitration and mediation, some civil courts require a settlement conference prior to trial. Often conducted by judges or volunteer attorneys, settlement conferences bring the parties together in an effort to resolve some or all of the issues without the necessity of trial.

Most cases never go to trial. The plaintiff may decide not to proceed with the lawsuit or the parties may reach a settlement of the claim.

Civil lawsuits filed on behalf of children are carefully reviewed by the court before any settlements are reached. Fearful that an adult may act without the child's best interests in mind, most courts require a review and court approval before a lawsuit filed by a child can be settled. Called minor's compromises, the court reviews any proposed settlement and ensures that the child

will receive the benefits of the settlement, even though an adult, usually a parent or caretaker, has participated in the process and may have access to the settlement monies before the child becomes an adult. The terms of a minor's compromise will usually describe in detail how and when the proceeds will be distributed to the child.

If all efforts to resolve the case fail, it may proceed to trial. The parties in a civil trial have the right to a jury, usually comprised of six to twelve persons. As the moving party, the plaintiff must prove the case by a preponderance of the evidence. A preponderance of evidence is sufficient evidence to make it more likely than not that the trier of fact is persuaded of the truth of the allegations. The defendant will have the right to present a defense. Of course, the child alleging the abuse may have to testify in the trial.

One special problem has to do with the statutes of limitations for the filings of lawsuits by children or adults who were abused as children. A statute of limitations is the time within which a lawsuit must be filed after the injury occurs. Failure to file a legal action within the statute of limitations for the type of injury suffered will end the legal proceedings before they start. The reasons for statutes of limitations are obvious. Lawsuits should be filed in a timely manner. The longer the delay in filing a lawsuit, the less able witnesses and the defendant are to remember the facts of the case and prepare a legal defense.

It seems unfair, however, to require a child to be held to the same legal standards as an adult. A young child is not in a position to make careful judgments about filing a lawsuit. Moreover, the child's caretakers may not be interested in taking legal action on behalf of the child, either because they do not have the child's interests in mind, and fail to take advantage of this opportunity, or because they are the persons who maltreated the child. As a result, the statute of limitations is extended in child abuse cases, often until the time a child reaches eighteen years of age. In addition, in any civil action the child plaintiff must encounter the same adult legal world that exists in criminal, juvenile, and domestic relations court settings. Thus problems of multiple interviews, sensitivity to child development considerations, and myths about the credibility of children are encountered in civil as in all other legal proceedings.

While there are many different situations in which child abuse may result in a civil action for damages, the three most recurring scenarios are lawsuits against the person who committed the abuse (and his or her insurance company), suits against a professional who has a responsibility to care for the child, and actions against the state for failure to protect after the state has assumed some responsibility over the child.

Case Example (*Gilbert v. Gilbert*, 1959)

A stepfather brutally beat his eight-year-old child, necessitating the removal of the child's spleen and one kidney. The child sued the stepfather through a guardian *ad litem*, alleging willful and malicious misconduct. The stepfather responded that he was immune from the legal action, since he was a parent and such a lawsuit would result in state involvement in family matters.

The trial court held that a child has the right to sue a parent for damages when the parent commits willful and malicious misconduct. The California Court of Appeals upheld the judgment of $30,000 in damages for the child (*Gilbert v. Gilbert*, 1959).

Discussion

In the *Gilbert* case, the stepfather relied upon the doctrine of parental immunity as his defense. That doctrine states that a child may not sue his parent, because such a lawsuit would result in

state intrusion in family matters. Underlying the doctrine is the notion that parents should have full care and control over their children and that such lawsuits would damage family relationships.

The doctrine of parental immunity has been seriously eroded in most states, particularly when the acts by the parent are willful and malicious. In some states, children may also sue their parents for acts of negligence. One reason given for the extension of liability to negligent acts is that there may be homeowner's insurance to cover the expenses related to the injury. Thus the state is not intruding into the parent/child relationship, but is facilitating a recovery for the family on behalf of the child.

Case Example (*Courtney v. Courtney*, 1991)

A child and his mother sued the mother's former husband for damages they suffered as a result of the defendant's physical abuse of the mother. One of the claims asserted that the defendant had intentionally inflicted emotional distress upon the child when he assaulted the mother in the child's presence. The trial court dismissed the claim. On appeal, the West Virginia Appellate Court ruled that the claim did state a cause of action for which damages could be sought. The court reversed the dismissal and returned the case for trial.

The appellate court wrote that the issue in the case was

> . . . whether a child can recover damages for severe emotional distress in the absence of physical injury because the child witnessed a third person verbally abusing and physically assaulting his mother.

In determining that damages are recoverable in such a situation, the court relied on Section 46(2) of the Restatement of the Law, Torts (1965).

> To establish a claim for emotional distress a plaintiff must show: (1) that the defendant's conduct

was "extreme and outrageous"; (2) that such conduct was directed at a third party; (3) that the plaintiff is a member of the third person's immediate family; (4) that the plaintiff was physically present when the extreme and outrageous conduct took place; (5) that the plaintiff suffered severe emotional distress as a result of the conduct; and (6) that if the emotional distress results in bodily injury, any person who was present at the time of the outrageous conduct may recover.

The court found that the complaint alleged that the child became emotionally disabled in his ability to communicate and socialize with his mother after he witnessed the beatings. Moreover, the plaintiff asserted his emotional distress was so severe it was necessary that he receive psychiatric care. Consequently, the plaintiff stated a recoverable claim for emotional distress.

Finally, the court found that the doctrine of parental immunity was not available to the defendant. The court sided with the majority of courts that have ruled on the issue, finding that parental immunity is not available to the defendant when the parent caused the injury from intentional or willful conduct (*Courtney v. Courtney*, 1991).

Discussion

After reading these cases, do you believe that there is anything left of the doctrine of parental immunity? Should a child be able to sue a parent for a spanking? A severe spanking? Should our court system permit juries to decide where the limits of legitimate parental discipline stop and child maltreatment begins? The juvenile dependency court addresses this issue regularly when it attempts to determine whether a "spanking" is reasonable corporal punishment or child abuse.

What if one parent was the abuser and the other parent knew of the abuse and did nothing to protect the child? Should the more passive parent also be liable for a civil claim for damages?

Several courts have recently held that the non-abusing parent is liable for damages if the child can prove that the parent knew of the abuse.

Actions Against Insurance Companies

Most abused children do not sue anyone. The maltreatment may never be discovered, no one may be interested or capable of bringing a legal action on behalf of the child, or the abuser may not have any assets. In the last situation, the child might prevail in a civil lawsuit, but there would be no ultimate recovery, since the defendant is without assets.

Some children bring legal actions against a parent or other person in the anticipation of insurance coverage for the damages. If the defendant has a homeowner's or other type of insurance policy, that policy may include coverage for maltreatment judgments against the defendant. The defendant might lose the civil suit, but would be indemnified for some or all of his losses by the insurance company.

Insurance companies have resisted such claims. They have asserted that their policies do not cover intentional acts and that such abuse is intentional.

> To state that a child molester intends anything but harm and long-term anguish to the child defies logic. (*Landis v. Allstate Insurance Co.*, 1989)

Rulings in California, Washington, and Wisconsin have supported this Florida appellate court opinion. In these states, if the acts of child abuse are willful or intentional, the insurance company is not obligated to represent the insured or to indemnify any recovery against him. Some plaintiffs' attorneys, however, continue to pursue these claims. If they can show that the acts by the defendant were made while he was unconscious, they have been able to overcome the "willful and intentional" barrier.

Actions Against Professionals

Courts have held that professionals are liable to a child if they fail to detect and report signs of child abuse in the course of their professional responsibilities. In *Landeros v. Flood* (1976), the California Supreme Court held that a child may sue a physician for injuries received from a parent after the physician examined the child. The court found that if the child can show that the physician should have detected signs of abuse on the child, the physician had a duty to report that abuse, so that the child would not have to return to the abusive environment.

The facts in this case reveal that the plaintiff was born on May 14, 1970. On repeated occasions during the first year of her life she was severely beaten by her mother and the mother's cohabitant. On April 26, 1971, when plaintiff was eleven months old, her mother took her to the hospital in San Jose, California, for examination, diagnosis, and treatment. The attending physician was defendant Flood, acting on his own behalf as an agent of defendant San Jose Hospital. At the time plaintiff was suffering from a comminuted spiral fracture of the right tibia and fibula, which have the appearance of having been caused by a twisting force. Plaintiff's mother had no explanation for this injury. Plaintiff also had bruises over her entire back, together with superficial abrasions on other parts of her body. In addition, she had a nondepressed linear fracture of the skull, which was then in the process of healing. Plaintiff demonstrated fear and apprehension when approached. Inasmuch as all plaintiff's injuries gave the appearance of having been intentionally inflicted by other persons, she exhibited the medical condition known as the battered child syndrome.

It was alleged that proper diagnosis of plaintiff's condition would have included taking X-rays of her entire skeletal structure and that such procedure would have revealed the fracture of her skull. Plaintiff claimed that the defendants negligently failed to take such X-rays and thereby negligently failed to diagnose her true condition. It was further alleged that proper medical treatment of plaintiff's battered child syndrome would have included reporting her injuries to local law enforcement authorities or child protective services. Such a report would have resulted in an investigation by the concerned agencies, followed possibly by placement of plaintiff in protective custody until her safety was assured. Plaintiffs alleged that the defendants negligently failed to make such a report.

The complaint further states that as a proximate cause of this negligence, plaintiff was released from the San Jose Hospital without proper diagnosis and treatment of her battered child syndrome and was returned to the custody of her mother and mother's cohabitant, who resumed physically abusing her until she sustained traumatic blows to her right eye and back, puncture wounds over her left lower leg and across her back, severe bites on her face, and second and third degree burns on her left hand.

On July 1, 1971, plaintiff was again brought in for medical care, but to a different doctor and hospital. Her battered child syndrome was immediately diagnosed and reported to local police and child protection authorities, and she was taken into protective custody. Following hospitalization and surgery she was placed with foster parents, and the latter subsequently undertook proceedings to adopt her. Plaintiff's mother and cohabitant fled the state, but were apprehended, returned for trial, and convicted of the crime of child abuse.

With respect to damages, the complaint alleged that as a proximate result of defendants' negligence plaintiff suffered painful permanent physical injuries and great mental distress, including the probable loss of use or amputation of her left hand.

The trial court ruled that the defendant owed no duty to the child and dismissed the complaint. The California Supreme Court reversed the trial court and remanded the case for trial. In its opinion, the supreme court noted that:

> . . . The standard of care in malpractice cases is well known. With unimportant variations in phrasing, we have consistently held that a physician

is required to possess and exercise, in both diagnosis and treatment, that reasonable degree of knowledge and skill which is ordinarily possessed and exercised by other members of his profession in similar circumstances. . . .

The first question presented is whether the foregoing standard of care includes a requirement that the physician know how to diagnose and treat the battered child syndrome.

. . . The plaintiff is entitled to the opportunity to prove by way of expert testimony that in the circumstances of this case a reasonably prudent physician would have followed those procedures.

. . . The second principal question in this case is proximate cause. Under the allegations of the complaint it is evident that the continued beating inflicted on plaintiff by her mother and Reyes after she was released from the San Jose Hospital and returned to their custody constituted an "intervening act" that was the immediate cause in fact of the injuries for which she seeks to recover. . . . Plaintiff is entitled to prove by expert testimony that defendants should reasonably have foreseen that their caretakers were likely to resume their physical abuse and inflict further injuries on her if she were returned directly to their custody.

. . . The judgment of dismissal in the trial court is therefore reversed.

Discussion

Do you think the physician should have been liable for injuries to the child in the *Landeros v. Flood* case? Is this asking too much of our medical community to be on the lookout for child abuse and to report that abuse when they detect it? The mandatory reporting laws in all states now require a physician to report such injuries to child protective services. In many states, there are criminal penalties for physicians who fail to report such injuries once they have been discovered (see California Penal Code section 11162).

Such a reporting requirement presents difficult choices for many physicians. If the physician has

a private practice and sees all members of a family, reporting suspected child maltreatment may jeopardize the relationship with the entire family. If the family is wealthy, the choice may be even more difficult because of the potential loss of future revenue.

Actions Against the State

When the state has legal control of a child, does it become liable for acts of maltreatment? As we learned in the chapter on Juvenile Court, the court may find that a child is a dependent child of the court and then make a placement determination. The state may permit the child to remain in parental custody with social services supervision or it can remove the child from the parents and place the child in foster, relative, or group care. If the state is supervising the child in any of those settings, does it become liable for abuse inflicted upon the child?

Liability When the Child Stays at Home

In order to better understand under what conditions the state is liable for failure to protect a child from abuse at home, we will turn to a description and analysis of the first United States Supreme Court case that addressed this issue: *DeShaney v. Winnebago County Department of Social Services* (1989). This case dealt with the liability of the state when a child is known to the social services agency but remains in his home under the supervision of a social services agency.

On March 8, 1984, four-year-old Joshua DeShaney was beaten so severely by his father that he lost nearly half the tissue in his brain and fell into a comatose state. Prior to that date, Joshua had been the victim of repeated acts of violence. As a result, he was left severely retarded and permanently confined to an institution. A neurosurgeon's examination revealed evidence of previous traumatic head injury, and scars of varying ages were found all over his body.

Joshua's sad story began in 1980 when his

parents divorced and his father was granted custody of Joshua. In 1982 the police department received a complaint from his father's second wife that he had hit the boy and caused "child abuse." The police department notified the Child Protection Unit (DSS) of the county. The unit interviewed the father, who denied the charges, and then closed the file.

The following January, Joshua was taken to the emergency room with multiple bruises and abrasions and was identified as a suspected victim of child abuse. The DSS was notified, and they placed Joshua in the temporary legal custody of the hospital while an investigation was conducted. Despite indications of abuse, the county attorney was not willing to pursue the case. Joshua was released back to his father because of "insufficient evidence," despite the fact that abuse was strongly suspected. The case was subsequently dismissed from court without a hearing. During the following year, however, DSS continued to monitor the family.

When Joshua was released back to his father, his father entered into a contract with DSS for his son's benefit. He was to receive counseling, remove an allegedly abusive girlfriend from the home, and enroll Joshua in Head Start, so that he could be monitored by DSS outside his home environment. Nothing came of this arrangement.

Over the next year, Joshua was treated for suspicious traumatic injuries on another occasion in a local emergency room. The hospital filed a written child abuse report on Joshua, but DSS neither interviewed the family nor observed Joshua. The caseworker visited Joshua's home only sporadically and did not press the matter when told that Joshua was unavailable to be seen. The caseworker, however, reported in her file that Joshua was in danger and that she did not believe the excuses given to her for the injuries to Joshua.

Although there were repeated signs of abuse, including several more visits to the emergency room with suspicious injuries, the DSS social worker assigned to the case took no action except

to visit the family sporadically, and during two of these visits she did not actually see the child. It was clear, however, that she believed Joshua to be at serious risk. Unfortunately, the father's violence culminated with the March 1984 events which sadly wrecked his son's life.

Joshua, through his guardian *ad litem* and his mother, brought suit under 42 U.S.C.A. section 1983 against Winnebago County, its Department of Social Services, the caseworker assigned to the case, and her supervisor, alleging that their failure to take action to protect Joshua constituted a deprivation of his liberty without due process of law, in violation of the Fourteenth Amendment.[1]

The District Court granted summary judgment in favor of the defendants. Summary judgment is a legal ruling that the plaintiff does not state a legal claim for which relief can be granted. In other words, the state and its agents, the social worker and the Department of Social Services, owed no duty to Joshua, so he could not recover damages from them. That ruling was affirmed by the Seventh Circuit Court and then by the U.S. Supreme Court. The Supreme Court held that the state's failure to protect Joshua from his father's beatings did not violate his substantive due process rights.

The Supreme Court held that the state had no constitutional duty to protect Joshua, because the harms Joshua suffered did not occur while he was in the state's custody. Thus, the state's failure to protect Joshua from his abusive father did not violate his substantive due process rights, because the state did not have "custody" of him. The Court further held that the state has no obligations

---

1. A remarkable number of constitutional claims are now litigated under 42 U.S.C.A. section 1983, which provides that: "Every person who, under color of any statute, ordinance, regulation, custom or usage, of any state or territory, subjects any other person to the deprivation of any rights, privileges, or immunities secured by the Constitution and laws, shall be liable to the party injured." Section 1983 was enacted by Congress as part of the Ku Klux Klan Act of 1871. The provision, however, remained obscure and underutilized for nearly a century.

to provide its citizens minimal levels of safety and security, or to protect them from the violence of private actors. The majority opinion held that the purpose of the due process clause was to protect people from the state, not to ensure that the state protected them from each other. The harm was inflicted by Joshua's father, not the state. While the plaintiff had argued that the failure of the state to intervene deprived Joshua of liberty within the meaning of the Fourteenth Amendment, the court's majority responded that this was a private action, not state action, even though the state had prior knowledge of the abuse.

The opinion stated that the state was not responsible for Joshua, because it had placed him in no worse position than that in which he would have been had it not acted at all. Although the child protective services had been aware of the dangers that Joshua faced, it played no part in their creation nor did it do anything to render him any more vulnerable to them. The court opined that the state was not responsible for the subsequent violence or tragedy that befell Joshua as a result of living within his own family environment. Thus, according to the U.S. Supreme Court's decision, children who are abused at home by their natural parents have no constitutional right to protection by the state.

Discussion

Do you agree with the U.S. Supreme Court's analysis? After how much involvement does the state become liable for the maltreatment a child suffers? If there had been an agreement signed by the father and by the social worker, would that be sufficient state involvement? What if there had been a court hearing, Joshua had been declared a dependent child of the court, and the juvenile court had placed him with his father under the supervision of the social services agency? Would that be sufficient state involvement to create liability?

In this case it appears that the hospital had detected abuse and reported it to the social services agency. According to the *Landeros v. Flood* case, the physician acted properly, so the hospital might not be liable for subsequent injuries to Joshua. Apparently, the social services agency was at least negligent in investigating and monitoring Joshua's situation. Should the agency be held to the same standard as the physician was in *Landeros v. Flood*?

Liability When the Child Is Removed from the Home

What would the U.S. Supreme Court's position have been had Joshua been abused by a foster parent rather than his natural father? The ruling in *DeShaney* suggested that had Joshua been removed from his father and placed in a foster home operated by the state's agents, there would have been a situation sufficiently analogous to incarceration to give rise to the affirmative duty to protect.

Case Example (*Norfleet v. Arkansas Department of Human Services*, 1993)

In the summer of 1991, a mother left for a two-day trip out of town. She left her two sons, eight and two, with a neighbor. On the morning after she left, the eight-year-old son experienced an asthma attack and was taken to a hospital, treated, and given medication to take with him. He was not released to the neighbor but instead was picked up at the hospital by a state welfare worker and put into a foster home.

The next day the mother returned from her trip and began looking frantically for her son. She called the agency, but received only a recorded message. Finally, someone told her that her son was all right and would be returned in the morning. The next morning the agency called and told the mother the boy had died at the foster home.

Her son had been placed at the home of an experienced foster care provider, but she had been given no medical information about the child. She did not know of the boy's asthma attack or of the medication he was to take. During the night, he told the foster mother he had no more medicine for the inhaler he was using. By morning he had stopped breathing and died.

The mother brought a civil rights action seeking damages from the Department of Human Services, the social services director, the caseworker, and the foster mother. She alleged that her child should have received medical care and supervision while in state care and that the defendants' deliberate indifference to her son's condition led to his death.

The defendants responded that they were entitled to qualified immunity. They said that they could not be held accountable, unless their conduct violated "clearly established statutory or constitutional rights of which a reasonable person would have known."

The Eighth Circuit rejected this defense and held that the Due Process Clause of the Fourteenth Amendment imposes duties upon state officials for the safety and well-being of children taken into foster care. Comparing the child's status to that of a person who was in a prisonlike setting, the Circuit Court found that a special custodial relationship had been created when he was placed in foster care. That special relationship created in the child enforceable rights to protection.

Discussion

Compare this case to the *DeShaney* facts. Here, the court permitted recovery and distinguished *DeShaney* because the child was in the care of the state. Since the state removed the child because it believed it could protect him better, it was held to have a duty to protect that child while he remained in state care.

Several other federal courts have agreed with the position taken in the *Norfleet* case. The U.S. Supreme Court has not yet ruled on this fact situation, but language in several of their cases, including the *DeShaney* case, indicates that it would uphold this finding.

The question as to whether a special relationship existed between the state and foster children had arisen only a few times before the *DeShaney* case reached the Supreme Court. In *Child v. Beame* (1976) the Southern District of New York had rejected the analogy of foster care to incarceration. But in *Doe v. New York Department of Social Services* (1981), the Second Circuit held that the child welfare system had an affirmative duty to protect the child plaintiff from abuse while in foster case. Also, the Northern District of Illinois court held in *Rubacha v. Coler* (1985) that the state had a duty to protect a foster child from attacks by other foster children.

In determining whether the state is liable for failure to protect a child from abuse in a foster home, the courts have made a distinction between "voluntary" and "involuntary" placement. Generally, if a child is found to have been voluntarily placed in a foster home, the state is not liable; if he or she has been placed involuntarily and abuse occurs, the state is liable.

One circuit court opinion held that a child involuntarily placed in a foster home is in a situation so analogous to a prisoner in a penal institution that a foster child's situation gives rise to an affirmative duty to protect (*Taylor v. Ledbetter* 1987).

In *Taylor v. Ledbetter* (1987), the court was presented with a case involving the severe beating of a foster child while the child was living in a county-approved foster home. In analyzing the child's due process rights, the court analogized a foster home environment to a "mentally retarded person involuntarily committed to a Pennsylvania state institution." The court stated that a person confined to a mental retardation facility had a due process right to reasonably safe living conditions. Similarly, if foster parents with whom the state places a child injure the child, and the injury results from state action or inaction, a balance of interests may show a deprivation of liberty. The court therefore concluded that where a state fails to meet its obligation to ensure safety and well-being in a home environment, the state is liable for that failure.

While acknowledging the difference in the inmate and foster child situations, the *Taylor* court held the difference only to be that the foster child would have a more difficult time proving that his injuries were caused by the agency's acts or omission. The court found that a foster child, involuntarily placed, is so much like an inmate that the Fourteenth Amendment applies to afford protection.

The *Taylor* decision dealt with children who were involuntarily placed in a foster home. What of the children who are voluntarily placed by their parents? Does the analysis as to their constitutional rights differ?

One court decision concluded that the state is not liable for failure to protect children from abuse when they have been voluntarily placed in a foster home. The Fourth Circuit Court of Appeals in *Milburn v. Anne Arundel County Department of Social Services* (1989) held that the situation of a child voluntarily placed in state supervised foster care by his parents is not analogous to prison inmates or institutionalized patients whose rights to reasonable safety are protected by the Fourteenth Amendment. The *Milburn* court referred to the footnote language in *DeShaney* and held that the state had not affirmatively restrained the child's liberty, but rather the child's parent "voluntarily" placed him in a foster home.

What does "voluntarily" mean? Do parents actually voluntarily place their children in foster homes? Do children voluntarily go there? Are children old enough to know whether their actions are voluntary or not? In most cases it seems that parents reluctantly agree to give up temporary custody of their child, because they are simply unable to care for their children by themselves. It would also seem that parents who cooperate with the authorities and voluntarily place a child in a foster home are giving up rights and protections for their child, while those that resist such a placement can sue on behalf of their child for damages should abuse occur. Moreover, social workers who investigate a case may threaten or coerce the parents with permanent loss of their child unless the parents "consent" to foster placement. This situation can often come up where the parents are poor, uneducated, and without legal counseling and therefore may be intimidated by the system into consenting to placement. Yet, in the *Milburn* court the decision was that the child had no constitutional rights to protection because he had been "voluntarily" placed in foster care.

In an earlier case, the Supreme Court had held that the distinction between voluntary and involuntary is not as clear-cut as it might initially seem. In *Smith v. Organization of Foster Families* (1977) the court noted that many "voluntary" placements are in fact coerced by threat of neglect proceedings and are not voluntary in the sense of informed consent.

Children are rarely asked whether they desire to be in foster care. Usually, the children have no choice about placement. They have no say with regard to placement, cannot realistically object to that placement, and are generally at the mercy of the social services system. Their placement therefore should be deemed involuntary.

It is also questionable whether children whose parents have "voluntarily" placed them in foster care are capable of giving adequate consent to their placement. Once the parent has "voluntarily" given up his child to the foster care system, the parent gives up many of his parental rights to the state. In many situations, once a parent has voluntarily placed his child in a foster home, he cannot regain custody without court approval (*In re George O.*, 1981). Because of the lack of alternatives and because parents cannot control the terms and conditions of placement once they give up custody of their children, foster placements are not voluntary in any meaningful sense.

It has been said that children are always in the "custody" of someone: their parents, their guardians, foster parents, or the state. Their dependence on others qualifies their freedom. A foster child is unique in that liberty for him or her means to be free from some abusive or neglectful environment. Their dependence on the state is reasonable, and the state should not act to abuse this dependence. Once it has acted to remove the foster child from an abusive environment, the state, through its foster care system, assumes a custodial position over that child.

The distinction as to the voluntary or involuntary placement of children into the foster care system really encompasses only how that child first came into foster care. Whether it is an involuntary removal from an abusive family or a voluntary placement by a parent, the child comes into the state's custody and should be afforded the same constitutional protections of the due process clause.

What do you think of the distinction between voluntary and involuntary foster care placement? Should children in foster homes be entitled to more protection than children who have been retained in their own homes with supervision?

CLASS ACTIONS

A class action is a lawsuit brought on behalf of a group of similarly situated persons addressing issues common to all members of that group and seeking relief for all group members. By their nature, class actions can have a significant impact on the social, business, and political organizations involved in the legal action. If the class of plaintiffs prevails in the lawsuit, the relief will have to address all persons in the class and those who might become members in the future.

Class actions on behalf of dependent children and children in foster care have been filed in federal courts throughout the United States. A

common theme through many of these lawsuits is that social service agencies are not adequately protecting, treating, or caring for children who have been placed in their care. There have been several theories utilized by the plaintiffs, but the common theme is that dependent children are being neglected by an overworked, understaffed social service agency and that those children may be worse off than they were in the abusive environment from which they were removed.

Case Example (*LaShawn A., et al., v. Sharon Pratt Dixon, et al.*, 1991)

A class action was brought on behalf of the children who were under supervision of the District of Columbia Department of Human Services (DHS) and children who, although not yet in the care of DHS, were known to the department because of reported abuse and neglect. The defendants included the mayor of the District of Columbia, at first Marion Barry and more recently Sharon Pratt Dixon, the director of the Department of Human Services, the director of the Commission of Social Services (CSS), the administrator of the Family Services Administration (FSA), and the chief of the Child and Family Services Division (CFSD). The last division had the primary responsibility for the administration and implementation of the child welfare system within the District, including the foster care system.

The plaintiffs were represented by the Children's Rights Project of the American Civil Liberties Union (ACLU). Their suit alleged both statutory and constitutional violations in the administration of the foster care system in the District of Columbia. Their allegations in their complaint charged that DHS had failed to do all of the following:

1. to provide services to families to prevent the placement of children in foster care;
2. to place children in foster care who could not safely remain at home;

3. to develop case plans for children in foster care; and

4. to move children into a situation of permanency, whether by returning them to their homes or freeing them for adoption (as required by the Adoption Assistance and Child Welfare Act of 1980, Public Law 96-272, discussed in chapters 1 and 5).

The trial lasted over two weeks, and the court heard testimony from a vast array of witnesses, including experts in the field, social workers and managers at the DHS, foster parents, and parents of children who had spent years in the custody of the welfare department. The complaint named seven children as plaintiffs on behalf of the class. As a result of all this testimony, the court had before it over a thousand statements that confirmed the plaintiff's allegations.

The Federal District Court judge summarized the scope of the lawsuit in his opinion.

> It is a case about thousands of children who, due to family financial problems, psychological problems, and substance abuse problems, among other things, rely on the District to provide them with food, shelter and day-to-day care. It is about beleaguered city employees trying their best to provide these necessities while plagued with excessive caseloads, staff shortages, and budgetary constraints. It is about the failures of an ineptly managed child welfare system. . . . Unfortunately, it is about a lost generation of children whose tragic plight is being repeated every day.

The defense had argued that public institutions cannot be expected to solve the problems brought about by poverty, neglect, and abuse until society addresses their causes. The court rejected this argument and entered a judgment of liability against the defendant officials. The court found that those agencies charged with operating the foster care system in the District of Columbia had not complied with either federal or District of Columbia law.

The court made a number of specific findings.

Timeliness of Investigations

The court found that staff shortages made it practically impossible to protect the children as mandated and that the children were at risk. The department failed to investigate many child abuse reports and on a yearly basis had a backload of over eight hundred cases for which investigations had not been completed. The court concluded that the DHS had failed both to initiate mandated investigations and to complete them on a timely basis.

Provision of Preventive Services

The court found that the DHS failed to provide services to prevent placement as mandated by the law. None of the cases studied contained a report on "reasonable efforts" determinations. Testimony of the social workers and administrators revealed that services were not provided because they were not available. Defendants admitted that they did not have the capability or the resources to provide the services mandated by the federal "reasonable efforts" requirements. The court therefore concluded that the Child and Family Services Division had failed to provide services or otherwise use "reasonable efforts" to prevent placement. The result was an increased risk of arbitrary or inappropriate placements, as well as an increased cost to the district.

Continuing Services

Placement

The court found serious deficiencies in the DHS placement of children. The law places limitations on the time period that a child can be in a voluntary placement without judicial determination that such placement is in the child's best interests. By the defendants' own admission, children had consistently remained in voluntary placement for much longer periods without the filing of an abuse or neglect petition with the court. In addition, children who needed placement often could not be placed anywhere. The defendants stated that the demand for foster homes had outpaced the supply, and that they frequently had been unable to place all of the children for whom they had received requests.

Case Planning

The court found there was a lack of case planning. Often the children would experience what is known as "foster care drift," with no consistent and clear plan. Foster care drift is the indefinite placement of children in a variety of foster care homes without the establishment of a permanent home. Reasonable standards require case plans to articulate specific goals with realistic strategies and time lines for accomplishing them. Case plans are necessary to ensure that children receive proper care, are placed in appropriate settings, and remain in foster care no longer than necessary. The court found that the CFSD frequently assigned inappropriate goals to the children in its foster care and consistently failed to prepare written case plans to enable the children to realize their goals.

Preventive Services

The court found that the CFSD often failed to provide any services to prevent the removal of children from their homes and that they failed to provide services to children or their families once children were removed from their homes and placed in foster care. The failure to provide the services designed to facilitate a child's return home was frequently due to the unavailability of those services. The CFSD workers were often unable to meet with the children "face-to-face." In some cases, there was no evidence to indicate that the children had ever been visited by their social worker.

Periodic Reviews

Although the federal law requires periodic reviews, the court found that the CFSD had consistently failed to comply with the requirements for judicial and administrative reviews.

Permanency Planning

The law requires that each child receive a permanent plan within twelve to eighteen months if the child cannot return home. The preferred permanent plan is that which will be most stable for the child. Thus, adoption after the termination of parental rights is the preferred plan, but guardianship and long-term foster or relative care are also available options. The court found that over 60 percent of the children who were considered for adoption had not been legally freed. This resulted in "at-risk adoptions," in which a potential adoptive parent takes a child into custody with the risk that parental rights will not be terminated and the potential parent will never be able to legally adopt the child. For half of the cases in which the children had not been legally freed for adoption, the CFSD staff had neglected to discuss the possibility of relinquishment of parental rights with their mothers.

System Infrastructure

The court also found that the various departments involved failed to adhere to federal and District law requirements regarding case tracking, case loads, supervision, and training.

Monitoring Foster Homes and Institutions

The law required that foster-care homes and facilities be licensed and inspected annually. The court found that the CFSD had not made the required inspections.

Missed Financial Opportunities

The defendants frequently claimed that they were unable to provide the services for lack of funding. According to expert and administrative testimony provided in the case, early prevention and the provision of preventive services is more effective than removing a child from the home. Yet, the court found that the DHS was not using its funds in a cost-effective manner, choosing instead to remove children from their homes and placing them in foster or institutional care without any reasonable efforts having been expended to permit them to remain at home.

Harm to the Children

The court also found that in failing to comply with the federal and District statutory requirements the DHS had caused harm to the young plaintiffs. Each of the named plaintiffs, as well as the rest of the members of the plaintiff class, had been and continued to be psychologically, emotionally, and physically harmed by the actions and inactions of the defendants.

Findings of Constitutional Violations

The *LaShawn* court opinion noted that the court would be limited to granting only conditional relief if the District were found to violate only statutory and not constitutional standards. The District could simply decide to forgo federal funding and continue its noncompliance without any further sanctions. The court therefore decided to consider the alleged constitutional violations.

The plaintiffs argued that they had been deprived of their due process rights, including

1. the right not to be harmed while in state custody;
2. the right to placement in the least restrictive, most appropriate placement;
3. the right to care that is consistent with competent professional judgment; and
4. the right not to be deprived of state or federally created liberty or property rights without due process.

In considering whether the defendants' actions or nonactions are indeed unconstitutional, the court noted that the *DeShaney* case presented the greatest obstacle to the plaintiffs' constitutional claims. As noted above, the District of Columbia had left many of the children in "voluntary" placement without the benefits of a judicial determination that would have put them into "involuntary" placement. Timely hearings and

reviews were simply not available. In many cases, children who should have been removed from their abusive homes and legally placed in foster homes were not removed, because foster homes were not available. According to the *DeShaney* decision, children who are still at home or who are put in voluntary placement are not covered by constitutional due process rights; in other words, the state is not liable for failure to protect these children from abuse. It would therefore seem that the *DeShaney* decision would limit the constitutional rights of the plaintiffs in *LaShawn*.

The court found, however, the *DeShaney* case was distinguishable from the *LaShawn* case for two reasons:

1. the plaintiffs in this case had clearly entered into the District of Columbia's custody, and
2. the District's own policies constitutionally protected liberty and property interests under the Fifth Amendment of the Constitution.

The District's violation of these policies consequently violated the due process rights of children in foster care. This argument had not been considered by the Supreme Court in *DeShaney* because it had not been argued in the courts below.

The court stated that it was indisputable that the plaintiffs had a liberty interest in safe conditions while in state custody, and that the rights of children in foster care were analogous to the rights of the involuntarily committed. These children were wards of the District, who relied wholly on the District to provide them with all of life's necessities. They were children who relied on the District to protect them from harm and ensure their well-being. Since specific services are necessary to prevent children from harm, the court concluded that the children in foster care had a constitutional liberty interest in those services. A child is entitled to the state's protection from harm, and to be protected in the manner provided by statute.

The court decision in *LaShawn* went further than the U.S. Supreme Court decision in *De-*

Shaney. In *LaShawn* the court held that the District had neglected its duties not only toward the children in foster care, but also toward those who were not yet in the District foster care custody. The court further added that the foster children who make up the plaintiff class in this case had done society no wrong and they deserved no punishment.

Finally, the court found that although the system's deficiencies may have been the result of staff shortages and excessive caseloads, this did not excuse the defendants, whose knowledge of these problems and failure to take action confirm that the problems were not isolated incidents but instead a persistent, pervasive practice. The court found that the evidence showed that the District had failed to comply with reasonable professional standards in almost every area of its child welfare system. The court considered that the evidence presented in the case was nothing less than "outrageous." Although these children had done no wrong, they were in effect punished as if they had. The court therefore held that the defendants had deprived the children of their constitutional rights in violation of section 1983 of Title 42 of the United States Code.

Discussion

Cases such as *LaShawn* give one pause. If our child welfare system is not protecting the children in their care and control, why do we have a child protection system at all? Sadly, there are a number of jurisdictions, principally large urban areas, in which the social services system is in similar disarray. An appellate court referred to the Cook County, Illinois (Chicago), child welfare system as an "abysmal failure," citing many of the same problems mentioned by the judge in the *LaShawn* case. (*In re Ashley K.*, 1991.)

Are the courts the best avenue for change? The defendants in all of these class actions ask the courts to excuse them because they are without the resources to do the tasks assigned them by the law. They argue that the legislature should allocate the resources to enable them to comply with the law. They point out that there are few satisfactory remedies. After all, the court cannot expect them to get more money from the legislature.

Yet this type of litigation has proven very effective. In many states, the social services agency, along with the political leaders, has agreed to make changes in their social services system, including the addition of more workers and services. These class actions can have a significant impact on the entire social services system and the children it serves.

Case Example (*Suter v. Artist M.*, 1992)

In 1989, a class of children in Illinois similar to that in Washington, D.C., filed a class action in the Illinois federal courts, alleging the same types of deficiencies in the Illinois child welfare system (*Suter v. Artist M.*, 1992). The lawsuit relied principally upon the language of federal law 96-272, the Adoption Assistance and Child Welfare Law of 1980. Specifically, the lawsuit alleged that the children removed from their parents' homes by the state were not receiving preplacement services, social worker supervision, reunification services, timely permanent plans, and other rights they alleged were guaranteed to them under the federal statute.

This case was heard by the District Court. After several days of testimony, it ruled that, while there had been some recent improvements in the social service agency operation, caseworkers were still not assigned in a timely fashion. The court ordered the agency to assign a worker for each child within three days of removal. The agency appealed that decision and the Seventh Circuit Court of Appeals upheld the order in a 2-1 decision.

The case was appealed by the State of Illinois to the U.S. Supreme Court. In 1992, the Supreme Court in a 7-2 decision reversed the trial court and held that the federal statute does not create an individual right enforceable in the federal court. The Supreme Court found the federal statute somewhat vague in its directive to the states, and therefore how the law would be carried out was to be left to the discretion of each state.

Discussion

Suter v. Artist M. would seem to limit severely the ability of a child or a class of children to sue the state for failure to provide the services outlined in the federal law. Several subsequent decisions have followed the *Suter* decision and have found in favor of the state social service agency and against the class of children suing the state.

However, *Suter v. Artist M.* is not the last word on such class actions. When the case of *LaShawn v. Kelly* (the new name for *LaShawn v. Dixon*) was appealed to the United States Court of Appeals for the District of Columbia, that court affirmed the trial court's decision. The Court of Appeals noted that *Suter v. Artist M.* did not create a private right to enforce the "reasonable efforts" provision of the federal Adoption Assistance and Child Welfare Act, but that there were independent legal grounds based on District of Columbia law which fully supported the trial court's decision. (*LaShawn A. v. Kelly*, 1993.) Thus the Court of Appeals found that two District of Columbia statutes, the Prevention of Child Abuse and Neglect Act and the Youth Residential Facilities Licensure Act, contained protections for the class of children sufficient to affirm the trial court's order in its entirety. *LaShawn v. Kelly* offers an avenue to continue class action litigation in the face of *Suter v. Artist M.* If state or local laws can be found which guarantee the same rights contained in the Adoption Assistance and Child Welfare Act, those state and local statutes can be the basis for relief.

Other class action litigation addresses similar issues for children in placement, including the frequency of visitation with their parents, special services for emotionally disturbed children, adequate medical care, caseload standards, and more. Such litigation will continue to have an impact on the way our social services system deals with the children in its care.

CONCLUSION

Many serious child abuse issues are raised and decided in the civil courts. Children can sue parents and other caretakers for abuse. Children can also sue professionals who detected their abused condition but failed to take action to protect them. In addition, they can sue social service agencies for failing to protect them, at least when the state agency has the children in its control.

Children as a class can sue social services agencies for failing to provide services and protections guaranteed by law. To be successful, such class action litigation will have to identify state laws which guarantee such services and protections, as the federal law may not support those claims.

Despite these opportunities, it remains true that few civil actions will be filed on behalf of abused children. First, in most cases, there is insufficient proof to identify the abuser in court proceedings. Second, even if that person is identified and proof can be gathered, the abuser may have no assets. Third, the child and family may conclude that a legal proceeding would be detrimental to the child. Reliving the abuse, facing the abuser in court, and traversing the legal system may persuade the child and family that it is better to put the matter behind them and take no further action.

CHAPTER 9

The Relationship of Different Legal Proceedings

In the previous four chapters we examined four different types of legal proceedings in which child abuse allegations can arise. In this chapter we summarize the differences between these types of proceedings and examine the relationships between cases that arise in more than one legal setting simultaneously. We also make suggestions about how the court system might better coordinate legal proceedings involving the same child or family.

Recall the hypothetical case that appeared at the beginning of this section. In that situation, there were legal proceedings in domestic relations court, juvenile court, criminal court, and civil court. While all of these proceedings could be taking place simultaneously, they would be distinctively different from one another. The differences are wide-ranging, from parties in the proceedings, to the purposes of the legal proceedings, to the procedures and evidentiary rules, to the possible outcomes. The first part of this chapter outlines many of the differences in the four types of legal proceedings.

PURPOSES OF THE COURT PROCEEDINGS

Juvenile, domestic relations, criminal, and civil proceedings were designed for distinctively different purposes. These different purposes dictate the ways in which each proceeding is conducted. Domestic relations proceedings are designed to permit parents to establish parenting and custody arrangements after they have separated. The assumption underlying these proceedings is that parents are capable of making these arrangements without court intervention or supervision. As a result, most custody agreements are reached without court involvement. Only in contested cases will the court resolve differences and establish the custody orders for the family. The possible outcomes in domestic relations proceedings range from one parent having exclusive custody of a child to an arrangement in which each parent shares in all aspects of child rearing.

The purpose of juvenile dependency proceedings is to protect children and preserve families. Juvenile proceedings occur only when parental care or lack thereof has resulted in child abuse or neglect. The focus of the proceedings is the well-being of the child. The state initiates juvenile proceedings in order to protect the child from further abuse or neglect. The preferred means of providing that protection is through social services designed to remove the problems which caused the abuse or neglect. If social services are not sufficient to protect the child, it may be necessary to remove the child from parental care and control. While in the majority of cases children are returned to one or both parents, in the most serious cases the child may never return to the parents, the court may terminate parental rights, and the child may be adopted.

Criminal proceedings are designed to determine whether a defendant has committed a crime and, if so, to punish the offender, to protect the community and the victim from further criminal behavior, and, if possible, to rehabilitate the offender. The state initiates criminal proceedings. The behavior of the accused is the focus of the proceedings. Possible outcomes range from a dismissal of the charges to conviction and a prison sentence for the defendant.

In civil proceedings the purpose is to compensate plaintiffs/victims for injuries they have received. The civil court will determine whether a particular defendant is responsible for injuries or losses to a plaintiff and the amount of any recovery for the plaintiff. Possible outcomes range from a large monetary recovery for the plaintiff to no recovery at all.

FIGURE 9.1: Overview of Court Proceedings

Court	Purpose	Parties	Investigation	Initiation of Proceedings	Time Frame	Evidence Proceedings	Testimony of Child Victim	Supervision and Enforcement
Juvenile Court	Protect children and preserve families	State, child, and parents	Social services agency	Petition by social services agency	Statutorily defined permanent plan within 18 months	Generally civil rules of evidence	Can be taken out of presence of accused in special cases	Social services monitoring
Domestic Relations Court	Permit parents to re-allocate parental rights after separation or marital dissolution	Parents; only rarely the child	The parents themselves	By one of the parents	Set by the parents	Generally civil rules of evidence	Can be taken out of presence of accused in special cases	Only that provided by the parents
Criminal Court	Punish offenders, protect society, deter other potential offenders	State and the defendent	Law enforcement	Prosecuting attorney or Grand Jury files charges	Statutorily defined, particularly if the defendant is in custody	Criminal rules of evidence	Most restrictive; child usually must testify in court	Probation department
Civil Court	Provide compensation for losses and damage caused by another person	Plantiff and defendent	The parties	Plantiff files legal action	Set by the parties	Civil rules of evidence	Can be taken out of presence of accused in special cases	Only that provided by the parties

PARTIES IN THE PROCEEDINGS

In each type of legal proceeding there are different parties and participants. A party is a person or entity with the legal right to appear, be represented by an attorney, and be heard in the proceedings. Participants may be witnesses or support persons, but they do not have the legal right to be represented by counsel, bring motions, and be heard by the court. For example, each parent is a party in a domestic relations proceeding. The state is not a party nor are relatives. The children of the marriage are not parties, although, as noted in chapter 4, in some jurisdictions the children will have a representative in these proceedings.

In juvenile dependency proceedings the parents and the state are parties. Since the state, usually in the form of a social services agency, is asserting that parental behavior has resulted in child abuse or neglect, it has the right to appear as a party in all legal proceedings brought on behalf of the child. The parents have the right to appear to respond to the state's allegations. In addition, the child is often a party in the proceedings and is represented either by a guardian *ad litem* or an attorney.

In criminal court proceedings, one or both parents may be defendants accused of criminal behavior. If only one parent is a defendant, the other may be a witness. The child will likely be a witness called by the prosecuting attorney. In the criminal case, however, only the accused is a party to the proceedings and entitled to have an attorney and be heard at all stages of the proceedings. The child victim or witness and the nonoffending parent are not parties and will appear in court only when called as witnesses.

In civil proceedings, there are usually two sides to the litigation, the plaintiff and the defendant. In a civil action alleging child abuse the child, through a guardian *ad litem*, would be the plaintiff and one or both of the parents might be the defendants. The guardian *ad litem* is an adult who represents the child's interests and appears on the child's behalf throughout the civil proceedings. If the defendant's conduct was covered by insurance, the insurance company may provide legal representation for the defendant and may reimburse the defendant for some or all of any recovery by the plaintiff.

THE STRUCTURE OF THE COURTS

The formal court structure and the relationship among each of these legal proceedings vary widely from jurisdiction to jurisdiction. For example, in some states each of the legal actions would be heard in a different court by a different judge. Those judges may or may not know about the other legal proceedings and may or may not coordinate their proceedings with the other actions. In other states the same judge in the same court might hear all four types of proceedings.

There is a national trend to coordinate and integrate legal proceedings which relate to children and families. Reflecting a sensitivity to the difficulties faced by children and families appearing in multiple proceedings, these court systems have attempted to combine or consolidate different parts of their legal activities. Most of these efforts have focused upon domestic relations and juvenile court actions. They have not included the criminal or civil dockets. The unified family court systems in Hawaii and New Jersey are examples of courts which have combined domestic relations, juvenile court, and some criminal cases in one court system.

In a recent overview of child and family legal proceedings, Rubin (1989) surveyed the court structure, statutes, and rules that relate to the integration of child and family legal proceedings. He found that the primary typology was that of a general jurisdiction court (twenty-five states). A general jurisdiction court is one in which the court has jurisdiction over many types of cases in addition to child and family proceedings. Six more states used a special jurisdiction trial court, and six more used a limited jurisdiction trial court. Special and limited jurisdiction courts hear only certain specified types of proceedings. For example, a special jurisdiction court might hear juvenile court matters, but no other types of legal proceedings. Thirteen states placed juvenile and domestic relations court jurisdiction in two or more courts.

The variations in court structure indicate the complexity in the manner in which the legal system responds to child maltreatment cases. Efforts to modify the court system to become more responsive to the needs of children and families in child maltreatment cases must include consideration of the court structure in which these cases are heard.

INVESTIGATION

As the hypothetical case indicated, there are several different persons and agencies who may investigate allegations of child maltreatment. In a domestic relations case, the parent who suspects the other parent has abused the child may be forced to investigate without assistance from the state. In the hypothetical case, the mother questioned the child, took her to a private therapist, and consulted an attorney. A parent without resources may have no ability to conduct any investigation.

In juvenile dependency proceedings it is the child protective worker who initially responds to the allegation of child maltreatment. If the case merits formal action by the social services agency, the CPS worker may turn the investigation over to a social worker with that agency.

Law enforcement personnel have the primary investigative role in criminal cases. They will respond to the initial call and conduct on-site

investigation and any follow-up work that is necessary. On occasion, the prosecutor will have a separate investigative staff to supplement law enforcement investigation.

In civil actions the plaintiff will conduct any investigation that is necessary in order to prepare the case for a court action. The investigation may include interviews, physical or mental health examinations, collection of reports made by other investigators, and information about any damages suffered by the child victim.

Resolution Without Court Action

Most reports of child maltreatment do not result in legal action of any kind. The investigation may reveal insufficient facts to take the matter any further or the case may be resolved for other reasons, without any legal action being filed. For example, the mother in the domestic relations portion of our hypothetical case may decide that she could not prove that the father molested her daughter and drop the matter. Or she might persuade the father to attend therapy, reduce his visits, or drop out of the children's lives. She could also decide that she does not have the resources to bring a legal action and do nothing at all.

In the juvenile dependency portion of the hypothetical case, the CPS worker may conclude that the allegations were unfounded, unprovable, or false. Even if the worker believed that the child had been abused, he or she might suggest that the mother take action in domestic relations court as an alternative to juvenile court. The worker might also persuade the father to reduce or terminate his visitation with his children or take other action that would resolve the matter in a manner that would ensure protection for the child. In each of these alternatives there would be no petition filed. The matter would be resolved short of formal legal intervention.

The criminal case also might be resolved without charges being filed. The law enforcement investigator might conclude that there was insufficient evidence to take the case to the prosecuting attorney. If the case were reviewed, the prosecutor might conclude that there was insufficient evidence to prosecute the case successfully. Such factors as the age of the child victim and the facts surrounding the contested custody proceeding might influence that decision not to prosecute.

The civil case might also be resolved without the initiation of legal proceedings. The plaintiff might conclude that there was insufficient evidence to prove the case in court. On the other hand, the plaintiff might persuade the defendant to pay damages for the maltreatment without the filing of any legal action.

Initiation of Proceedings

If there is no resolution short of legal action, formal proceedings may be initiated. Each of the four types of legal actions is initiated differently. In domestic relations actions, one of the parents initiates the legal proceedings. Domestic relations actions emphasize private ordering of legal relationships. The state offers a forum for the resolution of disagreements between parents. The state does not initiate domestic relations actions. If neither parent brings a legal action, there will be no change in the status quo.

In juvenile dependency court, it is the state, usually through a social services agency, that initiates proceedings on behalf of children. The juvenile case usually starts with the filing of a petition. This filing culminates an investigation by a child protective agency that has found that formal action is necessary to protect the child. The decision to file in the juvenile court rests initially with the child protection investigator or the social worker. The investigator must consider whether the child has been abused or neglected and whether either parent is able and willing to protect and provide for the child.

In criminal court it is the prosecutor representing the state who initiates a legal action by filing formal charges against a defendant. Depending on the state, the case may have to be reviewed by a grand jury or it may be filed directly by the prosecutor. If the district attorney refuses to prosecute, there will be no criminal action.

In a civil action it is the plaintiff who initiates legal proceedings by filing an action against the defendant. The legal papers will state the reasons for the action and the type of recovery sought by the plaintiff. After the action is served upon the defendant, the proceedings may commence.

The Time Frame

The time frame for each type of legal proceeding in the four courts is different. Domestic relations proceedings can take years to resolve. Because one of the parents must initiate legal action, these cases can be dormant for years, waiting for one of the parents to take further legal action. Since issues of child maltreatment involve investigation, it is likely that such cases will take extended periods of time in the domestic relations courts. Of course, if the parents reach agreement on the child custody and visitation issues, the case may be resolved quickly.

Juvenile dependency proceedings are guided by much more strict time guidelines. Because juvenile cases can involve the involuntary removal of children from their parents, most state statutes mandate immediate court review of the removal and a trial or jurisdictional hearing within thirty to ninety days after the removal.

Criminal court proceedings are governed by constitutional and statutory law. Because an accused person may be detained in jail awaiting trial, criminal cases come to trial usually in a matter of months. The United States Constitution guarantees a defendant the right to a speedy trial, and many state constitutions and statutes affirm that guarantee and spell out the details. In California, for example, a defendant is guaranteed a trial within sixty days of arraignment. If the case does not proceed to trial within that time, the case must be dismissed.

The defendant may waive his or her right to a speedy trial. This occurs often when the defendant wishes to investigate the case more thoroughly. In child abuse cases, some defendants will permit postponement of the case, believing that the child witness will become a less credible witness with the passage of time. If there is a likelihood of the child forgetting or otherwise becoming unavailable for trial, delay works in the interests of the accused. If there is a likelihood of conviction, the longer the delay, the more the punishment is put off. The accused may also have investigation and trial preparation which are the basis for requests for delay. For the child, however, a swift resolution of the case is preferable. Children, and particularly younger children, may forget what happened as time passes. More importantly, the longer the child has to wait until there is a resolution of the case, the longer the pressure of the upcoming trial remains on the child.

Some states have addressed the need to have a speedy trial by enacting legislation mandating trials within a specified time period when children are witnesses. For example, California Penal Code Section 1048 (Standard California Codes, 1988) states that all criminal matters in which the minor is a material witness shall be given precedence over all the other criminal actions in the order of trial, and that the trial shall be commenced within thirty days of arraignment in Superior Court, unless the court finds good cause for a continuance.

In civil cases the time frame is determined by the parties, their investigation, discovery, and negotiations. Civil cases can take years to reach trial. In most states, there is a statute which requires civil trials to be heard within five years from the time they are filed by the plaintiff. Often the court backlog is so great that a civil case will not come to trial until the five years have run. In some states, the judiciary or the legislature has taken steps to have civil trials resolved in a more timely fashion. The technique utilized is generally more court management of civil trials. Where these trial court delay reduction initiatives are operating, civil cases will generally be resolved in one to two years after filing.

Evidence and Procedures

The evidentiary rules and court procedures in the four different types of legal action are different. This is understandable, because the purposes and what is at stake in each court are different. The general rule is that the criminal defendant has the greatest legal protection. Because the criminal defendant faces a loss of liberty, both constitutional and statutory law offer him heightened security against state intervention. A criminal defendant must be proven guilty beyond a reasonable doubt, the highest standard of proof in the law. The criminal defendant has a right to confront his or her accusers, a right which may not be available to the parent in juvenile court dependency proceedings. This right of confrontation is discussed in greater detail in chapters 11 and 12.

The evidentiary and procedural rules governing domestic relations, juvenile dependency, and civil trials are generally similar. All are considered civil proceedings. There may be some variation in evidentiary and procedural rules based upon statutes and court rules. These vary from state to state.

Testimony of the Child Victim-Witness

The child maltreatment victim may have to testify one or more times in each type of legal proceeding. Changes in the law over the past decade have enabled a child's statements to be received in many court proceedings without having to testify in court. These changes have been most noticeable in civil proceedings, including domestic relations, juvenile dependency, and civil trials. In criminal cases, it is still difficult to admit a child's statements without the opportunity for the defendant to confront and cross-examine the child in open court. The issues surrounding confrontation and cross-examination will be discussed in chapters 11 and 12.

Most domestic relations court judges are reluctant to have a child testify in front of the parents. First, such testimony may not be necessary, since the child's statements may have been recorded in the custody evaluations. Second, the litigants may prefer to have the child speak to the judge in his or her chambers. However, if a parent insists on being present during the child's testimony, the judge may have to determine whether such testimony will be detrimental to the child.

Supervision and Enforcement

The power of the courts to supervise and enforce their rulings varies greatly among the four courts. The domestic relations court usually has no supervisory agencies to enforce its rulings. Only a parent can call the court's attention to noncompliance by the other parent and bring the case back to court. Once the case is before the court, it can enforce its orders by contempt. If a parent is found to be in contempt of a court order, the court can place the offending parent in jail or levy a fine.

The juvenile dependency court is in a much better position to supervise and enforce the orders it makes. Each dependency order is supervised either by a probation officer or social welfare worker. The case supervisor will bring to the court's attention any violation of court orders. When there is a violation, the principal power of the juvenile court is to remove the child from the custody of the parent or further restrict parental access to the child. This should occur only if the parental violation of the court order endangers the child. The juvenile court can also hold the parent in contempt of court if the parent willfully violates a court order.

The criminal court also has strong supervisory powers. Most convicted defendants in child maltreatment cases who are not sent to prison are placed under some type of probationary supervision. The probation officer monitors the progress of the defendant and reports any violations of court orders to the court. The principal power of the criminal court is to jail the abuser if probationary conditions are not met.

In civil proceedings the court has no supervisory powers. Once a judgment has been rendered for a plaintiff, it is up to the plaintiff to follow through and see that the monetary damages are recovered from the defendant. If the defendant refuses to pay the judgment, the plaintiff can use civil remedies to obtain the money. These remedies include attachment and placing liens on property and bank accounts.

THE RELATIONSHIPS AMONG THE COURTS

The same child maltreatment case with the same family members may appear in more than one setting simultaneously. The most frequently recurring situations arise in domestic relations and juvenile dependency court proceedings. In these cases a child maltreatment allegation arises in the midst of a child custody action in domestic relations court. The issues often become which court should hear the case and how should the two courts coordinate the two possible actions between each other.

The other frequent relationship is between the criminal and juvenile dependency courts. In these cases typically the adult parent is prosecuted for child maltreatment simultaneously with the dependency action in juvenile court. Sometimes the dependency court may be considering ways in which the child can be reunified with the offending family member, while the criminal court is fashioning a punishment for that same person. Sometimes the judge hearing the dependency action will decide that the allegations are untrue, and the defendant in the criminal case will ask that the charges be dismissed based upon the principle of collateral estoppel. In the following case examples, we examine each of these situations.

Recall in our hypothetical case that the mother

brought a legal action in domestic relations court to terminate visitation between the father and the children. She based her motion for modification on the father's alleged abuse of their daughter, Sally. Simultaneously, the child protection worker filed a petition in juvenile dependency court alleging that Sally needed the protection of the court. In the three cases that follow, the California appellate courts indicate possible guidelines for the management of cases that might arise in both domestic relations and juvenile dependency courts (Edwards, 1987).[1]

In the case of In re Jennifer P. (1985), the adoptive parents dissolved their marriage, Jennifer was living with her mother, and her father had reasonable visitation rights. When the mother suspected that Jennifer had been sexually molested by the father during visitation, she informed the social services department and cooperated with the police investigation and medical examinations. The mother contacted the juvenile court and cooperated in the criminal prosecution. She also went to the domestic relations court, secured a temporary restraining order prohibiting the father's visitation and entry to her house and requested a modification of the family law order to prohibit the father's contact with Jennifer on a permanent basis. The mother then objected to further juvenile court intervention.

Testimony at the juvenile court jurisdictional hearing revealed that the child psychiatrist believed the mother handled the entire matter superbly, and the social services department worker described the mother as having "demonstrated superior care and cooperation throughout [the investigation]" (p. 324). However, neither the family law modification proceeding nor the criminal proceeding had concluded, and the father had not expressed a willingness to stay away from Jennifer or the mother's house.

On these facts, the trial court sustained a dependency determination, only to have the court of appeals reverse that finding. The appellate court suggested that the juvenile court should have confidence in findings made by other superior courts, stating that "[w]e can hardly presume the domestic court would require or allow father-daughter contact where it would be detrimental to Jennifer's welfare" (p. 327). The appellate court concluded by adding that "our system, for better or for worse, presumes that parents are the best judges of their children's best interests" (p. 327).

Jennifer P. stands for the proposition that a custodial parent who becomes aware of abuse to the child can take sufficient protective steps so that juvenile court intervention will not be necessary or permitted. In Jennifer P., the juvenile court investigative worker decided incorrectly to have the juvenile court intervene for Jennifer's protection. Based upon the guidelines listed above, intervention was not necessary. The investigative worker had a strong suspicion as to the identity of the abuser, and the father apparently was not contesting the change of custody or restraining orders in domestic court. The mother retained custody of Jennifer throughout the proceedings, sought help from the domestic relations court, secured restraining orders, and terminated the father's visitation. The mother also initiated counseling for Jennifer. Finally, the investigating worker had nothing but praise for the way in which the mother handled the entire situation.

While there had been abuse, the nonabusing custodial parent took sufficient protective steps to ensure that the abuse was stopped and that Jennifer would receive appropriate therapy. The juvenile court could do no more, and intervention was therefore unnecessary. The investigating worker should have declined to initiate juvenile proceedings. However, the worker might have monitored the domestic relations court and criminal court proceedings to learn their outcome and ensure that the mother secured appropriate permanent protective orders.

In re Nicole B. (1979) presents a similar

---

1. The discussion of the following cases is adapted from L. Edwards (1987), "The Relation of Family and Juvenile Courts in Child Abuse Cases," *Santa Clara Law Review*, 27, 201-278.

factual context, yet a different result. In *Nicole B.* the parties stipulated to the facts that were submitted in support of a dependency petition. Those facts included: (1) a boyfriend of the mother struck Nicole while spending time with her in a park; (2) the striking was of the type contemplated by the California Welfare and Institutions Code section 300(d); (3) the boyfriend was subsequently taken to a psychiatric hospital; (4) the mother had no knowledge of the incident and was away when it occurred; (5) the boyfriend had been residing in the house for three months and had known the mother for six months; and (6) at the time of the hearing, the boyfriend no longer resided with the mother and was not allowed to come in or about the mother's residence.

On these facts the trial court sustained the petition and declared Nicole to be a dependent child of the court, and the court of appeal affirmed that finding. The appellate court stressed the fact that the boyfriend did not express an intent to remain away from Nicole or her mother's house. Given the close relationship between the mother and the boyfriend, the court concluded there was a basis for inferring a potential for the boyfriend's return. The court based its opinion on its overriding concern for the protection of the minor and not on parental unfitness.

The court noted that the unfitness of the parent is not the determinative issue under Welfare and Institutions Code section 300(d). Rather, the court must look to past events for aid in the determination of the present fitness of a child's home for the purpose of deciding whether the juvenile court should assume jurisdiction over the child.

Nicole B. held that a nonabusing custodial parent whose child is abused cannot prevent juvenile court intervention when she has not taken sufficient steps to protect the child from further abuse. It was the mother's live-in relationship with the abuser that was of continuing concern to the investigating worker and subsequently to the trial judge. Furthermore, although not specifically noted in the appellate court opinion, the mother had

taken no protective steps such as securing domestic relations court restraining orders. Finally, the opinion suggested that neither the investigating worker nor the judge had confidence in the mother's ability to protect the child from future contacts with the boyfriend. The child required supervision for a period of time.

A comparison of the rules enunciated in *Nicole B.* and *Jennifer P.* is instructive. If a parent, upon discovery of an abuse, takes adequate steps to protect the child from further abuse, and responds to the needs of the child, the juvenile court has no basis to sustain a dependency petition as a matter of law. If, on the other hand, the non-offending parent takes insufficient steps to protect the child or fails to respond to the needs of the child, dependency may be invoked. For example, if Nicole's mother had obtained a restraining order prohibiting the boyfriend from contacting Nicole or from coming to the house and had indicated that her relationship with him was over, the result might have been different.

The inquiry in each case centers around the mother's ability to protect the child and provide for the child's needs without state intervention and supervision. Dozens of similar decisions are made daily in cases throughout the state. Usually, an investigating worker decides whether to intervene based upon considerations similar to those discussed in *Nicole B.* and *Jennifer P.* The worker also evaluates the mother's attitude regarding the abuse allegations. In many of these cases, mother must make the difficult choice between protecting her child and deciding to maintain a relationship with a male who provides support for the family. A worker who detects ambivalence may remove the child from the mother's custody to insure the child's protection and to prevent the mother from attempting to persuade the child to change her story.

Nicole B. and *Jennifer P.* reflect situations in which juvenile court can and cannot assume jurisdiction. The case of *In re Christina T.* (1986) provides an example of a situation in which the juvenile court *must* assert its jurisdiction.

In *Christina T.*, dependency proceedings were brought on behalf of the minor, a five-year-old, alleging that the minor's father had subjected her to sexual abuse during the past six months (section 300[a] of the Welfare and Institutions Code) and that her home was unfit due to the depravity of her father (section 300[d] of the Welfare and Institutions Code). The parents, pursuant to a marital dissolution agreement, shared custody of the minor; the mother had nine days a month and the father the remainder. During time with the mother, Christian complained to her mother and the baby-sitter that her father made her take showers with him, rubbed her between her legs until it hurt, touched her buttock, and slept with her in the same bed. Christina later made a similar statement to an investigating detective. A doctor testified that the minor's hymen was not intact and that both her anus and vagina were dilated, all of which was consistent with sexual molestation. The evidence also included testimony from a psychiatric social worker who interviewed the minor utilizing anatomically correct dolls. The minor took the female doll and put its face between the male doll's legs saying, "[t]hat's what little girls do" (p. 634). The minor also told the social worker, "[t]hat's what daddy Peter [mother's cohabitating boyfriend] has me do" (p. 634). Later, the minor retracted this statement and said it was Chris, her father, who had done it. Her father denied any molestation.

At the conclusion of the trial, the court found both petitions untrue, stating "[t]here is no question that she has been sexually molested by somebody. . . . [But since] the allegations in this petition [have not] been proved by a preponderance of evidence, I find them both untrue" (p. 636-37).

The court of appeal reversed the finding, reasoning that once the trial court found that the minor had been molested, the statutory presumptions were activated, and the burden of producing evidence shifted to the parents. Since neither parent was able to establish that the abuse occurred in the home of the other parent, the petition must be sustained as a matter of law. The remaining question of who sexually abused the minor was relevant to the dispositional phase of the case and to any orders the court might fashion to assist the child. The appellate court remanded the case to the trial court for further dispositional proceedings.

Christina T. stands for the proposition that when a child has been sexually molested and the parents cannot satisfy a court as to the identity of the perpetrator, the juvenile court must intervene on behalf of the child. Where similar facts are discovered during a domestic relations court proceeding or in a juvenile court trial, the participants must recognize that the case belongs in juvenile court, and appropriate action should be taken to ensure that result.

Christina T. presents facts familiar to many domestic relations and juvenile court participants: the so-called unprovable child molestation. All participants agree that something has happened to the child, but no one can prove who was responsible for the abuse. Had the appellate court upheld the trial court's dismissal, further proceedings would have taken place in the domestic relations court. That forum would have decided issues of custodial time sharing, access to the child, and other relevant issues. But the appellate court held that these facts, as a matter of law, must result in the assertion of juvenile court jurisdiction.

If the juvenile court had found there was no molestation but that the child or someone else fabricated evidence of molestation or that the evidence of molestation was inconclusive, juvenile court jurisdiction would probably not have been necessary. The petitions would have been dismissed, and further proceedings would have taken place in the domestic relations court.

If, however, the court was unsure whether a molestation had occurred but found that the child was traumatized by something or someone and was behaving as though she had been sexually abused when there was no satisfactory explanation for her behavior, a more difficult problem would be presented. This type of case typically includes some sexualized statements by the child, inconclusive medical evidence, resistance to visitation (usually with the father), and signs of extreme stress after visitation (bed wetting, nightmares, and acting out behavior). This type of case also typically involves a bitter custody battle that has followed a bitter marital dissolution. The mother often claims that the father is abusing the child, while the father claims nothing is wrong during visitation and that the mother is programming the child to produce words and responses.

This last factual situation presents difficulties for the court process. The facts fall short of those necessary to invoke juvenile court jurisdiction while presenting complications that make it difficult, if not impossible, for the domestic relations court to meet the child's needs. Whether the juvenile court should invoke its jurisdiction should be measured by the needs of the child. In cases in which the child exhibits extreme stress and competent professional testimony declares that service or supervision is necessary, the juvenile court should assert jurisdiction. In other cases the juvenile court should decline to intervene.

When read together, *Nicole B.*, *Jennifer P.*, and *Christina T.* help define the jurisdictional line between the domestic relations and juvenile courts. Under the facts in *Jennifer P.*, the juvenile court did not have jurisdiction; the facts in *Nicole B.* were sufficient for the juvenile court to exercise its jurisdiction; and in *Christina T.*, the facts *demanded* that the juvenile court exercise jurisdiction. This spectrum of factual settings and appellate rulings will be of assistance in the effort to decide how the two courts should best relate to each other.

The other frequent relationship is between the criminal and juvenile dependency courts. In these cases the adult parent is prosecuted for child maltreatment simultaneously with the dependency action in juvenile court. Sometimes the juvenile court may be considering ways in which the child can be reunified with the offending family member while the criminal court is fashioning a punishment for that same person. Sometimes the judge hearing the dependency action will decide that the

allegations are untrue, and the defendant in the criminal case will ask that the charges be dismissed based upon the principle of collateral estoppel. In the following case examples, we will examine each of these situations.

Case Example (*State v. Cleveland*, 1990)

The following case example is from a Washington State of Appeals Court. A fact-finding trial was held in the juvenile court on a petition for dependency of eight-year-old K., the defendant's stepdaughter. The basis for the claimed dependency was the allegation that the defendant, Mr. Cleveland, had sexually abused K., and that Mrs. Cleveland, K.'s mother and Mr. Cleveland's wife, could not order Cleveland to live elsewhere. The trial court found that the State had not shown by a preponderance of the evidence that the alleged sexual abuse had occurred and dismissed the petition.

Before the dependency hearing was completed, Cleveland was charged with statutory rape and indecent liberties. Upon dismissal of the dependency petition, Cleveland moved for dismissal of the criminal charges on collateral estoppel grounds, asserting that the criminal charges were based on allegations of sexual abuse identical to those allegations heard and dismissed in dependency proceedings. The trial court denied the motion to dismiss, and Cleveland was convicted by a jury of indecent liberties and attempted statutory rape.

Mr. Cleveland appealed, asserting that the prosecution was barred by the doctrine of collateral estoppel. His argument was that once a court had determined that the abuse had not taken place, other courts were unable legally to find that the conduct had occurred.

At trial, K. testified that Mr. Cleveland had rubbed her "private parts" with his finger. She said he had not touched her bare skin nor touched her in any other way. She denied any penetration and said she could not recall specific occasions when sexual abuse occurred.

Detective Marsh testified, pursuant to the child hearsay statute, to statements made to him by K. describing three instances of sexual abuse. Several of K.'s school friends, the school nurse, two teachers, the caseworker, and the foster mother all testified to statements made to them by K. reporting sexual abuse by Cleveland.

Barbara Huffman, a family therapist, testified as an expert witness concerning characteristics and typical responses of child victims of sexual abuse. The testimony of Mr. Cleveland and Mrs. Cleveland was very similar to their testimony in dependency hearings.

The appellate court reflected upon the concept of collateral estoppel, stating that it stood for an extremely important principle in the adversary system of justice. The court said that collateral estoppel means simply that when an issue of ultimate fact has once been determined by a valid and final judgment, that issue cannot again be litigated between the same parties in any future lawsuit.

The court reviewed the law and noted that, for the doctrine of collateral estoppel to apply, four factors must be present: (1) the issue decided in the prior adjudication must be identical with the one presented in the second; (2) the prior adjudication must have ended in a final judgment on the merits; (3) the party against whom the pleas of collateral estoppel is asserted must have been a party or in privity with a party to the prior litigation; and (4) application of the doctrine must not work an injustice.

The court concluded that the first three factors were satisfied, stating:

> It is undisputed that the issue resolved in Cleveland's favor in the dependency hearing was identical to the issue on which he was convicted in the criminal proceeding. That issue was sexual abuse of his stepdaughter K. There is also no

question but that the dependency proceeding ended in a final judgment on the merits. The party against whom the plea of collateral estoppel is asserted is the State of Washington in both cases. It is immaterial that in the dependency proceedings, the State was represented by the Attorney General and in the criminal prosecution was represented by the county prosecuting attorney.

The court then indicated that overall considerations of public policy are determinative of the issue before it. The court stated that

> . . . dependency proceedings are often attended with a sense of urgency, are held as promptly as reasonably possible, and the entire focus of the proceeding is the welfare of the child. The focus being more narrow than in the typical felony case, the State normally does not need, nor does it perform, the extensive preparation typically required for felony trials.
>
> Furthermore, the prosecutor uses many more resources in developing a felony prosecution than those available in the typical dependency hearing. Dependency is decided by a judge, while felony trials are usually tried by a jury. In addition, if the State was faced with application of the doctrine of collateral estoppel to findings in dependency proceedings, there could well be a reluctance to conduct dependency proceedings in cases where one or more of the same issues would arise in subsequent criminal prosecutions. While the welfare of minor children is undeniably important, we are influenced by the desirability of not impeding enforcement of the criminal law when no overriding consideration requires it.

The court affirmed the judgment.

Discussion

What is the collateral estoppel doctrine? Does it make sense to limit the number of times that an issue can be tried before the court system? Is this doctrine similar to that of double jeopardy? According to the double jeopardy doctrine, a person may not be put in jeopardy (on trial) more than once for the same crime. Is an allegation of child maltreatment in a juvenile dependency proceeding similar to a criminal charge? Is not the loss of custody of one's child as serious as a loss of liberty?

The law in this area remains in conflict. In the case of *Lockwood v. Superior Court* (Cal App., 1984), a dependency petition was filed on behalf of an infant, alleging child abuse by the infant's parents. At approximately the same time, criminal proceedings were commenced against both parents. The juvenile dependency case was tried first, and the juvenile court dismissed the petition, finding that the State had failed to prove nonaccidental injury. Relying on that adjudication, the parents moved to dismiss the criminal charges. The California Court of Appeals held that the prosecuting attorney was collaterally estopped by the dependency adjudication from relitigating the abuse issue in the criminal case.

Other issues arise which focus upon the relationship among parallel child maltreatment proceedings. For example, the parties in one court proceeding may wish to have access to the investigative reports, court orders, testimony, and other information collected in an earlier proceeding. This often arises when a criminal defendant or a civil litigant requests information from a juvenile dependency proceeding. The matter is complicated by the fact that juvenile dependency proceedings are confidential and access to information by third parties is limited by statute in all states. In a series of cases, the U.S. Supreme Court has outlined the process by which the court system can determine whether to release such information. Generally, the process involves a judge reviewing the sought-after information *in camera* (privately) and deciding whether the relevance of the material to the pending case outweighs any confidentiality interest that the child or other family members might have in keeping the matter confidential (*Pennsylvania v. Ritchie*, U.S.S. Ct., 1987).

Changes in Court Structure

All four courts serve important functions. It is unlikely that the court system can be entirely restructured in order to better serve children and families in child maltreatment cases. However, some modifications in court structure and co-ordination seem desirable, both for the litigants and for the court process.

A number of states are considering restructuring their court systems in order to better accommodate the needs of children and families who appear before them. Some states have operated a unified family court for years. Others are experimenting with bringing legal actions involving children and families under the jurisdiction of one branch of the court system. For example, a report from the California Attorney General's Office on the child victim witness (1989) has called for a total reorganization of the juvenile and domestic relations court into a new Family Relations Division of the Superior Court. This new division would consolidate all matters relating to child abuse and violence, along with other traditional domestic relations and juvenile court matters in a new Superior Court structure. All child and family related matters would come under this division, including: domestic relations, juvenile delinquency, juvenile dependency, children in need of supervision, termination of parental rights, adoptions, probate, paternity, emancipations, and all other legal actions in which the child and the family are involved. Criminal actions against the perpetrator of child abuse and civil actions involving children suing adults for damages would still be handled in other courts.

Several states have already instituted such combined systems. Delaware, Rhode Island, Hawaii, New Jersey, and Washington, D.C., are the most notable examples (Edwards, 1992). The electorate in Nevada voted to create a statewide unified family court, while other states, including Florida and Virginia, are moving toward such a unified court. The National Council of Juvenile and Family Court Judges in Reno, Nevada, has created a Family Court Center which offers technical assistance to states considering such unification.

Even if a court system is unable to create some sort of a unified family court, changes should be made to ensure that legal actions involving the same children and family members are better coordinated. These changes can come from court rules, statutes, or protocols. Whatever the method, some coordination is necessary if the court system is to deal more efficiently and effectively with child maltreatment cases.

CONCLUSION

The present court structure in many states dealing with child abuse cases has led to unnecessary duplication of efforts, conflicting orders, and often great trauma to the children and family members involved. At the same time, the great influx of child abuse cases has made it more urgent that a new system of treating child abuse and neglect cases be created. This chapter has examined the sources of problems in the system and has suggested ways for reorganizing the structure and humanizing the treatment of the child victim. It is important that the functions of the various courts are clearly spelled out, and that the support staff in the legal system develop better guidelines for when to send a case to another court. They need to be prepared to work together in cases that overlap. The emphasis throughout should be on serving the best interests of the child victim, reducing the trauma caused by the system itself, and ensuring due process and fairness for all persons involved.

PART 3

In Part Two, we examined the different types of legal proceedings in which child abuse can arise. After discussing juvenile, domestic relations, criminal, and civil proceedings, we addressed the relationship among different court proceedings involving the same child.

In Part Three we turn to the legal issues surrounding a child's appearance in court. For any legal relief to be granted there must be evidence produced in a court of law that abuse had taken place. Often the only witness to that abuse is the child. But the legal system was not designed for children. Some children may be unable to appear in court and testify. They may not be competent to testify, or they may be too frightened to answer questions. Moreover, subjecting children to the legal process may result in reabuse by the very system designed to protect them.

The legal system has responded to the special needs of children who may have to testify in court. Legislatures have written statutes designed to support and protect children in child abuse cases. Courts have also attempted to reduce the trauma that children may experience in court proceedings.

The difficulty with many of these changes is that they may violate the constitutional rights of the accused. The alleged abuser is not interested in measures designed to help the child witness. The child's testimony may be the only evidence that will support a criminal conviction, a change

of custody, or a termination of parental rights. Failure of the child to testify may mean that the legal action cannot proceed.

Part Three examines various legal procedures that are designed to permit children to testify in a more protected environment or to have their words be admitted into evidence without giving testimony. Many creative procedures and evidentiary rules to reduce the potential trauma to children who must testify have been suggested. In Part Three these procedures and rules are examined through a discussion of selected cases and statutes.

In less than a decade federal and state legislatures and the courts have carved out a new area of law, one that deals with the child victim in court proceedings. Part Three focuses on the balance between the needs of children and the rights of accused persons. This balance has been established primarily by the U.S. Supreme Court, but other courts have contributed to the analysis. The balance is different depending on what type of legal proceeding is involved and the type of evidence and procedure proposed. The final word on many of the issues discussed in this part has not been heard. These cases and materials provide the foundation for developments to come.

CHAPTER 10

The Child Witness

The recent growth in the number of trials involving child sexual abuse allegations has precipitated an increase in the number of children called to testify in court. Often the child's statements in or out of court are the only evidence supporting the prosecution, making pretrial interviewing and courtroom preparation of the child a critical stage in the case.

The use of children's testimony has been accompanied by an interest in understanding the differences between adult and child testimony and in the special problems presented by children's testimony. Some experts charge that young children may be unable to separate truth from fiction, that they are very suggestible and unable to be competent witnesses in court. Others believe that children are very capable of rendering competent testimony. A major dilemma raised by children in court is, therefore, whether a young child abuse victim is legally competent to testify.

A child who is required to testify in court may experience severe psychological stress in reliving the witnessed event. As discussed in the chapter on criminal courts, criminal procedures that operate for the purpose of prosecuting the alleged offender often fail to take into account the psychological damage that can be done to a young child in the role of witness. While child abuse itself is emotionally damaging, the ordeal of bringing criminal charges and the subsequent court procedures can compound the victimization.

This chapter explores the special problems presented when children are witnesses. It includes an overview of issues related to child witness testimony, such as the competency of children to be witnesses, child development issues related to giving testimony, consistency in children's testimony, suggestibility of children and contamination by interviewers, children and lying, and perceptions of child witness testimony by jurors. Pertinent research findings are presented.

Finally, we address the issue of secondary victimization of child victims and describe some of the measures taken to meet the special needs of child witnesses. There is some overlap in this subject matter and the following chapters on confrontation (chapter 11) and hearsay evidence in child maltreatment cases (chapter 12).

TESTIMONIAL ISSUES

Competency

No discussion of children as witnesses can avoid the issue of the competence of the child to bear witness. Competency involves two separate questions: can the witness communicate with the court, and does the witness understand the duty to tell the truth? Each of these questions raises special considerations when the witness is a child. A major change in the relation of children to the legal system over the years has been an increasing presumption of competence (Garbarino, 1989).

Historically, the law's assessment of competency has reflected social assumptions and values. For many years slaves, women, and children were not allowed to testify in courts of law. While slavery has been abolished, and legal reforms over time have made it legal for women to testify, the assumption that children cannot give truthful testimony has continued to exclude many children from giving testimony in court. Often, competency rules have been illogical and discriminatory (Dziech and Schudson, 1989). While it is clear that many adults also may have problems separating truth from fiction and lies and may be unable to communicate with the court, the court process has focused almost entirely upon children's truthfulness and competency.

Ironically, an early U.S. Supreme Court Case, *Wheeler v. United States* (1895), found a five-year-old competent to give legal testimony in a criminal trial. The justices concluded in this trial that there is no precise age that determines the question of competency, and they established the rule that the witness must have capacity and intelligence to testify, appreciate the difference between truth and falsehood, accept the duty to tell the truth, and know the obligations of an oath.

States have used many different ways to meet the *Wheeler* standards. Some have automatic age limits on testimony, while others have left the competency issue to the court or the jury to decide.

Under common law, competency was established automatically at age fourteen. For example, in Illinois, the court must determine whether or not a child under fourteen is competent (*In the Interest of E. D.*, 1986). This approach has been changing, with only five states still adhering to the common law tradition. Thirteen states presume that children over ten are competent. Eighteen states require demonstration that the child understands the nature and obligation of the oath to tell the truth. In many states the court must make a determination as to the child's competency. For example, in *Hardy v. Commonwealth* (1986), a six-year-old sodomy victim was examined at a court-conducted competency hearing. The victim defined a lie as "something that really did not happen" and the truth as "something that happened." The judge asked if the story she had been telling about the appellant had been true, and she said yes. The court ruled that the victim was competent. In Georgia, a child is competent if he or she knows that he or she would be punished for lying. It is not necessary that the child understand the meaning of an oath (*Barnes v. State*, 1985). In summary, in order to be competent, a child must have sufficient mental capacity to observe, recollect, and communicate and have some sense of moral responsibility.

A second issue is how a child's competency should be decided. In *State v. Weisenstein* (1985), the defense counsel wanted to examine a five-year-old in detail concerning competency, with eleven written questions to test the victim's ability to observe, recollect, communicate, and express understanding of moral distinction. The trial court refused to permit this line of questioning. The appellate court affirmed the trial court, citing the

control of the examination for determining witness competency is within the trial court's discretion.

In 1974, the revised Federal Rules of Evidence abolished the competency rule for trials in federal courts. Federal Rule of Evidence 601 now dictates that every person is competent. This left to juries the responsibility for assessing the credibility of child witnesses. Many states followed the federal lead, and by 1985 twenty states had ruled that every person is presumed competent (Dziech and Schudson, 1989).

Several important cases exemplify this new procedure. In *State v. James* (1989), the Connecticut Supreme Court affirmed the constitutionality of a state law allowing complainants in child sex abuse cases to testify without a preliminary finding of competency. The court also held that the defendants are no longer entitled to have the jury instructed to consider the witnesses' youth in accepting their credibility. The court held that this statute was in line with the modern trend toward eliminating the threshold qualifications of witnesses.

In *State v. Superior Court Pima County* (1986), the Arizona Appeals Court stated that Arizona follows Federal Rule 606, which says competency is for the jury to decide, regardless of the witness's age. Competency does not require that a child comprehend the abstractions of truth, falsehood, or duty to testify truthfully. In cases of extreme youth, the judge must be convinced that no trier of fact could reasonably believe the witness could have observed, communicated, remembered, or told the truth. If the child is found incompetent, the child's out-of-court assertions may be admissible. There must be an *in camera* (in chambers) finding by the court as to the statement's reliability and some corroboration. Similarly, in *State v. Hunt* (1987), the Washington Appeals Court found that a child may be competent at the time of making a statement, but incompetent at the time of trial because of inability to remember at trial. The defendant contended that the child's out-of-court statements were not admissible because the child could not remember them at trial. The appeals court found that out-of-court statements were reliable, spontaneous, and a recitation of facts generally unknown to children.

In *Kentucky v. Stincer* (1987), the U.S. Supreme Court considered for the first time whether a judge could modify the procedures of a competency hearing to accommodate a child. In this case the defendant appealed his sexual assault conviction because the judge had excluded him from the competency hearing when the young victims became afraid to testify in his presence. The Supreme Court allowed the exclusion, and declared that the constitutional rights of the defendants must coexist with opportunities for children to testify. It should be noted that the defendant in this case did have the right to question the children during the trial.

Closely related to the competency issue is the requirement that every witness in criminal court take an oath or make an affirmation in the form prescribed by the law. A typical oath or affirmation is, "Do you swear (or affirm) that you will tell the truth and nothing but the truth in the matter pending before this court, so help you God?" "I do" or "I so affirm." Although the requirement applies to children as well as adults, the linguistic and legal complexity of the prescribed oath is beyond the ken of many children. Many states now do not require a particular form of oath or affirmation for children (e.g., *In re R. R.*, 1979, from New Jersey). A recent case from Arkansas, for example, *Waletz v. Dept. of Human Services* (1989), found that an oath is not required of a child if it is clear that he or she will tell the truth. In California, a child under ten years of age is required only to promise to tell the truth (California Evidence Code 710).

Finding a child competent to testify does not mean that the court assumes that the child's ability to communicate is the same as that of an adult. It simply means that juries or judges should be allowed to see and hear the child witness and evaluate his or her credibility.

Case Example (*People v. Vialpando*, 1990)

The first case example is taken from the Colorado Court of Appeals. A defendant was charged with sexually assaulting a fourteen-year-old, who, at that time, was baby-sitting at the home of a neighbor. At trial, one of the children for whom the victim was baby-sitting was called as a witness. The defendant was convicted, and he appealed on numerous grounds, including a challenge to the minor witness's competence.

The Colorado Court of Appeals affirmed the conviction in all respects. As to the competence of the child witness, the court noted that by statute, children under ten years of age were precluded from testifying only in cases where they "appear incapable of receiving just impressions of the facts respecting which they are examined or of relating them truly." Such a determination was left to the sound discretion of the trial court.

In this case, prior to receiving the seven-year-old's testimony, the trial court had conducted an inquiry into the witness's competency to testify. Along with correctly answering certain questions regarding herself and the defendant, the child also stated that she understood the difference between telling the truth and lying as well as the consequences that flowed from each type of behavior. Furthermore, the child promised the trial court judge that she would tell the truth in court. Finally, the defense did not question the witness's ability to observe and accurately recount the incident that she testified about. Accordingly, the appellate court noted that it could not be said that the trial court had abused its discretion in finding that the child had been competent to testify and allowing her testimony into evidence.

Case Example (*Wade v. State*, 1991)

The second case example is from the Florida District Court of Appeals. In this case, the child was not found competent to testify.

A man was charged with attempted sexual battery of a child in his neighborhood. The exact date of the incident was unknown, but it was alleged to have occurred within a one-year period between 1987 and 1988. The matter did not come to trial until 1990, when the child was six years old. During *voir dire*, the preliminary examination of the child to determine competency, the child was questioned by both the prosecutor and the defense counsel. She was asked some basic questions about school, her age, and what she was wearing in court. She also answered questions about Santa Claus, the Easter Bunny, and the difference between the truth and a lie. Based on her answers, the trial court found her competent to testify, and the defendant was ultimately convicted.

The defendant's conviction was reversed and the case was remanded for a new trial by the District Court of Appeals of Florida. The court ruled that the trial court failed to make the appropriate findings with respect to the child's competency. The trial court should have considered whether the child was (1) capable of observing and recollecting facts, (2) capable of narrating those facts, and (3) had a "moral sense of obligation to tell the truth." Although the child had been questioned with respect to her ability to recall certain events in the *recent* past, she had not demonstrated an ability to recall events which occurred as long ago as the time period in which the crime charged was alleged to have taken place. Thus, the court found, it was not clear that the child could separate fact from fantasy.

Moreover, the appellate court stated that the *voir dire* failed to indicate the child felt any moral obligation to tell the truth. The court recognized that the child had shown she knew the difference between the truth and a lie. However, according to the court, this was not enough: "Knowing the difference between the truth and a lie does not impute a moral obligation or sense of duty to be truthful." The questions asked of the child did not provide the trial court any basis for a finding that she felt morally compelled to tell the truth.

Finally, the court took note of several other factors which weighed against a finding of competency: the child's delayed disclosure; lack of spontaneity; and contradictions between her testimony in court and her out-of-court statements.

Discussion

The trend in the United States is to presume all witnesses to be competent, administer an oath or affirmation, and permit the jury to determine their credibility (believability). As noted earlier, the Federal Rules of Evidence take this position, as do many states (Federal Rules of Evidence, 1989). The Florida decision runs counter to this trend. A child in that case was expected to demonstrate she knew the difference between the truth and a lie and, in addition, understood her moral obligation or sense of duty to be truthful. These are sophisticated abstract concepts. It would not be difficult to confuse a child with questions concerning them. Indeed, many adults would stumble over these concepts if questioned closely in a courtroom setting.

We believe the better rule is to permit the child to testify and leave to the jury the questions of the child's credibility. In this fashion, the jury is the trier of fact capable of deciding what happened and whom to believe.

Child Development and the Giving of Testimony

Children have different cognitive and communicative abilities from adults. Attorneys may confuse children with abstract and complex questions or misinterpret their responses. When this happens, the truth-finding process is compromised, and the child is sometimes further traumatized (Child Victim Witness Manual, 1992). In order to understand the child witness's performance, it is necessary to understand the basic psychological processes occurring during the event about which testimony will eventually be elicited and the witness's subsequent recall of that event (Penrod, Bull, and Lengnick, 1989).

Early developmental theorists argued that children routinely confuse reality with fantasy (Freud 1959; Piaget 1932). Modern research, however, suggests that children are less likely than adults to differentiate fact from fantasy in some situations but not in others (Lindsay and Johnson, 1987). While children use pretend situations in their play, they seem to know when they are pretending. At this point, there is insufficient evidence to conclude that young children's testimony should be excluded because they cannot differentiate fact from fantasy (Myers, et al., 1989).

In order to understand how the interviewing process can affect a child witness's memory, it is important to have an understanding of the developmental stages of children's memory. A child between the ages of two and four is just learning to use language as a tool for communication. A four-year-old will mix together important details with irrelevant details. Most of the cognitive skills used to recall memories develop between the ages of five and ten. Younger children who lack the skills to recall memories may be at risk for accepting and taking advantage of memorization and recall strategies adults suggest to them (Brown, 1979).

Research on children's understanding of time indicates that it is not until adolescence that children fully master the concept of time (Cole and Lofthus, 1987). Preschoolers are aware of the timing of their routines, but they tend to place events in time based on their own experiences. It is not until they are eight or nine years of age that children understand that there is a constant flowing of time that applies to everyone and is independent of their own activities. However, the fact that children have very limited ability to specify the date and time of specific acts does not imply that what they recall is less accurate (Ceci, Ross, and Toglia, 1987). Children can often give enough specific information to enable others to place the events in time.

The perception and storing of information by children resemble perception and storing or encoding by adults. A witness must selectively attend to only certain stimuli, and these are the stimuli that may be encoded, stored, and retrieved. Thus, perception is a selective process. Many factors can affect recall and recognition of information. These factors can influence the process at any stage: perception, encoding, storage, or retrieval (Penrod, Bull, and Lengnick, 1989).

Children, like adults, store only fragments of their experiences. But children may be more problematic in this area, because they store less of their experiences than adults (Lofthus and Davies, 1984). Studies show that the less complete someone's memory is, the more susceptible that person is to suggestion (Goodman, 1984). Children may also have more difficulty than adults retrieving information from long-term memory (Lofthus and Davies, 1984).

Children bring both strengths and weaknesses to the witness stand. Under certain conditions, they do less well than adults in providing accurate reports, while under other conditions they may remember details that adults have given no attention to (Child Victim Witness Manual, 1992). Overall, children do not have a general memory deficit that renders their testimony untrustworthy. Even children below five years of age can testify when they are asked simple and direct questions. Children do not necessarily remember less than adults do, but they are less proficient at reproducing the information without guidance to stimulate memory.

Case Example (*People v. Jones*, 1990)

A defendant was charged with twenty-eight counts of sexual abuse, perpetrated against four children over an extended period of time. At trial, each victim testified regarding the nature of the sexual contact, the general frequency of the assaults, and the months and years in which the molestation took place. No testimony could be elicited, however, regarding the specific dates, times, or places of any particular assault. The defendant was convicted on twelve counts, and he appealed on the basis that the evidence was insufficient and that a conviction based upon such evidence was violative of his due process rights. The court of appeals reversed the convictions on several counts and affirmed as to others. Further review was then granted by the California Supreme Court.

The supreme court recognized that cases of this sort pose a troublesome conflict between the need to prosecute long-term, repetitive child abusers and the need to respect the accused's rights to tender a complete and vigorous defense to such charges. The supreme court noted that it was understandable that a child victim of long-term, repetitive sexual abuse would not be capable of recalling the specific dates, times, and places of every or any particular assault. On the other hand, the presentation of "generic" victim testimony clearly impaired the accused's ability to defend himself, particularly in terms of any alibi defense which might be raised. The court believed, however, that so long as the victim could describe the kind of sexual contact which had occurred, the number of assaults or their general frequency, and the general time period during which the assaults occurred, a sufficient quantum of proof had been tendered for the trier of fact's consideration and assessment of the weight such testimony would be given. (See also chapter 7.)

As for the defendant's due process claim, the court held that the filing of the information against the defendant, and the subsequent preliminary examination and pretrial discovery, afforded the defendant sufficient notice of the charges and evidence against him. The fact that certain pieces of the victim's story were equally unavailable to both the state and the defendant did not deprive the accused of the ability to defend himself against whatever state evidence was being presented for the trier of fact's consideration. The court therefore concluded that the appellate court's reversal was incorrect, and the convictions on those overturned counts were reinstated.

Discussion

In the *Jones* case, the child victim simply could not remember specific details of her experiences. She knew that she had been abused but could not give the specific time, day, or date of any single act. Even the details of any particular act were general. There were so many alleged acts of abuse that she could testify as to all of them in a general way, but none specifically.

Do you believe that her inability to remember specific details deprived the defendant of his right to cross-examine her effectively? Are there situations in which a child's testimony is so vague about the time that it would be unfair for the defendant to be asked to respond to the charges?

Consistency

Consistency in a child's testimony is an important factor. Generally, the fact that a child's story remains consistent over time increases the likelihood that it is true. But younger children are less able to remain consistent than older children. Children's reports often tend to appear less consistent than those of adults. Children have difficulty systematically evaluating their communications for possible errors, omissions, and contradictions. Children's normal developmental limitations in monitoring communications make it difficult for them to recognize inconsistencies in their stories. Apparent contradictions also may result from their immature reasoning skills.

Preschoolers may often generalize in illogical ways as they make up explanations for what they observe around them, and may not be able to see clearly what is cause and what is effect. For example, Singer and Revenson (1978) report that a preschooler insisted that a dog could cause a train to appear. The youngster reasoned that the train went by because the dog barked. The fact, however, that the child was mistaken about the causal relationship should not disqualify him as a witness; he was able to describe both the train and the dog. We must simply be aware of the limitations in his logical development and make a clear distinction between lies and mistakes.

Children may also try to suppress events that were very frightening for a long period of time. (See the discussion of the sexual abuse accommodation syndrome in chapter 13.) If the child later is able to communicate all the details of the abuse, the later account may appear inconsistent with the early account. In contrast, false accusations may not be accompanied by the same emotional trauma and may actually be more consistent over time (Jones and McQuiston, 1986).

Suggestibility

A major concern is children's purported suggestibility to misleading or inaccurate information. Suggestibility refers to the degree to which the report of an observer changes after the observation to include information that was not present during the event. Are children so suggestible that their testimony should be rejected?

An early study (Lofthus, 1979) indicated that preschool children are susceptible to the incorporation of misleading information at a very young age. More recent studies indicate that children may not necessarily be more suggestible than adults. Two experiments by Duncan, Whitney, and Kunen (1982) suggest that children may in fact be less susceptible than adults to the incor-

poration of misleading information into their existing memories. Furthermore, some research discloses that young children are more resistant to suggestive questioning than many adults believe (Everson and Boat, 1989). The research that has been conducted on the susceptibility of children to suggestive questioning is far from conclusive. Some studies indicate children are more susceptible to suggestion than adults; others point to the opposite conclusion, and some find no difference (Penrod, Bull, and Lengnick, 1989). Overall, studies have not converged on a simple relationship between age and suggestibility (Zaragoza, 1987).

Younger children, however, may be more susceptible to suggestions concerning the details of what they recall (Cohen and Harnick, 1980). Cues used to trigger recall may also contaminate the contents of the memories recalled. Younger children who lack the skills to recall memories will often accept and take advantage of memorization and recall strategies adults suggest to them (Brown, 1979). Leading questions, for example, may serve as cues which help a child recall memories otherwise out of reach (Berliner and Barbieri, 1984).

When a child is prone to susceptibility, it may be because of the child's inability to accurately distinguish among different sources of memories (Flavell, 1985). If an interviewer's words or procedures encourage the child to imagine some event or some of its details, the child may thereafter accept the fantasy as a memory. Children may be vulnerable to memory falsification through repeated interviews suggestively covering the same topic (Christiansen, Sweeney, and Ochalek, 1983). Repeated interviews often occur, and the children may perceive this as a demand for more or different information, feeling that the interviewer was not satisfied with what was already said. If false allegations are repeated often enough in an interview, the child may well come to believe them.

Children may also more readily accept suggestions from someone they see as of a relatively high social status (Ceci, Ross, and Toglia, 1987). Likewise, responses of disbelief or anger by adults may change what children say. In addition, the stress of the interview situation itself with potentially frightening authority figures may inhibit or distort the recounting of events. Feelings of loyalty to one's parents and the desire to protect parents from hearing about bad and painful experiences may also affect the way children give testimony. In many circumstances, children may say what they think adults want to hear (Garbarino and Stott, 1989). It is now standard police policy to interview a child victim out of the presence of the alleged perpetrator even if that person is a parent.

It is apparent that all humans are more susceptible to suggestive influences when their memory is incomplete because of poor encoding or memory deterioration, or when they perceive the interviewer has a high status in relation to themselves. These factors are more often present for the child witness than the adult witness, and it may be that children who are subjected to such investigations are more susceptible to suggestion than adults (Feher, 1988).

Due process requires that the state not convict a defendant upon evidence which is the product of suggestion (*United States v. Wade*, 1966). According to Feher (1988), child witnesses are highly susceptible to suggestion and often undergo suggestive interviews. He concludes that the testimony of children is not reliable enough to ensure due process.

There are two primary sources of contamination in child witness interviews: spontaneous reconstruction by the child alone and suggestive interviewing techniques. It is very important that child interviewers not influence the children either through verbal responses or through body signals. The lines between reassurance, cuing, and suggestion may often be difficult to draw. Since children are often very reluctant to talk about the alleged child abuse, the interviewer often applies some degree of encouragement to make the child respond. Often leading questions are asked. However, the importance of avoiding suggestive interviewing was clearly brought out by the verdict in the *McMartin* trial, where jurors stated that leading

interviews by child psychologists made it impossible for them to reach a guilty verdict, even though they were convinced that the children were in fact victimized. (*People v. Peggy McMartin Buckey*, 1990). There is, therefore, a real need for trained professionals to conduct child witness interviews in controlled interview surroundings.

A child's verbal reports are influenced by the child's age, by the setting in which the conversation takes place, by the person engaging the child in conversation, and by the child's understanding of the immediate situation that he or she finds himself or herself in. Understanding their messages requires information from observations and interactions with a child in more than one context (McNamee and Dowley, 1989).

One prominent innovation in child witness interviewing techniques is the use of anatomically correct dolls. Children are often encouraged to use these dolls to act out the events that they are telling about, on the assumption that such dolls will make the expression less verbal, more accurate, and less stressful for the child. The theory is that children will use the dolls to reveal the abuse without embarrassment even if the child is unwilling or, because of age, unable to verbalize it (Boat and Everson, 1988). The danger in the use of such dolls is that they might stimulate fantasy and play that later might be recalled as the truth. Moreover, the evaluator's personal values and biases may affect interpretations of children's play with the dolls.

The use of these new techniques for child witness interviewing and trial preparation poses a new set of problems for the criminal law system, a system organized around the paramount value of reliability (Christiansen, Sweeney, and Ochalek, 1983). A guiding principle of American criminal justice is that no one shall be branded as a criminal in the absence of demonstrably reliable evidence. If children can be misled by suggestions in pretrial interviews and by being unable to remember correctly, then this principle of reliable testimony is jeopardized. (See chapter 13 for a fuller discussion of some of these issues.)

Case Example (*Ochs v. Martinez*, Texas Court of Appeals, 1990)

A father moved to have the custody provisions of his divorce decree modified because of his belief that the mother's new husband was sexually abusing one of the parties' two children. At trial, the father presented the videotaped testimony of the allegedly abused child, who had been interviewed by a social worker through the use of anatomically correct dolls. Other evidence that supported the father's allegations came in the form of testimony by expert and lay witnesses regarding hearsay statements made by the child. Each of these witnesses was also allowed to state his or her opinion that the child was telling the truth. In opposition, the mother introduced evidence that the child had recanted her accusations during an in-chambers pretrial hearing and that there was no physical or medical indication that the child had been sexually abused. The trial court granted the motion to modify and transferred custody of both children to the father. The mother appealed.

The Texas Court of Appeals reversed the trial court's order and remanded the matter for a new hearing. Pursuant to statute, the videotaped testimony of a child sexual abuse victim could properly be admitted into evidence but only if the interviewer asked open-ended questions that did not suggest a response. Because many of the social worker's questions were leading, the video-taped testimony was impermissibly tainted and should not have been admitted without editing out the child's responses to the offending questions. The appellate court also criticized the admission of the lay and expert witness opinion testimony regarding the victim's veracity. Such testimony invaded the province of the trier of fact as the sole determiner of the credibility of any witness.

Discussion

In this case, the appellate court reversed the trial court's orders because of the unreliability of the truth-finding process. The court found that the interview of the child was conducted so inappropriately that the trier of fact (judge or jury) was receiving questionable information and was unable to reach a fair decision. The court instructed the trial court to edit the improper questions and answers when the case came to court for trial again.

But will this be possible? The child may now remember her earlier testimony as being the truth. She may give the same response to an open-ended question that she gave to the earlier leading question. In other words, once the truth-finding process has been tainted, it may be difficult to start over again with a clean slate. The memories of the leading and suggestive questions and answers may remain.

The appellate court also criticized the trial court because it permitted witnesses to give opinions as to the child victim's veracity. They were asked if they thought the child was telling the truth about the abuse allegations. Both the expert and lay witnesses stated that they believed she was telling the truth.

This is not proper witness testimony. The question whether a witness is telling the truth is one for the trier of fact, the judge or the jury, and no one else. To permit witnesses to give their opinions as to the child victim's veracity is error sufficient for an appellate court to overturn a lower court decision.

Do you agree that it should be left to the judge or jury as trier of fact to determine the credibility of witnesses? Is anyone better able to make that determination? Should that person be able to come to court and help the judge and jury?

Children and Lying

A related issue is whether children lie about being victims of child abuse. Many worry about the extent to which children may have been pressured to complain of being abused, especially in divorce and custody cases. According to Levy (1989), the "children never lie" thesis was dominant in the early explosion of child abuse proceedings. Since then, however, psychologists and other professionals have come to realize that in certain cases children may, in fact, fabricate stories of child abuse, often with the help of a custody-seeking parent (Myers, et al., 1989).

While there is a need for concern about fabricated allegations of child abuse in the context of child custody, our concern should not turn to exaggeration. Nor should it turn to automatic disbelief of a child by the professionals working in the system (Coleman, 1986). In fact, many children may first be abused during a marital breakup because of the stress involved for all concerned. In addition, a number of children may actually first disclose sexual abuse during the breakup of the family, even though it may have occurred prior to the breakup (Corwin, et al., 1987).

While children are capable of deliberate falsehood, there is also clinical experience and research which indicate that children rarely fabricate false accusations of sexual abuse (Berliner and Barbieri, 1984). Experienced mental health professionals must also use their skills to assist in detecting fabricated and coached allegations. Most young children lack the experience required to manufacture detailed and explicit descriptions of sexual abuse. It is important to note whether the child uses age-appropriate language and sentence structure and whether the emotional response and affect are consistent with what is being described. It is also important, however, to realize that some abused children may describe their abuse without apparent feeling, especially when they have been asked to tell their story over and over again to a series of interviewers. Moreover, children who have been severely traumatized may show an emotional numbness in all areas of their lives.

It is important to assess whether the child or parents had a motive to lie about the abuse or whether there are signs of mental illness or disorders that may have led to false accusations. No foolproof technique exists to detect fabricated charges of sexual abuse.

Perception of Child Testimony by Jurors

Myers et al. (1989) note that a child who is consciously and accurately telling the truth may nevertheless be disbelieved by a jury. Juries are typically impressed with testimony that is consistent and certain. If a child's testimony is inconsistent, the child may be disbelieved. A child may also appear timid and hesitant, and too easily influenced by questions from the attorney.

On the other hand, children may be perceived as sincere and less deceitful than adults. Jurors may find it hard to believe that children could have invented the details in an account of sexual abuse. A study by Goodman, Bottoms, Herscovici, and Shaver (1989) examined the effects of age on the perceived credibility of victims of sexual abuse. The researchers used a sexual assault trial scenario in which the victim's age varied from six to fourteen to twenty-two years of age. The testimony of the witness was identical irrespective of her age (although it seems that in reality the testimony of a six-year-old would be quite different from the testimony of a twenty-two-year-old). The study found that the six-year-old was perceived to be significantly more credible than the twenty-two-year-old, while the credibility of the fourteen-year-old did not vary significantly from either the six- or the twenty-two-year-old. The defendant was seen as significantly more guilty when the victim was young. The jurors also seemed to doubt that the youngest victim would fabricate her story, and they seemed to be moved by a need to protect the child from further victimization.

A jury's assessment of a child's credibility can be influenced by the phrasing of questions during direct and cross-examination (Myers, 1987). Children may be asked questions about abstract concepts that they do not understand. Their responses, in turn, may be seen as inconsistencies, rather than misunderstandings. Often the problem lies with the style of questioning, not with the child. If the jury does not see that the line of questioning is developmentally inappropriate, the child may be perceived as a poor witness. For example, what might happen to a child who is asked to respond how many times something happened if he has not yet learned how to count? He may respond with any number that he knows, which might be inconsistent with prior statements. The child is not lying; he is simply trying to give an answer. Yet the jury may perceive it as lying. At the same time, traditional, aggressive methods of cross-examination probably are more likely to promote sympathy for the child and irritation with the defense.

While it is heartening that jurors do not readily believe that young children will fabricate a story of abuse (e.g., Goodman, et al., 1989), it is also prudent to note that a well-rehearsed and coaxed child witness may be more readily seen by a jury as a credible witness. Jurors should not fail to consider the possible impact of suggestive and misleading examination techniques on younger children. The *McMartin* verdict indicated that juries do indeed take such factors into consideration. In general, a child may be more readily believed if the testimony involves description, if he or she was exposed to the defendant over a long period of time, or if the crime was violent (Goodman, Golding, and Haith, 1984).

Case Example (*People v. Stark*, 1992)

The district attorney of San Diego County charged Stark with twelve sexual offenses with Clayton T., a sixth-grade child, also known as "Tyker." All of the counts alleged Stark occupied a special position of trust and engaged in substantial sexual conduct with Clayton. A jury found all

charges and allegations true. Stark was sentenced to state prison for a total term of sixteen years, eight months. The sentence was later modified to a total term of fifteen years in state prison.

Stark had been a sixth-grade teacher since leaving the U.S. Navy and had had a long association with the Boy Scouts, having been a Boy Scout until entering the Navy and an assistant scoutmaster and thereafter scoutmaster of the largest Boy Scout troop in San Diego. Over time, more than a thousand boys had been involved in Stark's Boy Scout troops.

Clayton's oldest brother, Chris, was a member of Stark's scout troop, attaining the rank of Eagle Scout. In the summer of 1986, preparing to enter the sixth grade and celebrate his eleventh birthday, Clayton also joined Stark's scout troop. One of Clayton's first Boy Scout campouts with Stark was a trip to Camp Pendleton. On the trip Clayton slept in a tent next to Stark. Clayton awoke during the night because Stark was fondling his genitals. Clayton didn't know what to do, so he pretended to still be asleep. Clayton was confused because of his fondness for Stark who was "real nice to be around."

In the summer of 1987 Clayton and Stark attended a Boy Scout gathering in Mexico. On one of the nights at this camp-out, Stark reached inside Clayton's sleeping bag and fondled his penis. Then Stark leaned over, put his head inside Clayton's sleeping bag, and orally copulated Clayton. Similar incidents occurred several times over the next few years. Finally, one day Clayton felt he had to tell someone and he told his coach, who in turn got him to talk to the principal and the police. In a subsequent phone call between Clayton and Stark, Stark appeared to acknowledge the sexual abuse.

At the trial, the prosecution presented two other witnesses who also claimed to have been sexually molested by Stark numerous times while they were in his Boy Scout troop, as well as other boys who had noticed his inappropriate behavior. Stark appealed his conviction.

The appellate court noted that a review of the

transcript shows it was not merely Clayton's word against Stark's; to have acquitted Stark the jury would have had to believe not only that Clayton was lying, but that every other prosecution witness was lying as well. In contrast to many prosecutions for child molestations, the victim in this case was an articulate and credible witness whose testimony was fully supported both by his contemporaneous statements to others and the similar acts testimony of several other credible witnesses. As the trial judge stated:

> This case did hinge on credibility. Every one of the prosecutor's young witnesses I found to be very credible, and in particular the complaining witness was a highly credible witness. At one point when he was asked in this courtroom how he felt about the defendant, that was the one time when he emotionally broke down, to show us very spontaneously and clearly that he had the highest regard for this man and had trusted him and had looked up to him and that this testimony was very difficult for him. That rather emotional moment in the courtroom was a very telling one, I believe. (*People v. Stark*, 1992)

Discussion

The issues in the *Stark* case hinged exclusively on the credibility of the witnesses. There was no physical evidence. There were no eyewitnesses. The only evidence was a child victim and some other young boys stating that sexual abuse took place and the defendant stating that it did not.

The jury clearly believed the young victim and did not believe the defendant. It is likely that the testimony of the other boys who had similar experiences helped the jury make its determination.

Would the jury have reached the same decision if there had been no corroborating witnesses? What if the case had been presented simply as the child's statements against the defendant's denials? Would the jury have believed the child was more

credible? Would it have found guilt beyond a reasonable doubt? After all, in a criminal court it is not whether the jury is slightly persuaded of a defendant's guilt. The jury must be satisfied beyond a reasonable doubt. This high burden might have resulted in an acquittal for the defendant without the other child witnesses. Indeed, the district attorney might not have ever filed the charges had it been one victim's word against one respected adult's denials.

This one-on-one scenario is repeated in child sexual abuse cases. Sexual activity is usually private, and often there is only one victim alleging the abuse. The credibility of the child victim and the accused is the issue that the legal system must determine.

Interactions among Factors

It is important to realize that all of the factors discussed interact with many situational factors as well as the child's personality and family situation. Some children may have a better support system than others. An intrafamilial abuse situation may be experienced very differently from abuse committed by a stranger. Children of the same age differ in their temperament and their ability to cope with the traumatic situation that brought them to the court. Where one child might become depressed and anxious, another may react with anger and hostility. Where one child might be too shy or fearful to answer the questions of attorneys, another may be able to answer questions clearly and competently. These differences have nothing to do with the truthfulness of their testimony, and yet the jurors may judge such variations very differently (*Child Victim Witness Manual*, 1992).

SECONDARY VICTIMIZATION

Secondary victimization refers to the secondary trauma suffered by many children simply by having to participate in the investigation process and court hearings.

The Settings for Child Witness Testimony

Children who are alleged victims of child abuse are interviewed by law enforcement and social services investigators in a variety of settings during the course of an investigation. Although the initial contact may be in the child's home, subsequent interviews are generally conducted at the interviewer's work site, rather than in a setting that takes the needs of the child into consideration. As discussed in chapter 3, children may be interviewed by a variety of professionals, such as law enforcement officers, social workers, physicians, nurses, mental health professionals, prosecutors, defense attorneys, and probation officers. The children may also be questioned by curious onlookers, such as uninvolved agency personnel, neighbors, school authorities, and relatives. Children frequently suffer emotional trauma from the frequent requests from numerous interviewers to retell their stories. Such reinterviewing often can have a detrimental effect upon the child, who may refuse to answer further questions, purposely change his or her story, or even decide not to participate further in the prosecution.

In addition to the investigative process, children appear as witnesses throughout the court system. They may appear as the alleged victims in a criminal prosecution, as subjects of protective dependency actions and as subjects of a custody dispute in a domestic relations action. All of these settings can be intimidating or frightening to children.

Case Example (*Hochheiser v. Superior Court*, 1984)

A defendant was accused of two counts of lewd conduct with a minor under the age of fourteen. At a pretrial conference, the prosecutor requested that the two complaining witnesses be allowed to testify via closed-circuit television from the jury room instead of in open court. The prosecutor indicated that the witnesses would be able to see the defendant and the cross-examiner, and the defendant would be able to see the witnesses. The defense counsel objected, stating that the procedure would deprive the defendant of a fair trial.

The prosecutor presented testimony by the victims' parents in support of the motion. The father of ten-year-old T. B. testified that, at the time of the preliminary hearing, his son, who was shy about his "private parts," had said that he did not want to talk about the incident in front of a lot of people. After the preliminary hearing, T. B. "went through several nights of nightmares and a round of bed-wetting." The father said he had not discussed with his son anything about testifying in court for over a year.

The mother of nine-year-old S. W. testified that when her son exited the courtroom after the preliminary examination, he was "totally distraught . . . in tears and couldn't . . . talk" and "started reverting back to baby-like behavior," such as wanting to wear diapers. Over a year later, when she told him that he would be coming to court to testify, he burst into tears and went up to his room, indicating there was no way he was going back to court, and that if he did come to court he would say, "I don't know anything." She claimed he started to talk baby talk and picked up a diaper that his mother was using as a rag and waved it at her. He seemed to be eating less, which concerned her, because he had cystic fibrosis.

The trial court indicated it had the inherent power to permit such closed-circuit television. The defendant filed a writ of prohibition with the appellate court asking that court to prohibit the trial court from utilizing the closed-circuit television procedure.

The appellate court granted the writ and prohibited the trial court from utilizing the closed-circuit procedure. The appellate court ruled that the trial court had no authority to utilize the procedure and that the legislature should first authorize such an innovation. The court noted that there may be significant differences in the quality of witnesses' testimony over closed-circuit television and concluded by saying:

> The use of closed-circuit television for the main complaining witnesses in a criminal trial encompasses a drastic change in our system of jurisprudence. It, among other things, may impinge upon cross-examination, the very heart of the tools used for truth finding and described by the United States Supreme Court . . . as the "greatest legal engine ever invented for the discovery of truth." Such a major step should be taken, "if at all, only upon the considered judgment of the Legislature" (citing cases). (*Hochheiser v. Superior Court*, 1984)

Discussion

The facts of the *Hochheiser* case indicate the potential for secondary victimization of children who participate in the criminal court process. In addition to the investigatory process and the interviews they endured before the formal court proceedings, the two child victim witnesses appeared in court at the preliminary hearing, a formal hearing before a magistrate to determine if there is probable cause to believe that a felony has been committed and the defendant committed the crime. Then they had to appear in the jury trial for further examination and cross-examination about the alleged abuse.

If the stress of testimony were not enough, consider the fact that more than a year passed between the preliminary hearing and the trial. The fact that the criminal case could not be resolved more quickly is a different form of secondary victimization.

Addressing the Needs of Child Victim Witnesses

In recent years, several states have moved to accommodate the special needs of child victim witnesses. These measures have included changing the interview protocol to reduce the number of interviews, using specially trained interviewers, establishing a central location for the interviews, creating a child-oriented environment at the interview location, and using videotapes to preserve the interview. Many jurisdictions have already set up special prosecutorial units to deal with children.

While it is probably impossible to avoid suggestibility altogether in child witness interviewing, the use of videotapes can provide an objective means by which all parties involved can assess the degree of suggestibility that might have taken place. Whether or not such videotaped interviews can be admitted as evidence at the trial, they can provide evidence about the interview process itself and the procedures used. What takes place in the interviews may be the most important issue in a sexual abuse trial. Yet, the interviewing process is not always well documented. Without a record of the interview process, there is no way to determine whether the testimony is a product of actual experience or suggestion. To combat some of these problems, in recent years many studies have been conducted on how to interview abused children (e.g., Jones and McQuiston, 1986) and how to assess child abuse (e.g., Berliner, 1988; White, Santilli, and Quinn, 1988).

The American Bar Association advocates using a team approach in interviewing, a speedy trial, modifications of court procedures and protocols to accommodate young children, and legislative initiatives to change the law, (American Bar Association, 1988). The National Council of Juvenile and Family Court Judges (1986) recommends that alternative methods to testifying be used whenever possible. If children have to testify, however, the Council recommends that judges should not question the competency of the child, but rather let the jury decide credibility as they do for adults. Judges are encouraged to ensure sensitivity to children both in and out of the courtroom. Prosecutors may prepare the child to testify by bringing the child into an empty courtroom to become familiar with the setting. Many states will allow a special child advocate to accompany the child into the courtroom.

Once the child is on the stand and under oath, the attorneys involved should use simple questions and language designed to place the child at ease (Myers, 1987). Use of legal terminology should be avoided. Direct examinations should start with questions designed to put the child at ease. Many adversarial practices common in the courtroom have unintended effects on child witnesses and their testimony. The California Attorney General's Task Force on Child Victim-Witnesses recommended that guidelines for examining and cross-examining a child witness should be determined by the judge and discussed with counsel before children testify (California Child Victim-Witness Judicial Advisory Committee [1988]). For example, objections would be required to be argued when the child is excused or at the side bar out of the child's earshot. The judge should control the questioning of children by all attorneys to ensure that the questions are age-appropriate, and should be prepared to rephrase the question. The testimony should be scheduled with sensitivity to the child's daily routine to minimize fatigue and distractibility. The child should be given frequent regularly scheduled breaks, and the courtroom should be rearranged to make it a less intimidating place for children whenever necessary. Finally, juries should routinely be instructed that they cannot expect adult behavior from young children and that efforts to reduce a child's fear and stress are appropriate and have no bearing on credibility.

In California, several new laws call attention to the needs of the child victim in the courtroom. Penal Code Section 868.8 permits the court to take frequent recesses to accommodate the needs of the child (California Penal Code, 1991). The judge can also remove his or her robe if that is thought to be less intimidating. In addition, there is a provision for exclusion of the public from preliminary examinations when the child might suffer serious psychological harm. Similarly, Penal Code Section 868.5 provides that in certain cases a child may choose two support persons to accompany him or her. One of these may be a witness, and one may accompany the child to the witness stand.

A swift resolution of a criminal case is also in the best interest of a child victim. Children, particularly younger children, may forget what happened as time passes. More importantly, the longer the child has to wait for a resolution of a case, the longer he or she remains under pressure (Sagatun and Edwards, 1989). The accused, on the other hand, generally prefers to have the trial postponed. There are several reasons for this. The defense may have investigation to complete. Delay may make it harder for the child witness to recall details of the event, or the child may become unavailable for trial. The State of California has clearly resolved this issue in favor of the child victim witness by declaring that all criminal actions in which a child is a victim or a material witness shall take precedence over all other criminal actions. Such trials must commence within thirty days of arraignment unless the court finds good cause for continuance.

All of these procedures nationwide are designed to assist the child victim as he or she faces the criminal justice system. They are intended to reduce any unnecessary trauma he or she may suffer by repeated interviews, exposure to the courtroom, and other pressures related to the adjudication of the case. Many of these procedures have yet to be tested in the appellate courts. These procedures must always be balanced against the need to provide the defendant with a fair and impartial trial. It is the interaction between the child's needs and the defendant's right to a fair trial that we turn to in the next two chapters.

CONCLUSION

This chapter has described various ways in which the court system has tried to accommodate itself to the special needs of the child victim witness. The crucial issue is the capacity of the legal system to respond appropriately to the needs of children with different competencies without jeopardizing the reliability and truthfulness of the testimony and to reduce secondary victimization for child victim witnesses.

CHAPTER 11

Confrontation: The Rights of the Accused versus Protection of the Victim

Many child abuse cases are difficult to prove in court without testimony from the allegedly abused child. In physical abuse cases, it is usually clear from medical evidence that something has happened to the child. In sexual abuse cases, there is often nothing more than the words of a child. When that child is very young or reluctant to testify, proof of the abuse can become very difficult. Moreover, since the dramatic rise in child abuse cases in the 1980s, many observers have noted that the child who alleges that she or he has been the victim of sexual abuse may also suffer from her or his contacts with the legal system.

Legislators and courts have responded to the perception that some children are re-abused by the legal system. They have developed procedural and evidentiary changes that are designed to reduce the trauma a child might suffer while in the legal system. Five different types of changes have been proposed. The first type aims at reducing the number of times a child might have to be interviewed or examined, whether in or out of court. These changes include videotaped testimony and rules limiting access to a child, whether for interviews or examinations. The second type of change has been the expansion of rules of evidence so that the words of the child can be presented in court by another person. Examples of this include the broadening of the hearsay exceptions.

The third type of change has been to permit the child to testify outside of the presence of the accused under specified circumstances. That is the focus of this chapter. The fourth type of change has been the expansion of the use of expert witnesses to describe what they believe has happened to a particular child. That will be addressed in chapter 12. The fifth category of change has been to modify the court setting so that it is more sensitive to the needs of the child witness. Changes in the law include the addition of support persons for the child witness, frequent recesses for the child, and reducing the formality of the court setting.

Many of these changes are controversial. Some observers believe that the delicate balance between the power of the state and the rights of the individual should not be disturbed. Attempts to compensate for the needs of the child witness are perceived as unfairly tipping the balance against the accused.

The focus of much of the debate surrounding these changes has been the Confrontation Clause of the U.S. Constitution: "In all criminal prosecutions, the accused shall enjoy the right . . . to be confronted with the witnesses against him" (Amendment VI). Closely related to the right to confront one's accusers is the right to cross-examine those persons. These concepts of confrontation and cross-examination are fundamental in American jurisprudence.

When the confrontation and cross-examination involve a child who may have been the victim of abuse by the person who is present to face the child, many have reexamined the nature of the right. When the accused is a person who is in a position of authority in the child's life, such as a parent, the problem becomes even more complex.

Although the appellate courts have by no means answered all of the questions raised by the new statutes and lower court rulings in these cases, several conclusions can be drawn. First, the Confrontation Clause will probably not be significantly diluted by the new procedures. Second, in noncriminal cases (civil, juvenile, and domestic relations) the right to confront one's accusers is likely to give way to many of the new procedures if a sufficient showing is made on behalf of the child.

In this chapter we review the three most common ways of avoiding direct confrontation in different types of court settings:

1. taking live testimony out of sight of the accused;
2. use of simultaneous closed-circuit television; and
3. use of videotaped depositions or testimony.

TAKING LIVE TESTIMONY OUT OF SIGHT OF THE ACCUSED

Several different methods have been employed to take child testimony out of the sight of the accused, ranging from seating the defendant and victim back to back and rearranging the seating to the use of "high tech" protective shields. In the past, attorneys have often used their own bodies to shield the victim from the defendant or have asked their witnesses not to look directly at the defendant when testifying.

Criminal Court Proceedings

In *State v. Strable* (1981), an Iowa court held that the fact that the witness testified behind a blackboard was, at most, a harmless error. In a similar case the same year, however, an appellate court in California reversed the conviction of the accused because he had been hidden from the victim during her testimony, even though he had remained in the same room as the child witness (*Herbert v. Superior Court*, 1981). In another California case, *People v. Serna* (1989), the trial court rearranged the courtroom so that the six-year-old child victim, who was reluctant to testify, was seated with her back to the defendant during her testimony. The rearrangement was held to be in error but considered harmless. In a prelude to *Coy v. Iowa*, the U.S. Supreme Court decided in *Kentucky v. Stincer* (1987) that a defendant's confrontation rights were not violated by his exclusion from a hearing to determine the competency of two child witnesses in a sexual abuse case. Thus, prior to *Coy*, very different opinions appeared to have been reached over apparently similar circumstances.

In *Coy v. Iowa* (1988), the U.S. Supreme Court confronted the issue of shielding the victims from defendants through the use of screens in the courtroom. In doing so the Court, for the first time, considered the constitutionality of the new laws enacted across the nation to shield child victims from direct confrontation with their assailants.

Case Example (*Coy v. Iowa,* 1988)

The defendant was arrested and charged with sexually assaulting two thirteen-year-old girls while they were camping in the backyard of the house next to his home. The girls said that the defendant entered their tent after they were asleep wearing a stocking over his head, shined a flashlight in their eyes, and warned them not to look at him. Neither was able to describe his face.

At the trial, the prosecutor made a motion pursuant to a recently enacted Iowa statute to allow the complaining witnesses to testify either via a closed-circuit television or behind a screen. The trial court approved of the use of a large screen to be placed between the defendant and the witness stand during the girls' testimony. After adjusting the courtroom lighting, the screen enabled the defendant dimly to perceive the witnesses, but they could not see him at all.

The defendant objected to the use of the screen, arguing that it denied him his right to confront his accusers. He also noted that the screen denied him due process of law, since it made him appear guilty and thus eroded the presumption of innocence. The trial court rejected his claims and instructed the jury to draw no inferences of guilt from the screen.

The jury convicted the defendant. The Iowa Supreme Court affirmed the conviction and rejected the defendant's claims that his right to confrontation and his due process rights had been violated. The defendant appealed to the U.S. Supreme Court.

The Supreme Court reversed the trial court, overturning the conviction. Justice Scalia noted in the majority opinion that

We have never doubted that the Confrontation Clause guarantees the defendant a face-to-face meeting with the witnesses appearing before the trier of fact. . . . The perception that confrontation is essential to fairness has persisted over the centuries because there is much truth to it. . . . [F]ace-to-face presence may, unfortunately, upset the truthful rape victim or abused child; but by the same token, it may confound and undo the false accuser, or reveal the child coached by a malevolent adult. It is a truism that constitutional protections have costs.

The Supreme Court then addressed whether the right to confrontation was violated in the case at hand. The Court found that the screen was designed to deny the defendant his ability to confront the witnesses. As such, it was found to be a violation of the defendant's right to a face-to-face encounter.

Justice Scalia went on to explain that, for there to be an exception to the Confrontation Clause, there must be an individualized finding that the particular witnesses needed special protection. Since the procedure in the case was pursuant to a statute and not to any demonstrated need for protection by the witnesses, there was no exception which would permit the judgment to be sustained.

Justice Scalia wrote for a divided Supreme Court. Several justices concurred in his decision but not in the reasoning he utilized. Several justices dissented from his decision. Most significantly, in a concurring opinion Justice O'Connor stated:

> I agree with the Court that appellant's rights under the Confrontation Clause were violated in this case. I write separately only to note my view that those rights are not absolute, but rather may give way in an appropriate case to other competing interests, so as to permit the use of certain procedural devices designed to shield a child witness from the trauma of courtroom testimony. . . .
>
> While I agree with the Court that the Confrontation Clause was violated in this case, I wish to make clear that nothing in today's decision necessarily dooms such efforts by state legislatures

to protect child witnesses. . . . Moreover, even if a particular procedure runs afoul of the Confrontation Clause's general requirement, it may come within an exception that permits its use. . . .

> Thus, I would permit use of a particular trial procedure that called for something other than face-to-face confrontation, if that procedure was necessary to further an important public policy. The protection of child witnesses is, in my view and in the view of a substantial majority of the states, just such a policy. The primary focus, therefore, likely will be on the necessity prong. . . . But if a court makes a case-specific finding of necessity, as is required by a number of state statutes, our cases suggest that the strictures of the Confrontation Clause may give way to the compelling state interest of protecting child witnesses.

The Chief Justice and Justice Blackman dissented and argued that the statute should have been upheld because, while face-to-face confrontation is preferred, it can be waived by the mere fact of the state legislative presumption. In addition, they noted that the victim's testimony was given under oath, that there was unrestricted cross-examination in the presence of the defendant, and that the defendant could see and hear the testimony.

Discussion

The Supreme Court was more closely divided than is suggested by the 6-to-2 vote (Justice Kennedy did not participate). Four justices appeared to take the position that the Confrontation Clause requires a face-to-face meeting in almost all circumstances, while the other four were willing to recognize exceptions.

Obviously, this is not an easy issue to resolve. A defendant will have less of an opportunity to prevail in trial if he is not able to confront his accusers. On the other hand, some accusers may not be willing to undergo the ordeal of face-to-face confrontation and will refuse to testify. Recall the attitude of the children in the *Hochheiser* (1984) case discussed in the previous chapter.

Do you agree with Justice Scalia that there is an appearance of guilt if a screen is placed between the child witness and the defendant during the witness testimony? Should the jury be told that the children are afraid of the defendant? Will it be sufficient for the judge to instruct the jury to disregard the screen?

The decision in *Coy v. Iowa* at first glance suggests that innovations to help the child victim witness will not hold constitutional muster in the Supreme Court. Many saw it as a devastating blow for the crusade to help the child victim of abuse. However, the concurring opinion by Justice O'Connor makes it possible to see this decision in a different light. Justice O'Connor stated that the Confrontation Clause is not absolute and may give way in an appropriate case to other competing interests to permit procedural devices to shield a child witness from the trauma of courtroom testimony. Nothing in the *Coy v. Iowa* decision, she said, dooms two-way closed-circuit television or other efforts to protect the child witnesses. Thus, the high court left open the possibility that an exception could be justified with proof that individual child witnesses needed protection.

The Supreme Court's decision in *Coy* caused a number of states to reexamine their child witness protection statutes. Since *Coy*, the majority of state appellate court decisions have held their child witness protection statutes are not violative of the defendant's Sixth Amendment rights only if:

1. the statute does not contain a blanket presumption of trauma in all child witness cases; and
2. the state is able to establish a particularized showing of necessity warranting protection.

In these cases, the state's interest in protecting child abuse victim witnesses has been held as an important or compelling state interest, such that a balancing test needs to be employed to make the specific finding suggested in *Coy*. Although most state courts interpret *Coy* as requiring a particularized showing of necessity in upholding their child witness protection statute, there is some difference of opinion as to what constitutes a sufficient finding of trauma to protect the child rather than the defendant.

Juvenile Court Dependency Proceedings

Many of the difficulties with children testifying discussed under criminal court proceedings also hold true for child victim testimony in juvenile court. However, since juvenile court action for dependency matters typically is civil in nature, and does not involve the potential loss of liberty for the accused, the juvenile court judge is often able to relax the formal requirements.

In *In re Stanley F.* (1978), the mother's confrontation rights were not violated by her exclusion during her eight-year-old child's testimony when all counsel was present. In this case the child's testimony was transcribed by a reporter, and counsel for the mother was afforded an opportunity to discuss the testimony given in chambers with the mother.

In *In re Tanya P.* (1981), the California appellate court concluded that the lower court had properly excluded the stepfather during the minor's testimony. Based on allegations that an eight-year-old minor's stepfather sexually molested her on a number of occasions, the defendant was allowed to appear through her attorney, who thoroughly cross-examined her, and where the testimony was transcribed by a reporter and made available to the defendant. Likewise, in *In re Mary S.* (1986), the minor witnesses who were afraid to testify in front of their parents did not violate the parents' confrontation rights by testifying in chambers, outside their parents' presence but in the presence of all counsel. In *State v. John C.* (1986) the Maine appellate court found that the juvenile court may limit cross-examination of the victim when the evidence is simply calculated to embarrass or harass the witness and is only collaterally relevant.

In one of the first juvenile court cases after the *Coy* decision was handed down, a court in Rhode Island, in *In re Michael C.* (1989), determined that a child's testimony may be taken in chambers with only the judge and a reporter present. The adoption of a special procedure to protect the child, if the trial justice deems it appropriate, was seen as a discretionary matter. This court decided that *Coy v. Iowa* had no relevancy to the issues pending in this case, because it did not involve a criminal prosecution. These abuse and neglect actions were determined to be civil in nature. In civil abuse and neglect prosecutions such as this one, the court held that the parents possessed no rights to face-to-face confrontation. The court also held that due process was satisfied by the procedure utilized by the trial court, in light of the demonstrated likelihood of harm to the child if he were compelled to give face-to-face testimony. The fact that the child was thirteen years old did not insulate him from the possibility of traumatization.

Similarly, the decision in *In the Interest of J.D.S., A Child v. Iowa* (1989), rested on the finding that delinquency actions are not criminal, and that the same rights for defendants do not apply. In this case a sixteen-year-old was adjudicated a delinquent for sexually abusing a four-year-old boy. The court made particular findings that the victim would be traumatized by confrontation with the accused. The juvenile court ordered a protective screen, which was a one-way mirror that allowed the accused to see the victim but the victim could not see the accused. The court held that this was a juvenile delinquency proceeding and not a criminal prosecution, and that the criminal court rights did not apply. The one-way mirror was all right, because there were individualized findings that trauma would result without citing O'Connor's concurrence. In addition, counsel for the juvenile experienced great difficulty in cross-examining the four-year-old, but since there

was some cross-examination, the motion to strike his testimony was denied.

Domestic Relations Court Proceedings

While there are no statutes restricting testimony of the child in domestic relations cases, many judges are reluctant to have a child testify in court in front of his or her parents. Instead, children often testify in the judges' chambers. This can be done with or without attorneys or a court reporter and with any special rules to which the court and parties may agree. However, there are no provisions that specifically allow the judge to do this without the parents' permission or to take the child's testimony without the parents' presence. If a parent insists on being present during the child's testimony, the judge cannot prevent it (Edwards, 1987). Thus, there are fewer protections afforded the child in domestic relations court than in juvenile court or in criminal court.

THE USE OF SIMULTANEOUS CLOSED-CIRCUIT TELEVISION

The use of simultaneous closed-circuit television is a more common procedure than the use of screening devices or other means of keeping the defendant out of sight of the child victim. According to Justice O'Connor's concurring opinion in *Coy*, while Iowa appears to be the only state authorizing the type of screen used in that case, more than half of the states have authorized the use of one- or two-way closed-circuit television. Statutes sanctioning one-way systems generally permit the child to testify in a separate room in which only the judge, counsel, technicians and, in some cases, the defendant are present. The child's testimony is broadcast into the courtroom for viewing by the jury. Two-way systems permit the child witness to see the courtroom and the defendant over a video monitor. Closed-circuit television is one of the most important innovations to be used in child abuse trials. It is relatively simple to set up in courtrooms and the adjoining judges' chambers. It is the device that most closely resembles face-to-face confrontation.

Criminal Court Proceedings

By the end of 1989, thirty-two states had statutes that permit judges to allow certain child witnesses to testify via closed-circuit television to the court and jury (Whitcomb, 1992). In California, for example, the legislature has authorized the use of contemporaneous closed-circuit television under specified conditions (California Penal Code, 1991, section 1347). In specific cases, this statute permits the accused and the child to be in separate rooms while the child testifies, each being able to see the other through closed-circuit television monitors. This legislative reform has not been widely used in California, partly because of the costs involved and partly because many prosecutors are unwilling to try this procedure. Many prosecutors believe the procedure detracts from the persuasiveness of the child's testimony (Sagatun and Edwards, 1989).

In the Victims of Child Abuse Act of 1990, Congress provided for alternatives to live in-court testimony for the child victim, such as two-way closed-circuit television. According to subchapter IV, Federal Victim's Protections and Rights, (42 USC, Sect. 13031), testimony of the child shall be taken by closed-circuit television if the court finds that the child is unable to testify in open court in the presence of the defendant, for any of the following reasons:

(i)   The child is unable to testify because of fear;
(ii) There is a substantial likelihood, established by expert testimony, that the child would suffer emotional trauma from testifying;
(iii) The child suffers a mental or other infirmity;
(iv) Conduct by defendant or defense counsel causes the child to be unable to continue testifying.

The Act also provides that the court shall support a ruling on the child's inability to testify with findings on the record. In determining whether the impact on an individual child is so substantial as to justify the use of closed-circuit television, the court may question the minor in chambers, or at some comfortable place other than the courtroom, on the record, for a reasonable period of time, with the child attendant, the prosecutor, the child's attorney, the guardian *ad litem*, and the defense counsel present.

Prior to *Coy*, in a case from Kentucky, *Commonwealth v. Willis* (1986), a divided court held that a statute allowing testimony of a child under age twelve by videotape before trial, by closed-circuit during trial, or in-court screening, was constitutional under state and federal face-to-face confrontation clauses. The five-year-old victim refused to respond at a competency hearing held in chambers when the defendant was present. Even though the Kentucky confrontation clause requires "meeting witnesses face-to-face," the court held that there could be an exception to this provision, and that there was no constitutional right to eyeball-to-eyeball confrontation.

In 1987, in *Commonwealth v. Ludwig*, the Pennsylvania Superior Court reached the same conclusion, in affirming a sexual assault conviction when a five-year-old testified by closed circuit after she "froze emotionally and was unable to testify in the presence of her father." The court concluded that the "right to confront does not confer upon an accused the right to intimidate."

Since *Coy* most courts have held that a particular finding of trauma to the child in confronting the defendant must be made before the use of closed-circuit television is allowed. For example, the Kansas Supreme Court adopted a very strict criterion as to what constitutes a particularized showing in *State v. Chrisholm* (1989). While the statutory language in Kansas neither required a particular showing nor established criteria from which a court could base its decision, the

Kansas Supreme Court upheld the statute by reading into it a requirement that a particularized showing of necessity as specified in *Coy* be made. The court ruled that, in order to invoke the statutory procedure, the trial judge must first make an individualized finding that there is clear and convincing evidence that to require a child to testify in open court will so traumatize him or her as to prevent the child from reasonably communicating with the jury or render him or her unavailable to testify.

Similarly, the New Jersey Superior Court in *State v. McCutcheon* (1988) ruled that in order to use a statute permitting a child witness to testify by closed-circuit television, there must be a substantial likelihood that the child would suffer severe emotional or mental distress if he or she were to testify in open court. In *People v. Henderson* (1990), the New York Supreme Court reversed a baby-sitter's conviction, because the trial court's finding of the child's "vulnerability" necessitating the use of closed-circuit television was based solely on an expert's testimony that all sexually abused children would benefit from this procedure. The court ruled that a particularized finding is necessary to justify the use of closed-circuit television.

The *Coy* case and the subsequent cases discussed above left unclear exactly what was needed to establish a particularized showing of trauma to the child victim. The *Maryland v. Craig* (1990) case gave the U.S. Supreme Court the opportunity to spell out in more detail the means by which such a showing of trauma could be made. More importantly, this case tested the constitutionality of the frequent use of one-way closed-circuit television as a means of protecting the child victim witness.

Case Example (*Maryland v. Craig*)

Maryland v. Craig involved a highly publicized prosecution of a woman who owned a day-care

center near Washington, D.C. The trial judge relied on testimony by therapists, who had been working with the four children for a year and who stated that to be in the defendant's presence would be so traumatic for the children that they would not be able to testify at all. The children were allowed to testify using one-way closed-circuit television, and the defendant was found guilty. The appellate court, however, overturned the lower court conviction, and interpreted *Coy* to mean that the victim needed to be questioned in the defendant's presence to establish trauma, and that expert testimony alone was not sufficient.

In its appeal to the U.S. Supreme Court, the state attorney general argued that the Maryland appeals court had misunderstood the Supreme Court's *Coy v. Iowa* decision. The state's brief said that the state court had erroneously and illogically required that the child be exposed to the very psychological and physical trauma that the protective measure, suggested by O'Connor in *Coy*, was intended to prevent. The U. S. Supreme Court agreed; the majority vacated the Maryland Court of Appeals' finding and remanded the case.

The facts as recited by the U.S. Supreme Court majority were that:

> In October 1986, a Howard County jury charged respondent, Sandra Ann Craig, with child abuse, first and second degree sexual offense, perverted sexual practice, assault, and battery. The named victim in each count was Brooke Etze, a six-year-old child who, from August 1984 to June 1986, had attended a kindergarten and pre-kindergarten center owned and operated by Craig.
>
> In March 1987, before the case went to trial, the State sought to invoke a Maryland statutory procedure that permits a judge to receive, by one-way closed-circuit television, the testimony of a child victim who is alleged to be a victim of child abuse. To invoke the procedure, the trial judge must first determine that the testimony by the child victim in the courtroom will result in the child suffering emotional distress such that the child cannot reasonably communicate (Md. Cts. and Jud. Proc. Code Ann. section 9-102, 1989). Once the procedure is invoked, the child witness,

prosecutor, and defense counsel withdraw to a separate room; the judge, jury, and defendant remain in the courtroom. The child witness is then examined and cross-examined in the separate room, while a video monitor records and displays the witness's testimony to those in the courtroom. During this time the witness cannot see the defendant. The defendant remains in electronic communication with defense counsel, and objections may be made and ruled on as if the witnesses were testifying in the courtroom.

In support of its motion invoking the one-way closed-circuit television procedure, the State presented expert testimony that Brooke, as well as a number of other children who were alleged to have been sexually abused by Craig, would suffer "serious emotional distress such that they could not reasonably communicate" if required to testify in the courtroom.

The court noted that the defendant Craig objected to the use of the procedure, complaining that she would be denied her right to be face-to-face with her accuser. The trial court, however, overruled the defendant's objection, finding that if any one of the children was forced to testify in open court, it would result in serious emotional distress, which would have an impact on the child's ability to communicate.

The Maryland Court of Appeals reversed the trial court's decision regarding the use of closed-circuit television in this case, finding that the showing made by the prosecutor was insufficient to invoke the special procedure.

The U.S. Supreme Court reversed the Maryland Court of Appeals and affirmed the order of the trial court. Justice O'Connor gave the majority opinion of the court. She noted that in passing the law permitting closed-circuit television, the state had a substantial interest in protecting children who are allegedly victims of child abuse from the trauma of testifying against the alleged perpetrator. She went on to say:

> We conclude today that a State's interest in the physical and psychological well-being of child abuse victims may be sufficiently important to outweigh, at least in some cases, a defendant's right to face his or her accusers in court. Accordingly, we hold that, if the State makes an adequate showing of necessity, the state interest in protecting child witnesses from the trauma of testifying in a child abuse case is sufficiently important to justify the use of a special procedure that permits a child witness in such cases to testify at trial against a defendant in the absence of face-to-face confrontation with the defendant.

Justice O'Connor noted that the trial court must find that the child witness would be traumatized, not by the courtroom generally, but by the presence of the defendant. Moreover, the trial court must find that the emotional distress suffered by the child witness in the presence of the defendant is more than mere nervousness or excitement or some reluctance to testify. She then pointed out that the Maryland statute requires a determination that the child witness will suffer "serious emotional distress such that the child cannot reasonably communicate," a standard easily meeting the minimum showing necessary.

Discussion

In her opinion, O'Connor delineated four elements of confrontation: physical presence of the witness; testifying under oath; cross-examination; and observation of the witness's demeanor by the trier of fact. Since closed-circuit television incorporates all of these elements, the opinion implied that such testimony is functionally equivalent to "live" testimony. Do you agree? Do you also agree with the main conclusions in *Maryland v. Craig* that:

1. closed-circuit testimony did not violate the constitutional right to face-to-face confrontation if the procedure required that the child witness testify under oath, was subject to cross-examination, and the defendant, the jury,

and the judge could observe the witness's demeanor;

2. if the trial court finds (on a case-by-case basis) that the special procedure is necessary to protect the child's welfare, and that testifying in defendant's presence would cause the child trauma and emotional distress; and

3. the emotional stress that the child would suffer by having to testify without the closed-circuit television must be more than mere reluctance to testify, nervousness, or excitement, but it is not necessary to establish this through a face-to-face meeting between the defendant and the victim.

Maryland v. Craig was decided on a 5–4 vote. One of the most conservative justices, Justice Scalia, joined with the more liberal justices in dissent, stating that the Sixth Amendment applied to all criminal prosecutions and that exceptions cannot be carved for child witnesses in the interests of public policy. They asserted strongly that the Constitution does not permit the Court to balance the interests between the defendant and the child victim. They concluded that seldom has the Court failed so conspicuously to sustain a categorical guarantee of the Constitution against the tide of prevailing current opinion.

On remand from the Supreme Court, the Maryland Court of Appeals affirmed its previous holding in *Craig v. Maryland* (1991). In *Maryland v. Craig* (1990) the Supreme Court had rejected as a matter of federal constitutional law the Maryland court's requirement that the judge must question the child in the defendant's presence to determine whether the child would be traumatized. The Maryland court, however, reiterated its strict standard for a finding of emotional distress, and held that the judge should question the child personally, preferably in the defendant's presence. While it acknowledged that, under the Supreme Court's ruling, such a pretrial interview in the defendant's presence is not constitutionally required, the Maryland court chose to impose this discretionary requirement as a matter of state law.

According to the Court, the pretrial interview "should be the rule rather than the exception" under Maryland law (*Supreme Court News*, 1991).

While the Supreme Court decision in *Maryland v. Craig* has been applauded, many child advocates view *Craig* as a setback because of its focus on the presence of the defendant, and not the entire courtroom setting, for determining whether the child witness will suffer emotional trauma (McCarthy, 1992). According to McCarthy in the aftermath of *Craig*, many prosecuting attorneys may be reluctant to utilize child witness protection statutes, believing that they will not be capable of showing that the child's trauma would be caused solely by the presence of the defendant. Likewise, many prosecuting attorneys believe that having the child testify in a traditional courtroom, although emotionally difficult for the child, may increase the chances of a conviction. For these reasons and others, in most cases prosecution attorneys will be reluctant to file a motion to protect the child witness from a face-to-face confrontation with the defendant.

A case from Pennsylvania that was decided after *Maryland v. Craig* demonstrates the difficulties involved in allowing the child to testify by closed-circuit television (*Pennsylvania v. Ludwig*, 1991). In *Ludwig* the defendant was charged with sexually abusing his five-year-old daughter. At the preliminary hearing, the child testified in the defendant's presence that she did not remember what had happened. She was unresponsive to further questioning. Based on expert testimony that the child had experienced "emotional freezing" at the preliminary hearing, the court allowed the child to testify by closed-circuit television and the defendant was ultimately held for trial. The defendant was convicted, and his conviction was affirmed by the Pennsylvania appellate court. The appellate court held that the use of the closed-circuit procedure was proper, finding the need to protect the child's welfare outweighed the restriction on the defendant's constitutional rights.

On appeal to the Pennsylvania Supreme Court the conviction was reversed. The Supreme Court held that under the state constitution, the defendant's right of confrontation had been violated. Pennsylvania's confrontation clause contains explicit language guaranteeing an accused the right to meet the witnesses face-to-face. The court also pointed out that in this case the defendant did not have a chance to cross-examine the child face-to-face, and that the child was not even aware that the trial was occurring. Although it was not necessary for this court to address the federal constitutional issue once it found a violation of the state constitution, the court cited the reasoning of the dissent in *Maryland v. Craig* and rejected the use of the balancing approach advocated by the O'Connor opinion.

Juvenile and Domestic Relations Court Proceedings

There are no special provisions for the use of closed-circuit television for dependency and domestic relations court proceedings. In general, the careful balancing needed to protect criminal defendants is not necessary in dependency cases or in domestic relations court.

In *Seering v. Department of Social Services* (1977), the court held that a child may testify by closed-circuit television in an administrative hearing in which sexual abuse was alleged as the basis for revocation of a family day-care license. However, the alleged offenders were permitted to view the testimony on the closed-circuit television and to confer with their lawyers before cross-examination.

THE USE OF VIDEOTAPED DEPOSITIONS AND STATEMENTS

Another alternative to testimony in court is videotaping the child's statements and using the videotape as a substitute for direct testimony. Videotaped testimony has been utilized by some courts, but its use depends upon the type of case and the special needs, if any, of the child.

Criminal Court Proceedings

As of 1990, the use of videotaped depositions to avoid confrontation with the accused was legal in thirty-four states (*Maryland v. Craig*, 1990). In addition, in the Victims of Child Abuse Act of 1990, Congress also established uniform rules permitting videotaped or televised testimony by children under the same conditions as those established for use of closed-circuit television. If the court finds that the child is unable to testify for any of the reasons stated earlier, the court shall order that the child's deposition be taken and preserved by videotape. The trial judge shall preside at the videotape deposition of a child and shall rule on all questions as if at trial. The only other persons who may be present are the same persons as were permitted at a closed-circuit television proceeding.

The videotape of a deposition must become part of the court records and be kept by the court until it is destroyed. The Act gave additional clear instructions on how to handle the videotapes and on how to ensure the child's privacy.

Texas enacted a statute (subsequently held unconstitutional) providing for *ex parte* videotaping of the child victim's statement and for admissibility of the videotaped statement in court (Tex. Code, 1987). The statute required, however, that the child be made available for the defendant to call and examine in court and, presumably, cross-examine if the defendant chose to do so.

A Kansas statute provides for the admissibility of a child victim's videotaped statement made before the initiation of criminal proceedings if, among other things, no attorney is present during taping (Kansas Statute, 1986). In addition, a child must be available for cross-examination, either in the courtroom or during the videotaping of a separate statement. The Kansas law also provides for the admissibility of a child victim's videotaped statement made after the initiation of criminal proceedings if only the attorneys, the child, and any other persons important to the child's welfare are present, only the attorneys question the child, and the child neither sees nor hears the defendant, if the defendant is present. A child who has given videotaped testimony in accordance with the statute may not be compelled to testify.

The Kansas Supreme Court in *Johnson* (1986) concluded that these statutes did not violate the Confrontation Clause, because the statutes required the court to find sufficient indicia of reliability before admitting the videotaped testimony, and because the child must be available for cross-examination either in the courtroom or on videotape. The court found that because the child is subject to cross-examination during the video-taping, the attorneys had sufficient opportunity to bring out factors bearing on the trustworthiness and reliability of the child's statements.

In *Hardy v. Commonwealth* (1986), the Kentucky Supreme Court held that use of a videotaped deposition taken prior to the trial and used at trial was permissible. Similarly, in *McGuire v. State* (1986), the Arkansas Supreme Court concluded that, while testimony in person is almost always required in other cases, a videotaped deposition provides the best substitute in a child sexual abuse trial.

Several post-*Coy* cases have also upheld the constitutionality of the use of videotaped testimony. In *State v. Bonello* (1989), the defendant was convicted of sexual assault of a five-year-old child. The court granted the state's motion to videotape the complainant's testimony outside the defendant's presence. Prior to *Coy*, the Connecticut Supreme Court had approved this proceeding, providing that the state prove the compelling need to use such procedure in the individual case. The court based this on preserving the truth-seeking function of the trial court. The court said that, *Coy* notwithstanding, this procedure was proper when it enhanced the truth-seeking function of the criminal trial because of the witness's fear of the defendant. In addition, there were individual findings that there was a compelling need to use

this procedure. This case then adhered to the guidelines suggested by O'Connor in her concurring opinion in *Coy*.

Similarly, in a case from the Indiana appeals court, *Brady v. Indiana* (1989), the court adopted the O'Connor concurrence. In this case the defendant was convicted for the molestation of his four-year-old daughter. The victim's videotaped testimony was admitted at the trial. The defendant objected on the grounds that he was denied face-to-face confrontation under *Coy*. The Indiana court, however, stated that in this case there were individualized findings that testifying in open court for this four-year-old would be a traumatic experience. The taping was done in her bedroom, where the victim was more relaxed and willing to talk. The defendant was in the garage watching a video monitor and could communicate with his attorney by use of a two-way radio. The attorneys used flash cards to object. The defendant's attorney was present and was allowed to cross-examine the witness.

In a more recent case from Wisconsin, *State v. Tarantino* (1990), the use of videotaped prelimi-nary hearing testimony during trial was also upheld as not violative of the defendant's confrontation rights. The defendant argued that the state statute allowing for the admission of the videotaped statement of a child sexual abuse victim was inapplicable where the child's testimony was elicited during a preliminary hearing. The Wisconsin Court of Appeals rejected such a claim on the grounds that there was no reason to distinguish between testimony given at a preliminary hearing and that given during trial, and that the goal of protecting child sexual abuse victims from the trauma of live testimony was well served by the statute.

In *State v. Pilkey* (1989) a case from Tennessee, the use of *ex parte* videotaped statements was found violative of the defendant's confrontational rights. In reaching this conclusion the Tennessee Supreme Court drew upon the Supreme Court's ruling in *Coy v. Iowa* and analogous decisions from other state courts. While the state's interest in prosecuting child abuse cases was weighty, it did not warrant the admission of the victim's *ex parte,* unsworn testimony as substantive evidence. This was particularly true in this case, where there was no judicial determination whatever that the child witness would in any way be traumatized by appearing in court. The court concluded, however, that the error was harmless, and the defendant's conviction was affirmed.

While videotaped depositions may provide very useful evidence for a jury and may spare children court appearances, there are also some problems with this procedure. Some critics claim that a videotaped deposition merely substitutes one formal proceeding for another (Whitcomb, Shapiro, and Stellwagen, 1985, p. 65). They suggest that such a deposition can be far more harrowing to a child than giving testimony in court. Also, in a more recent overview of the legal issues involved, Whitcomb (1992) notes that critics have argued that videotaping the child's testimony at a proceeding apart from trial may threaten the defendant's right to a public trial with a jury because the jury and the public are not physically present when the videotape is made. No case testing the constitutionality of videotaped testimony has yet reached the U.S. Supreme Court.

CONCLUSION

This chapter has covered the various ways in which the legal system has tried to accommodate itself to the special needs of the child victim witness without unduly jeopardizing the confrontational rights of the accused. Both federal and state statutes have been enacted to provide protections for the child victim, although not all of the state statutes are consistent with the Supreme Court's requirement tying the child's trauma to specific confrontations with the defendant.

Generally courts have confirmed their willingness to accommodate the special needs of the child victim and to limit confrontation whenever it can be shown that the child would be traumatized by the presence of defendant. Only in a few state courts, where their constitutions specifically require a face-to-face confrontation, have the claims of the defendant been upheld.

Although the *Coy* decision stressed the right of face-to-face confrontation for the defendant, the *Maryland v. Craig* decision allowed for reasonable exceptions to this rule. Such flexibility is important if the courts are going to be able to handle the great volume of child abuse cases without causing widespread secondary victimization.

The *Coy* ruling that there must be individualized findings of trauma in each specific case before safeguards such as a shield can be used is typically seen as a ruling in favor of the defendant's right to confrontation. At the same time, however, this ruling may actually serve to limit the rights of the accused. If the court finds that testifying in front of the accused is so traumatic that the child needs to be protected, is that not somehow implying (at least to the jury) that the defendant is guilty? Along this line, defendants might actually be better served by a blanket rule that allows the use of protective devices without a finding of trauma than by a rule that allows for individualized exception situations.

Finally, the constitutional rights to confrontation have thus far been interpreted to apply only to the criminal courts, where the threat to a person's liberty is at stake. The decisions in juvenile and domestic relations courts have not yet resulted in the same constitutional protection for the defendant. Clearly, the founding fathers had no concept of the modern-day juvenile and domestic relations courts when the Constitution was written. At stake there is not the personal liberty of the defendant, but custody of a child. One could argue that many would perhaps rather give up their liberty than risk losing their child, and that a more precious value is at stake in the civil courts. Nevertheless, the constitutional debate on confrontation has not yet extended to dependency or domestic relations courts.

The dilemma posed by the special protections needed for children in court and the rights of the accused eludes easy resolution. Moreover, there are many unresolved issues awaiting determination by our legislatures and appellate courts. As technology becomes more sophisticated, new means of securing testimony may be developed. They, too, will have to be tested against the Constitution and its guarantees for a person accused of criminal behavior.

CHAPTER 12

Hearsay Evidence and the Child Witness

The prosecutor questions the mother of a child victim in a criminal trial:

PROSECUTOR: After you came inside and saw the child playing, what happened next?
WITNESS: I asked her what had happened to her.
PROSECUTOR: And what did she say?
WITNESS: She said . . .
DEFENSE ATTORNEY: Objection. Any statement from the witness about what the child told her would be hearsay and inadmissible as evidence.
THE COURT: I sustain the objection. Next question.

Child maltreatment is often difficult to prove. Typically the abuse occurs in secret, with the child and the perpetrator being the only witnesses. In most sexual abuse cases, there is no physical evidence. Thus, proof of maltreatment usually turns on the child's testimony. However, in many cases, the child may be too young or too frightened to testify fully, and in some cases the child may be unable to testify at all. In those cases, any relevant statement that the child has made out of court can be extremely important. It may be the only evidence available to prove the child maltreatment allegations.

Out-of-court statements offered as evidence present significant problems for the legal system. The trier of fact, the jury or the judge, may not be able to understand the meaning of the statement. Because the witness is not available for questioning, it may be difficult to judge the reliability of the statement. An accused is particularly interested in questioning the declarant in order to demonstrate that the statement is not trustworthy.

Case Example (*White v. Illinois*, 1992)

The defendant was convicted by a jury of aggravated criminal sexual assault, residential burglary, and unlawful restraint. The sexual assault related to S.G., then four years old. The testimony at trial revealed that in the early morning of April 16, 1988, S.G.'s baby-sitter, Tony DeVore, was awakened by S.G.'s scream. DeVore went to S.G's bedroom and witnessed the defendant leaving the room and thereafter the house. DeVore asked S.G. what happened. S.G. said that defendant had put his hand over her mouth, choked her, threatened to whip her if she screamed, and touched her in "the wrong places." S.G. then pointed to her vaginal area.

S.G.'s mother returned home about thirty minutes later. She said her daughter seemed scared and a little hyper. The mother testified that S.G. repeated her claims that the defendant choked and threatened her. She testified that S.G. also said that the defendant "put his mouth on her front part." The mother also noticed that S.G. had bruises and red marks on her neck that had not been there previously.

Officer Terry Lewis arrived a few minutes later and questioned S.G. alone in the kitchen. S.G. gave basically the same story to him as she had first reported to the baby-sitter and her mother, but added that the defendant had "used his tongue on her private parts."

A few hours later, S.G. was taken to the hospital and examined by an emergency room nurse and then by a doctor. Each testified at trial and each said that S.G. gave an almost identical account of the evening's events as she had to the baby-sitter, her mother, and the police officer.

S.G. never testified at trial. The prosecution attempted to call her on two occasions, but she apparently experienced emotional difficulty on being brought to the courtroom and each time left without testifying. The defense did not call the child, nor was there any request for the court to declare that S.G. was unavailable to testify.

The defendant objected to the admissibility of S.G.'s statements as reported by the baby-sitter, her mother, the police officer, the nurse, and the doctor. The defendant claimed that each statement was inadmissible hearsay testimony. The trial court overruled each objection. With respect to the first three, the court ruled the statements could be admitted as spontaneous declaration, a statement relating to a startling event or condition made while the declarant was under the stress of excitement caused by the event or condition. With respect to the latter two statements, the court ruled that each was admissible as a statement made in the course of securing medical treatment. Such a hearsay exception is permitted under Illinois statutory law when the statement is made by a victim to medical personnel for purposes of medical diagnosis or treatment.

The defendant appealed his conviction, and it was affirmed by the Illinois Appellate Court and by the United States Supreme Court. In affirming the trial court's evidentiary rulings, the Supreme Court discussed the reasoning for permitting exceptions to the hearsay doctrine.

> We note first that the evidentiary rationale for permitting hearsay testimony regarding spontaneous declarations and statements made in the course of receiving medical care is that such out-of-court declarations are made in contexts that provide substantial guarantees of their trustworthiness. But those same factors that contribute to the statements' reliability cannot be recaptured even by later in-court testimony. A statement that has been offered in a moment of excitement—without the opportunity to reflect on the consequences of one's exclamation—may justifiably carry more weight with a trier of fact than a similar statement offered in the relative calm of the courtroom. Similarly, a statement made in the course of procuring medical services, where the declarant knows that a false statement may cause misdiagnosis or maltreatment, carries special guarantees of credibility that a trier of fact may not think replicated by courtroom testimony.

Discussion

Hearsay evidence consists of statements made out of court that are offered in a court proceeding to prove the truth of the matter asserted. In a legal proceeding, hearsay evidence is usually inadmissible because the declarant is not before the court to be examined by the parties. Cross-examination is believed to be important to the truth-finding process. The Supreme Court referred to cross-examination as "the greatest legal engine ever invented for the discovery of truth." Since the declarant is not before the court, the real meaning of the statement cannot be tested by the cross-examination process.

In *White v. Illinois*, hearsay evidence formed the basis of the prosecution's case against the defendant. There were five persons who testified what S.G. told them. S.G. never testified. Thus, there was no opportunity for S.G. to be cross-examined by the defendant or for the judge or jury to have an opportunity to observe her demeanor when she made her statements. Nevertheless, each of the five statements was admitted by the trial court and that ruling was affirmed by the United States Supreme Court.

In spite of the strong policy of having the declarant available for cross-examination before a statement is admissible, there are many exceptions to the hearsay rule. The primary reason for the exceptions is that some out-of-court statements are inherently reliable and need not be tested by cross-examination in order to be admissible. The first three statements in the *White* case were made shortly after the event. The child made her statements spontaneously to each witness. The court reasoned that such statements were inherently reliable, since the declarant did not have an opportunity to fabricate her story. Critical to this analysis is the notion that the declarant was excited when she made her statements.

Does this reasoning make sense to you? Do you think that the statements immediately following a traumatic event are more reliable than those given days later?

The last two statements in the *White* case were made a few hours later at a hospital. Each was in response to a request for information from medical personnel, first a nurse and then a doctor. This type of statement is thought to be particularly truthful, because a person is assumed to be honest with medical personnel. How else is a nurse or doctor going to give one proper treatment if a patient gives them incorrect information?

This so-called medical diagnosis exception to the hearsay rule is available in some but not all states. In some states, the courts have ruled that a statement to a doctor by a patient seeking treatment is not inherently truthful. Which of the two positions do you find more persuasive? Have you ever lied to a nurse or doctor when seeking treatment? Do you believe such statements are inherently reliable?

Exceptions to the hearsay rule are a significant evidentiary strategy in child abuse cases. As the *White v. Illinois* case indicates, young children may not be able to testify in court. They may not have the sophistication to answer adult questions. They may not have the emotional strength to appear in the courtroom.

But if they have made inherently reliable statements outside the courtroom, the prosecutor may decide to prosecute, utilizing those statements as the main evidence in the case. The prosecutor is thus able to avoid traumatizing the child by subjecting him or her to the courtroom, while at the same time having available the words of the child for the judge and jury. Understandably, those accused of crimes based on hearsay statements are very concerned about these evidentiary rulings.

ADMISSIBILITY OF HEARSAY EVIDENCE

Case law and legislation have shaped the hearsay rule through the years. In *Ohio v. Roberts* (1980), the Supreme Court established a two-part test for determining the trustworthiness of out-of-court statements. First, in the usual case, it must be established that the witness is unavailable. The court reasoned that the Confrontation Clause establishes a preference for face-to-face confrontation with respect to prior testimony. Thus the party wishing to introduce prior statements must either

produce the witness or establish the witness's unavailability. Second, once a witness is shown to be unavailable, his or her statement is admissible only if it is reliable. Reliability can be inferred from the circumstances surrounding the statement. In making this determination, the court might examine what was happening to the declarant at the time the statement was made, what was the emotional condition of the declarant, or what reasons might the declarant have for lying or for telling the truth.

Unavailability

Generally, the Confrontation Clause requires that the party seeking to introduce hearsay evidence make a good faith effort to obtain the presence of the witness at trial before hearsay statements can be admissible as a substitute for direct testimony. The reasoning for this rule is obvious. The court should not permit hearsay testimony if the declarant is available to testify and be cross-examined.

The *Ohio v. Roberts'* standard of "unavailability" can be interpreted in several ways. For example, a distinction can be made between "physical" unavailability and "testimonial" unavailability. A witness may be physically available, but unable to provide testimony at trial, due to the stress or fear involved. *White v. Illinois* is an example of a case in which the child was present, but unable to testify. A child may have suffered a memory loss after the abuse and thus be unavailable for giving testimony. In determining unavailability, the critical factor is the ability of the witness to testify, not the witness's physical presence in court.

Federal Rule of Evidence 804(a) provides five possible grounds of unavailability of a competent witness's testimony. Under subsection (a)[1], a witness who is exempt from testifying about the subject matter of the statement on the grounds of privilege is unavailable. Thus, if a witness refuses to testify based upon an excuse of the privilege against self-incrimination, that would result in unavailability. Under subsection (a)[2], a witness who persists in refusing to testify concerning the subject matter of the statement despite a court order is unavailable. Under subsection (a)[3], a witness who testifies to a lack of memory of the subject matter of his or her statement is unavailable. Failed memory unavailability extends not only to witnesses who truly lack recollection, but also to those who feign lack of recollection. Under subsection (a)[4], a witness who is unable to be present or to testify at the hearing because of death or a then-existing physical or mental illness is unavailable. Under subsection (a)[5], in both civil and criminal cases, a witness who cannot be secured by process or other reasonable means is unavailable (Federal Rules of Evidence, 1991).

Although the *Ohio v. Roberts* case implies that a showing of "unavailability" is necessary, the court also stated that while the Confrontation Clause normally requires such a showing, competing interests such as public policy and the necessities of the case may warrant dispensing with confrontation at trial. The opinion added that parties need not demonstrate unavailability or produce the witness when the utility of confrontation is remote.

In 1986, in *United States v. Inadi*, the U.S. Supreme Court declared that "unavailability" was not a prerequisite to the admission of hearsay. The Court stated that it is not necessary to show that a witness is unavailable before out-of-court statements can be introduced. The justices argued that the purpose of the Confrontation Clause is to seek the truth, and that to exclude such statements would only impede the fact-finding process. This decision also challenged the notion that a statement made earlier and out of court was less trustworthy than one made before the jury. In fact, the court said that statements made out of court in a different context may be reliable and may be irreplaceable as substantive evidence. The decision asserted that hearsay evidence can have significant value for a jury "precisely because it provides statements from a different time and context without regard to their usefulness at trial" (*U.S. v. Inadi*, 1986, 399).

Since *Inadi*, this principle that statements out of court may be admitted even when the child

is available for testimony has been upheld in separate state supreme courts in Arizona (*State v. Robinson*, 1987), Arkansas (*Johnson v. State*, 1987), Vermont (*State v. Gallagher*, 1988) and Illinois (*White v. Illinois*, 1992). The Arizona Supreme Court concluded that a child's spontaneous statements about an unusual personal experience, made soon after the event, are at least as reliable as the child's in-court testimony, given months later after innumerable interviews and interrogations may have distorted the child's memory. Indeed, such out-of-court statements are valuable and trustworthy, in part because they exclude the naïveté and curiosity of a small child, and were made in circumstances very different from interrogation or a criminal trial. Not all courts adhere to this direction, however.

Case Example (*State v. Roman*, 1991)

The following case example took place in New Jersey. In the course of a child sexual abuse investigation, the police obtained a statement of a ten-year-old child who claimed to have been victimized by the suspect. The child also related that she had been threatened by the defendant regarding the disclosure of the abuse. Indictments were returned charging the defendant with sexual assault, terroristic threatening, and endangering the welfare of a child. Prior to trial, the victim and her mother moved to another state, partly out of fear of the defendant. A subpoena was issued to compel the child's appearance and testimony, but the mother refused to permit the child to return.

No further action was taken by the state in order to compel the child's attendance. Rather, the state moved for the admission of the child's hearsay testimony under a statutory exception to the rule against hearsay. Under this rule, a witness's hearsay testimony could be admissible in cases where the witness was "unavailable." The term "unavailable" was then defined as a witness who was beyond the jurisdiction of the court's process to compel his appearance or whom the state was unable to produce despite the exercise of due diligence. The trial court agreed that the child was unavailable as a witness and that the state's invocation of the Uniform Act to Secure the Attendance of Witnesses was unnecessary due to the fact that the child's mother had refused to obey the prior subpoena. It denied the state's motion, however, on the ground that the child was now over twelve years of age, making the hearsay exception inapplicable. The state appealed.

The New Jersey Superior Court, Appellate Division, affirmed the evidentiary ruling, though its rationale was different from that employed by the trial court. The court held that the trial court had erred in finding that the child was unavailable as a witness. The appellate court noted that the trial court clearly had the authority to compel the child's attendance at trial through the invocation of the Uniform Act to Secure the Attendance of Witnesses. The possibility that the mother might refuse to honor any such order did not detract from the trial court's authority to issue a summons to compel her attendance. Furthermore, the potential futility of invoking the Uniform Act did not relieve the state from its obligation to attempt to do so. Such a failure to attempt to secure the child's presence through this process was viewed as a lack of due diligence on the state's part. Because the child witness was available, the hearsay evidence should not have been admitted.

Discussion

This case addresses the steps that must be taken before a witness can be declared unavailable. If a witness has died, that person is clearly unavailable. If the witness has moved away from the local area, the circumstances will determine availability. If the witness moved to a foreign country and was unwilling to return to testify, it is likely that the court would find him or her unavailable. But if the witness has moved to another state, the Uniform Act to Secure the Attendance of Witnesses provides a mechanism to compel the attendance of that witness. The New Jersey appellate court found that the trial court should have enforced the Uniform Act before making the unavailability finding.

Requiring an out-of-state witness to attend a court proceeding is not an easy task. If the witness seeks relief in the other state and an out-of-state court makes an order protecting the witness from the subpoena, the matter could take months or years to resolve.

Do you believe that the mother's resistance to the court order in the New Jersey case made the child unavailable? What if you knew that it would take six months or a year to produce the witness? Is that sufficient for a finding of unavailability?

Reliability

The second important consideration in admitting hearsay evidence is whether it is reliable. Every hearsay statement, however relevant and material to a case, must be reliable to be admitted. If the declarant does not testify, then the court must inquire as to the reliability and trustworthiness of the out-of-court statements. Usually, reliability is inferred when the statement falls within a "firmly rooted hearsay exception" (*Ohio v. Roberts*, 1980). However, if it does not, then the court must consider whether the out-of-court statement has adequate indicia of reliability. In *Ohio v. Roberts* the court held that this would include cases where there was cross-examination on prior occasions, or where the hearsay is marked with such trustworthiness or such indicia of reliability that it may be placed before the jury without confrontation.

The issue of whether a statement that does not fall under an established hearsay exception is reliable and trustworthy was precisely the subject matter of a U.S. Supreme Court decision involving hearsay and child sexual abuse allegations.

Case Example (*Idaho v. Wright*, 1990)

Laura Lee Wright and Robert L. Giles were jointly charged with two counts of lewd conduct with a minor under sixteen. The alleged victims were Ms. Wright's two daughters, one of whom was five and a half and the other two and a half at the time the crimes were charged.

The facts of the case reveal that the children's mother and her ex-husband, Louis Wright, the father of the older daughter, had reached an informal agreement whereby each parent would have custody of the older daughter for six consecutive months. The allegations surfaced in November 1986, when the older daughter told another person that Giles had had sexual intercourse with her while Ms. Wright, the respondent, held her down and covered her mouth, and that she had seen the respondent and Giles do the same thing to the respondent's younger daughter. The younger daughter was living with her parents, Ms. Wright and Giles, at the time of the alleged offenses.

The older daughter's disclosures were reported to the police and the older daughter was taken to the hospital. A medical examination of the older daughter revealed evidence of sexual abuse. One of the examining physicians was Dr. John Jambura, a pediatrician with extensive experience in child abuse cases. Police and welfare officials took the younger daughter into custody that day for protection and investigation. Dr. Jambura examined her the following day and found conditions "strongly suggestive of sexual abuse with vaginal contact," occurring approximately two or three days prior to the examination.

At the joint trial of Ms. Wright and Giles, the trial court conducted a *voir dire* examination of the younger daughter, who was three years old at the time of trial, to determine whether she was capable of testifying. The court concluded, and the parties agreed, that the younger daughter was "not capable of communicating to the jury." The question before the Supreme Court was the admission at trial of certain statements made by the younger daughter to Dr. Jambura in response to questions he asked regarding the alleged abuse. Over objection by Ms. Wright and Giles, the trial court permitted Dr. Jambura to testify before the jury as follows:

Q. (By the prosecutor.) Now, calling your attention, then to the examination of Kathy Wright on November 10th. What—would you describe any interview dialogue that you had with Kathy at that time? Excuse me, before you get into that, would you lay a setting of where this took place and who else might be present?

A. This took place in my office, in my examining room, and as I recall, I believe in previous testimony I said that I recall a female attendant being present; I don't recall her identity. I started out with basically, "Hi, how are you," you know, "What did you have for breakfast this morning?" Essentially a few minutes of just sort of chitchat.

Q. Was there response from Kathy to that first—those first questions?

A. There was. She started to carry on a very relaxed, animated conversation. I then proceeded to just very gently start asking questions about, "Well, how are those things at home," you know, those sorts. Gently moving into the domestic situation, and then moved into four questions in particular, as I reflected in my records. "Do you play with daddy? Does daddy play with you? Does daddy touch you with his pee-pee? Do you touch his pee-pee?" And again we then established what was meant by pee-pee; it was a generic term for genital area.

Q. Before you get into that, what was, as best you recollect, what was her response to the question "Do you play with daddy?"

A. Yes, we play—I remember her making a comment about "yes, we play a lot" and expanding on that, and talking about spending time with daddy.

Q. "And does daddy play with you?" Was there any response?

A. She responded to that as well, that they played together in a variety of circumstances and you know, seemed very unaffected by the question.

Q. And then what did you say and her response?

A. When I asked her "Does daddy touch you with his

pee-pee?" she did admit to that. When I asked, "Do you touch his pee-pee?" she did not have any response.

Q. Excuse me. Did you notice any change in her affect or attitude in that line of questioning?

A. Yes.

Q. What did you observe?

A. She would not—oh—she did not talk any further about that. She would not elucidate what exactly— what kind of touching was taking place, or how it was happening. She did, however, say that daddy does do this with me, but he does it a lot more with my sister than with me.

Q. And how did she offer that last statement? Was that in response to a question or was that just a volunteered statement?

A. That was a volunteered statement as I sat and waited for her to respond, again after she sort of clammed up, and that was the next statement that she made after just allowing some silence to occur.

On cross-examination, Dr. Jambura acknowledged that a picture that he drew during the questioning of the younger daughter had been discarded. Dr. Jambura also stated that although he had dictated notes to summarize the conversation, his notes were not detailed and did not record any changes in the child's affect or attitudes. The trial court admitted these statements under Idaho's residual hearsay exception.

Ms. Wright and Giles were each convicted of two counts of lewd conduct with a minor under sixteen and were sentenced to twenty years' imprisonment. Each appealed only from the conviction involving the younger daughter. Giles contended that the trial court had erred in admitting Dr. Jamura's testimony under Idaho's residual hearsay exception. The Idaho Supreme Court disagreed and affirmed his conviction. Ms. Wright asserted that the admission of Dr. Jambura's testimony under the residual hearsay exception nevertheless violated her rights under the Confrontation Clause. The Idaho Supreme Court agreed and reversed Ms. Wright's conviction.

The Supreme Court of Idaho held that the admission of the inculpatory hearsay testimony violated Ms. Wright's federal constitutional right

to confrontation, because the testimony did not fall within a traditional hearsay exception and was based on an interview that lacked procedural safeguards. The court found Dr. Jambura's interview technique inadequate because "the questions and answers were not recorded on videotape for preservation and perusal by the defense at or before trial; and blatantly leading questions were used in the interrogation." The statements also lacked trustworthiness, according to the court, because "this interrogation was performed by someone with a preconceived idea of what the child should be disclosing." The court found that "the circumstances surrounding this interview demonstrate dangers of unreliability which, because the interview was not (audio or video) recorded, can never be fully assessed." The court concluded that the younger daughter's statements lacked the particularized guarantees of trustworthiness necessary to satisfy the requirements of the Confrontation Clause and that therefore the trial court erred in admitting them. Because the court was not convinced, beyond a reasonable doubt, that the jury would have reached the same result had the error not occurred, the court reversed Ms. Wright's conviction on the count involving the younger daughter and remanded for a new trial.

The U.S. Supreme Court affirmed the Idaho Supreme Court's decision excluding the hearsay testimony of the younger girl. The court noted that:

> The crux of the question presented is therefore whether the State, as the proponent of evidence presumptively barred by the hearsay rule and the Confrontation Clause, has carried its burden of proving that the younger daughter's incriminating statements to Dr. Jambura bore sufficient indicia of reliability to withstand scrutiny under the Clause.
>
> . . . The State responds that a finding of "particularized guarantees of unworthiness" should instead be based on a consideration of the totality of the circumstances, including not only the circumstances surrounding the making of the statement, but also other evidence at trial that corroborates the truth of the statement. We agree

that "particularized guarantees of trustworthiness" must be shown from the totality of the circumstances, but we think the relevant circumstances include only those that surround the making of the statement and that render the declarant particularly worthy of belief. In other words, if the declarant's truthfulness is so clear from the surrounding circumstances that the test of cross-examination would be of marginal utility, then the hearsay rule does not bar admission of the statement at trial.

. . . Thus, unless an affirmative reason, arising from the circumstances in which the statement was made, provides a basis for rebutting the presumption that a hearsay statement is not worthy of reliance at trial, the Confrontation Clause requires exclusion of the out-of-court statement.

. . . We think the Supreme Court of Idaho properly focused on the presumptive unreliability of the out-of-court statements and on the suggestive manner in which Dr. Jambura conducted the interview. Viewing the totality of the circumstances surrounding the younger daughter's responses to Dr. Jambura's questions, we find no special reason for supposing that the incriminating statements were particularly trustworthy.

. . . Given the presumption of inadmissibility accorded accusatory hearsay statements not admitted pursuant to a firmly rooted hearsay exception, we agree with the court below that the State has failed to show that the younger daughter's incriminating statements to the pediatrician possessed sufficient "particularized guarantees of trustworthiness" under the Confrontation Clause to overcome that presumption. . . . we therefore agree with that court that Ms. Wright's conviction involving the younger daughter must be reversed and the case remanded for further proceedings. Accordingly, the judgment of the Supreme Court of Idaho is affirmed.

Discussion

In *Idaho v. Wright*, the parties asked the U.S. Supreme Court to identify the procedural prerequisites to the admission of such hearsay statements at trial. The court declined to endorse a mechanical test for determining "particularized guarantees of trustworthiness," but found that admission should be based on a consideration of the totality of the circumstances. The court held that the relevant circumstances, however, should be those surrounding the making of the statement and not other evidence at trial. Thus, the fact that the older girl testified that she had been sexually molested by the same persons was not to be considered relevant to whether the younger girl was telling the truth when she talked to the doctor.

The *Idaho v. Wright* case was decided by a 5–4 vote. The dissent argued that excluding corroborating evidence apart from the statement itself flies in the face of common sense, legal precedent, and the considered wisdom of virtually the entire legal community that corroborating evidence is relevant to reliability and trustworthiness. Furthermore, Justice Kennedy, writing for the dissent, observed that it is preferable to consider other corroborating evidence, since that evidence can at least be examined by the defendant and the trial court in an objective and critical way.

Several of the factors discussed in *Idaho v. Wright*, such as increasing reliability by taping interviews and using the "totality of circumstances" guideline, have been raised in subsequent cases. A case from Georgia, *Smith v. State* (1991), is a good example.

A father was charged with several counts of physical and sexual assault which he had allegedly perpetrated on his children. At the time the alleged acts were committed, the children were eleven and twelve years old. During the course of their investigation into these crimes, the police conducted an audiotaped interview of the children during which they related the particulars of their father's assaults. At trial each child testified, though one of the children did so unwillingly. The audiotaped interview was also admitted into evidence over the defendant's objection. The father was convicted, and he appealed.

The Georgia Court of Appeals affirmed the conviction, rejecting numerous challenges to the trial court's admission of the audiotaped statement. Under the state's child sexual abuse hearsay exception, any statement made by a child victim who was under fourteen years of age could be admitted if the child was available to testify at trial and the court found that the circumstances surrounding the making of the statement provided sufficient indicia of its reliability. Accordingly, the defendant had not been denied his opportunity to confront and cross-examine these witnesses against him.

The court also refused to disturb the trial court's ruling regarding the existence of sufficient indicia of the statement's reliability. The fact that the police had failed to make a videotape recording of the interview, and that they may have conducted the interview with a preconceived idea of what the children should have been saying did not automatically render the audiotaped statement unreliable under a totality of circumstances analysis, which the trial court had conducted in this case. Accordingly, the trial court's ruling with regard to the admission of the audiotape was affirmed.

The *Idaho v. Wright* opinion was also followed in a case from Illinois, *People v. Deavers* (1991). A five-year-old girl was evaluated by a school psychologist to assess her intellectual and cognitive functioning and academic achievement. During the evaluation, the child spontaneously disclosed that she had been sexually abused by her stepfather. The next day, the psychologist reported the child's statements to the Department of Children and Family Services, and the child was interviewed at school by a detective in the presence of two investigators and the school principal. The stepfather was charged with sexual assault. At the trial, the psychologist and the detective testified as to the child's statements. Evidence was also admitted that the stepfather physically abused his wife and that he was sexually aroused by the victim. He was convicted.

On appeal, his conviction was affirmed by the Appellate Court of Illinois. The court held that, under the totality of the circumstances test articulated in *Idaho v. Wright* (1990), the trial court did not err in determining that the statement possessed "sufficient safeguards of reliability." The court specifically rejected the stepfather's claim that the child's delayed disclosure necessarily diminished the reliability of her statements. According to the court, the child's failure to report the abuse promptly was understandable. Not only was she probably afraid and embarrassed, but she knew her mother was aware of the abuse and had failed to stop it. The court emphasized that the time lapse between the child's statements and the abuse itself could have been considered as a factor by the trial court, but that the trial court was correct in not according that factor too much weight.

In addition, the court held that the admission of evidence that the stepfather physically abused the mother and that he was sexually aroused by the child was not prejudicial. The evidence of domestic violence was offered only after the mother had testified inconsistently with her previous statements incriminating her husband. Thus, this evidence was permissible because its purpose was to provide a possible explanation for her changed testimony, that is, that she was afraid of the defendant. The court also found proper the testimony of certain witnesses that the defendant told them he had become sexually aroused upon seeing his stepdaughter naked. The court stated that it viewed the evidence in question as strongly probative and suggestive of the state of mind that would be inclined to commit the crimes complained of. Since the child's hearsay statements were properly admitted, and the additional evidence was not prejudicial, the court affirmed the stepfather's conviction.

EXCEPTIONS TO HEARSAY RULES

Many states have already adopted exceptions to the hearsay rule for child victims of abuse which apply to both criminal and civil proceedings

(Eatman and Bulkley, 1987). Traditional hearsay rules have now been expanded to include the following exceptions, all important provisions for child maltreatment cases:

1. The "Prior Recorded Testimony" exception;
2. The "Excited Utterance" exception;
3. The "Complaint of Rape" exception;
4. The "Tender Years" exception;
5. The "Medical Diagnosis/Treatment" exception;
6. The "Probation Reports/Social Studies" exception;
7. The "Residual" exception; and
8. The "Sexually Abused Child" exception.

Additional exceptions exist in some states.

The "Prior Recorded Testimony" Exception

The prior recorded testimony exception is available only when the declarant is unavailable as a witness. Under this exception, former testimony may be admitted if it was offered against a party to the action who had the right and opportunity to cross-examine the witness at a former hearing or trial (e.g., California Evidence Code, sections 1290[a], 1291[a]{2}). The burden of establishing unavailability of the declarant is on the proponent of the evidence, and the showing must be made by competent evidence (*People v. Turner*, 1990).

Testimony given by a witness at a preliminary examination may be offered at trial, but only if the defendant had the opportunity for meaningful cross-examination at the preliminary examination. The former testimony remains subject to the same objections as though the defendant were testifying at the trial, including objections as to competency.

In *People v. Liddicoat* (1981), the court held that the transcript of the preliminary hearing testimony of a young child who had been adjudged competent at the preliminary hearing two months before the trial was admissible at trial. The trial judge had found the child to be unavailable to testify at the trial because of incompetency, despite the fact that the magistrate had found her to be competent to testify a short time earlier. The court of appeal held that the trial judge was correct both in ruling the child incompetent to testify at trial and in giving great deference to the magistrate's earlier determination of competency.

The California Penal Code (section 1346) allows the court to order that a child's testimony at preliminary hearings be videotaped so that it may be preserved for trial if necessary (California Penal Code, 1993). There is also a hearsay exception for the preliminary hearing testimony of a child who is a complaining witness if the former testimony is offered in a juvenile court dependency proceeding. The term "complaining witness" means the alleged victim of the crime for which the preliminary hearing was held. Again, for this former testimony to be admissible, the defendant must have had the right and opportunity to cross-examine the child at the preliminary hearing with motives and interests similar to those of the parent or guardian against whom the testimony is offered at the dependency hearing.

The "Excited Utterance" Exception

An "excited utterance" is testimony about a statement relating to a startling event or condition while under the stress of excitement caused by that event or condition. The first three declarants in the *White v. Illinois* case reported excited utterances from the child victim. This exception is quite often applicable to child sexual abuse cases. The three requirements of an excited utterance are (1) a sufficiently startling experience suspending reflective thought, (2) a spontaneous reaction, and (3) a statement relating to the startling experience (Whitcomb, 1992). The Federal Rule of Evidence 803 provides a hearsay exception for a present sense impression which is

> . . . a statement describing or explaining an event or condition made while the declarant was perceiving the event or condition, or immediately thereafter. (Fed. Evid. 808[1]

Courts applying the excited utterance exception must find that the statement is not a product of deliberation. Once the event or condition passes, the statements generally lose their reliability as "excited utterances" because the victim gains time to prepare, and possibly lie. Other factors that the court must consider in deciding whether to admit the statement under the excited utterance exception include the child's physical, mental, and emotional condition while making the statement, the circumstances of the event, and the statement's subject matter.

The excited utterance exceptions are often broadly interpreted in child abuse cases. For example, in *State v. Hanson* (1986) the court held that a child's statements and the pictures she drew immediately after seeing a film of child abuse were sufficiently excited to qualify as excited utterances. The initial disclosure of sexual abuse to a counselor was made spontaneously in response to a movie designed to educate children about child abuse. The child used words and pictures and also testified at trial. Even though the statement was not made shortly after the abuse, it was found to be spontaneous and therefore reliable, given the circumstances. In *State v. Bauer* (1986) the court determined that a child's excited utterances included not only words, but actions such as rubbing her vagina.

In child abuse cases the "excited utterance" exception may be applied to the child's first disclosure of abuse (*In re Interest of R. A.*, 1987), even if this takes place long after the event itself. A child may be afraid and unable to talk about the child abuse right away. According to the Child Sexual Abuse Accommodation syndrome, such behavior is quite common (Summit, 1983). Recognizing this phenomenon, a Massachusetts case, *Commonwealth v. McDonough* (1987), held that a child's statements to a policeman three months later were sufficiently prompt to qualify as an "excited utterance" because the child feared his mother and could not oppose her sexual abuse of him. In *Commonwealth v. Adams* (1987), a child told the mother of incest after seeing a TV show on the subject, but the mother waited four months to tell the police because of fear of the perpetrator. The court determined that the child's statements were still excited utterances because the delay was the mother's, not the child's. The defendant had visited with the victim off and on for ten years and had sexually assaulted her for five of those years. The victim had watched the film *Something about Amelia*, which dealt with father/daughter incest, and left the room crying. She later informed her mother of the sexual assault. The defendant left the child's home a few weeks later, and four months later the mother went to the police.

In another case, a child's statements to a mother four hours after the assault were not admissible because the mother was found to have prompted the child (*State v. Griffith*, 1986). In this case, the mother questioned the child for two hours, and the defendant's name came up in response to a leading question. The court found such circumstances did not produce a spontaneous declaration. Similarly, in *Souder v. Commonwealth* (1986), the court denied admission of statements made to the grandmother twenty-four hours after the alleged incident, when they were made in response to the grandmother's persistent questioning. In this case, where the defendant had been convicted of child abuse, partly based on statements from the grandmother and mother, the appeals court reversed the conviction, saying that the statements were simply too remote and unreliable to qualify as spontaneous.

The "Complaint of Rape" Exception

The "complaint of rape" exception has also been referred to as the "complaint of sexual conduct." This exception derives from the understanding that such hearsay helps to prove that the child's statements were not a fabrication and that the victim had not consented to the act.

Case Example (*State v. Campbell*, 1985)

In a prosecution for sodomy of a three-year-old victim, the defendant was convicted and appealed. The Oregon appellate court noted in its recitation of the facts that the prosecutor and the defense attorney stipulated that the child was incompetent to testify at the trial. Her mother testified that she asked her daughter a question and her daughter replied,

> Robin [the defendant] takes my clothes off every day.

The mother asked why he did that and the girl replied:

> He swings me around and stuff. . . . He licks my tee-tee [referring to her vaginal area].

The defendant objected to the testimony as hearsay, but the trial court admitted the evidence. The appellate court found that the testimony was admissible as a complaint of sexual misconduct, an exception to the hearsay rule. The court referred to the Oregon statute.

> Rule 803. Hearsay exception: availability of declarant immaterial. The following are not excluded by Rule 802, even though the declarant is available as a witness. . . .
> [18a] Complaint of sexual misconduct. A complaint of sexual misconduct made by the prosecuting witness after the commission of the alleged offense. Such evidence must be confined to the fact that the complaint was made.

The appellate court pointed out that in this case there were also circumstantial guarantees of reliability, because the statements were made immediately after the event and contained material which the three-year-old would have no knowledge of had the event not occurred.

Some critics say that this hearsay exception is not really relevant in child abuse cases where consent is clearly not an issue. Generally, the exception is used in adult forcible rape cases where a victim's failure to complain might be seen as "consent." Secondly, victims of child sexual abuse often do not make prompt complaints (Summit, 1983). Nevertheless, the exception has been used in several states.

The "Tender Years" Exception

Some states have adopted a "tender years" exception to the hearsay rule. The "tender years" exception traditionally has allowed the court to hear children's prior statements about abuse. It focuses attention on the age of the child, rather than on the content of the statement itself. As with all exceptions to the hearsay rule, there must be an indication of reliability.

Several cases address the issue of the "tender years" exception. In *In the Matter of W.D.* (1985), the Oklahoma court found its tender years exception to be constitutional. In this case, a five-year-old child made statements to a shelter care worker and others concerning the father's sexual abuse. These statements were admitted at trial under Oklahoma's "tender years" exception, where statements of children under ten that describe an act of sexual conduct by another are admissible if the court finds that the contents and circumstances of the statements provide sufficient indicia of reliability and the child either testifies at the hearing or is unavailable. The appellate court pointed out that all hearsay exceptions violate the Confrontation Clause, but those that have the circumstantial guarantee of reliability must be admitted, because of the sensitive consideration involved in confronting a child under ten years of age in a case of sexual abuse.

Similarly, in *State v. Robinson* (1987), the Arizona court found that a child's hearsay statements may be used under the "tender years" exception if they appear reliable and the child is unavailable to testify without undue trauma. In *U.S. v. St. John* (1988), the defendant was convicted of sexual assault on a ten-year-old boy. The victim was interviewed by a clinical psychologist and a social worker many months after the alleged occurrence. The court admitted the testimony based upon the "tender years" exception. In *State v. Wright* (1988), the defendant was convicted of the rape and sodomy of a six-year-old child. Utilizing the "tender years" doctrine, the court admitted statements made by the victim to a police detective who had interviewed the child shortly after the event. The appellate court affirmed the trial court, noting that the statements were made within two hours of the crime and were not the product of coercion or leading questions.

A Florida court has also found the "tender years" rule constitutional (*Perez v. Florida*, 1988). In this case, the defendant was charged with the assault upon a three-year-old child. The defendant made a pretrial motion to exclude the child victim's hearsay statements and compel the child to testify. The court refused to permit the child to testify, holding that to force the child to participate in the trial would create substantial likelihood of severe emotional and mental harm. This case also clarified the relationship between competency and hearsay exceptions by ruling that it is constitutional to allow a child's statements into evidence even though the child is not competent to testify. The court stated that the fact that a child is not competent to testify at trial does not necessarily mean that the child is unable to state the truth. It also rejected the argument that the trial judge must always personally examine the child before finding that the out-of-court statements of the child are reliable.

In a case from New Jersey (*R.S. v. Knighton*, 1991) the court ruled that the "tender years" exception could not be barred from admission in civil cases.

The "Medical Diagnosis/Treatment" Exception

Pursuant to the medical diagnosis/treatment exception, certain out-of-court statements by children describing to medical personnel present symptoms or medical history are sufficiently reliable to justify admission into evidence. Since a patient has a compelling reason to tell the truth to a doctor, these statements are considered by many courts to be reliable. According to Weinstein and Berger (1986), the majority of states admit statements of present symptoms or medical history when made to a physician in the course of securing treatment. It is interesting to note that Idaho did not have a medical diagnosis/treatment exception in the state codes, and that the *Idaho v. Wright* case (*supra*) might never have gone to the U.S. Supreme Court if it had had such an exception. The emphasis on the "trustworthiness" of the pediatrician's testimony in that case was due to the fact that the testimony did not fall under a firmly rooted hearsay exception. Illinois, on the other hand, did have such an exception in its law. The statements from the doctor and the nurse were therefore admitted in *White v. Illinois*. The Federal Rules of Evidence admit statements made for purposes of diagnosis, whether or not the patient seeks treatment from the diagnostician. According to rule 803[4] of the Federal Rules of Evidence:

> The following are not excluded by the hearsay rule, even though the declarant is available as a witness: statements made for purposes of medical history, or past or present symptoms, pain or sensations, or the inception or general character of the cause or external source thereof insofar as reasonably pertinent to diagnosis or treatment.

In applying the medical diagnosis/treatment exception several major issues have emerged: (1) whether to expand the exception to other professionals such as psychologists, social workers, and nurses; (2) whether the identity of the alleged abuser can be revealed in these statements; and (3) whether the child victim must be aware of and understand the diagnostic purpose of the examination.

Expansion of the Medical Exception

In *Matter of Helms* (1985), a child's statements made to a pediatrician and to a psychologist, both for the purpose of obtaining treatment, were found admissible. The five-year-old made statements to each as to abusive acts by her father, but at the criminal trial the child did not testify. The statements made to the psychologist for diagnosis or treatment were also admissible, even though the child was referred to the psychologist under court order. In *State v. Nelson* (1987) the court permitted a psychologist to testify about a three-year-old child's statements.

In *In re Freiburger* (1986) a child's statements as to child abuse made to a psychiatrist or social worker for the purpose of treatment were also found admissible. The child told the social worker how her daddy poked and gave her shots (referring to sexual penetration), and then she showed the social worker how on an anatomically correct doll. Nonverbal conduct was found to be a statement, since it was intended as an assertion. However, in a similar case, *Souder v. Commonwealth* (1986), the court found demonstrations by a child on an anatomically correct doll to a social worker investigating possible child abuse inadmissible.

In *In re Jean Marie W.* (1989) statements of a child to a nurse were allowed as a necessary part of a diagnosis. The court concluded that the medical diagnosis/treatment exception to Rhode Island's hearsay rule allows for the admission of statements made for the purposes of diagnosis or treatment, and that these statements do not need to be made to a physician. The admissibility hinges on whether what has been related by the child will assist or is helpful in the diagnosis or treatment of his or her ailment.

In *State v. Larson* (1991), the Minnesota Supreme Court held that the defendant's rights to confrontation had not been violated by the child's statements to a physician's assistant who had examined the child. Citing the lessons from *Idaho v. Wright* (1990), the court noted that the statements

made to the physician's assistant fell within the "firmly rooted" medical exception, as well as being accompanied by particular guarantees of trustworthiness. The manner in which the statements had been elicited was nonleading, and the nature of the child's description of the sexual contact was not the type of story that a four-year-old child would be expected to fabricate.

Identity of the Alleged Abuser

In *Souder v. Commonwealth* (1986), two physicians who examined the child victim testified based on statements made by others contained in the medical record. These statements identified the appellant as the abuser. The court held that the medical records exception was limited to statements "important to an effective diagnosis or treatment" and held the statements inadmissible. At issue here was whether the hearsay exception for medical diagnosis should apply only to the medical condition of the child or also to the identity of the alleged perpetrator. The court held that the identity of the perpetrator was not a necessary part of the information needed by the doctor to render treatment to the child, and, therefore, the identification information did not have the same trustworthiness as the other statements.

According to the traditional medical hearsay exception, physicians could testify about the "what" of the injuries, but not the "who" or who had committed the abuse. The diagnostic treatment exception could help confirm that the abuse has taken place, but could not substitute for a victim's testimony identifying the offender (Dziech and Schudson, 1989). In *United States v. Renville* (1985), however, the court allowed the doctor also to identify the abuser. The court stated that the exact nature and extent of the psychological problems often depend on the identity of the abuser, and that physicians have an obligation not to return an abused child to an environment in which he or she cannot be protected from recurrent abuse. Similarly, courts have admitted statements identifying the alleged perpetrator, reasoning that the perpetrator's identity is important to the child's treatment, particularly if the child is diagnosed with a sexually transmitted disease or if the alleged perpetrator shares the child's household (*State v. Robinson*, 1987). (These issues are discussed at greater length in chapter 13.)

Awareness of the Purpose of Diagnosis

Many critics argue that children may not know whether the person to whom they disclose can diagnose or treat their problem or, indeed, that children may not even understand what a diagnosis is. Courts have rendered conflicting opinions on this issue. The Washington Court of Appeals found that the possibility that a child's statements to a counselor were not motivated by a desire to obtain treatment should not bar admission of this evidence (*In the Matter of the Dependency of S.S.*, 1991). In this case a child was adjudicated as being dependent as a result of being sexually abused by her father. Evidence adduced at trial included hearsay statements regarding the offenses which the child had made to various family members, counselors, and the police. The statements had been admitted under the medical diagnosis/treatment exception.

On appeal, the father argued that his daughter, who was four years old, had been too young to understand that the social worker was questioning her with an eye toward providing treatment and that the underlying rationale for the medical diagnosis/treatment exception was therefore absent. The Washington court noted that the father's argument was not totally lacking in support, but that prior case law held that children who were even younger had made admissible hearsay declarations to health care providers. Corroborative evidence existed in the form of highly sexualized behavior which the victim had exhibited following the assaults by her father. In addition, the child's identification of the perpetrator was also allowed, because the effective treatment required an identification of the perpetrator.

However, in *R. S. v. Knighton* (1991), the Supreme Court of New Jersey held that for out-of-court statements to be admissible under the medical exception, the declarants (five boys between the ages of one and four) must have understood that they needed treatment and that such treatment depended on their truthfulness to the doctor. In order to evaluate whether the children thought they needed treatment, or whether they realized the importance of being truthful to their doctors, testimony from the therapists, the parents, or the children themselves was required.

The "Probation Reports/Social Studies" Exception

Investigators often prepare reports for the court regarding the underlying facts of the case the court is considering. They include reports from law enforcement, probation, social services, child protective services, domestic relations investigators, court staff, mental health professionals, and more. These reports usually contain statements from the witnesses to the events under consideration and thus contain hearsay evidence.

Such reports are usually not admissible as evidence, but in certain circumstances they can be admitted. Their admissibility depends on the type of legal proceedings and whether they fall within an exception to the hearsay rule. One of the most remarkable exceptions was outlined by the California Supreme Court.

Case Example (*In re Malinda S.*, 1990)

This case addresses the question of whether a juvenile court erred in admitting a social studies report containing hearsay at the jurisdictional hearing (trial) of a juvenile dependency petition. The minor, Malinda S., was born in 1983, shortly before her parents, Carol and Russell, were married in 1984. In 1986 they separated, with Malinda living with her father on weekdays and spending weekends with her mother, and with Russell's grandmother helping with day care.

Carol began noticing behavioral changes in Malinda in 1987. These included Malinda becoming more withdrawn and becoming upset when she saw people with no clothes on and throwing temper tantrums when it was time to return to her father's home. One night when Carol picked her up, she noticed a strong odor coming from Malinda's vagina. When she asked Malinda to wash her privates (Malinda's word for the vaginal area), she refused, saying "No, because they hurt." When Carol asked why her privates hurt, Malinda said, "Because my daddy has been touching my privates."

Carol filed a complaint with the San Diego County Department of Social Services (DSS), which then petitioned the juvenile court to find Malinda a dependent child of the court, pursuant to the California dependency law.

A social worker, Kathy Davis, interviewed Malinda about the allegations and Malinda reportedly told her, "My daddy touches my privates and I don't like it," and "Sometimes he kisses my private when I have an owie on it." A few days later Michelle Neumann-Ribner, another social worker, conducted a videotaped examination of Malinda. During this interview Malinda played with anatomically correct dolls and demonstrated familiarity with body parts. She also made several statements such as "I don't like my dad, because he pulled my private off." Later that day Susan Horowitz, M.D., examined Malinda's genitals and determined that an external redness and labial adhesion were consistent with a history of rubbing and external genital contact without penetration.

Investigating social worker George Wulff observed the second interview with Malinda, read the reports prepared by Ms. Neumann-Ribner and Dr. Horowitz, and interviewed Malinda and her parents. He included all of his observations, including the statements by Malinda. In addition, his report contained a summary of the facts, a social assessment, an evaluation, a reunification plan, and a series of recommendations.

After he had completed his report, he reinterviewed Malinda and she recanted her earlier statements, saying she had made them up. When Wulff asked her why she changed her story, Malinda said that her great-grandmother had warned her "not to say anything bad about my daddy." Thereafter, Ms. Neumann-Ribner reinterviewed Malinda and she reconfirmed that her father had touched her private parts with his hand and penis "lots of times."

At the jurisdictional hearing the juvenile court heard testimony from Carol, Russell's grandmother, and Wulff. Neither Malinda, Neumann-Ribner nor Dr. Horowitz was called to testify. In addition, the social study authored by Wulff was admitted into evidence over Russell's objection.

Russell appealed his case and the California Supreme Court affirmed the trial court's decision. The court examined several statutes and court rules to determine whether they created hearsay exceptions for social studies. The court pointed out the reliable nature of such reports.

> . . . [T]he social studies at issue here are prepared by disinterested parties in the regular course of their professional duties. These elements of objectivity and expertise lend them a degree of reliability and trustworthiness. . . .

The court concluded that as long as a meaningful opportunity to cross-examine and controvert the contents of the report is afforded, such reports constitute competent evidence upon which a court may base its findings.

Russell had claimed that, because juvenile dependency cases move so quickly, it would be impossible for him to subpoena the necessary witnesses to rebut the evidence within the social study. (A jurisdictional hearing must be held within fifteen judicial days from the detention hearing.) The California Supreme Court noted that a parent must have the opportunity to call witnesses, but that the time scheme was adequate to meet due process considerations.

Discussion

The *Malinda S.* case is limited to juvenile court dependency cases. The report is admissible only if the report is served on the other parties ten days before the hearing, so that they have an opportunity to subpoena any witnesses whose statements appear in the report and if the preparer of the report is present at the hearing to be cross-examined. Obviously, if the child's statements are contained in the report, they become evidence in the case.

The *Malinda S.* case has been criticized by attorneys who represent parents in dependency proceedings. They point out that social workers often are not the "neutral" investigators the California Supreme Court indicated they were. Moreover, they claim that it is unfair to expect the parents to utilize their resources to call witnesses whose statements are contained in the social worker's report. They suggest that, since the Department of Social Services is bringing the legal action to have a child declared a dependent of the court, that agency should produce its witnesses. Several local juvenile courts in California have adopted a local rule consistent with the latter suggestion.

The *Malinda S.* doctrine has been extended to include statements from a child contained in a social report, even though the child was later found to be incompetent to testify at the trial, because of her inability to distinguish truth from falsehood (*In re Kailee B.*, 1993). The appellate court in its decision noted:

> Historical analyses of the arcane judicial rules concerning hearsay and competency that have developed over the centuries in cases involving adults, whether civil or criminal in nature, are of little assistance in proceedings designed only to determine how best to safeguard the welfare of children of extremely tender years. Such children may be totally incapable of treating with the abstractions that underlie testimonial competency, yet are quite capable of observing and reporting on specific events to which they are privy. . . .

After holding that the statements contained within the social study were admissible, the appellate court went on to indicate how those statements should be utilized by the trial court.

> Although we have concluded the remarks attributed to Kailee in the reports were admissible for their probative value under the social studies exception to the hearsay rule, it is important to emphasize that, in order to ascertain and protect the best interests of the child in actions of this sort, the determinative question often is not the literal truth of every matter implied or potentially deducible from the child's statements, but rather whether those statements, in fact, were made, and if they were, what could have caused the child to utter them.

In domestic relations cases, there are often investigative reports prepared for the court's consideration. In California a custody investigation report and recommendation may also be prepared and submitted to the domestic relations court at trial (California Civil Code §4602). That report may contain hearsay evidence. The Civil Code provides that the court may consider this report, but may not admit it into evidence absent stipulation by the parties (*In re Marriage of Russo*, 1971). Hearsay evidence can be stricken from the report on motion by either party.

Case Example (*Hord v. Morgan*, 1989)

The parents of two children dissolved their marriage in 1983. They were awarded joint custody of the children, with the mother having primary physical custody during the school year and the father during the summer. Each parent also had reasonable visitation within those two periods. All pick up and delivery of the children was to be at a particular location in Fort Scott, Kansas. The mother remarried and moved to Clinton, Missouri, while the father moved to Oklahoma.

Shortly after the dissolution, problems developed between the parents. They complained of each other's conduct, and the custody and visitation issues were returned to court for modification. At that hearing, the court reduced the amount of time that the father had custody of the children and modified the joint custody to sole custody for the mother. During the hearing, a witness for the mother testified to a conversation she had with one of the children.

ATTORNEY: Okay. And who would make those statements?
WITNESS: His father.
ATTORNEY: And what type of statements were they?
WITNESS: Statements. "Your mother really doesn't care about you. Your mother is not a good mother." Along that line. That is about as specific as I can get.

The attorney also asked the witness about statements the child had made concerning his father inflicting punishment on him and causing bruises.

The father's attorney objected to all of these statements and appealed the decision to modify custody. The appellate court affirmed the trial court's decision, noting that

> It is also worthy of note that in dealing with custody matters there can be legitimate and relevant reasons for the trial court to have before it evidence of what children are saying to others concerning their relationship with their parents, i.e., other than for the truthfulness of what has been said. The trial court can receive this evidence, in the nature of background information, in an effort to determine whether to exercise its discretion to conduct an in-chambers interview with the child, pursuant to section 452.385, RSMo 1986.

The court went on to note that there is a recent trend toward increased flexibility regarding the admission of statements made by a child to others.

For example, in a case from Iowa, *Lorenza v. State* (1988), the court found that the trial judge in a divorce proceeding can require presentation and dissemination of a child abuse report despite administrative regulations to the contrary.

The "Residual" Exception

The Federal Rules of Evidence 803[24] and 804[b]5 allow for the admission of statements not specifically covered by any other exception so long as they have the equivalent circumstantial guarantees of trustworthiness. These other types of statements are referred to as residual hearsay exceptions.

To establish the guarantee of trustworthiness the courts will consider criteria such as the credibility of the statement and the child at the time the statement was made in light of the child's persona, knowledge, the availability of time to fabricate, the child's bias, and the suggestiveness created by leading questions. Courts further consider other corroborating factors such as the credibility of the person testifying to the statement, the availability of the child at trial for cross-examination, whether the child has recanted or reaffirmed the statement, and the existence of corroborating physical evidence. According to Graham (1988) in child abuse cases, courts should also consider whether the child's statement discloses an embarrassing incident that a child would not normally relate unless true, is a cry for help, employs appropriate childlike language, or describes a sexual act beyond a child's normal experience. Also relevant are the child's age and maturity and the child's relationship with the accused. (*State v. Myatt*, 1985).

Most states have either adopted the federal residual exceptions or have adopted similar ones. This is a great resource for child maltreatment cases, since these exceptions can be applied when none of the others seem to fit. For example, several states now admit statements by children to parents which are not excited utterances under this exception (e.g., *State v. McCafferty*, S.D., 1984). However, as described earlier, in *Idaho v.*

Wright (1990) the U.S. Supreme Court found that the residual exception was not a firmly rooted exception and that statements allowed under this exception must have additional indicia of trustworthiness to be held reliable.

The "Sexually Abused Child" Exception

Since not all the hearsay exceptions specifically focus upon child maltreatment cases, many states have passed special statutory hearsay exceptions for child sexual abuse prosecutions. At least twenty states have now passed statutes creating special hearsay exceptions which permit the admissibility of a child victim's hearsay statements when the equivalent circumstances of trustworthiness or reliability required by the Federal Rules of Evidence are present. These statutory exceptions do not need to fall under a traditional hearsay exception to be admissible.

Although state statutes or rules differ in the procedures they establish for determining the admissibility of child testimony, they generally require that the statements possess the guarantees of trustworthiness required under the Confrontation Clause. This criterion is determined by corroborating facts such as physical evidence, and the assessed credibility of the witness.

State v. Ryan (1984) illustrates the Supreme Court of Washington's search for particularized guarantees of trustworthiness. In *Ryan* two children first told one story to their mothers, then recanted it after questioning by the mother. The court reversed the trial court's admission of these statements, concluding that the children had been too susceptible to the mother's influence.

While such "sexually abused child" exceptions may be helpful when traditional hearsay exceptions are inadequate, they can also introduce some problems. For example, how the age of a child is defined could mean that children over a certain age would be excluded from this protection. Many state laws follow the traditional confrontation interpretation, and require that the child be "unavailable" before the exception can be used. Also, a child's statements to police officers, social workers or anyone else trained to interview children may not be included, because the courts have not found that such statements possess circumstantial guarantees of trustworthiness.

CONCLUSION

The special problems presented by having children testify in court are being met by creating special court procedures for children and allowing exceptions to the hearsay rule. The changing needs of present-day litigation brought about by the many cases of child maltreatment have made such liberalizations in court procedure necessary. Without hearsay exceptions, important or crucial evidence might not ever be presented in court, especially if the child is unavailable as a witness. Even when the child is available, such out-of-court statements can provide important and valuable information for the jury. These provisions, however, must always be balanced against the confrontational rights of the accused and the risks that hearsay evidence may be based on misperception, faulty memory, or insincerity.

CHAPTER 13

Expert Witnesses in Child Abuse Cases

A significant means of proving that child abuse has occurred is through the testimony of an expert witness. As we learned in the previous chapter, statements by the allegedly abused child can be received into evidence through a number of exceptions to the hearsay rule. Such statements may also be admissible from an expert witness. In addition, the expert may be able to give opinions on whether abuse has taken place, how the abuse occurred, and, in certain circumstances, who was the likely person to have abused the child.

As we have noted, child abuse is difficult to prove. The child may be too young to testify or the testimony may be suspect precisely because the victim is a child. These problems are often compounded by a lack of physical evidence. If the child is not able to testify, there may be very little, if any, evidence to present in court.

The rules of evidence govern who can be qualified as an expert witness, what types of issues the expert can address and what types of opinions the expert can give. In this chapter we examine the legal framework in which expert witnesses give testimony in child abuse cases. We will first discuss who can be an expert witness. Then we will address the admissibility of expert testimony. In addition, we will give examples of the ways in which expert testimony has played a part in a variety of child abuse cases.

WHO CAN BE AN EXPERT WITNESS?

The rules of evidence in each jurisdiction describe who can be qualified as an expert witness. According to the Federal Rules of Evidence:

> A person is qualified to testify as an expert if he/she has special knowledge, skill, experience, training, or education sufficient to qualify him or her as an expert on the subject to which his/her testimony relates. Against the objection of a party, such special knowledge, skill, experience, training,

or education must be shown before the witness may testify as an expert. (Section 720)

In an actual case, the judge will decide whether a person is qualified to testify as an expert. Typically, an attorney will call a person as a witness and ask the judge to qualify the witness as an expert in a particular area. For example, the attorney may ask that the witness be qualified as a medical doctor with expertise in the causes of physical injuries to children. The attorney will then offer evidence, usually testimony from the doctor, that supports the conclusion that the doctor is an expert. Those questions might address any of the following:

- Education
- Experience with the subject matter
- Publications
- Recognition within the field
- Specialized training
- Familiarity with relevant professional literature
- Membership in professional organizations
- Prior qualification as an expert witness in other court proceedings.

The attorneys for the other parties will also have an opportunity to examine the witness on any qualifications.

After the examination regarding qualifications concludes, the judge will decide whether the witness is an expert and in which areas the witness is qualified to testify as an expert. Thereafter, the questions regarding the case before the court will commence.

ADMISSIBILITY OF EXPERT TESTIMONY

To be admissible at trial, expert testimony must be relevant to the issues at hand, and it must be based upon scientifically valid reasoning properly applied to the facts of the case. To be relevant means that the court must find a logical connection between the evidence offered by the expert and the issues to be proven. In addition, the court must balance the probative value of the evidence against legal rules which might exclude that testimony. For example, the expert may be prepared to give an opinion that a particular person caused the abuse or that a child was telling the truth when he talked to the doctor. Those opinions are relevant to the issues before the court, but the law will not permit an expert to give that type of opinion because of other legal policy reasons.

The final requirement for admissibility is that the expert's opinion be based on valid reasoning. If the expert is relying upon scientific evidence, there must be a preliminary showing that the reasoning or methodology utilized is valid. The United States Supreme Court explained this last requirement in a recent case.

Case Example (*Daubert v. Merrill Dow Pharmaceutical, Inc.*, 1993)

Two minor children had serious birth defects. They and their parents sued the defendant pharmaceutical company, alleging that the birth defects had been caused by the mother's ingestion of Bendectin, a prescription antinausea drug marketed by the defendant. The defendant made a motion for summary judgment, alleging that it could not be proven that the drug caused the birth defect.

In support of its position, the defendant submitted an affidavit of an expert well-credentialed on the risks from exposure to various chemical substances. He stated that he had reviewed all of the literature on Bendectin and human birth defects and concluded that no study had found that Bendectin was capable of causing malformations in fetuses. He concluded that maternal use of Bendectin during the first trimester of pregnancy

has not been shown to be a risk factor for human birth defects.

The plaintiffs responded with eight expert witnesses of their own, each with impressive credentials. They concluded that Bendectin can cause birth defects. Their opinions were based on animal studies that found a link between Bendectin and malformations, pharmacological studies, and "reanalysis" of previously published epidemiological (human statistical) studies.

The district court granted the motion for summary judgment and the U.S. Court of Appeals affirmed that decision. Each noted that scientific evidence is admissible only if the principle upon which it is based is "sufficiently established to have general acceptance in the field to which it belongs," and each cited case law.

The U.S. Supreme Court reversed the district court and relied principally upon the Federal Rules of Evidence, Rule 402, which states:

> All relevant evidence is admissible, except as otherwise provided by the Constitution of the United States, by Act of Congress, by these rules, or by other rules prescribed by the Supreme Court pursuant to statutory authority. Evidence which is not relevant is not admissible.

The Supreme Court noted that the Federal Rules go on to describe expert testimony in Rule 702:

> If scientific, technical, or other specialized knowledge will assist the trier of fact to understand the evidence or to determine a fact in issue, a witness qualified as an expert by knowledge, skill, experience, training, or education may testify thereto in the form of an opinion or otherwise.

The Court held that these rules do not require that there be "general acceptance" in the scientific community as a prerequisite to admissibility, pursuant to the *Frye* case. Instead, the Court stated that the trial judge must ensure "that any and all scientific testimony or evidence admitted is not only relevant, but reliable."

The Court went on to explain that a trial

judge facing proffered expert scientific testimony must determine whether the witness is an expert and whether the expert will testify as to scientific knowledge that will assist the trier of fact (judge or jury) to understand or determine a fact in issue.

> This entails a preliminary assessment of whether the reasoning of methodology underlying the testimony is scientifically valid and of whether that reasoning or methodology properly can be applied to the facts in issue.

The Court concluded its decision with some advice to trial judges facing admissibility issues, adding that the justices were confident the trial judges "possess the capacity to undertake this review."

Discussion

This case modified the test by which most courts admit expert testimony. The previous test, based on the *Frye* standard (*Frye v. U. S.*, 1923), focused upon whether the technique was "generally accepted" as reliable in the relevant scientific community. This test was seen as protecting the courts from untested scientific theories unless and until those theories had been accepted within the scientific community which would normally examine them.

The Supreme Court found that the Federal Rules of Evidence did not incorporate the *Frye* standard, but left the matter to the trial judge, who must determine whether the proffered testimony is relevant. The Court recognized that judges are not scientists, but suggested that through the use of the adversary process they will be able to determine which scientific theories are relevant to the issues at hand and which are not.

The *Daubert* case may have a major impact upon child abuse cases in court. Expert witnesses are often called to testify on behalf of one of the parties in these cases. The theories they bring have been subjected to the *Frye* test. Now they will apparently have to be reexamined in light of the new Supreme Court ruling.

THE SCOPE OF EXPERT TESTIMONY

In most child abuse proceedings several issues are raised. The trial may include descriptive and diagnostic issues, issues of witness credibility, and issues regarding the legal facts of the case: for example, was the child abused, or who committed the abuse? In order to address these issues, the attorneys may offer expert testimony.

Descriptive and Diagnostic Issues

Descriptive and diagnostic issues that may be presented in child maltreatment litigation include:

1. What are the characteristics of child abuse and neglect?
2. What are the behaviors commonly observed in abused and neglected children?
3. Does the alleged victim exhibit these characteristics and does he or she fit the profile of an abused or neglected child?
4. Does the alleged offender fit an offender profile?

Case Example (*People v. Gray*, 1986)

Gray was charged with two counts of lewd and lascivious conduct upon a child under the age of fourteen years. At the trial the defendant's nine-year-old stepdaughter testified that the defendant had sexually abused her on two occasions between January and June of 1985. She did not reveal these incidents until the summer of 1985 when she visited her father and stepmother. Some of the details of the incidents were revealed only to the investigating police officer.

Dr. Mosman, a child psychologist, testified about the traits and characteristics of child sexual abuse. He gave opinions about experiences and behavioral traits common to child abuse victims. Dr. Oliver, a defense expert, testified that delayed reporting is not unusual in child molestation cases. The defendant denied he touched the child with any sexual motivation.

The defendant was convicted of both counts. He appealed, arguing in part that Dr. Mosman's testimony was improper. The court affirmed the conviction, stating that the expert testimony was allowable, since:

> Here, Doctor Mosman's testimony was not admitted "as a means of proving—from the alleged victim's post-incident trauma—that a [molestation] had, in fact, occurred." It was admitted after Tosha testified she did not tell anyone about touching appellant's penis, except in response to Detective English's questioning, she did not tell anyone until she testified in court that appellant said, at the time, "it won't bite you," and she told her mother she might have been incorrect about some incidents, but agreed with her father, because she feared his anger. Doctor Mosman said that delayed reporting and inconsistency is not unusual, with victims of child molestation, a statement concurred in by the defense expert, and explained what causes children to react differently to molestation than adults might expect.

The court noted that both experts had acknowledged that there are certain behavioral traits commonly seen in molestation victims, including delayed reporting, increased disclosure over time, accommodation in the sense of outward affection toward an adult the child also fears, and increased likelihood of immediately reporting a stranger than a family member. The court permitted the expert testimony because:

> The subject of child molestation and, more particularly, the sensitivities of the victims, is

knowledge sufficiently beyond common experience such that the opinion of an expert would be of assistance to the trier of fact.

Discussion

In the *Gray* case, the appellate court permitted the expert witness to testify as to commonly observed behaviors in victims so long as the expert did not offer an opinion whether Tosha had, in fact, been abused. It was up to the jury to decide from the facts of the case whether Tosha had been abused. This type of testimony, however, has its limits because the reactions of victims to abusive behavior vary widely, and there are no fully established or agreed-upon observable indicators of "abused child victim profile."

Witness Credibility

Expert witnesses are generally not permitted to give testimony concerning whether a witness is telling the truth. This issue is one for the jury to determine. Appellate courts have been called on to review expert opinion evidence on numerous occasions.

Case Example (*State v. Batangan*, 1990)

The defendant was charged with sexual abuse of his seven-year-old daughter. The daughter testified that when she was six or seven years old, on four or five occasions, the defendant performed sexual acts on her. The daughter could give no times or dates, nor could she give specific details as to any one incident. There was no physical injury and no third-party witness. The daughter did not report the incidents until several months after the occurrences. She later recanted her allegations.

At trial, however, she testified that she had been sexually abused by the defendant.

At the trial the State presented Dr. John Bond as an expert witness in the field of clinical psychology with a subspecialty in the treatment of sexually abused children. He testified that he had evaluated the child (her personality, intelligence, behavior) and what she had related to him regarding the incidents of sexual abuse. He testified about the behavior of child sexual abuse victims in general. Finally, he testified how he evaluates whether a child is telling the truth and then implicitly testified that the child in this case was believable and that she had been abused by the defendant.

The defendant objected to Dr. Bond's testimony, but the trial court overruled the objection and permitted him to testify. The defendant was convicted and appealed.

The Hawaii Supreme Court reversed the conviction and held that admission of the expert testimony was in error. While the court acknowledged that expert testimony may play a useful role in disabusing the jury of some widely held misconceptions about the behavior of child victims, it held that such evidence must assist the jury without unduly prejudicing the defendant.

> Thus, while expert testimony explaining "seemingly bizarre" behavior of child sex abuse victims is helpful to the jury and should be admitted, conclusory opinions that abuse did occur and that the child victim's report of abuse is truthful and believable is of no assistance to the jury, and therefore, should not be admitted. . . . The jury is fully capable, on its own, of making the connections to the facts of the particular case before them and drawing inferences and conclusions therefrom.

Case Example (*State v. Mazerole*, 1992)

The parents of three children were charged with sexually abusing them. The two older children,

seven and nine years of age, were qualified to be witnesses by the trial court. They testified about their parents' abusive conduct.

In their defense the parents called an expert in child psychology to testify on the issue of fabrication and related psychological issues. The expert intended to testify that the children's allegations could be childhood fantasies because they involved factors not usually found in child abuse.

Before the expert testified, the trial court conducted a hearing outside of the presence of the jury. At that hearing, the court concluded that the expert should not be allowed to testify on those issues. The parents were convicted of the charges and appealed to the Maine Supreme Court.

The supreme court affirmed the trial court. It noted that that expert's opinion would have been based on his own experience and a review of the literature. It held that such opinions were not better than any held by lay people sitting on the jury.

> The jury was capable of making its own conclusions about the believability of the children's allegations without the need for expert testimony on the possibility that the children were making them up.

Discussion

These two cases offer examples of issues about which an expert may not testify. The trier of fact, in these cases the jury, is asked to determine the facts of the case. When there is conflicting evidence, it is the duty of the jury to determine the credibility of the witnesses. On the issue of credibility, the law considers jurors just as capable as experts. Therefore, when an expert proposes to give an opinion concerning credibility, the court will ordinarily exclude that testimony.

Case Example (*People v. Nelson*, 1990)

The defendant was accused of aggravated criminal sexual assault and aggravated criminal sexual abuse of a child. At the trial the child testified that he went on fishing trips with the defendant, a family friend. During one of those trips, the child said, the defendant touched his penis with both his hands and mouth. Thereafter he refused to go on any further fishing trips, but did not tell anyone until the next year when he was questioned by his mother. The mother testified that the child no longer wanted to go fishing with anyone, his grades in school had dropped, and he was often afraid and would sleep on the floor of his parent's bedroom. The defendant denied the allegations.

During the trial, Dr. Hoffman, a psychologist and expert in the field of child abuse, was called to testify in rebuttal for the limited purposes of the victim's credibility, which had been attacked by the defendant on cross-examination. Dr. Hoffman explained how children act when they have been sexually abused, how offenders act when they are trying to lure children into a situation where they may be sexually abused, and how the characteristics exhibited by the child in this case were consistent with those to be displayed by a victim of sexual abuse. She did not testify concerning who might have abused the child, nor did she indicate that the child had, in fact, been sexually abused or that he was telling the truth. She also testified that the "unusual behaviors" exhibited by the child could have been triggered by factors other than sexual abuse. The defendant also presented an expert witness who disputed Dr. Hoffman's knowledge and testimony.

The jury convicted the defendant of both counts, and the defendant appealed. The Illinois appellate court affirmed the conviction, noting that such testimony is admissible in rebuttal after the defendant has attacked the victim's credibility.

At this time, we choose to limit the admissibility of such testimony to rebuttal after the victim's credibility has first been attacked. Under such circumstances, defendant's own actions have necessitated the use of syndrome testimony, especially when defense counsel emphasizes some unusual aspect of the victim's behavior such as recantation or delayed reporting.

Discussion

The appellate court in the *Nelson* case concluded that, while the prosecution may not address the issue of credibility of the child witness initially, it may respond to claims by the defendant that the child was not telling the truth by offering expert witness testimony about the behavior of child abuse victims in general. The defense had attacked the child's credibility by emphasizing that the child had delayed his report of the abuse. The appellate court acknowledged that jurors may not understand that it is common for child sexual abuse victims to delay reporting victimization and permitted an expert witness to explain how child victims as a group generally behave. Since the expert's testimony was limited to an explanation of the behavior generally, without reference to the defendant or to the child's credibility, it did not amount to an improper bolstering of the victim's testimony. Finally, the expert testified that the victim's unusual behavior patterns could have resulted from something other than being sexually abused. Expert testimony in this form was proper, the court held, since it allowed the jury to give whatever weight it deemed appropriate to the testimony.

Legal Conclusions about the Alleged Facts

Courts of law must determine ultimate conclusions about the cases before them. These are legal conclusions, such as: was the alleged victim abused, and did the alleged offender commit the abuse? Normally, expert testimony may not be offered to prove legal conclusions (*State v. Batangan*, 1990).

What is permissible expert testimony varies considerably, depending on the type of court involved, the issue involved, the stage of the proceedings, and which side is presenting the expert witness. In order to examine in more detail when experts have been allowed to address and answer the questions listed above, we will now focus specifically on the different use of expert testimony in physical and sexual abuse cases. First, we will look at the field of physical child abuse and testimony on the battered child syndrome. Second, we will look at the field of sexual child abuse, the child sexual abuse accommodation theory, and the use of anatomically correct dolls.

PHYSICAL ABUSE

Physical child abuse is legally defined as nonaccidental physical injury to a child. The law often turns to experts in order to determine whether a child has been physically abused. Expert medical testimony may be indispensable to counter claims that the child's injuries were accidental (Berliner, et al., 1988). When allegations of physical abuse are tried in court, the prosecution must first prove that the child's injuries were nonaccidental and, second, establish the identity of the perpetrator. In the past, expert testimony on physical abuse was restricted to a description of the nature of the injuries, and conclusions regarding whether a particular pattern of injuries was the result of abuse were left to the jury to make. In the last two decades, however, expert testimony on "the battered child syndrome" has been used to establish that a child's injuries were not accidental.

The Battered Child Syndrome

The term "battered child syndrome" was first coined by Kempe and his colleagues (1962). As described in earlier chapters, the battered child syndrome refers to a child who has received repeated and/or serious injuries by nonaccidental means. Children with battered child syndrome usually show signs of repeated abuse, with injuries in different stages of healing. Characteristically, these injuries are inflicted by someone who is ostensibly caring for the child. Several elements are included in the "battered child syndrome." They are:

1. The child is usually under three years of age.
2. There may be evidence of bone injury at different times.
3. There may be subdural hematomas with or without skull fractures.
4. There is a seriously injured child who does not have a history that fits the injuries.
5. There may be evidence of soft tissue injury.
6. There may be evidence of neglect.

The battered child syndrome simply indicates that a child found with the type of injuries outlined above has not suffered those injuries by accidental means (Kempe, et al., 1962).

Case Example (*People v. Jackson*, 1971)

The defendant was accused of beating his child. During the trial the child's mother testified that she left the child with the defendant. The child suffered injuries and was taken to a hospital and examined by a pediatrician. The doctor testified at the trial that the child suffered from burns, a previous head injury with a subdural hematoma (a liquefied blood clot on the brain), a swollen forearm, a distended abdomen diagnosed as injury to the liver, two recent fractures in the right forearm and one recent fracture in the left forearm (revealed from X rays), scratches, and ten broken ribs. The doctor concluded that the child suffered from the battered child syndrome.

Despite the defendant's denial he was found guilty of the charges and appealed. He claimed that the expert testimony was improper.

The appellate court affirmed the conviction, noting that:

> A finding, as in this case, of the "battered child syndrome" is not an opinion by the doctor as to whether any particular person has done anything, but, as this doctor indicated, "it would take thousands of children to have the severity and number and degree of injuries that this child had over the span of time that we had" by accidental means. In other words, the "battered child syndrome" simply indicates that a child found with the type of injuries outlined above has not suffered those injuries by accidental means.

Against the claim that the expert was giving an opinion that the defendant was the person who inflicted the injuries, the court said:

> The additional finding that the injuries were probably occasioned by someone who is ostensibly caring for the child is simply a conclusion based on logic and reason. Only someone regularly "caring" for the child has the continuing opportunity to inflict these types of injuries; an isolated contact with a vicious stranger would not result in this pattern of successive injuries stretching through several months.

Discussion

Appellate courts have uniformly permitted expert testimony on the battered child syndrome. Since the *Jackson* case, courts have allowed medical expert testimony on the battered child syndrome to address the following:

1. describe what the characteristics of abuse look like;
2. express an opinion as to whether the child in question exhibits the characteristics; and

3. express a professional opinion as to whether the child in question has been abused.

In addition, many courts permit expert physicians to give opinions on the means used to inflict injuries (*State v. Jurgens*, 1988; *State v. McClary*, 1988; *State v. Tanner*, 1983).

Case Example (*People v. Newlun*, 1991)

The defendant was charged with fifteen counts of lewd and lascivious acts with a child under the age of fourteen. The evidence at trial revealed that when the child, M., was fourteen months of age she was examined by her pediatrician who discovered warts around the child's anal opening. In the doctor's experience, such warts in a young child were likely to be venereal warts. She referred M. to a dermatologist who determined that the warts were probably contracted by contact with an infected penis. But, since the medical literature at that time suggested other possible means of transmission, and M.'s mother denied any possible molestation, the doctor did not report the case to child protective services.

The evidence further showed that M.'s parents separated when M. was about three, and about a year later the mother noticed that M. was unusually dirty and had scratches after a visit with her father, the defendant. The mother took M. immediately to see the same pediatrician, who noticed that M.'s hair was streaked and matted, her elbows and legs had many abrasions, her buttocks and upper thighs were covered with red crisscross marks, and the areas around her rectum and vagina were red. M. made no statements to the doctor, did not like being examined, and became upset when her father's name was mentioned.

The next day, in domestic relations court, the mother made an unsuccessful attempt to have the father's visitation suspended. Two months later the mother testified that after she picked M. up at her father's home, the child came into her room crying. She took her clothes off, climbed on top of the mother's naked body, moved the mother's legs apart, and put her body in between the mother's legs. She said "This is the way Daddy makes me sleep."

The next day the mother took M. to be seen by child protective services. That same day M. was examined by Dr. Pugno, the medical director of the Shasta General Hospital, who had examined several hundred children for suspected molestation. Dr. Pugno observed that the child's vaginal region had suffered injuries consistent only with repeated penetration by an adult penis. The doctor testified that there was no reasonable possibility the injuries could have been accidentally self-inflicted, and intentional self-infliction was equally unlikely because of the painfulness of the injuries. At an absolute minimum it would have taken half a dozen sexual assaults to produce these injuries.

The doctor also examined the child's anal region and noticed that the anal opening was almost an inch. The doctor testified that this so-called "wink reflex" is typical in children who have been repeatedly sodomized. He said that it would have taken at least twelve to fourteen to as many as thirty penetrations over a six-month period to establish such a pronounced opening.

The defendant was convicted of all fifteen counts by a jury and appealed the verdict. On appeal he contended that there was insufficient evidence to prove that he committed fifteen separate acts of molestation. The appellate court rejected his claim, stating:

> In the present case, the minimum number of acts committed was established by the unrebutted testimony of Dr. Pugno that it would have taken at least six vaginal penetrations and at least twelve to fourteen anal penetrations to produce the injuries and abnormalities he detected on examining M. The competency of Dr. Pugno as an expert witness on this subject was never questioned. Given that expert medical testimony about the physical characteristics of an injury is generally competent

to prove the cause of the injury, it would be anomalous if a reviewing court could not consider such testimony as substantial evidence of molestation.

The appellate court concluded by affirming the conviction.

Discussion

This is an example of an expert witness describing to the jury both the type of injury (sexual abuse by another person) and the minimum number of separate assaults. The expert rendered an opinion based on viewing hundreds of young persons suspected of being sexually abused. With this background, the doctor was able to testify as an expert in the diagnosis of physical injuries consistent with being sexually abused. His testimony concerning the type of injury and the number of assaults was believed by the jury. Moreover, his testimony was found by the appellate court to be a sufficient basis for multiple counts of sexual abuse.

It is clear that the *People v. Newlun* case would not have been possible fifty years ago. The justice and child protective systems would have been unable to respond to the mother's concerns about her daughter. Until very recently, there would have been no child protective services investigation available, no medical expertise on the type of injuries suffered or on the number of times the child was assaulted, and no charges filed by a district attorney.

The father argued that there was insufficient evidence to convict him on any specific time or day or any specific sexual assault. Since the child did not testify as to the day or date of any assault, the father claimed that he was not given sufficient notice so he could adequately prepare his defense. He alleged that he was therefore denied due process of law.

Do you believe that a conviction for a crime

such as that charged in the *Newlun* case must be supported by proof that it occurred at a specific time or on a specific date? Do you believe it is fair to the accused to be charged with fifteen counts of abuse alleged to have occurred during a general time period? Is the doctor's testimony about the minimum number of assaults a sufficient basis for the jury to convict the defendant?

An expert testifying on the battered child syndrome may not express an opinion as to whether the defendant in the case had committed the abuse, that is, an opinion about the identity of the perpetrator. Thus, even in the case of the battered child syndrome which represents the most "objective" medical criteria to ascertain the existence of abuse, expert testimony may not be used to establish the guilt of a particular defendant.

In *State v. Phillips* (1991) the court held that jury instructions which allowed for the inference that a child suffering from the battered child syndrome had been injured by a caretaker did not unlawfully shift burden of proof to defendants. In this case, a married couple was charged with first degree murder in the death of a foster child and felony abuse stemming from certain injuries which an adopted child had suffered. Part of the state's case included the testimony of a doctor who qualified as an expert witness in the field of pediatrics and child abuse. During his testimony, the expert explained the battered child syndrome. At the conclusion of the case, the trial court instructed the jury that, if it found that a child had suffered from the battered child syndrome, it was permissible to infer that the child's injuries were inflicted by a caretaker. The defendants were convicted, and they appealed on numerous grounds, including a challenge to the admission of the expert witness testimony and the jury instruction regarding the battered child syndrome.

The Supreme Court of North Carolina rejected each of the defendant's claims and affirmed the convictions. In addressing the defendants' challenge to the expert witness testimony and the related jury instruction, the court found that the type of expert witness testimony which had been elicited fell within that which was authorized by the state's rules of evidence and prior case law. With regard to the jury instruction given by the court, the court noted that a finding that a child suffered from the battered child syndrome allowed for only a permissible inference that the child's injuries had been inflicted by a caretaker, and did not create a mandatory inference or presumption to this effect. Thus, the burden of proof remained on the state to prove beyond a reasonable doubt that the injuries were inflicted by the defendants.

CHILD SEXUAL ABUSE

Where there is medical evidence of sexual abuse, physicians also serve as expert witnesses in sexual abuse cases. In recent years, pediatricians and other medical experts on child sexual abuse have learned more about the medical manifestations of sexual abuse. Typically, the major evidence sought is sperm or seminal fluid on the victim's skin, body openings, or clothing, or damage to vaginal and rectal areas (DeJong, 1989). When such medical evidence exists, it is generally admissible (DeJong and Rose, 1988).

For example, in the case of *People v. Mandibles* (1988), the prosecutor called an expert witness to testify that the child victims had been sexually abused. The expert, Dr. Astrid Heger, had examined the children with a binocular colposcope. She testified that trauma could be observed visually by a trained individual. She described one scar in particular which is classic in very young children for a certain type of sexual abuse. According to her, it appears consistently in almost 90 percent of the girls who describe painful vaginal penetration.

Dr. Hager found scarring and a hymenal opening which was twice the normal size for a ten-year-old female. She testified the findings were consistent with sexual abuse and specifically with penile penetration. Other experts testified during the trial and gave differing views.

The jury convicted the defendant, and he appealed. He claimed that it was improper to permit Dr. Hager to testify because she used a new technique which the prosecution had failed to demonstrate was generally accepted as reliable in the scientific community.

The appellate court affirmed the trial court. It held that the use of a magnifying device was not a new scientific method.

> In contrast, the expression of expert medical opinion as to the cause of a wound or injury falls... outside the realm. Indeed, it is settled by "a long line of California decisions" that an expert medical witness is qualified "to give an opinion of the cause of a particular injury on the basis of the expert's deduction from the appearance of the injury itself."

Since the colposcope only magnified the injured area, it permitted the doctor to examine the injury more closely. As such, the use of the colposcope was not a new scientific technique within the meaning of the *Frye* rule.

Frequently, however, there is no medical evidence of abuse. In these cases, proof is sometimes offered from mental health experts. These experts are prepared to offer several different types of testimony which might lead the trier of fact to conclude that the child has been sexually abused.

Child Sexual Abuse Accommodation Syndrome

The most frequently utilized theory to explain children's reactions to sexual abuse is that supporting the child sexual abuse accommodation syndrome (Summit, 1983). This theory describes the purportedly typical behavior of children who have been victims of repeated sexual abuse by a family member or an adult with whom the child has a trusting relationship. The proposed syndrome is comprised of one or more of five elements: secrecy, helplessness, entrapment and accommodation, delayed disclosure, and retraction (Summit, 1983). According to the child sexual abuse accommodation syndrome, it is typical for sexually abused children to exhibit one or more of these behaviors.

A child who is molested by a trusted adult is often faced with intimidation to keep the molestation a secret. This atmosphere of secrecy conveys to the child that the molestation is bad and must not be exposed. Similarly, a child often fears punishment or loss of the adult's approval if sexual demands are not met and may react with submission and helplessness. According to Summit, the child may also learn to adjust to the traumatic situation and may not display outward manifestations of sexual abuse (Summit, 1983, p. 185). For all of these reasons, sexually abused children may delay disclosure of the molestation and may often retract an accusation because of the traumatic reactions to disclosure (Summit, 1983, p. 188).

Some of the behaviors described in the child sexual abuse accommodation syndrome may be inconsistent with a judge's or jury's understanding of how a victim would respond to repeated sexual abuse. The judge or jury might conclude that it is likely that the child fabricated the story, since he or she did not report it immediately or retracted an accusation. The child sexual abuse accommodation syndrome is therefore typically used to explain the child's behavior to the judge or jury and to establish a victim's credibility in light of such peculiar behavior.

Case Example (*People v. Beckley*, 1990)

This case represents two separate appeals to the Michigan Supreme Court on the same issue, namely, whether an expert witness can testify as to the characteristics and patterns of behavior typically exhibited by sexually abused children. In the first case, the fifteen-year-old child testified that her father had sexual intercourse with her and told her not to tell anyone. The act of intercourse was not alleged until about a year later. During that time she continued to see her father. During cross-examination of the child, the defense attorney stressed the delayed disclosure, the medium of disclosure (a high school essay), the child's continual desire to see her father, and her initial tendency to deny any sexual intercourse.

The prosecution then called Robin Smietanka as an expert witness. The court limited the testimony to the victim's behavior observed by the expert which would be consistent with the profile of an incest victim. The expert commented on the four instances of behavior and said that each was typical of a victim of sexual abuse.

In the second case, the defendant was accused of sexual abuse of her six-year-old daughter. The child accused her mother of holding her arms and legs and forcing her to perform fellatio on the mother's live-in boyfriend. Initially, the child only implicated the boyfriend. Some months later, she accused her mother of participating in the incident.

The prosecution's first witness was Lynn Butterfield, a psychiatrist. She testified relating to sexually abused children generally, as well as an opinion relating to the observable behavior of the child. On cross-examination, she indicated that some of the observed behavior might be attributable to the child's placement in foster care. On redirect examination, she testified that children generally have no knowledge of sexual acts, and therefore there is no way a child could invent a specific sexual act without experiencing it.

The prosecution called a second expert, Dr. Shinedling, who testified about the behavior patterns of children who were sexually abused. Dr. Shinedling also testified as to what expectations persons could have when dealing with a child and his or her precision as to dates and sequences of events. Dr. Shinedling testified that children are very imprecise and have a hard time conceptualizing days, weeks, or months.

In each case the defendant was convicted and appealed, based, in part, on the admissibility of the expert testimony. The supreme court addressed the issues in each case by a review of the law, first summarizing their position regarding the admissibility of evidence relating to behavioral patterns of sexually abused children.

Accordingly, we would hold that evidence of behavioral patterns of sexually abused children is admissible "for the narrow purpose of rebutting an inference that a complainant's post-incident behavior was inconsistent with that of an actual victim of sexual abuse, incest or rape." Therefore . . . we would hold that only those aspects of "child sexual abuse accommodation syndrome," which specifically relate to the particular behaviors which become an issue in the case are admissible.

The court went on to examine the child sexual abuse accommodation syndrome, referring to it as a set of symptoms which tend to occur together, but which do not resolve the question whether abuse occurred. As such, the court held that the syndrome is unreliable as an indicator of sexual abuse. Rather, the expert must focus upon whether the specific behavior at issue is commonly or uncommonly associated with sexually abused children as a class. In this manner, the expert will assist the jury to dispel any popular misconception commonly associated with the demonstrated reaction.

The Michigan Supreme Court went on to state that:

> . . . [A]ny testimony about the truthfulness of this victim's allegations against the defendant would be improper because its underlying purpose would be to enhance the credibility of the witness.

Finally, the supreme court analyzed the facts of each case in light of the legal principles it enunciated and concluded that the conviction of defendant Beckley would be affirmed while the conviction of Ms. Badour would be reversed.

Discussion

The child sexual abuse accommodation syndrome has been permitted as evidence in several criminal court cases (e.g., *Keri v. State*, 1986; *People v. Gray*, 1986; *People v. Luna*, 1988; *People v. Payan*, 1985), while in other proceedings it has not been admitted (e.g., *Johnson v. State*, 1987; *Lantrip v. Commonwealth*, 1986; *People v. Bowker*, 1988; *People v. Roscoe*, 1985; *State v. Haseltine*, 1984). Whether such testimony was allowed depended on the type of proceeding, when in the proceedings the testimony was offered, and for what purpose.

In *People v. Roscoe* (1985) the appellate court held that the lower court had been in error to admit a psychiatrist's testimony on the child sexual abuse accommodation syndrome but decided that the error was harmless. The court held that, although expert testimony is admissible for certain purposes other than to establish defendant's guilt, the rule authorizing expert testimony to rehabilitate a complaining witness's credibility is limited to discussion of victims as a class, supported by references to literature and experience. It does not extend to a diagnosis and discussion of the witness in the case at hand (*Roscoe*, p. 1093). In reaching this decision the court relied heavily on *People v. Bledsoe* (1984), which had noted that psychological syndromes relating to victims were developed not to determine whether a victim had been abused but to assist mental health professionals in treating victims. Similarly, *State v. Haseltine* (1984) and *Johnson v. State* (1987) also rejected testimony that sexual abuse occurred based on the accommodation syndrome.

In summary, the child sexual abuse accommodation syndrome has been admitted in criminal court proceedings primarily as rebuttal to dispute the notion that the child's behavior was inconsistent with sexual abuse. Courts have rejected expert opinion on Summit's accommodation syndrome when such testimony is offered to prove that abuse had occurred. In addition, such testimony has been rejected because there was no showing that the syndrome was generally accepted in the relevant scientific community (*Lantrip v. Commonwealth*, 1986; *People v. Bowker*, 1988).

Expert testimony has also been offered to describe what a typical incest family would resemble. In *People v. Lucero* (1986), the defendant was charged with sexual assault of a child. A twelve-year-old daughter accused her father of sexual contact. The father denied the accusations. In addition to the daughter and her mother, the prosecution offered a psychologist as an expert in the field of psychology as it relates to incest victims and families and sexual abuse of children. The witness then testified as to what the typical incest family resembles. The witness offered no opinion whether the defendant's family was a typical incest family or whether the child was credible.

The defendant was convicted and appealed, claiming that because the expert had not interviewed the defendant's family, the testimony was irrelevant. The appellate court affirmed the conviction, stating that the probative value of the testimony outweighed any prejudicial effect it might have had on the process.

The Lucero case seems consistent with the reasoning in the child sexual abuse accommodation syndrome cases. The expert witness may describe classes of persons or families but may not offer an opinion on whether the particular person or family fits the description. That question is left for the jury to decide.

In general, criminal court proceedings have stricter rules for admitting evidence than juvenile dependency and family court proceedings. In dependency proceedings at the trial stage, experts may address both diagnostic and credibility issues. However, even in such proceedings the expert may not address the legal issue of whether the defendant is the perpetrator. For example, in *In re Cheryl H.* (1984), while an opinion that the child had suffered abuse was permitted, the testimony of a psychiatrist that a child was sexually abused *by the father* was ruled inadmissible. The appellate court held that it was error to admit the expert opinion that Cheryl's father was the person who had committed the abuse, because this testimony impermissibly drew inferences about conduct by a third party based primarily on hearsay. The court said that the psychiatrist should only have been permitted to express an opinion that Cheryl believed her father was the one who abused her (*Cheryl*, at p. 1119).

Whether testimony on the child sexual abuse accommodation syndrome should be allowed to prove that sexual abuse has occurred is a hotly debated issue. Hensley (1986) believes that the child sexual abuse accommodation syndrome meets all the criteria for the *Frye* rule. He suggests that testimony on the syndrome is appropriate, both to enhance the credibility of the child witness, and to prove that the alleged familial sexual abuse occurred in cases in which the victim has been sexually abused by a relative or other trusted adult in a nonviolent manner.

Levy (1989), on the other hand, concludes that evidence based on the child sexual abuse accommodation syndrome should never be admitted in court proceedings. According to Levy, the symptoms of the syndrome are too broad and overlapping, unmeasurable and based on impressionistic findings rather than scientific data. There is not enough information to determine whether the symptoms are indicative of sexual abuse.

Other experts contend that while the syndrome has a place in the courtroom, it should not be used for diagnostic purposes in court. Myers, Bays, Becker, Berliner, Corwin, and Saywitz (1989) note that many professionals simply assume that, just like the battered child syndrome, the child sexual abuse accommodation syndrome could be used to detect abuse. However, while the battered child syndrome is medical in nature, based on "objective" evidence, the problem with the accommodation syndrome is that some of the components are not necessarily indicative of abuse. The purpose of the syndrome therefore is not to diagnose, but to help explain why so many children

delay reporting the abuse and why so many recant and deny allegations of abuse (ibid. 67–68).

Buckley (1988) also notes that expert testimony on psychological reactions of child abuse victims should not be used to prove that a child was abused, because of the fact that there is such great variation in how children react to being abused. Many of the so-called common effects of abuse may be attributed to other trauma or may exist in normal children.

The Use of Anatomically Correct Dolls

Case Example (*In re Amber B.*, 1987)

A petition was filed in the Solano County Juvenile Court alleging that a child, Amber, had been sexually abused by her father and that her sister was at risk of similar abuse. At the trial on the petition, the Department of Social Services offered an expert witness, Dr. Raming, who had examined Amber on three occasions. Over objection, he testified that in his opinion Amber had been sexually molested and that she believed she had been molested by her father.

Dr. Raming's opinion was based on two factors. First was the nature of Amber's reports of abuse, in which she described instances of abuse in varying ways. Dr. Raming testified that children who have been molested will

> talk about being abused, but they will do this by consistently giving the . . . same facts or the essence in different words, such that they have an event or an experience in their minds and are not merely repeating . . . rote by rote, someone else's words. . . .

The second factor was the nature of Amber's behavior with an anatomically correct doll in Dr. Raming's office. During two of Dr. Raming's examinations, Amber placed her index finger in the vaginal and anal openings of the doll and pushed and twisted her finger vigorously. According to Dr. Raming, Amber's behavior with the doll

> is fairly consistent with molested children. This is not the usual type of behavior one would see in children who are in a stage of age-appropriate sex exploration. . . . [W]hen children this age describe or graphically demonstrate anal or vaginal penetration, it's pretty much assumed that the child learned that from experience and not from . . . sex exploration with other children.

Amber did not testify at the trial. Her father testified and denied the abuse. The juvenile court sustained the petition, alleging that Amber had been molested while in the care of her parents, although it did not find that the father had molested her. The court placed her and her sister with their mother, afforded the father supervised visits, and required counseling for Amber and both parents.

The father appealed the juvenile court decision, claiming that the expert testimony was improperly admitted, since it was based on a new scientific method of proof that had not been shown to satisfy the *Kelly-Frye* test of admissibility (*People v. Kelly*, 1976).

> Under the *Kelly-Frye* rule, evidence based on a new scientific method of proof is admissible only upon a showing that the procedure has been generally accepted as reliable in the scientific community in which it was developed.

The appellate court noted that, while the test is usually applied to novel devices or processes involving the manipulation of physical evidence such as lie detectors, experimental systems of blood typing, voiceprints, identification by human bite marks, and microscopic analysis of gunshot residue, it can also be utilized for a new scientific process operating on purely psychological evidence offered to the courts.

The appellate court stated that:

> The purpose of the *Kelly-Frye* test is to prevent fact-finders from being misled by the "aura of

infallibility" that may surround unproven scientific methods.

The appellate court first determined that the *Kelly-Frye* rule applied to juvenile court dependency cases, since proof in these cases must be supported by evidence that is legally admissible in the trial of civil cases. The court then addressed whether the technique employed by Dr. Raming for detecting child sexual abuse is a new scientific method of proof which satisfied the *Kelly-Frye* rule. It concluded that it was a new scientific method and therefore subject to the *Kelly-Frye* test. It held that the trial court erred when it failed to require a showing of general acceptance in the relevant scientific community in accordance with *Kelly-Frye*.

> We conclude that the practice of detecting child sexual abuse by (1) observing a child's behavior with anatomically correct dolls, and (2) analyzing the child's reports of abuse is . . . "a new scientific process operating on purely psychological evidence" and is subject to the *Kelly-Frye* test.

The dependency finding was reversed and the matter referred back to the juvenile court.

Discussion

Amber B. is an example of expert witness testimony which offered an improper opinion. The expert witness was permitted to testify that he believed Amber had been sexually molested, based upon her play with anatomically correct dolls, without first establishing that there had been some acceptance within the scientific community that such doll play was indicative of sexual abuse. The case was sent back to the trial court for retrial. If there were a retrial and such evidence could be produced by the party calling Dr. Raming, he would be able to give the same testimony he did at the first trial. It is unlikely, however, that such evidence would be produced. Most studies indicate that such behavior with anatomically correct dolls does not indicate that the child was sexually abused (White and Santilli, 1988).

Amber B. reflects the state of the law in California and in many states before the *Daubert* case was handed down by the United States. Whether the test announced in *Daubert* will be adopted by the states remains to be seen.

The scientific literature on the degree to which children's behavior with anatomically correct dolls can correctly assess whether abuse has occurred is rather scant. Three studies are commonly cited. In the first conducted by White, Strom, Santilli, and Halpin (1987), two groups of children (N = 25 in each group) were interviewed to elicit their reactions to anatomically correct dolls. Significant differences were found between the reactions of children who had not been referred for suspected sexual abuse and those who had. Children who had not been referred for abuse revealed very few behaviors indicative of abuse, whereas suspected abused children demonstrated significantly more sexually related behaviors when presented with the dolls. Younger children were more responsive to the dolls than older children. The study, however, has been criticized for its methodology. It never specified whether the group referred for suspected child abuse had prior interviews with dolls or whether the experimenters who scored the behavior knew which of the groups the children belonged to, and the scoring categories were general and vague (Levy, 1989).

The second study also involved an assessment, using anatomically correct dolls, of the behavior of sexually abused children and the behavior of children who had not been sexually abused (Jampole and Weber, 1987). In this study a comparison was made between one group of children (N = 10) who all had been judged by the child protection workers or the police to have been sexually abused, with another group (N = 10) of children who were not abused. Of the children who had been sexually abused, nine demonstrated sexual behavior with the dolls; one did not. Of the children who had not been sexually abused, eight did not demonstrate

sexual behavior, two did. The authors concluded that anatomically correct dolls are a significant investigative tool. Although the differences between the two groups were clear, it should be noted that the N was very small. Second, all the children in the abused group had already been removed from their homes and had previously been interviewed and interrogated regarding their victimization. Such previous experiences may have affected the way they played with the dolls. Third, no information was given about the nature of the researcher's behavior with the children (Levy, 1989).

The third study (Aman and Goodman, 1987) was somewhat different. Again the goal of the study was to assess the inferential value of children's reactions to anatomically correct dolls. The researchers focused on whether anatomically correct dolls facilitate children's abilities to report events accurately or whether they lead to false reports of abuse. A group of three-year-olds (N = 30) and a group of five-year-olds (N = 30) who were screened to eliminate any suspicions of sexual abuse participated in a real-life play situation with a male confederate for ten minutes. One week later the children were interviewed by a female researcher under three different conditions. In the anatomically correct doll condition children were questioned with the use of four anatomically correct dolls. In the second condition the children were questioned with dolls that looked just like the anatomically correct dolls, but without the secondary sexual characteristics. In the third group no dolls were used. All groups were asked several misleading questions implying a sexually inappropriate or abusive behavior on the part of the male confederate.

The researchers found that children's suggestibility did not significantly differ with use of the dolls. There were no significant differences in the children's interactions with or without the dolls. The five-year-olds answered the abuse questions more accurately than the three-year-olds. On the basis of these findings the authors of the study concluded that playing with anatomically correct dolls does not lead to false reports of sexual abuse in children. However, this still doesn't answer the question of whether sexually abused children would make false statements or not. So far, a clear profile that clearly distinguishes abused children's play with dolls from nonabused children's play has not been developed.

The use of anatomically correct dolls in child abuse cases was developed primarily as a therapeutic tool, not as a means of investigation. It is still uncertain whether children who have been abused play with the dolls differently from children who have not been abused. The dolls in use are by no means standard, and investigators may use many different protocols in handling the play interviews and have little or no training. Despite their value as a therapeutic tool in evaluating suspected sexual abuse of young children, evidentiary use of anatomically correct dolls in dependency or criminal proceedings has become increasingly controversial and not yet well accepted.

Given the lack of clarity in the interpretation of children's play with dolls, their use in court proceedings should be limited. A noted legal expert in this area has concluded that the dolls should be used only as an investigative tool or as demonstrative evidence to aid children in testifying, not as a diagnosis of sexual abuse (Bulkley, 1988). Levy (1989) asserts that dolls testimony should be inadmissible altogether, even as an aid in a child's testimony. The fact that there is very little scientific evidence to support inferences about abuse from a child's play with anatomically correct dolls, combined with the possibility that such testimony by experts may nevertheless carry an "aura of infallibility" with jurors, warrants the exclusion of expert testimony as a descriptive tool.

MEDICAL NEGLECT

Expert witnesses are sometimes utilized in medical neglect cases. These cases usually arise in the context of a juvenile court dependency proceeding in which the state is seeking to protect the child from substandard parental care. The issue in medical neglect situations is whether the parent is providing adequate medical care for the child.

Case Example (*In re Troy Z.*, 1992)

Juvenile court dependency petitions were filed on behalf of Troy alleging that he had suffered serious physical harm inflicted nonaccidentally by his parents and/or by his parents' willful or negligent failure to provide food, clothing, shelter, or medical treatment, and that he was under five and had suffered severe physical abuse by a parent. The facts revealed that the mother noticed that the eyes of her six-month-old son, Troy, were rolled back. When paramedics arrived, Troy had stopped breathing. At the hospital the admitting doctors found him to have no palpable blood pressure and a body temperature of 89 degrees axillary. He was flaccid and appeared severely emaciated and foul smelling.

The parents explained to the social worker that at his third month they had stopped feeding Troy expensive baby formula in favor of boiled milk and other types of food. They said Troy had no medical care because it was a nuisance. Another doctor who examined Troy after admission found he displayed profound emaciation and weighed only seven pounds, five ounces, less than his birth weight. His overall appearance was that of a starved infant.

After a week Troy gained on average more than three ounces a day. The physician concluded that:

> [I]t seems definite that Troy has no illness that would cause him to become undernourished and that his nutritional problem which almost killed him was, with reasonable medical probability, due simply to his being deprived of sufficient feedings by his caretakers.

The parents pled no contest to the petitions. Thereafter, a dispositional hearing was held to determine what plans should be made for Troy. At that hearing, two expert witnesses testified. Dr. Clark, a psychologist who had treated parents involved in similar cases, testified that there was a 50 to 60 percent chance that the parents would reunify with Troy and that neither parent had a close personal relationship with Troy. Thus, Troy would not suffer serious emotional detriment if he were separated from them.

Dr. David Chadwick testified that Troy suffered from an extreme case of nonorganic failure to thrive and that he came within a hairbreadth of dying of starvation. He also testified that the photos taken of Troy shortly before the court hearing accurately reflected that he weighed twenty pounds, which was close to normal in development.

The juvenile court decided not to offer the parents reunification services with Troy, and the parents appealed. The California Supreme Court affirmed the orders of the trial court.

Discussion

Troy Z. exemplifies how medical experts can demonstrate that a child is failing to thrive. Through their expertise, doctors can inform the court what developmental stages a child should display at any age. By observing the child in an out-of-home setting the medical experts can determine whether the low weight and other vital signs are the result of organic causes and possibly beyond the control of the parents or are the result of inadequate parental care. In this case, when Troy gained weight regularly after removal from the parents, it became clear that he was failing to thrive because of parental neglect.

CONCLUSION

In many cases in which the issues of child abuse are raised, an expert's opinion may be offered concerning abuse generally or the facts of the case. Since the evidence at the hearing may not include testimony of the alleged victim, the expert's views may be determinative. For this reason the critical questions in these cases often are whether the expert can testify and on what issues he or she may render an opinion.

It is apparent from the cases cited above that there are some situations and issues for which an expert may testify and some for which he or she may not. A properly qualified expert may discuss the characteristics of an abused child, the characteristics of victims as a class, and the observed behavior of the child in question. However, that testimony may not be offered until someone has challenged the assertion that the child has been abused. Only medical experts have been allowed to link testimony on general characteristics about abuse and victims as a class to conclusions that the alleged victim has been abused. Although in certain circumstances an expert may address the issue of a witness's credibility, it is not permissible for an expert to conclude that someone is or is not telling the truth.

Expert testimony presented by the prosecution on typical characteristics of sex offenders or by the defense that the defendant does not fit the profile of an abuser has generally been excluded. The defendant, however, has more freedom in establishing that he or she does not fit the profile of an abuser by raising the issue of his or her character and his or her alleged propensity to engage in sexually deviant behavior. In no case may an expert conclude that a certain individual is the perpetrator. This issue is left to the trier of fact, the judge or jury.

Generally the courts have permitted medical experts to address the issue of whether the child has been abused. Mental health experts have not been permitted to give that opinion. The child sexual abuse accommodation syndrome may only be used to describe behaviors that are typical of abused children.

The purpose of expert testimony is to assist the trier of fact by providing a resource for ascertaining truth in areas outside the knowledge of ordinary persons. Although such testimony may often be helpful, the possibility always exists that the trier of fact may be unduly influenced by the expert's testimony, especially if the knowledge has not yet been accepted by the relevant scientific community. Courts must proceed with caution in admitting expert testimony in child maltreatment cases. The trial court must be satisfied that the witness is indeed an expert and that the expert knowledge offered is recognized as valid and reliable by the relevant professional community.

Allegations of child abuse are difficult to prove, but they are equally difficult to defend against. Testimony that could be clearly prejudicial

to the defendant must therefore be carefully considered, and accepted only when it rests on sound scientific evidence.

These issues are far from resolved. More studies may call into question the child sexual abuse accommodation syndrome and observations of behavior with the anatomically correct dolls, or determine that these do in fact meet the new federal standard. New techniques may be developed to provide better diagnostic tools to ascertain abuse.

It is important that the social sciences and the law work hand in hand on these critical issues. The law has made some use of the battered child syndrome. It remains to be seen whether syndromes developed by mental health professions and the use of tools such as the anatomically correct dolls will be as useful. We need to develop better knowledge that will ensure a greater number of successful legal actions to protect children and punish their abusers without violating the rights of those who are accused.

PART 4

New types of child abuse issues continue to arise. Fetal abuse occurs when a mother ingests dangerous substances during pregnancy. Hundreds of thousands of pregnant women ingest such substances each year. The results can be devastating for the newborn baby.

Some children fight back against child abuse. They utilize violence against their parents and then argue that they were justified in doing so.

Some adults recall abuse they suffered as children. After they "discover" that they were abused, they may seek treatment, criticize their abusers, sue them, or even go to the media with their claims. Some of those who are accused of this abuse assert that mental health professionals have helped create fantasies by using suggestive questioning during therapy. They state that the memories of abuse are false.

Part Four focuses on these new questions. Because these are emerging issues, there has been little guidance from either legislatures or courts. But because child abuse is endemic in our population, these and other issues will continue to challenge us as a society.

"Fetal Abuse": The Case of Drug-Exposed Infants

National hospital studies estimate that from 10 to 25 percent of all babies born in the United States are exposed to drugs before birth (Dixon, 1989). The number of infants born exposed to illicit drugs has grown dramatically to an estimated 375,000 children in 1988 (Select Committee on Children, Youth and Families, 1989, p. 7). The California State Department of Alcohol and Drug Programs estimates that between 72,000 and 85,000 of the 570,366 live births in the state in 1989 involved prenatal alcohol or drug exposure (Report of the Select Committee on Perinatal Alcohol and Drug Use to the Department of Alcohol and Drug Programs, Sept. 1991).

Perinatal substance abuse can cause a wide range of serious medical complications for the infant, including withdrawal, physical and neurological deficits, low birth weight, growth retardation, cardiovascular abnormalities, spontaneous abortion, and premature delivery, as well as long-term developmental abnormalities (Howard, Kropenske, and Tyler, 1986; Petitti and Coleman, 1990; Weston et al. 1989).

Although drug exposure during pregnancy does not harm every child, those that are affected may become "problem children" for their parents and schools, who may be unable to meet the children's special needs (Faller and Ziefert, 1981). For example, many drug-exposed babies resist cuddling and cry easily. Their symptoms of irritability, lethargy, poor feeding, and poor sleeping are extremely stressful for their caretakers. They are severely disturbed by changes in routine and are easily aroused, overreacting to any stimulation. They don't like to be touched. It is frequently difficult to form a strong attachment to such babies (Lacayo, 1989). Many children are separated from their mothers while undergoing treatment or as a result of child protective services interventions, which may make later bonding difficult. In addition, substance-abusing parents often have difficulty in providing minimal adequate care for even healthy babies.

Such long-term problems also have an impact upon public health, social welfare, education,

and the courts. The long-term costs to society of care for substance-exposed infants are staggering and may continue for the rest of their lives. Often the direct drug-related effects are compounded by family poverty and parental substance abuse. The educational system is just now beginning to experience the tremendous problems that these children represent in the schools in terms of learning disabilities and behavioral and psychological malfunctions.

There has been a legal response to the incidence of drug-exposed infants. Women have been criminally charged with "fetal abuse" or with the crime of endangering their child while still in the womb. Such fetal abuse usually involves the use of drugs during pregnancy, which in turn affects the fetus. These children may later be born with multiple handicaps and suffer prolonged pain and frustration, and they may require continuous services from an already overburdened society. In addition, the child welfare system has dealt with thousands of drug-exposed infants.

Numerous public policy issues are raised by the births of drug-exposed or drug-addicted infants. Should the state intervene on behalf of the baby? Should the child welfare system take action to protect the baby? Should the criminal justice system be utilized to punish the mother for her conduct? Or should it be left to the medical and public health system to deal with the mother and the baby?

The concept of fetal abuse also raises complex legal and ethical questions. Meeting obligations to the unborn child may require placing limitations on the mother's conduct that would not be there if she were not pregnant (Robertson, 1989). The mother's right to privacy and her autonomy must be balanced against her baby's welfare. Should the rights of the fetus be recognized at the risk of sacrificing the rights of the mother? Is the mother's right of privacy worth the lifelong suffering of the child and the staggering costs to society?

This chapter covers the legal issues involved in expanding the concept of child abuse to include fetal abuse and neglect. We will discuss whether mandatory reporting laws apply to the use of illegal drugs during pregnancy and to drug-exposed infants. We will also address social services and juvenile court intervention, criminal court responses, civil court litigation, and the availability of treatment.

APPLICATION OF MANDATORY REPORTING LAWS

The point of entry into the legal system for most drug-exposed infants and their families is immediately after birth. Many hospitals now routinely perform neonatal toxicology screens when maternal substance abuse is suspected. Typically, such screens are performed when the newborn shows signs of drug withdrawal, when the mother admits to drug use during pregnancy, or when the mother has had no prenatal care. If the results of the toxicology test are positive, the hospital may report the results to child protective services, which, in turn, may ask the court to prevent the child's release to the parents until an investigation is conducted.

Most states have passed laws which require people who, in their work, come into regular contact with children to report to the authorities any reasonable suspicion of child maltreatment. Failure to report is typically a misdemeanor criminal offense.

Mandatory reporting laws did not until recently include the discovery of a drug-exposed infant as a reportable event. Since the "abuse" took place before birth and could not take place in the same form after birth, it did not appear to be covered by the law. In the past five years the dramatic rise in the number of drug-exposed infants has led to a number of changes in these laws with regard to these children. Legislation specifically requiring physicians to test newborns and immediately report the child and the mother for illicit substance abuse has already been passed in several states. For example, the District of Columbia, Indiana,

Minnesota, Florida, Massachusetts, Oklahoma, Utah, Illinois, Nevada, New York, Rhode Island, and California have all included or made references to drug-exposed newborns and children under their mandatory child abuse reporting laws (English, 1990). Eight of these states generally require that reports be made to child protective services when toxicology tests on newborns are positive (Marshall, 1991). The Minnesota legislation is perhaps the most far-reaching of these laws. The Minnesota statute requires physicians to test both the mother and the newborn if they think the mother has used a controlled substance for a nonmedical purpose prior to birth (Minnesota Stat., sections 626.5561 and 626.5562, 1990). Three states, including California, mandate a further assessment by a health practitioner or medical social worker before the infant is released from the hospital (California Penal Code section 11165.13, 1991, and California Health and Safety Code section 10901, 1991).

The new law in California modified the existing child abuse reporting laws to specify that a positive toxicology screen at the time of delivery of an infant is not in and of itself a sufficient basis for reporting child abuse or neglect. Under the new law, however, any indication of maternal substance abuse mandates an assessment of the needs of the mother and her infant. Any indication of risk to the child as determined by the assessment must be reported to the county welfare departments. The law further requires the health and welfare agency to develop and disseminate a model needs assessment protocol for pregnant and postpartum substance-abusing women, and for the referral of a substance-exposed infant to a county welfare department. The law also specifies that the purpose of the needs assessment is to identify services for the mother, child, and family, and to determine the level of risk and the corresponding level of services and intervention needed to protect the newborn. In contrast to many laws passed in other states, the law in California does not endorse automatic reporting of positive toxicology screens to child protective services, and it emphasizes the desirability of treatment and medical services rather than criminal prosecution.

There are several factors that argue against mandatory reporting of positive toxicology tests on newborns. Most of the toxicology screens currently in use can accurately detect only about 30 percent of drug exposure in babies, depending on when the test was administered, when the mother used drugs, and which drugs were used (Bean, 1990). The unreliability of drug tests (specifically, the high incidence of false positives) makes them questionable for initiation of state investigative processes. Testing is both under- and over-exclusive. Some newborns who were drug-exposed in utero will not test positive; others that do test positive may not actually be substance exposed.

The tests are also limited in what they can detect. According to Gomby and Shiono (1991), standard urine tests for cocaine metabolites in the urine can detect cocaine for no more than three days after it is ingested. In general if a woman who used drugs up until the last three weeks prior to delivery were tested only on delivery of her baby, the tests would not detect any drug use. Such tests, may, therefore, be too inaccurate to trigger presumptions of neglect.

Racial background may have a major impact on which cases are reported by the hospitals to the child protective services. In a study from Florida, Chasnoff, Landress, and Barrett (1990) found that African-American women were almost ten times as likely to be reported to county health authorities for alcohol and drug abuse during pregnancy as Caucasian women. This occurred in spite of the fact that urine samples of the pregnant women collected at their first prenatal visit revealed no significant differences between patients of different races, and between low-income and upper-income women. African-American women, however, were more likely to use crack cocaine, while Caucasian women were more likely to use marijuana and alcohol.

COURT DECISIONS RELATED TO REPORTING

A few state appellate and supreme courts have addressed the issues of whether positive toxicology tests performed on newborns should come under the mandatory reporting laws and whether drug use during pregnancy is probative of future child abuse and neglect. In *In re Steven S.* (1981), a California appellate court overturned a juvenile court decision finding that an unborn fetus was not a person within the meaning of the child abuse or neglect statutes. In contrast, a similar case from New York (*In the Matter of "Male" R.*, 1979) found that the prenatal conduct of the mother bears on the right of a child to begin life with a sound mind and body. According to the New York court, a newborn suffering narcotics withdrawal symptoms as a consequence of prenatal drug addiction may properly be considered a neglected child within the jurisdiction of probate court.

Case Example (*In re Troy D.*, 1989)

Baby Troy was born prematurely, and urine toxicology screens performed both on him and his mother revealed the presence of illegal drugs. Less than a week later, the Department of Social Services filed a petition in juvenile court alleging that Troy was a dependent child. They requested that Troy be detained and not be allowed to return home with his mother. This request was granted the following day. While Troy was allowed to go home after about a month, at the dispositional hearing the court declared him a dependent child of the court and placed Troy with his paternal grandmother.

Troy's mother challenged the admission in juvenile court of her medical records as evidence that Troy was exposed to drugs. The juvenile court and the appellate court, however, found that medical information about the baby was properly disclosed, under an exception to the physician-patient privilege contained in the child abuse reporting law. According to that law, once a hospital social worker has made the decision that the results of the drug tests raise a reasonable suspicion of child abuse, he or she is then obligated to disclose appropriate medical information, such as the toxicology test results, as part of the abuse report (p. 874). At the same time, the *Troy* decision specifically noted that the case involved injury to a "living child," and that it was not reaching a decision on the reporting of harm to an "unborn fetus." Thus, the *Troy* case did not answer directly the question of whether drug exposure to an unborn child or a fetus is covered by the mandatory reporting laws.

The *Troy* case also addressed the issue of whether fetal drug exposure should be seen as a form of child abuse and presumptive of future abuse. Troy's mother had argued that the juvenile court had no jurisdiction over her baby, because the dependency petition alleged conduct with respect to a fetus, not a child. Although the court agreed that a dependency petition could not be sustained with respect to a fetus, it said that this case was concerned with the protection of a living child, not with a fetus. In addressing this issue, the court noted both the growing number of drug-addicted babies nationally, and the reasoning from the earlier *Baby X.* case from Michigan (see below). It found that prenatal drug use was indicative of future harm to the living child.

In Michigan (*In re Baby X.*, 1980), a juvenile court took temporary custody of a newborn who had exhibited symptoms of heroin withdrawal within twenty-four hours of his birth, as a result of the mother's drug addiction during her pregnancy. The appellate court in Michigan later affirmed the juvenile court's jurisdiction over the baby born with drug withdrawal symptoms. The court reasoned that, since prior treatment of one child can support neglect allegations regarding another

child, prenatal treatment can be considered probative of a child's neglect. The court said that a newborn suffering narcotics withdrawal symptoms as a consequence of prenatal drug addiction may properly be considered a child within the jurisdiction of the juvenile (probate) court (*In re Baby X.*, 1989, p. 739).

Discussion

This approach has been criticized by Robin-Vergeer (1990). According to Robin-Vergeer, by law the state should concern itself with future harm, and there is no reason to assume that pregnant drug users will be incapable of raising their own children. While the criminal justice system is inherently backward-looking and could, indeed, punish a woman for "fetal abuse" if such a crime existed, the juvenile system is forward-looking and must look for real indicators of future risk to the child. Juvenile courts and legislation intended to protect children cannot automatically characterize as abuse to the child the harm inflicted upon the fetus.

In *Troy*, however, the California Supreme Court let stand the decision that the use of illicit drugs during pregnancy was a sufficient basis alone to trigger a child abuse report. Note that this decision was later eroded by the subsequent revisions in the California Child Abuse and Reporting Law.

What do you think about these issues? Do you think that substance abuse during pregnancy that affects the child should automatically be reported? What type of statute would you draft to protect infants? Would you support legislation that would restrict a pregnant woman's conduct in order to protect an unborn child?

SOCIAL SERVICES AND JUVENILE COURT INTERVENTION

The role of social services and the juvenile court is governed by federal law, Public Law 95-272 and the Adoption Assistance and Child Welfare Act of 1980, which require states to exercise reasonable efforts to avoid out-of-home placement in order to receive federal funding (Adoption Assistance and Child Welfare Act, 1980). Under this law, which was described in chapters 1 and 5, it is assumed that children develop best in their own families and that most families are worth preserving.

Preliminary data indicate that the majority of infants leave the hospital to be returned to their mothers or other family members as caretakers (Office of Inspector General, 1990). However, with the increased reports of drug-exposed infants, the social welfare system has become seriously overtaxed. According to McCullough (1991), in some communities there has been as much as a 3,000 percent increase in the number of drug-related dependency petitions granted from 1985 to 1989. Drug-exposed infants endangered by parental drug abuse have become the fastest growing foster care population.

The federal requirement for family preservation may be particularly difficult to accomplish with the drug-exposed infant cases. Many of these infants have a hard time identifying with caretakers, and it is difficult to reunify or maintain family contact with parents who have other problems, such as drug addiction or criminal law obligations. Some physicians and commentators advocate that federal law be reexamined to allow for earlier out-of-home permanent placement for these children (Bean, 1990; Besharov, 1989). Others have noted that families may be referred to the welfare and court system because this is the only way that services can be made available to them (Larson, 1991). Sometimes money may be available for foster care, but not for drug treatment.

A recent study focused on how drug-exposed infants are handled in the social welfare and juvenile court systems (Sagatun-Edwards and Saylor, 1995). The study tracked 284 cases from the initial reports to the child protective services through investigations and court hearings in juvenile court. In the sample studied, both African-American and Hispanic cases were overrepresented compared to the population statistics in the county, while both Caucasians and Asians were underrepresented. Mothers were also predominantly single, unemployed, and with a poor education. One quarter of the fathers were incarcerated.

Figure 14.1 shows how these cases proceeded through the social services and the juvenile court systems. It is important to note that some records were incomplete, and missing data prevented a complete tracking of all cases. In addition, at each decision point more and more cases were either closed or not applicable for review at that stage.

At the initial review, 7 percent of the cases were closed. In 186 of the remaining cases, the child was removed from the mother or parents. At the intake investigation, 14 cases were settled and 93 cases were referred for informal supervision (voluntary services) out of court. A petition to make the child a dependent of the court was filed in 47.5 percent of the initial cases, and in 3 cases the child was immediately relinquished by the parents. Cross-tabulations of these decisions with ethnicity show a statistically significant relationship between ethnicity and the decision either to settle the case at intake, refer to informal supervision, or file a petition. A greater proportion of Caucasian women (52 percent) was referred for informal supervision, while a greater proportion of the African-Americans (71 percent) and Hispanic women (65 percent) had court petitions filed ($X^2 = 17.61$, P = <.001). Similarly, a higher proportion of cocaine cases (the drug of choice for African-Americans) in this study continued through the court hearings, while amphetamine cases (a drug used mainly by Caucasians) were less likely to be referred to court.

FIGURE 14.1: Case Progression

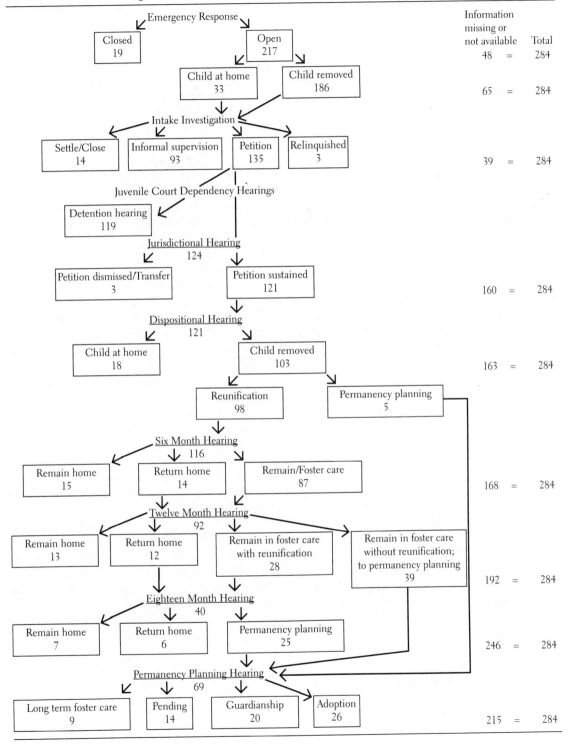

At the jurisdictional hearing, nearly every petition was substantiated, and at the dispositional hearing 76 percent of the children from the petitioned cases were removed from home. Reunification services were ordered for 96 cases, while 5 cases were too serious to warrant reunification services and immediately went to permanency planning proceedings. Thus, in 80.9 percent of the substantiated cases the child was removed and placed in a reunification program. Of the initial 135 petitions to court, 38.5 percent (N = 42) cases resulted in the child placed at home, while 51.1 percent (N = 69) ended with permanent placement outside the home. Of the initial 284 cases, 24.3 percent ended with placement away from the mother.

These data show that about one-third of the cases that go through reunification services are in fact returned to the family. How this rate of return for reunification cases compares to other types of cases in reunification is hard to determine, because of lack of comparable data. In recent years, however, the nationally accepted policy on reunification has come under increasing attack, with some authors expressing strong reservations about the ability of abusive parents to become caring and nurturing parents (e.g., Gelles, 1993). According to Gelles, the assumptions on which reunification policies are built, namely, that children are harmed in foster placements, may not always hold true. Whether parents who have been using drugs and/or are still using drugs can be good parents or learn to be good parents through reunification is an issue that needs further study. The low socio-economic background also indicates that special attention must be directed at the importance of social background in the processing of these cases.

CRIMINAL COURT RESPONSE

Some states have attempted to utilize the criminal sanction to punish mothers for exposing their fetuses to drugs. Some of these attempts to prosecute women criminally for illicit drug use during pregnancy have foundered on the question of nonrecognition of fetal personhood by the law (Chavkin, 1990). Fetuses have few, if any, legal rights since, as fetuses, they are not considered children. The nonrecognition of the fetus as a legal entity is embodied in the "born alive" rule, which states that the fetus has to be born alive as a precondition to legal personhood. Underlying this rule is the assumption that the mother and fetus constitute a unit whose legal interests are coextensive (McNulty, 1987).

In one of the first cases involving this issue (*Reyes v. Superior Court*, 1977), a woman was charged with two counts of felony child endangerment after she had twins who were born addicted to heroin displaying withdrawal symptoms. However, the court found that the child endangerment statutes did not apply to prenatal conduct, since this was not expressly stated in the relevant statute (California Penal Code section 271 a[1], 1991). The court distinguished the type of conduct punished by the statute, conduct which harms a child after birth, from the materialization of the danger after birth that was inflicted *in utero* (*Reyes v. Superior Court*, p. 216). To be actionable child abuse under traditional criminal law, the conduct that causes the injury or creates the dangerous situation must occur after the birth of a live child.

In a more recent case, (*People v. Stewart*, 1987), the prosecutor charged the mother with "fetal abuse" under California Penal Code section 270, which requires a parent to provide food, clothing, and medical attention and is one of the few statutory provisions that specifically include a fetus. The prosecution said that Stewart had deprived her unborn child of medical necessities by failing to get adequate prenatal care or medical attention for a *placenta previa* condition that may have been caused by her drug usage. As a result, the mother hemorrhaged for a significant period of time and the baby was born brain dead. Stewart was charged with criminal responsibility for harm to her fetus which had allegedly occurred because she had not followed her doctor's orders. However, the trial court dismissed the case after arguing that the Legislature did not intend for section 270 to be used in such a way. In both *Stewart* and *Reyes v. Superior Court* the trial courts dismissed the charges of "fetal abuse" because the statutes under which the women were charged were not intended for punitive use against the mother. Both courts expressly left open the possibility that if a criminal law existed specifically directed at prenatal harm to a fetus, such prosecutions might be allowed.

No state has passed legislation that specifically makes it a crime to use a controlled substance during pregnancy (Marshall, 1991). Instead, criminal prosecutions have been based on existing criminal laws, which were never designed or intended to govern prenatal conduct. These include statutes that prohibit drug use, sale, possession, or delivery of drugs to minors, which apply to all adults—males and females. According to Paltrow (1990), such statutes should not be used to apply to the pregnant woman because of her special relationship to the fetus (e.g., "pushing" drugs through the umbilical cord). Women in states such as Florida, Massachusetts, and South Carolina have faced criminal prosecutions stemming from their use of cocaine, heroin, or alcohol while pregnant.

Case Example (*Johnson v. Florida*, 1992)

On October 3, 1987, the defendant mother delivered a son. About one and one-half minutes elapsed from the time the baby's head emerged from the mother's birth canal to the time the umbilical cord was clamped. The obstetrician who delivered the baby testified he presumed that the umbilical cord was functioning normally and that it was delivering blood to the baby after he emerged from the birth canal and before the cord was clamped. The mother admitted to the baby's

pediatrician that she had used cocaine the night before the delivery. A toxicology test performed after birth on both the mother and son proved positive for a product of cocaine.

In December 1988, the mother was pregnant again. She suffered a crack cocaine overdose and said she was concerned about the effect of the drug on the unborn child. In January at the time of delivery of that baby girl, the mother told the obstetrician that she had used rock cocaine earlier that morning. Again during delivery approximately sixty to ninety seconds elapsed from the time the baby's head emerged until the umbilical cord was clamped. The mother also acknowledged to social workers and doctors that she had been using cocaine throughout both pregnancies.

The mother was prosecuted under Florida's criminal statutes for delivering a controlled substance to her two minor children. At the trial the facts of the births were described and the second obstetrician testified that there would have been blood passing from the mother to the child in the short period after each had emerged from her womb and before the umbilical cord was clamped. A pathologist and toxicologist testified that given the time from her ingestion of cocaine until each delivery, there would have been cocaine in the mother's blood after the birth of each baby. Other expert witnesses contested the conclusion that blood containing cocaine would actually have flowed through the umbilical cord during the sixty- to ninety-second interval.

The mother was convicted of two counts of delivering a controlled substance to another person, that is, to her two babies during the short interval after birth before the umbilical cords were clamped.

The mother appealed and the appellate court affirmed her convictions. The Florida Supreme Court, however, reversed the convictions. That court held that the legislature did not intend the word "deliver" to include the passage of blood through the umbilical cord. The Florida Supreme Court adopted the language of the justice who dissented in the lower appellate court decision when she wrote that

... the Legislature never intended for the general drug delivery statute to authorize prosecution of those mothers who take illegal drugs close enough in time to childbirth that a doctor could testify that a tiny amount passed from mother to child in the few seconds before the umbilical cord was cut. Criminal prosecution of mothers like Johnson will undermine Florida's express policy of "keeping families intact" and could destroy the family by incarcerating the child's mother when alternate measures could protect the child and stabilize the family.

The court acknowledged that drug abuse is a serious national problem and that there is particular concern about the rising numbers of babies born with cocaine in their systems as a result of maternal substance abuse. The court pointed out the negative aspect of such prosecutions.

However, prosecuting women for using drugs and "delivering" them to their newborns appears to be the least effective response to this crisis. Rather than face the possibility of prosecution, pregnant women who are substance abusers may simply avoid prenatal or medical care for fear of being detected. Yet the newborns of these women are, as a group, the most fragile and sick, and most in need of hospital neonatal care. A decision to deliver these babies "at home" will have tragic and serious consequences.

Discussion

Do you agree with the Florida Supreme Court's opinion? Do you believe that passage of drugs through the mother's umbilical cord is "delivery" within the meaning of the criminal statute?

Some courts have dismissed similar prosecutions on constitutional grounds, finding that they violated the women's constitutional rights to due process and privacy (*Massachusetts v. Pellegrini* [1989]; *Michigan v. Bremer* [1991]; *Stallman v. Youngquist* [1988]).

The view that the mother cannot be prosecuted criminally for abuse to the fetus was also given support in a 1988 Illinois Supreme Court decision (*Stallman v. Youngquist*, 1988). In 1984, a lower court in Illinois had held that the child, who was a five-pound fetus at the time of her prenatal injuries, was a legal person for purposes of maintaining a negligence action after birth against her mother (*Stallman v. Youngquist*, 1984). However, this decision was reversed. In 1988, the Illinois Supreme Court refused to adopt "the legal fiction" that the fetus is a "separate legal person with rights hostile to the woman" (*Stallman v. Youngquist*, 1988). The court found that holding a mother liable for negligent infliction of prenatal injuries infringes on her right to privacy and bodily autonomy.

Some who favor prosecution of maternal substance abuse argue that the use of alcohol, tobacco, and illicit drugs during pregnancy is not a "fundamental right" and not protected as is the right to privacy or even the right to an abortion. According to Balisy (1987), the use of alcohol and tobacco is a mere privilege, and the use of illicit drugs is a crime. The state, he argues, has a compelling interest in protecting "potential life." Such compelling state interests include both preventing the societal costs of a mother's conduct and preventing injury to the fetus. States, therefore, should be permitted by statutory interpretation to proscribe a pregnant woman's tobacco, alcohol, and drug abuse to protect a viable fetus (Balisy, 1987).

Opponents of criminalizing "fetal abuse" argue that prosecuting women for their conduct during pregnancy is not only unconstitutional, but a waste of resources (Paltrow, 1989). From this perspective, no criminal statute could be tailored narrowly enough to protect a woman's right to privacy or her due process rights. At all stages of pregnancy, the fetus is completely dependent on the woman. According to Paltrow (1989), recognizing "fetal abuse" as a crime moves us toward criminalizing pregnancy itself because no woman can provide the perfect womb. A woman should not give up her legal rights just because she chooses to become pregnant. In addition, criminal prosecution of pregnant drug-using women and not of drug-using male partners may be a form of gender discrimination where women are punished simply for their biological difference from men.

There are many practical arguments against criminalization as well. For example, if criminal prosecution were possible, the mother might go underground at birth. How can one control the mother during pregnancy? If she should be locked up, when should the incarceration start? Should it start at three months or six months? What if the mother changes her mind about carrying the fetus to term and wants an abortion instead?

Traditionally, criminal laws require that punishment be imposed when there is both a criminal act and a culpable mental intent. Assuming that the state has a right to maintain a reasonable standard of fetal health, it seems logical that the state could only punish those women who willfully, intentionally, or knowingly create a substantial risk of harm to their fetus. However, women who harm their fetuses generally do not do so because they want to. Sometimes women do not even know that they are pregnant when they use the harmful drugs. Therefore compliance with a principle of "fetal health" would require that women be criminally punished for unintended or unknowing harm to their fetuses. Often women who are addicted to drugs or use drugs may be unaware of the harm done to their babies. They may be too poor to afford proper prenatal care, they may be afraid to seek such care for fear of being reported and having their babies taken away, or such prenatal care may not be available. A reasonable community standard of care is hard to determine under such adverse conditions. The state should not impose punishment for conditions over which a pregnant woman has no practical control, such as lack of access to prenatal care or substance abuse treatment (McNulty, 1987). Fetal abuse laws could easily result in discriminatory enforcement against the poor. Moreover, women are only reported and prosecuted for using illegal

substances during pregnancy. Alcohol, the drug of choice for many women, may have far more severe effects on the newborn, such as the fetal alcohol syndrome (Report of the Select Committee on Perinatal Alcohol and Drug Use, 1991). Yet, since alcohol is a legal drug, hospitals do not commonly test for alcohol in their toxicology screens. This, combined with the fact that poor patients in public hospitals are more likely to be tested and reported, introduces a clear class bias in the prosecution of prenatal drug exposure.

Thus, not only can criminalizing the effects of drugs on the fetus be seen as an intrusion on women's fundamental rights, it may also further no interest in the woman's health or well-being. Prosecution might discourage a woman from seeking prenatal care and dissuade her from providing accurate information to health-care providers.

Many professional organizations with an interest in the legal reactions to drug-exposed infants have come out with strong statements against criminal prosecution, including the American Medical Association, the American Public Health Association, the American College of Obstetricians and Gynecologists (1987), the American Society of Law and Medicine (Paltrow, 1990), and the National Association for Perinatal Addiction Research and Education (Chasnoff, 1991). The National Council of Juvenile and Family Court Judges states that criminal prosecution should be used only as a last resort (National Council of Juvenile and Family Court Judges, 1991).

Do you think that use of illicit drugs during pregnancy should be prosecuted? What about the use of legal drugs, such as alcohol, that might result in even more harm to the child, such as the "fetal alcohol syndrome"?

CIVIL COURT ACTION

In civil law fetal rights have already been well established. A majority of states already consider fetuses that have died *in utero* to be "persons" under wrongful death statutes, and therefore parents may sue people who harmed the fetus *in utero*, causing the death (McNulty, 1987). Courts have also long recognized "wrongful life" actions.

In *Grodin v. Grodin* (1981), a child brought suit against his mother for prenatal injuries because of the mother's negligence in failing to secure prenatal care. The court held that the injured child's mother should bear the same liability as a third person for negligent conduct that interfered with the child's rights to begin life with a sound mind and body (Balisy, 1987). In holding that a child could recover damages from the mother for prenatal injuries, the court did not discuss the relevance of the unique physical relationship between the woman and the fetus at the time of the "injury" (Johnson, 1987).

Some case law demonstrates that in contexts other than maternal substance abuse, the courts have already found that the state's interests in protecting the fetus may overcome a woman's autonomy rights. In 1964, the New Jersey Supreme Court recognized the rights of a fetus to have the mother submit to blood transfusions against her religious beliefs (*Raleigh Fitkin-Paul Morgan Memorial Hospital v. Anderson*, 1964). In another case, the Georgia Supreme Court affirmed a lower court's order authorizing the hospital to perform a caesarian section in the event that the woman could not safely deliver the child naturally (*Jefferson v. Spalding County Hospital Authority*, 1981). In this case, the court found that the interests of the fetus outweighed those of the pregnant woman.

TREATMENT FOR PREGNANT SUBSTANCE ABUSERS

If the mother were encouraged to undergo residential treatment for her problems and given training to cope with her infant's special needs, the cycle of repeated drug abuse might be interrupted. According to Finnegan, Connaughton, Emich, and Wieland (1992), pregnant addicts who receive proper prenatal care have significantly fewer neonatal problems. Rehabilitative programs that provide comprehensive medical and social services such as drug treatment, obstetric, pediatric, gynecological and educational counseling, child development and parenting skills programs have reported some success (Suffet and Brotman, 1984). According to Griffith (1991), with specialized training for parents in how to handle their drug-exposed infants from the time of the baby's birth, many problems associated with prenatal cocaine exposure can be corrected by age three.

However, often drug treatment centers deny women admission for several reasons. A survey by Chavkin (1990) revealed that 54 percent of treatment programs categorically excluded the pregnant. Most centers have no provisions for child care. Very few residential treatment centers are available for pregnant women. Once the baby is born, even if the mother has been placed in residential treatment, there are few such facilities that also allow children. Older children and sometimes even the newborn need to be placed in foster care, thereby disrupting family bonds. Many expectant mothers are faced with the choice of giving up care of their existing children by putting them in foster care in order to undergo treatment. Finally, the waiting lists for centers that do take pregnant women are often so long that the woman's baby may well be born by the time she is placed, thereby making it impossible for the treatment to have a positive effect on the fetus.

In addition to the lack of spaces available, there is also the problem of how to treat pregnant women. Since more facilities were created to deal with nonpregnancy addiction, most have no expertise on how the treatment might damage the fetus and fear malpractice suits. Many obstetricians have voiced concern about detoxification during pregnancy unless biochemical monitoring of fetal status could be assured (Zuspan, Gumpell, and Mejia-Zelaya, 1975). Others have found that the use of methadone to cure addiction may cause severe neonatal withdrawal symptoms (Chasnoff, 1989; Ostrea, Chavez, and Strauss, 1976).

With better medical technology in perinatal medicine, the fetus has become more accessible to treatment and diagnostic procedures. A medical treatment approach which treats the pregnant woman and her fetus as an entity with the mother in charge will in most cases be the best alternative. Providing better services to poor women would go very far towards improving the health of their children. Drug treatment and obstetric and pediatric care should be coordinated with day care, job training, and education. While such programs will be costly, they are far less costly than long-term foster care for the children and incarceration of the mother.

CONCLUSION

The growing incidence and awareness of drug-exposed infants warrant careful examination and efforts by policy makers, the legal system, and service providers. In the past few years a wide variety of responses has emerged. Efforts range from the criminalization of "fetal abuse" to a mandatory reporting under child protective laws, with possible referral to the juvenile court, to discretionary reporting with a medical-service oriented (nonpunitive) approach (English and Henry, 1990).

The use of criminal prosecution for fetal abuse, the automatic reporting of positive toxicology screens and the deprivation of custody based on unreliable drug tests punish women for their drug use without necessarily helping the child or the family. While we all feel sympathy for infants born addicted to drugs and damaged from birth, punishing the mother for the prenatal conduct is not going to help the child nor improve the mother's health care.

The desirability of postbirth sanctions should depend on the gains to the children relative to the harm that might arise from such a policy. While the health of the fetus is important, criminalizing "fetal abuse" would not serve the intended purpose. It would probably jeopardize rather than secure the fetal health. Women at risk would not seek medical advice for fear of being punished and of losing their children. In addition, the mother's important constitutional guarantee of rights to liberty and privacy would be violated. Criminalization of maternal conduct during pregnancy would also violate a woman's right to equal protection under the law. The creation of "fetal rights" mandating state intrusions in regulating a woman's conduct during pregnancy would necessarily intrude in the most private areas of a woman's life.

Protection of children after birth is important. The state should have the right to intervene under juvenile court jurisdiction, once voluntary services and other forms of treatment have been explored. Infants who have severe symptoms of drug addiction and whose mothers appear unable to care for them for other reasons should be covered by the mandatory child abuse reporting statutes. Legal sanctions should be a last resort, not a substitute for adequate treatment programs. Any intervention on behalf of the drug-exposed infant must be predicated on other indications of future harm, not just the past prenatal drug use. Such indicators might include the mother's care of siblings, her willingness and ability to participate in drug treatment, parenting classes, and the availability of a support system. The goal should be to provide pregnant women with effective drug treatment and comprehensive prenatal care with continued services after birth, so that they may maintain custody of their own children. Intervention should be limited to protect children who are at great risk, so that loss of constitutional rights and societal costs may be prevented.

CHAPTER 15

Other Developments in Child Abuse and the Legal System

In recent years there have been several other important developments in the area of child abuse and the legal system. In this final chapter we will discuss some of these, including the use of the "battered child syndrome" as a defense for children who attack or kill their abusive parents, legislation and debate around the issue of extending the statute of limitations to adult victims of childhood abuse, the "false memory syndrome," and finally the issues and allegations surrounding the so-called "backlash movement."

ABUSED CHILDREN WHO FIGHT BACK

Children rarely kill their parents (Blodgett, 1987). In 1992 there were 343 cases in the United States in which a child killed a parent or someone in a guardianship position. In a study of the relationship between victims and their murderers, it was found that the child as a murderer and the parent as a victim was the least likely in homicide situations (Wilson and Daly, 1993). When a child kills a parent (parricide), the killing usually follows a history of violent abuse by that parent (Mones, 1985).

According to a recent FBI report, in 1992 there were 343 parricides in the United States, only 1.6 percent of all homicides (Angel, 1993). In spite of the relatively small numbers, these are all tragic cases, and there is a growing concern over how these cases are handled in the courts and whether applicable laws and legal definitions need to be formally changed. Many sad case histories have been published about how such children have been found guilty of murder in spite of overwhelming evidence of child abuse preceding the homicide (Mones, 1991). When an abused child kills a parent, he or she often faces a criminal justice system and a society that cannot accept the notion that a child could kill his or her mother or father under any circumstances (Layton,

1993). It may make little or no difference that the abused child kills the abuser after many years of severe and chronic abuse. To some it may be hard to believe that a child could endure any abuse without telling an outsider and asking for help. According to Mones (1991), an attorney specializing in defending children in parricide cases, everyone immediately asks the question, "Why didn't the child get help?" (Mones, 1991, p. 33).

As we pointed out earlier in this book, there are compelling sociological and psychological reasons that inhibit abused children from seeking help. Abused children may attach themselves to and identify with their abusers. Children may also struggle with overt threats from abusers. Abusers may tell children that if they ever tell anyone they will be beaten or killed or some other family member may be harmed. Even when the abuse has been reported and social services and juvenile courts have become involved, the full extent of the abuse suffered by a child may be unknown because of these fears.

If the child believes there is no escape and that he or she will continue to be abused, the child may take desperate action. Some children run away from home. In a few cases a child may finally fight back by killing the abuser.

Many prosecutors charge first-degree murder in parricide cases despite evidence of long-standing abuse by the parent and psychological studies showing the effects of such abuse on the defendant's mental state. As with most criminal cases, the matter is usually settled through a plea bargain. Defense counsel traditionally have been more than satisfied if they have secured a plea bargain for second-degree murder. The result in these cases is usually a prison term (if the child's case was transferred to adult court) or a term in a maximum security juvenile institution.

Although most parricide cases are resolved by plea bargain, in a few cases that have been tried, the jury or the judge found the child defendant not guilty on all counts of attempted murder even though the child freely admitted to the act. For example, in a case involving a child who had several times (unsuccessfully) attempted to kill his father, the jury learned during the trial that from early childhood the defendant's father had kept him in handcuffs and chains and had raped him as a teenager. After six weeks of such testimony, the jury found the child not guilty (Chambers, 1986). In this case, the graphic evidence presented to show the abuse persuaded the jury to reject the traditional legal rules, finding them inadequate to deal with the circumstances (Angel, 1993).

Several defense experts in parricide cases have tried to broaden the traditional definitions of self-defense to include the "battered child syndrome," a concept similar to the "battered woman syndrome" used in domestic violence cases of chronic abuse. Such arguments have slowly become accepted by appellate courts in some states.

The Battered Child Syndrome

Originally, the term "battered child syndrome" was developed to describe a child who had been consistently physically abused by nonaccidental means (see chapters 2 and 13). The term connoted a series of physical symptoms discernable by medical specialists to indicate that a child had suffered severe physical injuries nonaccidentally. The new usage of the term as a defense, however, takes the concept further, namely, using the diagnosis of battery (e.g., the evidence of the battered child syndrome) as a way to explain why a child who has been chronically abused would see no other way to defend him- or herself except by killing the abusive parent. In addition, the battered child defense is extended to include all kinds of maltreatment—physical, sexual, and emotional abuse—as well as severe neglect cases. The battered child syndrome as a defense in parricide cases is similar to that used in the battered woman defense in domestic violence cases where the long-time victim ends up killing her batterer. Many argue that such a "battered person defense" may be equally if not more appropriate for abused children.

Scobey (1992) notes that self-defense theories for homicide defendants have always been limited and usually involve scenarios in which acting in self-defense is justified. The traditional self-defense doctrine typically involves a man-to-man, stranger-to-stranger confrontation, which is characterized as immediately violent and physically threatening. Courts have carefully outlined requirements which a defendant must prove in order to fall within the class of people for whom self-defense is a viable argument. Normal self-defense theory is based on the principle that a person who is unlawfully attacked by another and who has no opportunity to resort to the law for his defense should be able to take reasonable steps to defend himself (Moreno, 1989). The court in a homicide case must conclude that the defendant perceived an imminent deadly or serious attack and that the perception was reasonable.

Such traditional interpretations of the "reasonable fear" requirement as well as an "endeavoring to escape" requirement fail to account for the complicated psychological environment created by an abusive family member (Scobey, 1992). These self-defense doctrines ignore the perceptions of women and children, particularly those who may feel helpless due to persistent abuse and battering. The circumstances in violent and abusive family situations call for an expanded definition of self-defense, despite the fact that the traditional requirements are not obvious or apparent (Crocker, 1985). The times that abused women and children fear their abusers are not limited to immediately before and during beatings. Their fear of death or great bodily harm may persist throughout most of their daily life.

The effects of family violence on the perceptions and behavior of its victims have already been recognized in the context of spousal abuse (Moreno, 1989). The battered woman syndrome was developed by Walker (1979) to describe the psychological characteristics of abused women and the battering relationship. According to Walker, the battering relationship is composed of three distinct and recurring phases: a tension-building stage, followed by an acute battering incident, and finally a period of contrition and affection. The battered woman feels trapped in the relationship and suffers from a "learned helplessness," making it impossible for her to believe that she can ever escape the batterer, except by killing him. The batterer promotes this perception of being trapped by controlling the victim's life and not permitting her any freedom. The battered woman syndrome has been used successfully in many court cases to explain why a battered woman does not simply walk away from such an abusive relationship. Many states allow testimony on the syndrome as a self-defense argument (Schneider, 1986).

In criminal cases involving women who have killed their batterer, experts have been called to testify as to the effects of violent abuse on the battered person. These experts describe the battered woman syndrome and suggest that a woman may believe it necessary to kill her abuser in order to escape the abuse. Such testimony has been judged to be "beyond the ken" of the average juror and has been permitted to educate the judge and jury about the common experience of battered women and why such women do not simply leave their abusive partners (see chapter 13 on expert testimony). This expert testimony is also used to explain why women might kill their spouses or partners in a seemingly "safe" situation not calling for immediate "self-defense," such as when the partner is sleeping. According to Walker (1979), even in such situations the battered victim perceives herself to be in danger and is indeed acting in a self-defense mode.

The function of this type of expert testimony relating to the battered woman syndrome is offered to assist the trier of fact in evaluating the reasonableness of the degree of force used by the defendant. That the defendant is a victim in a battering relationship is probably not sufficient evidence to submit to the jury in support of self-defense. It is the perceived imminence of danger, based on the appearance of some threatening behavior or communication, which supplies the justification to use deadly force under a claim of self-defense.

Similar expert testimony could be used to explain why abused children might kill their parents even when apparently no immediate danger to the child exists. For example, many killings occur when the parent is asleep or otherwise not an immediate threat to the child (Angel, 1993). However, abused children, like battered women, are likely to perceive the behavior of the batterer in the context of a history of abuse and threats and believe they are in imminent danger even in "nonthreatening" situations. Indeed, the abused child may well feel that his or her very existence is in danger at all times. Children perceive their parents, especially abusive parents, as very powerful—perhaps omnipotent. Because victims of abuse know their abusers and their capacities for violence, they may strike back at times with a force that seems unreasonable to the outsider.

Admission of testimony on the battered child syndrome defense does not, of course, end the inquiry or necessarily mean that the defendant will be acquitted. This information is merely intended to help the jury interpret how the defendant might have perceived and responded to threats of imminent danger. It still remains for the jury or judge to decide whether or not as a "battered child" the defendant behaved reasonably in the self-defense context.

Judicial acceptance of the battered child syndrome defense has been slow in gaining acceptance. For example, in *State v. Holden* (1985) an Ohio appellate court considered the issue of the admissibility of expert testimony concerning the psychological effects of child abuse. The young defendant claimed that he killed his father in self-defense and offered expert testimony regarding the psychological effects of the past abuse to support his claim. However, the court refused to admit expert testimony on the "battered person syndrome." The court stated that there was ample evidence to show that the child was abused by his father and found that admission of expert testimony on the battered child syndrome (as used here) would have permitted the jury to make determinations based on stereotypes of abused children and not the factual situation.

In the last few years a few appellate and state supreme courts have allowed such defenses, and in some instances where such testimony was excluded and the defendant convicted, have returned cases to the trial court for further hearing. Following is an example of such a case.

Case Example (*State of Washington v. Janes*, 1992)

The following case is taken from an appeals court decision in the state of Washington. On August 30, 1988, Andrew Janes (Andy) who was seventeen years old at the time, shot and killed his stepfather, Walter Jaloveckas, as Jaloveckas walked through the front door of their home. Andy then triggered the alarm system in the home to summon the police and fire department. When the police arrived, Andy fired at them as well as at some empty cars and at the telephone in his house. A police officer and a bystander were slightly injured in the shooting.

Andy was charged with one count of murder in the first degree (premeditated) and two counts of assault in the second degree. The trial court found that Andy had suffered a pattern of ongoing abuse at the hands of the stepfather and therefore imposed an exceptional sentence of ten years on the murder conviction. Andy appealed the conviction with respect to all three counts.

The facts at the trial revealed that the stepfather, Walter Jaloveckas, had moved in with the Janes family when Andy was seven years old after Andy's biological father had abandoned the family earlier that year. After the family moved into a home of their own two years later, Jaloveckas became increasingly abusive and subject to sometimes physically violent outbursts of anger. Testimony at the trial showed that the abuse included incidents where Jaloveckas beat or hit Andy, his brother, and Gale Janes, their mother, smashed a stereo and bicycles with a sledgehammer, and threatened

to torture, kill, or send the boys away for such transgressions as being tardy in completing chores or taking some of his marijuana. While Jaloveckas's actions were reported to child protective services on three occasions, CPS did not follow up on those reports. On at least two of these occasions Ms. Janes or Andy requested that CPS not follow up out of fear of reprisal by Jaloveckas.

On the evening of August 29, an incident occurred that Andy said triggered the events of the next day. Ms. Janes testified that when Jaloveckas used a low tone, it usually meant that he was making a threat. She did not hear what he actually said, and Andy could not remember what was said. The next morning Ms. Janes woke Andy up after Jaloveckas left for work and told him that he should be sure to get all his work done because his stepfather was still angry.

One of Andy's school friends testified that he stopped by Andy's home on the way to school. Andy brought out a shotgun and loaded it, showed it to his friend, and told him he was going to kill Jaloveckas. Andy left the shotgun under some clothes in his room, went to school, and left after two classes. After returning home, Andy broke a padlock off the door to the bedroom shared by Ms. Janes and Jaloveckas in which Jaloveckas kept his supply of alcohol and marijuana. Andy drank whiskey, smoked marijuana, retrieved his shotgun, and loaded a 9mm handgun that belonged to Jaloveckas. When Jaloveckas returned at 4:30 P.M., Andy shot him as he entered the home. Jaloveckas died from two gunshot wounds to the head.

There was no dispute that Andy killed his stepfather. The defense counsel sought to base Andy's defense on a theory of justifiable homicide. The defense argued that Andy acted in self-defense because he perceived himself to be in imminent danger of serious bodily harm in a condition analogous to the "battered woman syndrome," stemming from ten years of abuse he had suffered at the hands of his stepfather. The trial court ruled, however, that in the absence of evidence showing that Andy was in fact in imminent danger at the time of the shooting, there was an insufficient factual basis to support giving an instruction regarding self-defense. The court held that evidence of the battered child syndrome could not, as a matter of law, support a finding of self-defense because, it concluded, there was no "imminent threat" to Andy at the time of the shooting. It therefore excluded the testimony.

Although the court did not permit testimony supporting the defense of justifiable homicide, it did permit defense experts to testify on the defense of diminished capacity. They testified that Andy suffered from post-traumatic stress disorder, primarily as a result of the abuse at the hands of Jaloveckas, and that as a result of this disorder, Andy's capacity for premeditation was "impaired." The court instructed a jury that it could consider a mental illness or disorder where the existence of a particular mental state was a necessary element of a particular crime.

The Washington Court of Appeals subsequently ruled that the trial court was in error to exclude testimony concerning the battered child syndrome and to refuse to submit the issue of the reasonableness of Andy's perception in light of expert testimony on the battered child syndrome. The court stated:

> In analyzing the question of whether the jury should have been permitted to hear expert testimony concerning the battered child syndrome in the context of the defendant's claim of self-defense here, we consider 1) whether scientific understanding of the battered child syndrome is sufficiently developed so as to be generally admissible, and 2) whether the expert testimony offered would have been helpful to the trier of fact in the context.
>
> While no Washington case has yet recognized the "battered child syndrome" in this context, the pertinent literature indicates that there is sufficient scientific basis to justify extending the battered woman syndrome to analogous situations affecting children. . . . Washington courts have held that expert testimony with respect to the battered woman syndrome is admissible to explain a woman's perception that she had no alternative but to act in the manner that she did. . . . Neither law nor logic suggests any reason to limit to women recognition

of the impact a battering relationship may have on the victim's actions or perceptions. We have noted in other contexts that children are both objectively and subjectively more vulnerable to the effects of violence than are adults. For that reason, the rationale underlying the admissibility of testimony regarding the battered woman syndrome is at least as compelling, if not more so, when applied to children.

Children do not reach the age of majority until they are 18 years of age. Until then, they have virtually no independent ability to support themselves, thus preventing them from escaping the abusive atmosphere. Further, unlike an adult who may come into a battering relationship with at least some basis on which to make comparisons between current and past experiences, a child has no such equivalent life experience on which to draw to put the battering into perspective. There is therefore every reason to believe that a child's entire world view and sense of self may be conditioned by reaction to that abuse.

As a result of this reasoning, the Washington appeals court recognized that the battered child syndrome is the functional and legal equivalent to the battered woman syndrome. It held that the scientific understanding of the battered child syndrome was sufficiently developed to make testimony concerning that syndrome admissible in appropriate cases.

The court also concluded that the information concerning the battered child syndrome and its application would have been helpful to the jury in this case. Without it, the jury could not adequately evaluate the reasonableness of Andy's perception that he was in imminent danger of death or serious bodily harm at the time he killed his stepfather. Without such testimony, the jury might have a difficult time understanding how counterintuitive and difficult the dynamics between a batterer and a victim can be. For example, one of the experts had been allowed to testify on the condition of hypervigilance in the battered child. Hypervigilance refers to a heightened ability to discern preaggressive behavior in others, a condition which occurs with long-term abuse. Without such testimony, the jurors could not understand the significance of Andy's claim that he acted in self-defense.

The court wrote in its conclusion:

> Battered children live in an environment wholly different from the safe and nurturing home depicted by traditional values and social values and societal expectations. The impact of long-term abuse on a child's emotional and psychological responses is a matter that is beyond the average juror's understanding. Without expert testimony to put the child's perceptions into context, a jury cannot fairly evaluate the reasonableness of the child's perception of the imminence of the danger to which he or she reacted. The jury, in this case, should, on remand, be permitted to hear the testimony and evaluate the reasonableness of Andy's perceptions and actions in light of the battered child syndrome evidence.

Discussion

How is the use of the battered child syndrome here different from that described in chapter 13? Do you agree that the battered child syndrome as defined here is the legal equivalent to the battered woman syndrome? Do you agree that it should have been allowed in this case? Should this syndrome be held to be a total defense exonerating Andy or just permitted to diminish the length of the sentence? The question raised in this case is a serious one: should children be allowed to use as a form of self-defense the fact that they have been abused even when they appear not to be in imminent danger?

In the past chapters we have focused primarily on the victimization of children and the trauma that they experience. In this case we see an example of a victim striking back. While we must be sympathetic to the abuse suffered by the victim, can the abusive history "excuse" the new crime

committed? While we do not mean to imply that child victims should go out and attack and murder their abusers, we believe that this is an important development in the approach to parricide cases. The "battered child syndrome" can help the jury to understand how a child can be driven to such desperate actions as a form of self-defense. The presentation of such information is important in assisting the trier of fact to evaluate the reasonableness of the use of force.

The new societal awareness of child abuse and the legislation and developments designed to protect child victims now seem to have paved the way for an increased willingness to accept the battered child defense in parricide cases. Although legislation incorporating such defenses for abused children killing their parents have not yet been developed, the fact that the battered woman defense now is widely incorporated in legal codes may also lead the way for new legislation on the battered child syndrome defense.

EXTENDING STATUTES OF LIMITATIONS TO ADULTS VICTIMIZED AS CHILDREN

Many adults who were physically or sexually abused as children never told anyone about the abuse until they reached adulthood. Other adults may have repressed the memory of the abuse and only remember it much later through therapy or particular memory-triggering incidents.

In child abuse cases, there are a number of special considerations concerning the statute of limitations. First of all, by its very nature child abuse involves a person who is not yet an adult and therefore unable to take legal action. Moreover, there are many factors that prevent a child victim from disclosing the abuse to others. In some situations the abuse may be the only form of love and attention the victim receives. In others the child may fear that people would not believe him or her or blame him or her for the abuse. In many situations, the victim may not disclose because of fear and threats made by the abuser.

Regardless of why the abuse was not disclosed, the silence prevents the victim from venting fears, anger, and shame. Many victims suffer emotional repercussions their entire lives. Studies have shown that sexual abuse victims are more likely than persons in the general population to experience serious mental health problems and dysfunctional behavior, including depression, anxiety, somatization disorders, substance abuse and addiction, suicide attempts, sexual dysfunction, and problems in interpersonal relationships (Gordon and Alexander, 1993). Adults who were sexually victimized in childhood represent a significant proportion of individuals with psychiatric disorders. Even adults who were abused as children and who have no recollection of the abuse also often suffer from the same emotional and behavioral problems. Loss of memory is a defense mechanism which may allow a victim to live with the fact that abuse has occurred without being overwhelmed by it. In some cases, after seeking professional help, the cause of the problems may eventually be uncovered. For all adult victims of child abuse, at issue is whether the statute of limitations for bringing actions relating to the abuse should be extended.

Statute of Limitations

A statute of limitations is a legislatively established time limit within which legal actions must be filed. The legal system is designed to offer aggrieved persons an opportunity to have redress before the courts of law. But there should be some limit on the length of time within which legal actions should be filed. With the passage of time memories fade, evidence is lost or forgotten, and witnesses disappear or become unavailable. Thus it is important to set a time limit during which legal actions must be filed or forever be blocked.

The statute of limitations is longer for the more serious types of conduct. Thus, in many states a misdemeanor (a less serious crime) must be prosecuted within a year from its commission. For homicide and other similar crimes there is no statute of limitations.

The statute of limitations for a personal injury claim normally commences when the cause of action accrues. A plaintiff then has a designated number of years, specified by statute and usually from one to six years, in which to bring the claim. However, the term "accrue" is not usually defined in the relevant statute and consequently is subject to judicial interpretation.

The courts are usually guided by a so-called discovery rule whereby the statute of limitations does not commence until a victim discovers or should have discovered the injury (Rodgers, 1993). A separate but related rule is the delayed discovery rule. Like the general discovery rule, this rule also provides that a cause of action accrues when the plaintiff knew or reasonably should have known that he or she had been injured. But it also adds an additional element of causation, namely that the action accrues when the plaintiff knew that the wrongful act of the defendant was the cause of the injury.

These rules assist adult victims of child abuse who may not remember being abused until years after the statute of limitations has run. In *Johnson v. Johnson* (1988), a victim, an adult woman of thirty-two years of age, filed a complaint and requested damages under several tort theories for injuries sustained as a result of her father's alleged abuse and her mother's failure to protect her from such alleged abuse (*Johnson v. Johnson*, p. 1364). The plaintiff claimed that she had suppressed all memories of the alleged sexual abuse and was ignorant of the causal connection between the abuse and her injuries until she entered therapy as an adult. In the course of therapy she was able to begin to remember and understand the scope and nature of her injuries and the causal connection to abuse by her father.

In its ruling the court distinguished between two situations and referred to them as Type One and Type Two. The Type One group of plaintiffs (the adult victims of childhood abuse) were those who, as children, were aware of the abuse at the time that it occurred but were unaware that their subsequent psychological problems resulted from the incidents of abuse. The second group of plaintiffs (Type Two) were those who claim that the trauma of abusive experience caused them to repress their memories of abuse. These victims claim that a recent significant event such as therapy has only now enabled them to recollect the fact that they were once violated. In cases involving a Type Two plaintiff, the federal court observed that "the strictures of the statutes must sometimes be loosened in order to give the substantive law room to develop" (*Johnson v. Johnson*, 1988, p. 1369). Applying the delayed discovery rule (discussed above), the federal court determined that in this case the factors clearly weighed in favor of the plaintiff.

In a later case in California, using the same distinctions between Type One and Type Two, the court decided that the statute of limitations bars Type One plaintiffs from filing actions after the statute has run, while Type Two plaintiffs do have that right. The court stated that the Type One plaintiffs knew of their abuse and could have filed a legal action while the Type Two plaintiffs did not know of their abuse and that the statute should be extended (*Mary D. v. John D.*, 1989).

Case Example (*Mary D. v. John D.*, 1989)

A twenty-four-year-old plaintiff sued her father for psychological injuries she allegedly suffered from his sexual abuse when she was a child. She alleged that the abuse occurred when she was five years old and younger and that because of the nature of the abuse she developed various psychological coping mechanisms including denial, repression, and disassociation from the experiences. She further alleged that she was not aware that the mental and emotional disturbances and distress

from which she suffered as a youth and a young adult were causally connected to her father's acts of sexual molestation. She alleged that because of the father's acts she suffered from childhood mental and emotional health problems, low self-esteem, distrust of people, self-destructive behavior, alcohol and drug abuse, sexual promiscuity, suicidal tendencies and attempts, and related injuries. Mary D.'s complaint also alleged that not until she began therapy approximately one year before filing the lawsuit was she aware of the abuse.

The defendant, John D., filed a motion for summary judgment, stating that an action for injury or illness based upon the alleged incest must be brought not later than three years after the injury or illness. The plaintiff conceded that the statute of limitations would not begin to run until her eighteenth birthday. However, since the complaint was filed approximately six years after her eighteenth birthday, the suit could not legally be heard.

The trial court granted the motion for summary judgment and ruled that the plaintiff had not filed her action within the proper time limits. Mary D. appealed that decision and the appellate court reversed the trial court.

The appellate court first addressed the question whether the delayed discovery doctrine would permit the statute of limitations to be tolled (extended) if the plaintiff had no memory of the alleged abuse. Referring to this situation as a Type Two case, the appellate court concluded

> . . . that the doctrine of delayed discovery may be applied in a case where plaintiff can establish lack of memory of tortious acts due to psychological repression which took place before plaintiff attained the age of majority, and which caused plaintiff to forget the facts of the acts of abuse until a date subsequent to which the complaint is timely filed.

The second issue raised in the appeal was whether the plaintiff had proof that in fact she had repressed the alleged events. The defendant asserted that some sort of showing from mental health experts was necessary to support the repression theory. The appellate court agreed that the plaintiff may be required to present such evidence, but that such proof would be offered before the trial court.

Discussion

Do you agree with the decision in this case? Should the delayed discovery rule have been applied in this case? Do you agree that such rules should be used at all? Different observers have expressed varying views on this issue. Rodgers (1993), who favors extension of the statute of limitations, argues that these rules still leave too much discretion to the courts in determining when the statute of limitations has run out. She argues that a neutral third party, such as an experienced psychologist, should determine how the rules should be applied in each case. Clevenger (1991–92) argues that if a plaintiff is able to present enough compelling evidence to meet the burden of proof, her claim should not be summarily dismissed on statute of limitations grounds.

Gardner (1993), on the other hand, argues that statute of limitations rules were created to protect the rights of defendants and that current efforts to extend the statute of limitations for child abuse crimes are dangerous erosions of defendant's rights. Statutes of limitations, he writes, were designed to (1) protect defendants against irrational and excessive punishments that are likely to be meted out in times of hysteria and (2) increase the likelihood that defendants will be able to avail themselves of credible witnesses. The modifications of statute of limitations law would deprive defendants sued by adult victims of alleged childhood abuse of their constitutional rights. He blames the "hysteria" surrounding child abuse as the cause behind extending the statute of limitations in child abuse cases.

Following the *Johnson* decision in 1988 the Illinois legislature passed a new statute which provided that an action for childhood sexual abuse may commence no more than twelve years after the victim attains the age of eighteen unless the victim was under some sort of legal disability during that time (Illinois Ann. Stat., 1991). After the new law was passed, the defendant moved again for summary judgment, arguing that under the new code the complaint was time-barred and should be dismissed with prejudice. The plaintiff, Ms. Johnson, urged the court to deny the motion, arguing that cases such as hers should be exempt from the twelve-year limit imposed by the new law, and alternatively, that she suffered from a legal disability at age eighteen (as provided for in the new statute).

In considering this issue the court did not try to determine the truth of the daughter's allegations but simply focused on how the new statute applied to this case. Finding that Ms. Johnson did not file her action till she was thirty-six years of age, and that she did not suffer from a legal disability at age eighteen that had recently been removed, the court found that her action now was time-barred and overturned their earlier ruling. The court noted that Ms. Johnson was not legally disabled simply because one therapist (whom the court characterized as having questionable qualifications) had found her to suffer from a multiple personality disorder.

In the second *Johnson* case the federal court used a strict interpretation of the new statute of limitations law to grant the defendant's summary judgment and thus to dismiss the adult victim's claims. In California the legislation in this area attempts to strike a balance between the competing rights of the survivors and their alleged perpetrators (California Civil Procedure Code, section 340.1, 1991). This statute gives a plaintiff an absolute right to file her claim until the time she reaches twenty-six. However, if after that time she discovers an injury or illness that was directly caused by the childhood abuse, she has an additional three years to commence the action. If this discovery occurs after the plaintiff has reached the age of twenty-six, the statute requires that affidavits be filed by the plaintiff's attorney and by a mental health professional, both of whom have reviewed the facts of the case and reasonably believe that the plaintiff was a victim of child sexual abuse at the hands of the defendant. The defendant is protected in that he may not be named as a party to the action until the judge has conducted an examination of the affidavits and has concluded that the action may proceed. The statute allows for pretrial discovery by the court, allowing the court to determine if the action has been initiated in an ethical manner. Thus, this legislation strives to address the concerns both of those who favor strict limitations, as well as those who want to protect victims' rights.

Most cases involving adult victims of child abuse pursuing action in court have involved civil court actions for damages. As noted in earlier chapters, it is more difficult to prove a case in criminal court than in civil court, because of the rules of evidence and the standard of proof involved. In cases involving homicide, however, there is no statute of limitations.

In a criminal case in California which received national attention the defendant was found guilty of murder after his grown daughter testified that she had repressed the grisly memory of her father murdering her childhood friend twenty years earlier (*People v. Franklin*, 1992). The centerpiece of the prosecution's case was the testimony of the suspect's daughter, Eileen Franklin-Lipsker, who told investigators she had repressed for twenty years the memory of seeing her father rape and bludgeon to death her childhood friend (Chiang, 1993). Franklin-Lipsker said her memory was triggered in 1989 by a look on her five-year-old daughter's face. She said she had repressed the memory because her father had physically and sexually abused her as a child and had threatened to kill her if she told anyone what she had seen. The body of her friend was found soon after the killing, but the case went unresolved for twenty years until Franklin-Lipsker stepped forward, made her allegations, and her father was arrested. The

California appellate court upheld the conviction, after finding the daughter's testimony "convincing, corroborated and credible." The California Supreme Court unanimously refused to review the murder conviction, and thus let stand the trial court guilt determination and the lengthy prison sentence.

THE "RECOVERED MEMORY" CONTROVERSY

The changes in the statutes of limitations described above make it possible for adult survivors of abuse to seek redress in the civil and criminal courts years after the alleged abuse took place. These extended delays present significant problems. There is no question that many victims of child abuse become adults without ever telling anyone about the abuse and that others have repressed it until therapy or some significant event brings out "recovered" memories. However, many commentators state that some adults are making false or mistaken accusations. Given the lapse of time and the lack of evidence it is extremely difficult to distinguish between true and false accusations of childhood abuse by adults. Extensions of statute of limitations have created great controversy. On the one hand, some have great doubts about the veracity of the charges and believe that the accused has no opportunity to defend himself. On the other hand, many believe that it is important that those who have been abused have the opportunity to seek redress for past acts.

According to Pezdek and Banks (1994) the veracity of childhood memories and the reality of memory repression is perhaps the most significant concern among psychologists today. Within the past ten years, there have been dozens of celebrated cases and many thousands of everyday cases of individuals who, in their adulthood, come forward with memories of having been abused as children. In response to these claims, some commentators argue that memory of childhood trauma is not reliable, that memory repression does not occur, and that memory is vulnerable to the suggestive influence of overzealous therapists, investigators, and self-help groups. For example, the book *Accusations of Child Sexual Abuse* (Wakefield and Underwager, 1993) has become a rallying point for many parents who feel that they have been unfairly accused, while the book *Courage to Heal* (Bass and Davis, 1988) has become popular with adult survivors of childhood sexual abuse.

Pezdek and Banks (1994) are the editors of a special issue of *Consciousness and Cognition* devoted exclusively to this issue. Some of the research suggests that "memories" can be fabricated or altered through repeated suggestions and interrogations, while other studies suggest that delayed recall is quite common and false accusations are rare. Lofthus (1994) has conducted several studies to determine whether false memories can be implanted and believed with the same assuredness as one believes real memories. Lofthus maintains that human memory is far from reliable. People often confuse what happened at one time with what happened at another time. In particular, Lofthus believes that misinformation can lead people to develop false memories of childhood trauma. For example, she cites the example of how one of her assistants told his younger brother, Chris, aged fourteen, that he (Chris) had been lost in a shopping mall at the age of five. Chris had no memory of ever being lost in a shopping mall, but when he was told this story by a person he regarded as an authority, his older brother, his usual resistance to influence fell away. Just two days later, when Chris was asked to recall being lost, he had already attached feelings to this non-event. According to Lofthus, this is an example of how therapists and investigators can lead people to develop false memories of childhood trauma.

Ceci, Crotteau, and Smith (1994) have conducted several studies on children's recall of "non-events." In their studies children were asked to "think real hard" about ten events. Some of the events were actual experiences whereas some were fictional. Children were asked to think about each

of the real and fictional events once per week for ten consecutive weeks. Each week, the experimenter asked the children to indicate whether the event had actually happened to them. Preliminary findings indicated that by the eleventh interview (conducted by a new interviewer who was "blind" to the children's prior answers), 68 percent of preschoolers claimed that at least one non-event had actually occurred to them. Children often provided ample details and a coherent internal structure for non-events that had been repeatedly suggested. The researchers conclude, however, that there are limits to this phenomenon. Specifically, children are most believing when the non-event taps into some familiar structure.

These generally nontraumatic "memories" manufactured in the above experiments may not be comparable to the recollections of real traumatic events such as childhood sexual abuse. According to Harvey and Herman (1994), delayed recall of childhood abuse is a relatively common factor in the clinical presentation of trauma survivors, and they further claim that verification of such recall is frequently possible. Freyd (1994) proposes a "Betrayal-Trauma Theory" to explain why the seemingly incredible nature of "memory recovery" might not be so incredible after all. Pursuant to this theory, traumatic amnesia need not be dependent on a purposeful suppression process; instead Freyd (who also describes herself as an adult survivor of childhood sexual abuse; Freyd, 1993) emphasizes that some memories are *safer* not to acknowledge and that defenses can be understood as cognitive information processing blockages.

In an innovative study of the memory of women who had documented childhood histories of sexual abuse, Williams (1994) found that many of these could not recall their victimization seventeen years later. In this study, 129 women with documented histories of sexual victimization were interviewed and asked about their abuse history. At the time of the interview (seventeen years following the report of the abuse), 80 of the women recalled the victimization. Of these women,

16 percent reported that at some time in the past they had forgotten about the abuse. These women with "recovered memories" were more likely to have been victimized by a family member than the women who reported that they "always remembered" their victimization. These data which show that women whose childhood abuse was a matter of public record often had repressed their victimization lend support to the claims of recovered memories of adult victims.

A commonly held belief is that painful or dangerous memories of past events are repressed. These repressed memories may lurk in the person's unconsciousness and may cause a person to act in an irrational and even self-defeating manner. The person then may seek counseling and therapy. The whole point of some therapies, including psychoanalysis, is to bring repressed material into consciousness where it can be identified and disarmed. Once the patient has learned what caused the problem, presumably most of the behavioral and emotional dysfunctions will be corrected. According to the repression theory, patients may recover memories of childhood trauma in therapy, or such memories may simply be triggered by some similar incidents. The point of contention in this context is whether adults can be led to believe that they have repressed such trauma and come to recover "memories" of events that never happened through leading suggestions and pressure from therapists and others.

The unprecedented case of Paul Ingram, eloquently recounted by Wright (1993a, 1993b), suggests that such false memories could possibly be created not only in the victims but also in the alleged offenders. According to Wright, the Ingram case has come to symbolize a growing controversy in this country over the validity of "recovered" memories, especially memories of what has come to be called "satanic-ritual abuse." Paul Ingram, his wife, Sandy, and several others were accused by their two adult daughters of sexual molestation going back to their early childhood years. After initially denying the charges, Ingram, at the urging of investigators and his pastor, began to produce memories not only of molesting his daughters but also of subjecting them to horrifying abuse at the hands of a satanic cult. A psychologist who participated in the investigation assured Ingram that memories of the abuse would come back to him once he confessed, and the pastor suggested images of the abuse before Ingram could recall any details. The Ingram family were members of a fundamentalist religion that believed in Satan and the works of the devil. Ingram implicated in the crimes two of his friends and former colleagues in the sheriff's department.

Before long, the two daughters, neither of whom had mentioned satanic abuse initially, elaborated upon their father's gruesome memories. The wife, along with an older brother, both of whom at first had no memories, also began to describe various forms of abuse. Only the two colleagues steadfastly denied the accusations. The father eventually pled guilty to the charges, and although he later tried to retract his guilty plea, the higher courts refused to hear his case. In his article, Wright implied that through their willingness to believe and protect the victims, police investigators and the pastor assisting in the interrogations went too far when asking leading and suggestive questions. As a result a nightmarish tale was created that in the end was too absurd and logically inconsistent for the investigators to believe. The author's conclusions must be tempered by the fact that Ingram remains in jail after having pled guilty of sexually abusing his daughters.

The False Memory Syndrome Foundation (FMS) was created based on the founders' skepticism regarding the disclosures of adults whose memories of abuse occur long after the alleged events. The initial membership of the foundation was drawn from over two hundred families who had contacted defense expert Ralph Underwager's Institute for Psychological Therapies (False Memory Syndrome Foundation, 1992). According to the FMS Foundation, it is therapists who are most responsible for manipulating adult patients into believing they were sexually abused during childhood. The FMS mission statement declares:

Increasingly throughout the country, grown children while undergoing "therapeutic" programs have come to believe that they suffered from "repressed memories" of incest and sexual abuse. While some reports of incest and sexual abuse are surely true, these "decade-delayed memories" are too often the result of False Memory Syndrome caused by a disastrous "therapeutic" program. False Memory Syndrome has a devastating effect on the victim and typically produces a continuing dependency on the very program that creates the syndrome. False Memory Syndrome proceeds to destroy the psychological well-being of not only the primary victim but—through false accusations of incest and sexual abuse—of other members of the victim's family. (False Memory Syndrome Foundation, 1992)

According to the FMS Foundation, the families contacting it show these similarities: (1) 80 percent of the accusations are made by daughters twenty-five to forty-five years old; (2) 90 percent of the charges stem from so-called "recovered" memories; (3) 17 percent of the families are being sued by their grown children; (4) 15 percent of the accusations involve satanic ritual abuse; (5) the children are advised to have no contact with their parents; (6) the majority of the siblings don't believe the accusations; (7) more than 80 percent of the parents are still married to their first spouse; (8) median income of the parents is more than $60,000; (9) 60 percent of the parents completed college and 25 percent have advanced degrees. The executive director of the foundation, Pamela Freyd, states that accusations of childhood abuse are usually made after the adult child goes to therapy for a number of reasons; the therapist suggests that sexual abuse occurred and the adult child is encouraged to analyze her dreams, undergo hypnosis, and attend self-help groups; the woman begins to remember abuse and is encouraged to confront her family; if abuse is denied, the woman cuts herself and her children off from the family, and the parents have no way to prove themselves innocent ("False Memory Profiles," 1993).

The founders, Pamela Freyd and her husband, Peter Freyd, state that they started the False Memory

Syndrome Foundation to seek the reasons for the spread of false memories, to work for the prevention of new cases, and to aid what they call the syndrome's primary and secondary victims (children and parents). They claim that nice families (such as themselves) are being destroyed by false accusations toward older parents by adult children who have been manipulated by overzealous therapists (Mitchell, 1993).

However, is the False Memory Syndrome Foundation a truly scientific organization? The founders' daughter, Jennifer Freyd, a psychologist at the University of Oregon, states that the FMS Foundation is based on a personal vendetta and active denial, coasting on legitimate issues about the validity of memory and taking advantage of the frequent disagreement among clinical and research psychologists. While the Freyds' denial of their daughter's allegations (which had not been made public prior to the founding of the organization), has turned into a crusade for all who say they are unjustly accused, their daughter, Jennifer Freyd, has publicly stated that the False Memory Syndrome Foundation is simply an attempt to cover up the fact that her father had sexually abused her as a child (Freyd, 1993). She claims that her parents have continued a pattern of behavior toward her which started in childhood: "a pattern of boundary violation, invasion and control, inappropriate and unwanted sexualization, family and relationship dysfunction" and of intimidation and manipulation. According to Jennifer Freyd there is no scientific basis for the term "false memory syndrome." In her opinion, it is simply a term conveniently coined to sound "scientific" and negatively label those who claim to have memories of childhood abuse. Others also view the foundation as a calculated legal defense strategy (Mitchell, 1993).

The creation of the False Memory Syndrome Foundation as well as another parent group, Victims of Child Abuse Laws (VOCAL), is seen by many as symptoms of a "backlash" movement against the protection of children from child abuse. Professionals who intervene in child sex abuse cases can be expected to be subjected to this "backlash," suggesting that children and now adults have been brainwashed into claiming abuse by parents and caretakers.

According to the National Center for Prosecution of Child Abuse, to ensure that only valid accounts are pursued in court, it is critical that allegations are investigated promptly, thoroughly, and objectively by trained law enforcement and other professionals ("False Memory Profiles," 1993). Sensitivity and skill are necessary not only for reliable interviews but to avoid unnecessary trauma for victims and those accused.

CONCLUSION

The ramifications of child abuse in the legal system seem to be never ending. In this chapter we have reviewed the situation faced by children who kill a parent possibly because of years of abuse. They ask the courts to accept a "battered child syndrome" theory similar to the "battered woman's syndrome" defense. Adult survivors of sexual abuse have argued that statutes of limitations should be extended so that victims who remember abuse years later can seek legal redress. Many oppose these extensions, claiming that the accused is unfairly asked to defend actions years later when evidence is unavailable. Groups have been formed, such as the False Memory Syndrome Foundation, providing support for parents accused of abusing their children and suggesting that the memories are the result of suggestive therapeutic techniques. Those who claim to have been abused answer that such groups are unscientific support groups for child abusers who have been exposed.

These issues will not be resolved in the legal system or anywhere else. No one other than the persons in the allegedly abusive relationship will ever know if it really took place. If we are to believe the Ingram case, even those involved may not know what happened.

All that we can expect of the legal system is to develop laws, rules, and procedures so that such claims can be addressed fairly in the context of our legal institutions. The legal system will never give us the "real" truth, but it will give us a process to determine to the best of our ability what claims can be heard, what evidence will be considered, and what redress will be offered to victims of child abuse.

CONCLUSION

Child abuse will never disappear. Despite our best preventive efforts, children will continue to be abused and neglected by the adults in their lives.

By their nature children are dependent upon their parents and guardians. To survive they must have adult support and assistance for the necessities of life, including food, shelter, clothing, health care, and emotional nurturing. Parents and other caretakers cannot or will not always provide what children need, and when they do not, the state must intervene on behalf of the child.

When and how the state takes action on behalf of abused children is a matter of some concern. The definition of child abuse has changed considerably. Some treatment of children which would have been ignored fifty years ago is today considered abuse or neglect. The physical disciplining of a child two generations ago might be considered child abuse today. The definition of abuse will continue to change as our attitudes toward family autonomy, individual rights, and child rearing evolve.

As we have seen in this text, abused and neglected children appear in many settings within the legal system. The state may intervene to protect a child in a juvenile court proceeding. The state may prosecute in a criminal court proceeding the person accused of maltreating the child. Parents may litigate child abuse allegations in the context of their marital dissolution proceedings. The child through a guardian *ad litem* may sue the person or the agency which has caused the abuse or neglect.

These interventions, moreover, have changed dramatically in the past few years, in both quantity and nature. Child abuse proceedings have increased greatly in number and now appear regularly in our legal system. Moreover, the legal system has had to respond to the needs of the children who appear in these proceedings. The legal system was not created for children, and many aspects of legal proceedings can be traumatic to children and unfair to the claims that they bring. As a result, many changes have been proposed and implemented in order to make the legal system more sensitive to the needs of the child.

These changes have been the subject of heated controversy throughout the legal system. Special exceptions to the hearsay rule, closed circuit television, the use of anatomically correct dolls, support persons in the court, and other innovations have resulted in numerous appellate court decisions. The appellate courts have struggled with many issues, but principally with the balance between the due process rights of an accused person and the needs of children in the legal system.

The legal system has made some significant accommodations to the needs of children. Some of the innovations have been rejected by the courts, but others have been affirmed as legitimate modifications in court procedures. These changes indicate that the legal system is capable of responding to the mounting claims of abused and neglected children.

As a society we have made a significant commitment to the protection of children. Through our mandatory reporting laws we have put on alert all of the people who regularly come into contact with children. We have instructed them to report suspected child abuse and neglect. Our law enforcement and social service agencies have developed expertise in the investigation of child abuse. Our prosecuting attorneys have specialized in child abuse cases. A new generation of lawyers and volunteers has committed itself to the representation of children in a variety of legal settings. Judges have been trained to deal appropriately with children as they come into the courtroom.

The changes have not ended. The incidents of child abuse continue to grow, and many legal issues surrounding child maltreatment remain unresolved. In addition, many communities still do not have the resources to provide adequate representation and support for children in the legal system. Fortunately, it appears that there is a commitment within the legal and volunteer communities to meet the needs of children in the legal system. Our goal must be to make the legal system available to claims of child abuse, while ensuring that any action taken by our legal system will be consistent with our traditions of due process and fairness to all persons affected.

APPENDIX

Introduction to Legal References

A number of references to cases and legislation occur in this text. Following is a brief introduction to legal research and how to read legal citations and find statutes. Court cases referred to in this text may come from state trial courts, state appeals courts, and state supreme courts, as well as federal district courts (e.g., the federal trial courts), federal circuit courts (e.g., the federal appeals courts), and the U.S. Supreme Court. Statutes and laws are at both the state and federal level.

READING LEGAL CITATIONS

Decisions made by the U.S. Supreme Court can be found in the *United States Report*, which is issued by the federal government, in the *United States Supreme Court Reports* published by Lawyers Co-Op, and in *West's Supreme Court Reporter*.

Federal appellate court decisions can be found in West's *Federal Reporter*, which contains decisions made by the U.S. Court of Appeals, the U.S.

Temporary Courts of Appeal, the U.S. Court of Customs and Patent Appeals, and the U.S. Court of Claims. U.S. District Court decisions are published in the *Federal Supplement*. Federal court decisions that deal with civil and criminal procedural matters, such as rules of evidence, expert witness testimony, and appeals procedure are also reported in West's *Federal Rules Decisions* (Stein, 1991).

State court decisions are published within each state and by West Publishing Company through their regional publications. West's *National Reporter System* divides the country into seven regions, with special reporters for California and New York, for the publication of decisions by state appellate courts. The reporters include the *Atlantic Reporter*, *North Eastern Reporter*, *North Western Reporter*, *Pacific Reporter*, *South Eastern Reporter*, *South Western Reporter*, *Southern Reporter*, *New York Supplement*, and *California Reporter*. State court decisions are issued officially by each state court and reported unofficially in West's *Regional Reporter Series* and in *American Law Reports*, published by the Lawyer's Co-Op Publishing Company. The West *Regional Reporter* contains only appellate

FIGURE A.1: Examples of a Case in the U.S. Supreme Court

Coy v. Iowa	410	U.S.	1012	1988
Case Name	Volume Number	Abbreviation for *U.S. Reports* where all Supreme Court decisions appear	Page number where legal decision begins	Year

OR

Coy v. Iowa	108	S. Ct.	2798	1988
Case Name	Volume Number	Abbreviation for the *Supreme Court Reporter*	Page number	Year

FIGURE A.2: Example of a Case in a U.S. Court of Appeals

Rouse v. Cameron	373	F.2d	451	(D.C. Cir. 1966)
Case Name	Volume Number	*Federal Reporter*, second series	Starting page	Decided in the U.S. Circuit Court for the District of Columbia

FIGURE A.3: Example of Case in a State Supreme Court

Carter v. General Motors, 361 Mich. 577, 106 N.W. 2d 105 (1969).

This case was decided by the Michigan Supreme Court in 1969. It can be found in volume 361 of the *Michigan Reports* starting on page 577 or in volume 106 of the second series of the *North Western Reporter* (*APA Publication Manual*, 1990).

FIGURE A.4: Example of Case in a Federal District Court

Lessard v. Schmidt, 349 F. Supp. 1078 (E.D. Wisc. 1972).

This case was tried in the Federal District Court for the Eastern District of Wisconsin and was decided in 1972. It appears in volume 349 of the Federal supplement, starting on page 1078 (*APA Publication Manual*, 1990).

FIGURE A.5: Example of Case in State Trial Court

In re Lee, No. 68 C.J.D. 13.62 (Cook County Cir. Court, Juv. Div., Ill. Feb. 29, 1972).

This case was tried in the Juvenile Division of the Cook County Circuit Court in Illinois. The case was decided on February 29, 1972. *In re* means "in the matter of " (*APA Publication Manual*, 1990).

and state supreme court decisions, whereas official state court reports may include selected state trial court decisions.

All legal citations begin with the case name, followed by the volume number of the document in which the case is reported, the source in which the report is found, the page number of the volume where the case begins, and the year in which the decision was made.

FEDERAL STATUTES AND REGULATIONS

A *statute* is a law passed by a legislative body declaring, commanding, or prohibiting something.

An *act* is the document that contains the statute (Harmon, 1989). The *Congressional Record* is published each day that Congress is in session and contains the text of bills, including legislative debates on bills that are introduced. *Statutes at Large* publishes federal legislation in pamphlet form, called slip laws, at the end of each legislative session. The *U.S. Code* is the official version of federal statutes and reports legislation by subject matter. The *U.S. Code Congressional and Administrative News* and the *United States Codes Annotated* as well as the *U.S. Code Services* are unofficial sources of the text of public laws.

A federal statute contains:

1. a public law number, e.g., P.L. 96-272, 1980;
2. a citation, e.g., 96 Stat. . . . ;
3. a popular name, e.g., Adoption Assistance and Child Welfare Act;
4. parallel citations for the U.S. Code, e.g., 42 USC 420, etc.;
5. a preamble; e.g., to provide for better care for children;
6. provisions: the text of the act or statute; and
7. legislative history—where the act originated and the related documents.

STATE STATUTES AND REGULATIONS

Every state compiles and publishes the laws that are passed during each legislative session. These collections are similar to those published in *Statutes at Large* and are published in chronological order. *Shepard's* also compiles a citator to state laws.

A state statute contains:

1. a citation, e.g., 1983 ch. 1297;
2. a preamble—to amend, repeal, and add sections;
3. parallel citations to the State Code(s): e.g., to add sections 11105.05 to the Penal Code; and
4. provisions—the text of the act or statute.

LEGAL RESEARCH

Legal encyclopedias, digests, loose-leaf services, and citators are good places to find legal materials. Case digests organize subject matter alphabetically and cite relevant court decisions chronologically. One such digest is the *Federal Practice Digest*, published by the West Publishing Company. *Shepard's Citations* provide references to all sources where a court decision, statute, and regulation can be found. Loose-leaf services are organized by subject area. In addition, there are computer services that cover legal cases, such as Lexis and West Law.

GLOSSARY

Adoption: The permanent relationship of parent and child created by legal action of the court rather than by birth.

Adoption Assistance and Child Welfare Act: A federal act passed in 1980 to establish a program of adoption assistance, to strengthen the program of foster care assistance for needy and dependent children, and to improve the child welfare, social services, and aid to families with dependent children programs.

Adjudicatory hearing: Same as a jurisdictional hearing—to determine whether the facts alleged in a petition are true.

Admissibility: Determination as to whether something may be used as evidence. A statement is admissible if a court concludes that it is to be used as evidence in a particular case.

Affirm: To ratify or uphold.

Affirmation: A solemn and formal declaration that an affidavit is true, that a witness will tell the truth. An affirmation can be an alternative to an oath for witnesses in legal proceedings.

Battered Child Syndrome: (1) Repeated physical abuse that could not have been inflicted by nonaccidental means. (2) Repeated physical abuse, usually by a parent, inflicted on a child.

Battered Woman's Syndrome: Repeated physical abuse of a woman, usually by a partner. The syndrome includes three stages: the build-up or tension, battering, and making up.

C.A.S.A.: Court-Appointed Special Advocates. A national program of trained volunteers who are appointed to represent abused and neglected children in the child welfare system.

Child abuse: Physical, sexual, or emotional child maltreatment.

Child advocate: A person who speaks on behalf of a child in a legal proceeding.

Child neglect: Failure to provide adequate physical, medical, and emotional care.

Child Sexual Abuse Accommodation Syndrome: Theory used to describe children's reactions to repeated sexual abuse by a family member or trusted adult; elements of the syndrome include secrecy, helplessness, entrapment and accommodation, delayed disclosure, and retraction.

Civil contempt proceedings: Proceedings to impose punishment on a person who is not complying with a court order.

Collateral estoppel: The doctrine of preventing an issue from being decided in more than one legal proceeding. If the parties were the same in the earlier legal proceeding, the issue is deemed to have been decided.

Colposcope: Magnifying device that enables physicians to examine vaginal openings for signs of trauma.

Competent: Able to understand, to communicate, and to understand the obligation to tell the truth.

Conflict of interest: Having different or opposing interests simultaneously. The representation of two parties each with a different interest.

Confrontation: The act of setting a witness face-to-face with the accused, in order that the latter may make any objection to the witness, ask questions of the witness, or that the witness may identify the accused.

Confrontation Clause: The Constitutional Sixth Amendment right of confrontation; it includes the privilege to cross-examine a witness.

Credibility: The quality in a witness that renders his or her evidence worthy of belief.

Cross-examine: To question an opposing party or witness in a hearing or trial.

Delayed discovery: The realization by a person that he or she was abused as a child. The discovery often takes place during therapy or at a significant event in the person's life.

Dependency cases: Child maltreatment or child welfare cases heard in the juvenile court.

Dependency Division (court): The part of juvenile court that handles child maltreatment cases.

Dependent child: Any child who is a ward of the court or under the protection of the court.

Deposition: A pretrial meeting of legal parties at which witnesses give testimony. Deposition testimony may be admitted as evidence in subsequent legal proceedings.

Detention hearing: A hearing in juvenile court to determine if a child should continue to be kept from the parents and placed in protective custody. Also referred to as a shelter care or probable cause hearing.

Dispositional hearing: A hearing to decide what is to be done as a result of proven child abuse or neglect.

Evidentiary rulings: Decisions by the judge concerning the admissibility of evidence offered at a trial or hearing.

Examine: To investigate, search, or interrogate.

Ex parte order: An order outside the context of a hearing given without the other party present.

Family Court: A division or part of a court system which deals with family matters. Usually the jurisdiction of the court includes juvenile and domestic relations cases and may also include emancipation, paternity, and related court calendars. In California, family court refers to domestic relations cases which include child support, spousal support/alimony, property division, child custody, and visitation.

Foster home: Substitute placement for a child who cannot live in his or her own home. The foster home is a temporary placement before a child returns to a parent or is placed in a more permanent setting.

Guardian *ad litem* (GAL): A legal representative for a child in legal proceedings.

Hearsay evidence: Evidence of a statement that was made other than by a witness while testifying at a hearing and that is offered to prove the truth of the matter stated.

In camera: In a judge's chambers, or in private.

Indictment: The formal document charging a defendant with criminal conduct. The indictment is brought by a grand jury after hearing evidence presented by a prosecutor.

Informal supervision: The provision of services by a social services agency to a family without formal court intervention.

In propria persona: A person representing him- or herself in court. Also *pro se*.

Judicial days: Days on which the court is in session. Excludes holidays and weekends.

Jurisdictional hearing: A hearing to decide whether a child comes under the statutory language describing a dependent child; also, a hearing to determine whether the facts alleged in the petition are true.

Juvenile court petition: Petition to allege that a child is neglected or abused and should be a dependent of the court.

Kelly-Frye test of admissibility: Evidence presented at trial must have general acceptance in the scientific community as a prerequisite to admissibility.

Mandatory Reporting Law: State law requiring professionals and others who regularly come into contact with children to report suspicions of child abuse or neglect to child protective services.

Oath: The statement by a witness that he or she promises to tell the truth in a legal proceeding.

Parens patriae **doctrine:** The power of the state to act in the parents' place for the purpose of protecting a child and his or her property.

Parricide: The killing of a parent by a child.

Percipient witness: A witness who was present when the event took place. A witness with firsthand knowledge of the event in question.

Permanency planning: Court action which provides a long-term placement for a dependent child. Adoption and guardianship are two types of permanent placement for a dependent child.

Permanency planning hearing: Hearing within eighteen months from the time a child is removed from parental care to determine the long-term placement for the child.

Petition: A legal document alleging that certain events have taken place and that the court should take action based upon the allegations. A petition initiates juvenile court proceedings.

Probate court: A division of the court system which deals with wills, estates, guardianships, and conservatorships. In some states, probate court also handles juvenile court matters.

Probative: Relevant, helpful to the trier of fact, as in a "probative question."

Pro bono: Free; without costs.

Reasonable efforts: The minimum level of services which should be provided by social services to prevent removal of a child from parental custody or to reunify a child with parents after removal. Under the federal law, the social services agency must show that "reasonable efforts" have been offered to a family before removing a child from parental custody.

Reliability: Trustworthiness; worthy of confidence.

Residual exception to the hearsay rule: Unspecified exceptions to the hearsay rule.

Reunification services: Services provided to reunite a child with parents after removal.

Review hearings: Court hearings held to monitor progress after court orders have been made.

Spontaneous declaration: A statement relating to a startling event or condition made while the declarant was under the stress of excitement caused by the event or condition; excited utterance.

Standing: Having legal status in a particular case. A person with standing is usually able to be assisted by counsel, to be heard, and to participate fully in the legal proceedings.

Status offense: An illegal act by a minor that is not a criminal offense.

Statute of limitations: The statute setting the time frame during which legal actions must be filed. If a person waits until after the statute of limitations has run, the law will generally preclude any court from hearing the matter.

Subpoena: A command to appear at a certain time and place to give testimony upon a certain matter.

Substantive evidence: Evidence presented for the purpose of proving a fact in issue, as opposed to evidence given for the purpose of discrediting or corroborating a testimony.

Suggestibility: Offering the answer in the question.

Summary judgment: Early resolution of a legal case based on legal issues. A judgment without a trial.

Termination of Parental Rights: The determination that a parent no longer has legal rights with regard to a child.

Totality of circumstance: Consideration of all aspects of the situation as opposed to one or two critical factors.

Trier of fact: A judge or jury.

Uniform Act to Secure the Attendance of Witnesses: Legislation setting out a standard means to ensure that witnesses attend legal hearings.

Voir dire: To tell the truth; the preliminary examination of a child to determine competency.

Volunteer *ad litem:* Volunteer appointed to appear on behalf of a child.

REFERENCES

Chapter 1: Scope and Historical Overview

Aries, P. (1962). *Centuries of Childhood: A Social History of Family Life*. New York: Knopf.

Besharov, D. (1983). Child protection: past progress, present problems, and future directions. *Family Law Quarterly*, 17, 151.

California Penal Code. (1991). St. Paul, MN: West.

Coy v. Iowa, 487 US 1012, 101 L.Ed.2d 857, 108 S.Ct. 2798 (1988).

Daro, D. (1988). *Confronting Child Abuse: Research for Effective Program Design*. New York: Free Press.

Daro, D., and Mitchell, L. (1990). *Deaths Due to Maltreatment Soar: The Results of the Eighth Semiannual Fifty State Survey*. Chicago, IL: National Committee for the Prevention of Child Abuse.

deMause, L. (1988). *The History of Childhood: The Untold History of Child Abuse*. New York: Peter Bedrick.

Dorne, C.L. (1989). *Crimes Against Children*. New York: Harrow and Heston.

Federal Bureau of Investigation. (1989). *Uniform Crime Reports for the United States, 1988*. Washington, DC: U.S. Government Printing Office.

Federal Bureau of Investigation. (1991). *Uniform Crime Reports for the United States, 1990*. Washington, DC: U.S. Government Printing Office.

Flicker, B. (1987). History of jurisdiction over juvenile and family matters. In F. X. Hartman (Ed.), *From Children to Citizens*. New York: Springer-Verlag.

Fredericksen, H., and Mulligan, R. (1972). *The Child and His Welfare* (3rd ed.). San Francisco, CA: Freeman.

Gelles, R. (1977). Violence towards children in the United States. Paper presented at the meeting of the American Society for the Advancement of Science, Denver, CO.

Gil, D. (1969). Physical abuse of children: Findings and implications of a national survey. *Pediatrics*, 44(5), Part 2, 857-864.

Gil, D. (1970). *Violence Against Children: Physical Child Abuse in the United States*. Cambridge, MA: Harvard University Press.

Gil, D. (1971). Violence against children. *Journal of Marriage and the Family*, 33(4), 637-648.

Gomby, D., and Shiono, P. (1991). Estimating the number of substance-abused infants. *The Future of Children*, 1(1), 17-25.

Grotberg, E. (Ed.). (1977). *Two Hundred Years of Children*. Washington, DC: Offices of Human and Child Development, Dept. of Health, Education and Welfare.

In re Gault, 387 U.S. 1 (1967).

Hardin, M. (1990). Ten years later: Implementation of Public Law 96-272 by the courts. American Bar Association Center on Children and the Law. Washington, DC: American Bar Association.

Hardin, M. (1988). Federal laws of special interest to attorneys handling civil child abuse and neglect cases. American Bar Association Center on Children and the Law. Washington, DC: American Bar Association.

Kelling, G. (1987). The historical legacy. In M. Moore (Ed.), *From Children to Citizens*, vol. 1. New York: Springer-Verlag.

Kempe, C., Silverman, F., Steele, B., Droegemuller, W., and Silver, H. (1962). The battered child syndrome. *Journal of the American Medical Association*, 181, 107-112.

Kent v. United States, 383 U.S. 541 (1966).

Kimmick, M. (1985). *America's Children: Who Cares? Growing Needs and Declining Assistance in the Reagan Era*. Washington, DC: Urban Institute Press.

Lloyd, D. (1991). What do we know about child sexual abuse today? National Resource Center on Child Sexual Abuse. Washington, DC: National Center on Child Abuse and Neglect, U.S. Dept. of Health and Human Services.

Marshall, A.B. (1991, Sept.). State-by-State legislative review. *Perinatal Addiction Research and Education Update*. Chicago, IL: National Association for Perinatal Research and Education.

National Center on Child Abuse and Neglect. (1988). *Study Findings: Study of National Incidence and Prevalence of Child Abuse and Neglect*. Washington, DC: U.S. Dept. of Health and Human Services.

National Institute of Justice. (1992, Oct.). *Report of Annual State Survey on Child Abuse and Neglect*. Washington, DC: National Committee for Prevention of Child Abuse.

Nelson, G. (1984). *Making an Issue of Child Abuse: Political Agenda Setting for Social Problems*. Chicago, IL: University of Chicago Press.

Page, S. (1982). The law, the lawyer, and medical aspects of child abuse. In E. Newberger (Ed.), *Child Abuse*. Boston: Little, Brown.

People v. Peggy McMartin Buckey and Ray Buckey (No. 14750900 Los Angeles Cty. Super. Ct., 1990).

Pfohl, S. (1977). The "discovery" of child abuse. *Social Problems, 24*, 431-433.

Platt, A. (1969). *The Child Savers: The Innovation of Delinquency*. Chicago, IL: University of Chicago Press.

Proceedings of the Conference on the Care of Dependent Children. (1909). Washington, DC: U.S. Government Printing Office.

Pumphrey, R., and Pumphrey, M., (Eds.). (1961). *The Heritage of American Social Work: Readings in Its Philosophical and Institutional Developments*. New York: Columbia University Press.

Radbill, S. (1987). Children in a world of violence: A history of child abuse. In R. Helfer and R. Kempe (Eds.), *The Battered Child* (4th ed.). Chicago, IL: University of Chicago Press.

Rosenheim, M. (1974). The child and the law. *Review of Child Development Research, 3*, 509.

Stein, T. (1991). *Child Welfare and the Law*. New York: Longman.

Strauss, M., and Gelles, R. (1986). The national family violence survey: Societal change and change in family violence from 1975-1985 as revealed by two national surveys. *Journal of Marriage and the Family, 48*, 465-479.

U.S. Advisory Board on Child Abuse and Neglect. (1990). *Child Abuse and Neglect: Critical First Steps in Response to a National Emergency*. Washington, DC: Dept. of Health and Human Services.

Victims of Child Abuse Act, 1990. Crime Control Act of 1990, Title II, 42 U.S.C. 13001, section 211.

Wadlington, W., Whitebread, C., and Davis, S. (1987). *Children in the Legal System*. Mineola, NY: Foundation Press.

West's California. (1991). *Juvenile Laws and Court Rules*. St. Paul, MN: West.

Whitcomb, D. (1992). *When the Victim Is a Child* (2nd ed.). Washington, DC: U.S. Dept. of Justice, Office of Justice Programs, National Institute of Justice.

Chapter 2: Types of Child Abuse and Neglect

Besharov, D. (1988). Child abuse and neglect reporting and investigation: Policy guidelines for decision making. *Family Law Quarterly, 22*, 1-15.

Bourne, R., and Newberger, E. H. (1977). "Family autonomy" or "coercive intervention"? Ambiguity and conflict in the proposed standards for child abuse and neglect. *Boston University Law Review, 57*, 670-683.

Bulkley, J. (1988). Legal proceedings, reforms and emerging issues in child sexual abuse cases. *Behavioral Sciences and the Law, 6*(2), 153-180.

California Penal Code. (1990). St. Paul, MN: West.

California Welfare and Institutions Code. (1990). St. Paul, MN: West.

Child Abuse Manual. (1989). Police Academy Training Manual. Sacramento, CA: POST.

Conte, J. and Berliner, L. (1988). The impact of sexual abuse. In L. Walker (Ed.), *Handbook on Sexual Abuse of Children*. New York: Guilford Press.

Daro, D. (1988). *Confronting Child Abuse: Research for Effective Program Design*. New York: Free Press.

Dean, D. (1979). Emotional abuse of children. *Children Today, 8*, 18-20.

Dumpson v. Daniel M. (1974). *New York Law Journal*, Oct. 16, p. 17, c. 7.

Faller, K. C. (1990). *Understanding Child Sexual Maltreatment*. Newbury Park, CA: Sage.

Garbarino, J. and Garbarino, A. (1986). *Emotional Maltreatment of Children*. Chicago, IL: National Committee for the Prevention of Child Abuse.

Gilpin v. McCormick, 921 F2d 928 (1990).

Giovannoni, J., and Bacerra, R. (1980). *Defining Child Abuse*. New York: Free Press.

In re Cheryl H., 153 Cal. App. 3d 1098 (1984).

In re E.G., 549 N.E.2d 322 (Ill.1989), 133 Ill.2d 98, 139 Ill. Dec. 810.

In re Edward C., 126 Cal. App. 3d 193; 178 Cal. Rptr. 694 (1981).

Juvenile Court Petition. (1985). Santa Clara County Superior Court.

Kadushin, A. (1974). *Child Welfare Services*. New York: Macmillan.

Kempe, C., Silverman, F., Steele, B., Droegemuller, W., and Silver, H. (1962). The battered child syndrome. *Journal of the American Medical Association, 181*, 107-112.

Lane, I., and Davis, A. (1987). Child maltreatment and juvenile delinquency: Does a relationship exist? In J. Burchard and S. Burchard (Eds.), *Prevention of Delinquent Behavior*. Newbury Park, CA: Sage.

Lloyd, D. (1991). What do we know about child sexual abuse today? Washington, DC: National Center on Child Abuse and Neglect, U.S. Dept. of Health and Human Services.

Matter of Theresa C., 576 N.Y.S. 2d 937 (1991).

Metropolitan Court Judges Committee Report: Deprived Children, A Judicial Response: 73 Recommendations. (1986). Reno, NV: National Council of Juvenile and Family Court Judges.

New York Social Service Law. (1991). Section 371.

People v. Jackson, 18 C.A. 3d 504, 95 Cal. Rptr. 919 (1971).

Polansky, C., Chalmers, A. and Bettenwiser, W. (1981). *Damaged Parents: An Anatomy of Child Neglect*. Chicago, IL: University of Chicago Press.

Rogers, P. (1992). Father gets six-month jail term in child endangerment case. *San Jose Mercury News*, April 8, p. 8B.

Stein, R. (1991). *Child Welfare and the Law*. New York: Longman.

Steinbach, A. (1989). The neglected child: A quiet crisis. *Baltimore Sun*, June 25, p. 1.

U.S. Advisory Board on Child Abuse and Neglect. (1990, June 27). Child abuse and neglect: Critical steps in response to a national emergency. Washington, DC: U.S. Dept. of Health and Human Services.

Victims of Child Abuse Act, 1990. Crime Control Act of 1990, Title II, 42 USC 13001.

Wadlington, D., Whitebread, C., and Davis, S.M. (1987). *Children in the Legal System*. Mineola, NY: Foundation Press.

Wald, M. (1975). State intervention on behalf of "neglected" children: A search for realistic standards. *Stanford Law Review*, 27, 987-1040.

West's California. (1990). *Juvenile Laws and Court Rules*. St. Paul, MN: West.

Chapter 3: Roles of Professionals Involved with Child Abuse and Neglect

Adoption Assistance and Child Welfare Act. (1980). Public Law 96-272, 42 U.S.C. Section 670 *et seq.*

Attorney General's Commission on the Enforcement of Child Abuse Laws. (1986). *Final Report*. Sacramento: California Attorney General's Office.

Barthel, J. (1992). *For Children's Sake: The Promise of Family Preservation*. New York: Edna McConnel Clark Foundation.

Besharov, D. (1985). *The Vulnerable Social Worker: Liability for Serving Children and Families*. Silver Spring, MD: National Association of Social Workers.

Besharov, D. (1988). The need to narrow the grounds for state intervention. In D. Besharov (Ed.), *Protecting Children from Abuse and Neglect: Policy and Practice*, pp. 47-90. Springfield, IL.: C. C. Thomas.

Besharov, D. (1990). Gaining control over child abuse reports: Public agencies must address both underreporting and overreporting. *Public Welfare*, 48(2), 34-47.

California Child Victim Witness Judicial Advisory Committee. (1988). *Final Report*. Sacramento: Crime Prevention Center, California Attorney General's Office.

California Penal Code. (1990). St. Paul, MN: West.

Child Abuse and Neglect. (1990). *Police Training Manual*. Sacramento, CA: POST

Child Abuse Prevention and Treatment Act. (1973). 42 U.S.C., Child Abuse Prevention, Adoption and Family Services Act. (1988). Public Law, 100-294.

Darryl H. v. Coler, No. 83 C 0628, U.S. District Court, N.D. Illinois, E.D. (25 Apr. 1984).

Edwards, L.P. (1992). The juvenile court and the role of the juvenile court judge. *Juvenile and Family Court Journal*, 43(2), 1-45.

Edwards, L.P. (1987). The relationship of family and juvenile courts in child abuse cases. *Santa Clara Law Review*, 27(2), 202-278.

Ehret v. New York City Department of Social Services, CV 81-2042 U.S. District Court, E.D. New York (19 Apr. 1985).

E.Z., et al. v. Coler, et al., 82 C 3976, U.S. District Court, N.D. Illinois, E.D. (March 12, 1985).

Faller, K.C. (1990). *Understanding Child Sexual Maltreatment*. Newbury Park, CA: Sage.

In re Christopher B., 82 CA3d 608, 147 CR 390 (1978).

In re Robert P., 61 CA3d 310, 132 CR 5 (1976).

Landeros v. Flood, 17 Cal. 3d 399, 131 Cal. Rptr. 69, 551 P.2d 389 (1976).

Miranda v. Arizona, 384 U.S. 436, 86 S. Ct. 1602, 16 L. Ed.2d 694 (1966).

National Center on Child Abuse and Neglect. (1984). The role of law enforcement in the prevention and treatment of child abuse. Washington, DC: U.S. Government Printing Office.

Stein, T. (1991). *Child Welfare and the Law*. New York: Longman.

Stein, T., and Comstock, G.D. (1987). *Reasonable Efforts: A Report on Implementation by Child Welfare Agencies in Five States*. Washington, DC: American Bar Association.

Stein, T., and Rzepnicki, T. (1983). *Decision Making at Child Welfare Intake: A Handbook for Practitioners*. New York: Child Welfare League of America.

Wald, M. (1992). Child Abuse and Neglect Materials 6. Course Materials, Stanford Law School, Stanford, CA.

Wald, M. (1988). Family preservation: Are we moving too fast? *Public Welfare*, Summer, pp. 33-38.

Wald, M., and Woolverton, M. (1990). Risk assessment: The emperor's new clothes? *Child Welfare*, 69(6), 483-511.

Chapter 4: Who Speaks for the Child?

Adoption Assistance and Child Welfare Act. (1980). 42 U.S.C., §§420 *et seq.*

Ballard v. Anderson, 4 Cal. 3d 873, 884 (1971).

California Standards of Judicial Administration: Judicial Council Recommendations. (1993). St. Paul, MN: West.

California Welfare and Institutions Code. (1993). St. Paul, MN: West.

Child Abuse Prevention and Treatment Act. (1974). (Public Law No. 93-247, 42 U.S.C. §5103.

Child Victim Witness Judiciary Advisory Committee. (1988). *Final Report.* Sacramento: California Attorney General's Office.

Cohen, C.P., and Davidson, H.A. (Eds.). (1990). *Children's Rights in America: U.N. Convention on the Rights of the Child Compared with United States Law.* Washington, DC: American Bar Association, Center on Children and the Law.

Deprived Children: A Judicial Response: 27 Recommendations. (1986). Reno, NV: National Council of Juvenile and Family Court Judges.

Duties of a Guardian Ad Litem. (1991). Family Court, First Circuit, State of Hawaii.

Edwards, L. (1993). A comprehensive approach to the representation of children: The child advocacy coordinating council. *Family Law Quarterly,* 27(3), 417-431.

Hardin, M. (1987). Guardians ad litem for child victims in criminal proceedings. *Journal of Family Law,* 25(4), 687-728.

History of the CASA Program. (1987). *Office of Juvenile Justice and Delinquency Prevention Juvenile Justice Bulletin.* Washington, DC: U.S. Dept. of Justice, Office of Justice Programs.

In re Christina D., 525 A.2d 1303, R.I. (1987).

In re Gault, 387 U.S. 1 (1967).

In re J.V. and C.W., Jr., 464 N.W.2d 887, Iowa App. (1990).

In re Lisa G., 504, A2d 1, N.H. (1986).

In re Patricia E., 174 Cal. App. 3d 1; 219 Cal. Rptr. 783 (1985).

In re Tanya H., 17 Cal. App. 4th 825 (1993).

Juvenile Justice Standards. (1980). Standards relating to counsel for private parties. Standard 3.1 (b). Washington, DC: American Bar Association.

National Study of Guardian Ad Litem Representation. (1990). Washington, DC: CSR, Inc.

Ramsey, S.H. (1983). Representation of the child in protection proceedings: The determination of decision-making capacity. *Family Law Quarterly,* 17(3), 287-326.

Riemer v. Riemer, 270 N.W.2d 93, 83 Wisc.2d. 375 (1978).

Siroky, G. (1993). Letters. *Youth Law News,* July-Aug.

Solender, E.K. (1976). The guardian ad litem: A valuable representative or an illusory safeguard? *Texas Tech Law Review,* 7, 620.

State Child Abuse and Neglect Statutes: A Comparative Analysis. (1985). Washington, DC: Clearinghouse on Child Abuse and Neglect.

State v. Freeman, 203 N.J. Super. 351, 496 A.2d 1140 (1985).

State v. Walsh, 495 A2d 1256 NH (1985).

United Nations Convention on the Rights of the Child. (1990). *United Nations Proceedings,* Sept. New York: United Nations.

Whitcomb, D. (1988). *Guardians Ad Litem in Criminal Courts.* Washington, DC: U.S. Dept. of Justice, Office of Communication and Research Utilization, National Institute of Justice.

Wisconsin Statutes Annotated. (1993). Section 767.045. St. Paul, MN: West.

Chapter 5: Juvenile Court: The Child Protective Function

Adoption Assistance and Child Welfare Act. (1980). Public Law 96-272, 42 U.S.C., paragraph 620 *et seq.* and §§670 *et seq.*

American Public Welfare Association. (1990) *Report.* Washington, DC: APWA.

Bearrows, T., Bleich, J., and Oshima, M. (1987). The contemporary mandate. In M. Moore (Ed.), *From Children to Citizens: 1. The Mandate for Juvenile Justice,* pp. 52-53. New York: Springer-Verlag.

Besharov, D. (1988). The need to narrow the grounds for state intervention. In D. Besharov and C. Thomas (Eds.), *Protecting Children from Abuse and Neglect.* Springfield, IL: C.C. Thomas.

California Welfare and Institutions Code. (1990). Sections 300 *et al.* St. Paul, MN: West.

Court-approved alternative dispute resolution: A better way to resolve minor delinquency, status offense and abuse/neglect cases. (1989). Reno, NV: National Council of Juvenile and Family Court Judges.

Edwards, L. P. (1987). The relationship of family and juvenile courts in child abuse cases. *Santa Clara Law Review,* 27 (2), 201-278.

Edwards, L. P. (1992). The juvenile court and the role of the juvenile court judge. *Juvenile and Family Court Journal,* 43(2).

Fox, E. (1970). Juvenile justice reform: An historical perspective. *Stanford Law Review,* 22, 1187.

Gladstone, W. (1990). Juvenile justice: How to make it work. *Miami Herald Viewpoint,* June 3, Sect. C.

Goldstein, I., Solnit, R., and Freud, A. (1980). *Before the Best Interests of the Child.* San Francisco, CA: Free Press.

In re Gault, 387 U.S.1, 87 S. Ct. 1428, 18 L. Ed. 2d 527 (1967).

In re Malinda S., 51 Cal. 3d 368, 272 Cal. Rptr. 787, 795 P. 2d 1244 (1990).

In re Mary S., 186 Cal.App.3d 414 (1986).

In the Interest of Ashley K., a Minor (1-90-3635), Appellate Court of Illinois, First District (17 April, 1991).

In the Interest of J.R.T., 427 So. 2d 251 (FLA, 1983).

Iruste-Montes, A. M., and Montes, F. (1988). Court-ordered versus voluntary treatment of abusive and neglectful parents. *Child Abuse and Neglect,* 12, 33-39.

Juvenile Justice and Delinquency Prevention Act of 1974, 42 U.S.C.A., sec. 5601-5751.

Kent v. United States, 383 U.S. 541, 566 (1966).

La Shawn A., et al. v. Sharon Pratt Dixon, et al., Civ. No. 89-1754 (D.C., 1991).

Moore, M. H. (1987). *From Child to Citizen: The Mandate for Juvenile Justice*. New York: Springer-Verlag.

National Committee for the Prevention of Child Abuse. (1986). *Child Abuse: Prelude to Delinquency?* Washington, DC: U.S. Dept. of Justice, Office of Juvenile Justice and Delinquency Prevention.

National Committee for the Prevention of Child Abuse. (1990). Survey. Chicago, IL: NCPCA.

National Council of Juvenile Court Judges. (1964). *Directory and Manual*. Reno, NV: NCJCJ.

Platt, A. (1977). *The Child Savers: The Invention of Delinquency* (2nd ed.). Chicago, IL: University of Chicago Press.

Prince v. Massachusetts, 321 U.S. 158 (1941).

Seymor, G. (1990). The juvenile justice system: Visions for the future. *Juvenile and Family Court Journal*, 41(2), 15-21.

Springer, C. (1991). Rehabilitating the juvenile court. *Notre Dame Journal of Law, Ethics and Public Policy*, 5(2), 397-420.

Stapleton, V., Aday, D., and Ito, J. (1988). *American Journal of Sociology*, 88(3), 549-564.

Sutton, J. (1988). *Stubborn Children: Controlling Delinquency in the United States 1640-1981*. Berkeley: University of California Press.

Szymanski, L. (1990). *Juvenile Code Purpose Clauses*. Pittsburgh, PA: National Center for Juvenile Justice.

Teitelbaum, L., and Gough, A. (1977). *Beyond Control: Status Offenders in the Juvenile Court*. Cambridge, MA: Ballinger.

Wexler, R. (1990). *Wounded Innocents: The Real Victims of the War Against Child Abuse*. Buffalo, NY: Prometheus.

Wolfe, D., Aragona, J., Kaufman, K., and Sandler, J. (1980). The importance of adjudication in the treatment of child abusers: Some preliminary findings. *Child Abuse and Neglect*, 4, 127-135.

Chapter 6: Domestic Relations Court

Bulkley, Jr. (1988). Legal proceedings, reforms and emerging issues in child sexual abuse cases. *Behavioral Sciences and the Law*, 6(2), 153-180.

California Civil Code. (1991). St. Paul, MN: West.

California Penal Code. (1991). St. Paul, MN: West.

Cantwell, H. (1981). Sexual abuse of children in Denver, 1979: Reviewed with implications for pediatric intervention and possible prevention. *Child Abuse and Neglect*, 5, 75-85.

Cauble, A. E., Thoennes, N., Pearson, J., and Appleford, R. (1985). A case study: Custody resolution in Hennepin County, Minnesota. *Conciliation Courts Review*, 23, 27-36.

Child Witness Manual. (1991). Emeryville, CA: California Center for Judicial Education and Research.

Coleman, L., and Clancy, P. E. (1990). False allegations of child sexual abuse: Why is it happening? What can we do? *Criminal Justice*, Fall, 14-47.

Corwin, D. L. (1986). Allegations of child sexual abuse in family court. Paper presented at Family Court Services, Alameda County Superior Court, Alameda, CA, May.

Corwin, D. L., Berliner, L., Goodman, G., Goodwin, J., and White, S. (1987). Child sexual abuse and custody disputes: No easy answers. *Journal of Interpersonal Violence*, 2, 91-105.

Edwards, L. (1987). The relationship of family and juvenile court in child abuse cases. *Santa Clara Law Review*, 27, 202-278.

Ellibee v. Ellibee, 826 P.2d 462 (Idaho, 1992).

Finkelhor, D., Hotaling, G., and Sedlack, A. (1991). Children abducted by family members: A national household survey of incidence and episode characteristics. *Journal of Marriage and Family*, 53, 805-817.

Gordon, C. (1985). False accusations of abuse in child custody disputes. *Massachusetts Family Law Journal*, Nov., 54-56.

Gray, L. (1986). The use of false accusations. Paper presented at the Fourth National Conference on the Sexual Victimization of Children, New Orleans, LA, May.

Green, A. H. (1985). True and false accusations of sexual abuse in child custody disputes. *Journal of the American Academy of Psychiatry*, 25, 449-456.

Grein v. Grein, 364 N.W. 2d 383 (Minnesota 1985).

G.S. v. T.S., 582 A.2d 467, 23 Conn.App.509 (1990).

Harmer, D. J. (1990). Limiting incarceration for civil contempt in child custody cases. *BYU Journal of Public Law*, 4(2), 239-291.

Heatherington, E., Cox, M., and Cox, R. (1978). Play and social interaction in children following divorce. Paper presented at the National Institute of Mental Health (NIMH) Conference on Divorce, Washington, DC.

Hogobom, E., and King, D. (1991). *California Practice Guide: Family Law*. San Francisco, CA: Rutter Group.

Horowitz, J., Salt, P., Gomes-Schwarts, B., and Sauzier, M. (1984). Unconfirmed cases of sexual abuse. In Tufts New England Medical Center, Division of Child Psychiatry, *Sexually Exploited Children: Service and Research Project*. Final Report for the Office of Juvenile Justice and Delinquency Prevention. Washington, DC: U.S. Dept. of Justice.

Huntington, D. (1986). Parental kidnapping: A new form of abuse. Center for the Family in Transition, Corte Madera, CA.

In re M. M., 650 P.2d 784 (Mont.Supp.Ct. 1982).

Johnston, J. R., and Campbell, L. E. G. (1988). *Impasses of Divorce: The Dynamics and Resolution of Family Conflict.* New York: Free Press.

Jones, D., and McCraw, M. J. (1987). Reliable and fictitious accounts of sexual abuse of children. *Interpersonal Violence,* 2, 27-45.

Leupnits, D. (1978). Children of divorce: reviews of the psychological literature. *Law and Human Behavior* 2(2), 167-169.

Marriage of Okum, 195 CA3d 176, 180, 240 CR 258 (1987).

Marriage of Rosson, 178 CA3d 1094, 1100, 224 CR 250 (1986).

Maryland Family Code Annual Supplement. (1990). Charlottesville, VA: Mitchie Co.

Mnookin, R. (1975). Child custody adjudication: Judicial functions in the face of indeterminacy. *Law and Contemporary Problems,* 39, 220-227.

Moffat v. Moffat, 27 Cal.3d 645; 165 Cal.Rptr.877, 612 P.2d 967 (1980).

Morgan v. Foretich, 846 F.2d 941 (4th Cir. 1988).

Mullins v. Mullins, 490 N.E.2d 1375 (Ill. App. 1 Dist.), 1986.

Nicholson, E. B. (1988). Child abuse allegations in family court proceedings: A survey of legal issues. In E. B. Nicholson and J. Bulkley (Eds.), *Sexual Abuse Allegations in Custody and Visitation Cases.* Washington, DC: American Bar Association.

People v. Peggy McMartin Buckey and Ray Buckey, No. A750900 (Los Angeles County Superior Court, 1990).

Peters, J. (1976). Children who are victims of sexual assault and the psychology of offenders. *American Journal of Psychotherapy,* 30, 398-421.

Public Law No. 101-97 (1989) 103 Stat. 633.

Raskin, D. C., and Yuille, J. C. (1989). Problems in evaluating interviews of children in sexual abuse cases. In S. J. Ceci, D. F. Ross, and M. P. Toglia (Eds.), *Perspectives on Children's Testimony.* New York: Springer-Verlag.

Romer, S. (1990). Child sexual abuse in custody and visitation disputes: Problems, progress and prospects. *Golden Gate University Law Review,* 20(2), 647-680.

Rubin, T. (1989). Child and family legal proceedings: Court structure, statutes and rules. Denver, CO: National Center for State Courts.

Sagatun, I. J., and Barrett, L. (1990). Parental child abduction: The law, family dynamics and legal system responses. *Journal of Criminal Justice* 18, 433-442.

Seymour v. Walter, 423 So. 2d 770 (LA Ct. App. 1982).

Sink, F. (1986). Studies of true and false allegations: A critical review. In E. B. Nicholson and J. Bulkley (Eds.), *Sexual Abuse Allegations in Custody and Visitation Cases.* Washington, DC: American Bar Association.

State in the Matter of Williams, 447 So.2d 1211, *Writ Denied* 449 So.2d 1357 (Louisiana, 1984).

Steagall v. Steagall, 442 So.2d 732 (Louisiana, 1983).

Thoennes, N., and Pearson, J. (1986). Summary of findings from the sexual abuse allegations project (Washington, DC: Association of family and conciliation courts research units). In E. B. Nicholson and Bulkley, J. (Eds.), *Sexual Abuse Allegations in Custody and Visitation Cases.* Washington, DC: American Bar Association.

Wallenstein, J., and Kelley, J. (1980). *Surviving the Breakup.* New York: Basic Books.

Chapter 7: Criminal Court and Child Abuse

American Humane Association. (1988). *Highlights of Official Child Abuse and Neglect Reporting.* Denver, CO: American Humane Association.

Arizona Revised Statutes. (1991). Title 13. Criminal Code. Chapter 6. Classifications of Offenses and Authorized Dispositions of Offenders, section 13-604.01.

Besharov, D. (1987). Child abuse: Arrest and prosecution decision-making. *American Criminal Law Review,* 24, 315-318.

Besharov, D., and Asamoah, H. (1988). The statutory framework for police activities in cases of child abuse. Washington, DC: American Enterprise Institute.

California Evidence Code. (1993). Sacramento, CA: Matthew Bender.

California Penal Code. (1991). St. Paul, MN: West.

Chapman, I., and Smith, L. (1987). Response to social service and criminal justice agencies to child sexual complaints. *Response to the Victimization of Women and Children,* 10(3), 130-135.

Child sex abuse should be decriminalized. (1991). *The Australian.* (Sydney), Feb. 2, p. 3.

Child Victim Witness Judicial Advisory Committee. (1988). Final Report. Sacramento: California Attorney General's Office.

Child Victim Witness Manual. (1992). *California Center for Judicial Education and Research Journal,* 12(1).

Dorne, C. (1989). *Crimes Against Children.* New York: Harrow and Heston.

Faller, K. (1990). *Understanding Child Sexual Maltreatment.* Newbury Park, CA: Sage.

Harshbarger, E. (1987). Prosecution is an appropriate response in child sexual abuse cases. *Journal of Interpersonal Violence,* 2, 108-109.

Martin, S. E., and Besharov, D. (1991). *Police and Child Abuse: New Policies for Expanded Responsibilities.* Washington, DC: U.S. Dept. of Justice, Office of Justice Programs.

Myers, J. (1985-86). The legal response to child abuse: In the best interest of children. *Journal of Family Law,* 24, 149-269.

Newberger, E. H. (1987). Prosecution: A problematic approach to child abuse. *Journal of Interpersonal Violence, 2,* 112-115.

Peters, J. M., Dinsmore, J., and Toth, P. (1989). Why prosecute child abuse? *South Dakota Law Review, 34*(3), 649-659.

People v. Harlan, 222 CA3d 439, 451, 454, 271 CR 653 (1990).

People v. Peggy McMartin Buckey and Ray Buckey, No A750900 (Los Angeles County Superior Court, 1990).

People v. Pitts, 223 CA3d 606, 869, 273 CR 757 (1990).

People v. Superior Court (Caudle), 221 Cal.App. 3d, 1990.

Richmond Newspaper Inc., v. Virginia, 448 US 555, 573, 65 KLK Ed 2d 973 (1980).

Runyan, D., Everson, M., Edelsohn, G., Hunter, W., and Coulter, M. (1988). Impact of legal intervention on sexually abused children. *Journal of Pediatrics, 113,* 647-650.

Spencer, J. R., and Flin, R. H. (1990). *The Evidence of Children: The Law and the Psychology.* London: Blackstone.

State v. Freeman, 496 A. 2d 114 (1985).

State v. Johnson, 528 N.E. 567 (Ohio App., 1986).

State v. Suka, 777 P.2d 240 (Hawaii), 1989.

Tedesco, J., and Schnell, S. (1987). Children's reactions to sex abuse investigation and litigation. *Child Abuse and Neglect, 11,* 267-271.

Whitcomb, D. (1986). *Prosecuting Child Sexual Abuse—New Approaches.* Washington, DC: U.S. Dept. of Justice.

Whitcomb, D. (1988). *Guardians ad Litem in Criminal Courts.* Washington, DC: National Institute of Justice, Office of Communication and Research Utilization, U.S. Dept. of Justice.

Chapter 8: Civil Court: Recovering Damages and Changing the System

Adoption Assistance and Child Welfare Act. (1980). Public Law 95-272, 42 U.S.C. 620 *et seq.*

California Civil Code. (1991). St. Paul, MN: West.

California Penal Code. (1993). St. Paul, MN: West.

Child vs. Beame, 412 F. Supp. 593 (S.D. N.Y. 1976).

Courtney vs. Courtney, Supreme Court of West Virginia, 413 S.E.2d 418 (19 Dec. 1991).

DeShaney v. Winnebago County D.S.S., 109 S. Ct. 988, 1005 (1989).

Doe v. New York City Department of Social Services, 649 F.2d 134 (2d Cir. 1981), *cert. denied,* 464 U.S. 864 (1983).

Gilbert v. Gilbert, 168 C.A.2d 102, 335 P. 2d 736 (1959).

In re Ashley K., 571 N.E.2d 905 (1991).

In re George O. 115 Misc. 2d 782, 791, 455 N.Y.S. 2d 146, 153 (N.Y. Fam. Ct., 1981).

Landeros v. Flood, 17 Cal 3d 399, 131 Ca. Rptr. 69, 551 P.2d 389 (1976).

Landis v. Allstate Insurance Co., 546 So 2d 1051 (Fla. 1989).

LaShawn A. v. Sharon Pratt Dixon, et al., Civil Action No. 89-1754, U.S. District Court for the District of Columbia (18 Apr. 1991).

LaShawn, A., v. Kelly, 990 F.2d 1319 (D.C. Circuit, 1993).

Milburn v. Anne Arundel County Dept. of Social Services, 871 F. 2d 474, *cert. denied,* 110 S. Ct. 148 (4th Cir. 1989).

Norfleet v. Arkansas Department of Human Services, 989 F.2d 289 (8th Cir. 1993).

Restatement of the Law, Torts (2nd ed.). (1965). Washington, DC: American Law Institute.

Rubacha v. Coler, 607 F. Supp. 477 (N.D. Ill. 1985).

Smith v. Organization of Foster Families, 432 U.S. 816 (1977).

Suter v. Artist M., 112 S.Ct. 1360 (1992).

Taylor v. Ledbetter, 818 F. 2d 791 (11th *cert. denied,* 109 S.Ct. 1337 (11th Cir. 1987).

Witkin, D. (1988). *Summary of California Law, 5* (9th ed.). San Francisco, CA: Bancroft-Whitney.

Chapter 9: The Relationship of Different Legal Proceedings

Child Victim Witness Judicial Advisory Committee. (1989). *Task Force Report.* Sacramento: California Attorney General's Office.

Edwards, L. (1987). The relationship of family courts in child abuse cases. *Santa Clara Law Review, 27,* 201-278.

Edwards, L. (1992). The role of the juvenile court judge. *Juvenile and Family Court Journal, 43*(2), 1-45.

In re Christina T., 184 Cal. App. 3d 630, 229 Cal. Rptr. 247 (1986).

In re Jennifer P., 174 Cal. App. 3d 322, 219 Cal. Rptr. 909 (1985).

In re Nicole B., 93 Cal. App. 3d 874, 155 Cal. Rptr. 916 (1979).

In re William T., 172 Cal. App. 3d. 790, 218 Cal. Rpt. 720 (1985).

Lockwood v. Superior Court, 160 Cal. App. 3d 667 (1984).

Pennsylvania v. Ritchie, U.S.S.Ct., 1987, 480 U.S. 39.

Rubin, T. (1989). *Child and Family Legal Proceedings: Court Structure, Statutes and Rules.* Denver, CO: National Center for State Courts.

Standard California Codes: Penal and Selected Provisions of Other Codes. (1988). New York: Matthew Bender.

State v. Cleveland, 794 P.2d 546 (Wash. App. 1990).

Chapter 10: The Child Witness

American Bar Association. (1988). Child victim witness guidelines (American Bar Assn., Criminal Justice Section, Report to the House of Delegates, July 1985). In B. E. Nicholson and J. Bulkley (Eds.), *Sexual Abuse Allegations in Custody and Visitation Cases* pp. 287-291. Washington, DC: American Bar Association.

Barnes v. State, 328 S.E. 2d 583 (Georgia App. 1985).

Berliner, L. (1988). Deciding whether a child has been sexually abused. In E. B. Nicholson and J. Bulkley (Eds.), *Sexual Abuse Allegations in Custody and Visitation Cases*, pp. 48-71. Washington, DC: American Bar Association.

Berliner, L., and Barbieri, M. K. (1984). The testimony of the child victim of sexual assault. *Journal of Social Issues*, 40(2), 125-137.

Boat, B. W., and Everson, M. D. (1988). Interviewing young children with anatomical dolls. *Child Welfare*, 67, 337-385.

Brown, A. L. (1979). Theories of memory and the problem of development: Activity, growth and knowledge. In L. Cermak and F. I. M. Craik (Eds.), *Levels of Processing in Memory*. Hillsdale, NJ: Erlbaum.

California Evidence Code. (1992). St. Paul, MN: West.

California Penal Code. (1991). St. Paul, MN: West.

Ceci, J., Ross, D., and Toglia, M. (1987). Age differences in suggestibility: Narrowing the uncertainties. In S. J. Ceci, M. P. Toglia, and D. F. Ross (Eds.), *Children's Eyewitness Memory*. New York: Springer-Verlag.

Child Victim Witness Judicial Advisory Committee. (1988). *Final Report*. Sacramento: California Attorney General's Office.

Child Victim Witness Manual. (1992). *California Center for Judicial Education and Research Journal*, 12(1), 5-154.

Christiansen, R. E., Sweeney, J. D., and Ochalek, K. (1983). Influencing eyewitness descriptions. *Law and Human Behavior*, 7, 59-65.

Cohen, R. L. and Harnick, M. A. (1980). The susceptibility of child witness to suggestion. *Law and Human Behavior*, 4(3), 201-210.

Cole, C. B., and Loftus, E. (1987). The memory of children. In S. J. Ceci, M. P. Toglia, and D. F. Ross (Eds.), *Children's Eyewitness Memory*. New York: Springer-Verlag.

Coleman, L. (1986). False accusations of sexual abuse: Have the experts been caught with their pants down? *Forum*, 12 (Jan.-Feb.).

Corwin, D. L., Berliner, L., Goodman, S., and White, S. (1987). Child sexual abuse and custody disputes: No easy answers. *Journal of Interpersonal Violence*, 2, 91-105.

Duncan, E. M., Whitney, P., and Kunen, S. (1982). Integration of visual and verbal information in children's memory. *Child Development*, 53, 1215-1223.

Dziech, B. W., and Schudson, C. (1989). *On Trial: America's Courts and Their Treatment of Sexually Abused Children*. Boston, MA: Beacon Press.

Everson, M. D., and Boat, B. W. (1989). False allegations of sexual abuse by children and adolescents. *Journal of the American Academy of Child and Adolescent Psychiatry*, 28, 230-235.

Federal Rules of Evidence. (1989). St. Paul, MN: West.

Feher, T., (1988). The alleged molestation victim, the rules of evidence and the Constitution: Should children really be seen and not heard? *American Journal of Criminal Law*, 14, 227-255.

Flavell, J. H. (1985). *Cognitive Development* (2nd ed.). Englewood Cliffs, NJ: Prentice-Hall.

Freud, S. (1959). Two principles of mental functioning. In J. Strachecy (Ed.), *The Standard Edition of the Complete Psychological Works of Sigmund Freud*, Vol. 9, pp. 143-153. London: Hogarth. (Original work published in 1911.)

Garbarino, J. (1989). Children as witnesses. In J. Garbarino and F. Stott (Eds.), *What Children Can Tell Us*. San Francisco, CA: Jossey-Bass.

Garbarino, J., and Stott, F. (Eds.). (1989). *What Children Can Tell Us*. San Francisco, CA: Jossey-Bass.

Goodman, G. S. (1984). The child witness: Conclusions and future directions for research and legal practice. *Journal of Social Issues*, 40(2), 157-175.

Goodman, G. S., Bottoms, B., Herscovici, B. B., and Shaver, P. (1989). Determinants of the child victim's perceived credibility. In S. J. Cici, M. P. Toglia, and D. F. Ross, (Eds.), *Perspectives on Children's Testimony*. New York: Springer-Verlag.

Goodman, G. S., Golding, J., and Haith, M. (1984). Jurors' reactions to child witnesses. *Journal of Social Issues*, 40(2), 139-156.

Hardy v. Commonwealth, 719 S.W. 2d 727 (KY 1986).

Hochheiser v. Superior Court, 161 CA 3d. 777 (Cal. Ct. Appeals) Nov. 1984.

In the Interest of E. D., 495 N.E. 2d 1334 (Illinois App. 1986).

In re R. R., 79 N.J. 97, 398 A. 2d 76 (N.J. 1979).

Jones, D., and McQuiston, M. (1986). *Interviewing the Sexually Abused Child* (2nd ed). Denver, CO: Kempe Center, University of Colorado School of Medicine.

Kentucky v. Stincer, 107 S. Ct. 2658 (1987).

Levy, R. (1989). Using "scientific" testimony to prove child sexual abuse. *Family Law Quarterly*, 23(3), 383-411.

Lindsay, D. S., and Johnson, M. K. (1987). Reality monitoring and suggestibility: Children's ability to discriminate among memories from different sources. In S. J. Ceci, M. P. Toglia, and D. F. Ross (Eds.), *Children's Eyewitness Testimony*. New York: Springer-Verlag.

Loftus, E. (1979). *Eyewitness Testimony*. Cambridge, MA: Harvard University Press.

Loftus, E., and Davies, G. M. (1984). Distortions in the memory of children. *Journal of Social Issues* 40(2), 57-67.

McNamee, S., and Dowley, G. (1989). Language development. In J. Garbarino and F. Stotts (Eds.), *What Children Can Tell Us*. San Francisco, CA: Jossey-Bass.

Myers, J. (1987). The child witness: Techniques for direct examination, cross-examination and impeachment. *Pacific Law Journal 18*, 801-941.

Myers, J., Bays, J., Becker, J., Berliner, L., Corwin, D., and Saywitz, K. (1989). Expert testimony in child sexual abuse litigation. *Nebraska Law Review 68*(1), 3-145.

National Council of Juvenile and Family Court Judges. (1986). Court procedures in child sexual abuse: Improving the system's responses. *Juvenile and Family Court Journal, 37*, 31-36.

Ochs v. Martinez, 789 S.W.2d 949 (Tex. App. 1990).

Penrod, S., Bull, M., and Lengnick, S. (1989). Children as observers and witnesses: The empirical data. *Family Law Quarterly, 23*(3), 411-433.

People v. Jones, 270 Cal. Rptr. 611, 792 P. 2d 643 (1990).

People v. Peggy McMartin Buckey and Ray Buckey (No. 14750900 Los Angeles Cty. Super. Ct., 1990).

People v. Stark, 92 C.D.O.S. 2672 (27 Mar. 1992).

People v. Vialpando, 804 P.2d 219 (Colorado App. 1990).

Piaget, J. (1932). *The Moral Judgment of the Child*. London: Kegan-Paul.

Sagatun, I. J., and Edwards, L. P. (1989). The child as witness in criminal courts. *Police Chief, 26*(4), 123-127.

Singer, D. and Revenson, T. (1978). *How a Child Thinks*. New York: Plume.

State v. Hunt, 741 P. 2d 655 (Wash. App. 1987).

State v. James, 211 Conn. 555, 560 A. 2d 424 (1989).

State v. Superior Court Pima County, 719 P. 2d 283 (Ariz. App. 1986).

State v. Weisenstein, 367 N.W. 2d 201 (S.D. 1985).

United States v. Wade, 388 U.S. (1966).

Wade v. State, 586 So.2d 1200 (Fla. Dist. Ct. App. 1991).

Waletz v. Dept. of Human Services, 768 S.W. 2d 41 (Ark. App. 1989).

Wheeler v. United States (1895) 159 U.S. 523, 524-26.

White, S., Santilli, G., and Quinn, K. (1988). Child evaluators' role in child sexual abuse assessments. In E. B. Nicholson and J. Bulkley (Eds.), *Sexual Abuse Allegations in Custody and Visitation Cases*. Washington, DC: American Bar Association.

Zaragoza, M. (1987). Memory, suggestibility and eyewitness testimony in children and adults. In C. J. Ceci, R. F. Ross, and M. P. Toglia (Eds.), *Children's Eyewitness Testimony*. New York: Springer-Verlag.

Chapter 11: Confrontation: The Rights of the Accused versus Protection of the Victim

Brady v. Indiana, 540 N.E. 2d 59 (Ind. App. 1989).

California Penal Code. (1991). St. Paul, MN: West.

Commonwealth v. Willis, 716 S.W. 2d 224 (KY, 1986).

Commonwealth v. Ludwig, ·Sup. Ct. PA, No. 02883 (PA, 1987).

Coy v. Iowa, 487 U.S. 1012, 101 L.Ed. 2d 857, 108 S. Ct. 2798 (1988).

Craig v. Maryland, 560 A.2d 1120 (1989), aff'd No. 110 (MD. Ct. App. 4/8/91).

Edwards, L. P. (1987). The relationship of family and juvenile courts in child abuse cases. *Santa Clara Law Review, 27*(2), 201-278.

Hardy v. Commonwealth, 719 S.W. 2d 727 (KY, 1986).

Herbert v. Superior Court, 117 Cal. App. 3d 661 (1981).

Hochheiser v. Superior Court, 161 Cal. App. 3d 777 (1984).

In re Mary S., 186 Cal. App. 3d 414 (1986).

In re Michael C., 557 A. 2d 1219 (R.I., 1989).

In re Stanley F., 86 Cal. App. 3 568 (1978).

In re Tanya P. 120 Cal. App. 3d 66 (1981).

In the Interest of J.D.S., A Child, v. Iowa, 436 N.W. 2d 342 (IA, 1989).

Johnson, 240 Kan. 326, 326-27, 729 P. 2d 1169, 1170-71 (1986).

Kansas Statutes Ann. (Supp. 1986) Paragraphs 22-3433, 22-3434.

Kentucky v. Stincer, 107 S.Ct. 2658 (1987).

Maryland v. Craig, 497 U.S., 111 L. Ed. 2d 666, 110 S. Ct. 3157 (1990).

McCarthy, P. J. (1992). *Educating the criminal court on the needs of the child witness*. The Guardian, *12*(1), 1, 15.

McGuire v. State, 706 S.W. 2d 360, 362 (AR, 1986).

Pennsylvania v. Ludwig, slip op., J-100-1989 (PA, 1991, May 10).

People v. Henderson, 156 A.D.2d 92 554 N.Y.S. 924 (1990).

People v. Serna, 214 Cal. App. 3d 299 (1989).

Sagatun, I. J., and Edwards, L. P. (1989). The child as witness in criminal courts. *Police Chief, 26*(4), 123-127.

Seering v. Department of Social Services, 194 CA3d 298, 303, 239 CR 422 (1987).

State v. Bonello, 554 A. 2d 277 (CT, 1989).

State v. Chrisholm, 777 P.2d 753 (KS, 1989).

State v. John C., 503 A. 2d 1296 (ME, 1986).

State v McCutcheon, 234 N.J. Super. 434, 560 A.2d 1303 (1988).

State v. Pilkey, 776 S.W. 2d 943 (TN, 1989).

State v. Strable, 313 N.W. 2d 497 (IA, 1981).

State v. Tarantino, 157 Wis. 2d 199; 458 N.W. 2d 582 (1990).

Supreme Court News. (1991). *ABA Juvenile and Child Welfare Law Reporter, 10*(4), 63-64.

Texas Code of Criminal Procedures. (1987). Ann. Art. 38.071, paragraph 2. Vernon Supp.

Victims of Child Abuse Act of 1990. (1990). Title II, 42 USC, 13001.

Victims Protections and Rights. (1990). Subchapter IV of the Victims of Child Abuse Act of 1990, 42 USC, 13031.

Whitcomb, D. (1992). *When the Victim Is a Child* (2nd ed.). Washington, DC: U.S. Dept. of Justice, Office of Justice Programs, National Institute of Justice.

Whitcomb, D., Shapiro, E. R., and Stellwagen, L. D. (1985). *When the Victim Is a Child*. Washington, D.C.: Office of Justice Programs, National Institute of Justice.

Chapter 12: Hearsay Evidence and the Child Witness

California Civil Code. (1993). St. Paul, MN: West.
California Evidence Code. (1993). St. Paul, MN: West.
California Penal Code. (1993). St. Paul, MN: West.
Commonwealth v. Adams, 503 N.E. 2d 1315 (Mass. 1987).
Commonwealth v. McDonough, 511 N.E. 2d 551 (Mass. 1987).
Dziech, B. W., and Schudson, C. B. (1989). *On Trial: America's Courts and Their Treatment of Sexually Abused Children*. Boston, MA: Beacon Press.
Eatman, L., and Bulkley, J. (1987). *Protecting Child Victim/ Witnesses*. Washington, DC: American Bar Association, National Legal Resource Center for Child Advocacy and Protection.
Federal Rules of Evidence. (1991). St. Paul, MN: West.
Graham, M. H. (1988). The confrontation clause, the hearsay rule and child sexual abuse prosecutions: The state of the relationship. *Minnesota Law Review, 72,* 523-601.
Hord v. Morgan, 769 S.W. 2d 443 (Mo. App. 1989).
Idaho v. Wright, (1990) 497 U.S.—, 111 L. Ed. 2d 648, 110 S. Ct. 3139.
In re Freiburger, 395 N.W. 2d 300 (Mich. App. 1986).
In re Interest of R.A., 403 N.W. 2d 357 (Neb. 1987).
In re Jean Marie W., 559 A. 2d 625 (R.I. 1989).
In re Kailee B., 93 C. D. O. S. 6658 (1993).
In re Malinda S., 51 C3d 368, 272 CR 787 (1990).
In re Marriage of Russo, 21 Cal. App. 3d 72, 98 Cal. Rptr. 501 (1971).
In the Matter of the Dependency of S.S., 61 Wash. App. 488 (Wash. Ct. App. 1991).
In the Matter of W.D., 709 P.2d 1037 (Oklahoma 1985).
Johnson v. State, 732, S.W. 2d 817 (Ark. 1987).
Lorenza v. State, 434 N.W. 2d 923 (Iowa App. 1988).
Matter of Helms, 335 S.E. 2d 917 (NC App. 1985).
Ohio v. Roberts, 100 S. Ct. 2531 (1980).
People v. Deavers, 580 N.E.2d 1367 (Ill.App.Ct.1991).
People v. Liddicoat (1981) 120 CA3d 512, 515, 174 CR 649.
People v. Turner (1990) 219 CA3d 1207, 1213, 268 CR 686.
Perez v. Florida, 536 S.O. 2d 206 (Fla. 1988).
R.S. v. Knighton, 592 A.2d 1157 (N.J. 1991).
Smith v. State, 405 S.E.2d 78 (GA.Ct.App.1991).
Souder v. Commonwealth, 719 S.W. 2d 730 (KY 1986).
State v. Bauer, 704 P. 2d 247 (Wash.App.1986).
State v. Campbell, 705 P. 2d 694 (Oregon, 1985).
State v. Gallagher, Vt. Sup. Ct., No. 86-174 (1988).
State v. Griffith, 727 P. 2d 247 (Wash. App. 1986).
State v. Hanson, 382 N.W. 2d 872 (Minn. App. 1986).

State v. Larson, 472 N.W. 2d 120 (Minn. 1991).
State v. McCafferty, 356 N.W. 2d 159 (S.D. 1984).
State v. Myatt, 237 Kan. 17, 22, 697 P. 2d 836, 841 (1985).
State v. Nelson, 406 N.W. 2d 385 (Wisc. 1987).
State v. Robinson, 735 P. 2d 801, 814 (Ariz. 1987).
State v. Roman, 590 A. 2d 686 (N.J. Super, Ct. App. Div. 1991).
State v. Ryan, 103 Wash. 2d 165, 691 P.2d 197 (1984).
State v. Wright, 751 S.W. 2d 48 (MO 1988).
Summit, R. (1983). The child sexual abuse accommodation syndrome. *Child Abuse and Neglect, 7,* 177-193.
U.S. v. Inadi, 475 U.S. 387, 392-400 (1986).
U.S. v. Renville, 779 F. 3d 430 (8th Cir. 1985).
U.S. v. St. John, 851 F. 2d 1096 (8th Cir. 1988).
Weinstein, J., and Berger, M. (1986). *Weinstein's Evidence: State Adaptations of the Federal Rules of Evidence*. Vol. 5. New York: Matthew Bender.
Whitcomb, D. (1992). *When the Victim Is a Child* (2nd ed). Washington, DC: U.S. Dept. of Justice, Office of Justice Programs, National Institute of Justice.
White v. Illinois, 112 S.Ct.Rpt. 736 (1992).

Chapter 13: Expert Witnesses in Child Abuse Cases

Aman, C., and Goodman, G. S. (1987). Children's use of anatomically detailed dolls: An experimental study. Paper presented at the National Center on Child Abuse and Neglect, Symposium on Interviewing Children, Washington, DC.
Berliner, L. (1988). Deciding whether a child has been sexually abused. In E. B. Nicholson (Ed.), *Sexual Abuse Allegations in Custody and Visitation Cases*. Washington, DC: American Bar Association.
Bulkley, J. (1988). Legal proceedings, reforms and emerging issues in child sexual abuse cases. *Behavioral Sciences and the Law, 6(2),* 153-180.
California Welfare and Institutions Code. (1991). St. Paul, MN: West.
Daubert v. Merrell Dow Pharmaceuticals, Inc. 113 S. Ct. 2786; 125 L. Ed. 2d 469 (1993).
DeJong, A. R. (1989). Principles and pitfalls in forensic evidence data collection. *The Advisor, 2(4),* 8-9.
DeJong, A. R., and Rose, S. (1988). The frequency and significance of physical evidence in legally proven cases of child sexual abuse. *American Journal of Diseases in Children, 142,* 406.
Federal Rules of Evidence. (1990). St. Paul, MN: West.
Frye v. United States, 293 F. 1013, 54 App. D.C. 46 (1923).
Hensley, K. L. (1986). The admissibility of "child sexual abuse accommodation syndrome" in California criminal courts. *Pacific Law Journal, 17,* 1361-1391.
In re Amber B., 191 CA App.3d 682, 236 CP Rptr. 623 (1987).

In re Cheryl H., 153 CA App.3d 1098, 200 CA Rptr. 789 (1984).

In re Troy Z., 3 Cal.4th 1770 (1992).

Jampole, L., and Weber, M. K. (1987). An assessment of the behavior of sexually abused and nonsexually abused children with anatomically correct dolls. *Child Abuse and Neglect*, 11(2), 187-192.

Johnson v. State, 292 AK 632, 732 S.W.2d 817 (1987).

Keri v. State, 179 GA App. 664, 347 S.E.2d 236 (1986).

Kempe, C. H., Silverman, F. N., Steele, B. F., Droegemueller, W., and Silver, H. K. (1962). The battered child syndrome. *Journal of the American Medical Association*, 181, 17-24.

Lantrip v. Commonwealth, 713 S.W.2d 816 (KY, 1986).

Levy, R. (1989). Using "scientific" testimony to prove child sexual abuse. *Family Law Quarterly* 23(3), 383-411.

Myers, J., Bays, J., Becker, J., Berliner, L., Corwin, D., and Saywitz, K. (1989). Expert testimony in child sexual abuse litigation. *Nebraska Law Review*, 68(1), 1-145.

People v. Beckley, 434 MI 691, 456 N.W. 2d 391 (1990).

People v. Bledsoe, 36 CA 3d 236, 203 CA Rptr. 450, 681 P.2d 291 (1984).

People v. Bowker, 203 CA App. 3d 385, 249 CA Rptr. 886 (1988).

People v. Gray, 187 CA App. 3d, 231 CA Rptr. 658 (1986).

People v. Jackson, 18 CA App. 3d 504, 95 CA Rptr. 919 (1971).

People v. Kelly, 17 CA 3d 24, 130 CA Rptr. 144, 549 P.2d 1240 (1976).

People v. Lucero, 724 P. 2d 1374 (CO App., 1986).

People v. Luna, 204 CA App.3d 776, 250 CA Rptr. 878 (1988).

People v. Mandibles, 199 CA3d 1277 (1988).

People v. Nelson,—IL App. 3d,—, 561 N.E. 2d 439 (1990).

People v. Newlun, 227 Cal.App.3d 1590 (1991).

People v. Payan, 173 CA App. 3d 27, 220 CA Rptr. 126 (1985).

People v. Roscoe, 168 CA App. 3d 1093, 215 CA Rptr. 45 (1985).

State v. Batangan, 71 Haw. 552, 799 P.2d 48 (1990).

State v. Haseltine, 120 WI 2d 92, 352 N.W.2d 673 (1984).

State v. Jurgens, 424 N.W.2d 546 (MN App., 1988).

State v. Mazerole, 614 a.2d 69, Maine (1992).

State v. McClary, 207 CT 233, 541 A.2d 96 (1988).

State v. Phillips, 399 S.E. 2d 293 (NC, 1991).

State v. Tanner, 675 P.2d 539 (UT, 1983).

Summit, R. (1983). The child sexual abuse accommodation syndrome. *Child Abuse and Neglect*, 7, 177-193.

White S., and Santilli, G. (1988). A review of clinical research data on anatomically correct dolls. *Journal of Interpersonal Violence*, 3, 430-432.

White, S., Strom, G. A., Santilli, G., and Halpin, B. M. (1987). Interviewing sexual abuse victims with anatomically correct dolls. *Child Abuse and Neglect*, 10, 519-529.

Chapter 14: "Fetal Abuse": The Case of Drug-Exposed Infants

Adoption Assistance and Child Welfare Act. (1980). Public Law 96-272. 42 U.S.C. paragraph 420 *et seq.*, 670 *et seq.*, as amended by the Omnibus Budget Reconciliation Act of 1987, Public Law 96-271.

American College of Obstetricians and Gynecologists. (1987). Patient choice: Maternal-fetal conflict. *Committee on Ethics Opinion*, 55 (Oct.).

Balisy, S. (1987). Maternal substance abuse: The need to provide legal protection for the fetus. *Southern California Law Review*, 60, 1209-1238.

Bean, Z. (1990). Infant drug addiction. Paper presented at the annual meeting of the National Council of Juvenile and Family Court Judges, San Jose, CA, July.

Besharov, D. (1989). The children of crack: Will we protect them? *Public Welfare*, 47, (Fall), 6-11.

California Health and Safety Code. (1991). St. Paul, MN: West.

California Penal Code. (1991). St. Paul, MN: West.

California Welfare and Institutions Code. (1991). St. Paul, MN: West.

Chasnoff, I. J. (1991). President's message. *Perinatal Addiction Research and Education Update.* Chicago, IL: National Association for Perinatal Addiction Research and Education.

Chasnoff, I. J. (Ed.). (1989). *Drugs, Alcohol, Pregnancy and Parenting.* Boston, MA: Kluwer.

Chasnoff, I. J., Landress, H. J., and Barrett, M. E. (1990). The prevalence of illicit drugs or alcohol during pregnancy and discrepancies in mandatory reporting in Pinellas County, Florida. *New England Journal of Medicine*, 322 (17), 1202-1206.

Chavkin, W. (1990). Drug addiction and pregnancy: Policy crossroads. *Public Health and the Law*, 80(4).

Dixon, S. (1989). Effects of transplantal exposure to cocaine and methamphetamine on the neonate. *Western Journal of Medicine*, 150, 436-442.

English, A. (1990). Prenatal drug exposure: Grounds for mandatory child abuse reports? *Youth Law News*, 11(1), 3-8.

English, A., and Henry, M. (1990). Legal issues affecting drug-exposed infants. *Youth Law News*, 11(1), 1-2.

Faller, K. C., and Ziefert, M. (1981). Causes of child abuse and neglect. *Social Work with Abused and Neglected Children*, 32, 43-44.

Finnegan, A., Connaughton, A., Emich, B., and Wieland, T. (1992). Comprehensive care of the pregnant addict and its effects on maternal and infant outcome. *Contemporary Drug Problems*, 1, 795-895.

Florida v. Johnson, No. E-89-900-CFA (Fla. Cit. Ct. 1989).

Florida v. Johnson, 578 So, 2d 419 (Fla. App. 5 Dist. 1991).

Gelles, K. (1993). Opinion: The doctrine of family reunification: Child protection or risk? *The Advisor* (American Society on the Abuse of Children), 6(2), 9-11.

Gomby, D., and Shiono, P. (1991). Estimating the number of substance-exposed infants. *Future of Children*, 1(1), 17-26.

Griffith, D. (1991) Strengthening the mother-infant relationship: Lessening the impact of prenatal substance abuse. Presentation at the National Training Forum on Drugs, Alcohol, Pregnancy and Parenting, National Association for Perinatal Addiction Research and Education, Chicago, IL, Dec.

Grodin v. Grodin, 102 MI App. 369, 301 N.W. 2d 869 (1981).

Howard, J., Kropenske, V., and Tyler, R. (1986). The long-term effects on neuro-development in infants exposed prenatally to PCP. *National Institute of Drug Abuse Monograph Series*, 64, 237-251.

In re Baby X., 97 MI App. 111, 293 N.W. 2d 736 (1980).

In re Steven S., 126 CA 3d 23 (1981).

In re Troy D., 215 CA App. 3d 889, 263 CA Rptr. 868 (1989).

In the Matter of "Male" R, 422 N.Y.S. 2d 819 (Kings Cty. Fam. Ct. 1979).

Jefferson v. Spalding County Hospital Authority, 247 Ga. 86, 274 S.E. 2d 457 (1981).

Johnson, D. (1987). A new threat to pregnant women's automony. *Hastings Center Report*. San Francisco, CA: Hastings Center.

Johnson v. Florida, 1992 W.L. 171213 (Fla.).

Lacayo, R. (1989). Nobody's Children. *Time*, Oct., 91-92.

Larson, C. (1991). Overview of state legislative and judicial responses. *The Future of Children*, 1(1), 73-83.

Marshall, A. B. (1991). State-by-state legislative review. *Perinatal Addiction Research and Education Update, September, 1991*. Chicago, IL: National Assn. for Perinatal Addiction Research and Education.

Massachusetts v. Pellegrini, No. 87970 (MA Sup. Ct., Aug. 21, 1989).

McCullough, C. (1991). The child welfare response. *The Future of Children*, 1(1), 61-72.

McNulty, M. (1987-1988). Pregnancy police: The health policy and legal implications of punishing pregnant women for harm to their fetuses. *Review of Law and Social Change*, 16(2), 277-319.

Michigan v. Bremer, No. 90-32227-FH (MI Cir. Ct., Muskegon County, Jan. 31, 1991).

Minnesota Statutes Annotated. (1990). West Supplement. St. Paul, MN: West.

National Council of Juvenile and Family Court Judges. (1991). *Protocol for Making Reasonable Efforts in Drug-Related Dependency Cases*. Reno, NV: NCJFCJ.

Office of Inspector General, Office of Evaluations and Inspections. (1990). *Crack Babies*. Washington, D.C.: U.S. Dept. of Health and Human Services.

Ostrea, E. M., Chavez, C. J., and Strauss M. E., (1976). A study of factors that influence the severity of neonatal narcotic withdrawal. *Journal of Pediatrics*, 88, 642-645.

Paltrow, L. (1989). Fetal abuse. *American Bar Association Journal*, Aug., 38-39.

Paltrow, L. (1990). When becoming pregnant is a crime. *Criminal Justice Ethics*, 9(1) 41-47.

People v. Morabeto, 580 N.Y.S.2d 843 (N.Y. Cty. Ct. 1992).

People v. Stewart, no. M508097, slip. opin. (San Diego County Ct. Feb. 23, 1987).

Petitti, D., and Coleman, M. (1990). Cocaine and the risk of low birth weight. *American Journal of Public Health*, 80(1), 25-28.

Raleigh Fitkin-Paul Morgan Memorial Hospital v. Anderson, 42 N.J. 421, 201 A.2d (1964).

Reyes v. Superior Court, 75 CA 3d 214 (1977).

Robertson, J. (1989). Fetal Abuse. *American Bar Association Journal*, Aug. 38-39.

Robin-Vergeer, R. (1990). The problem of the drug-exposed newborn: A return to principled intervention. *Stanford Law Review*, 42(3), 745-809.

Sagatun-Edwards, I. J., and Saylor, I. C. (1993). Early intervention with high risk infants: Final research report. Sacramento, CA: Office of Criminal Justice Planning.

Select Committee on Children, Youth and Families, U.S. House of Representatives. (1989). No place to call home: Discarded children in America. Washington, D.C.: U.S. Government Printing Office.

Select Committee on Perinatal Alcohol and Drug Use. (1991). *Perinatal Alcohol and Drug Use: Strategies for Prevention, Intervention and Treatment*. Sacramento: State of California Dept. of Alcohol and Drug Programs.

Shaver, D. (1989). Prosecute the mothers of addiction. *California Lawyer*, Nov., 72-73.

Stallman v. Youngquist, 129 IL App. 3d 859, 473 N.E. 2d 400 (1984).

Stallman v. Youngquist, 531 N.E. 2d 355 (1988).

Suffet, F., and R. A. Brotman. (1984). A comprehensive care program for pregnant addicts: Obstetrical, neonatal and child development outcomes. *Journal of Addiction*, 19(2).

Weston, D. R., Ivens, B., Zuckerman, B., Jones, C., and Lopez, R. (1989). Drug-exposed babies: Research and clinical issues. *National Center for Clinical Infant Programs Bulletin*, 9(5), 7.

Zuspan, F. P., Gumpell, J. A., and Mejia-Zelaya, A. (1975). Fetal stress from methadone withdrawal. *American Journal of Obstetrics and Gynecology*, 122, 43.

Chapter 15: Other Developments in Child Abuse and the Legal System

Angel, C. (1993). Cases that nullify the law: Evidence of abuse becoming key to parricide trials. (When kids kill: A special report). *Los Angeles Daily Journal*, Oct. 18.

Bass, E., and Davis, L. (1988). *The Courage to Heal*. San Francisco, CA: Harper and Row.

Blodgett, A. (1987). Self-defense: Parricide defendants cite sexual abuse as justification. *American Bar Association Journal*, June, 36-46.

California Civil Procedure Code. (1991). St. Paul, MN: West.

Ceci, S., Crotteau, M. L., and Smith, E. (1994). Recalling nonevents: An experimental investigation of source attribution errors. *Consciousness and Cognition* (Special Issue), Jan.

Chambers, C. (1986). Children citing self-defense in murder of parents. *New York Times*, Oct. 12, p. 38.

Chiang, H. (1993). Conviction in rape-slaying let stand. *San Francisco Chronicle*, July 15.

Clevenger, N. (1991-92). Statute of limitations: Childhood victims of sexual abuse bringing civil actions against their perpetrators after attaining the age of majority. *Journal of Family Law*, 30, 447-469.

Crocker, P. L. (1985). The meaning of equality for battered women who kill men in self-defense. *Harvard Women's Law Journal*, 8, 121-132.

"False Memory Profiles." (1993). *Sunday Oregonian*, Aug. 8, p. L6.

False Memory Syndrome Foundation. (1992). *Update*, 5(2). National Center for Prosecution of Child Abuse. Washington, D.C.

Freyd, J. (1994). Betrayal-trauma theory: A cognitive science approach to dissociation and traumatic amnesia. *Consciousness and Cognition* (Special issue), Jan.

Freyd, J. (1993). Theoretical and personal perspectives on the delayed memory debate. Paper presented at the Continuing Education Conference: Controversies around recovered memories of incest and ritualistic abuse, Ann Arbor, MI, Aug. 7.

Gardner, R. (1993). Child abuse cases should not have extended statutes of limitations. In *How Should the Legal System Respond to Child Abuse?* San Diego, CA.: Greenhaven Press.

Gordon, M., and Alexander, P. (1993). Special issue: Research on treatment of adults sexually abused in childhood. *Journal of Interpersonal Violence*, 8(3), 307-429.

Harvey, M., and Herman, J. L. (1994). Amnesia, partial amnesia, and delayed recall among adult survivors of childhood trauma. *Consciousness and Cognition* (Special issue), Jan.

Illinois Annotated Statutes, ch. 110, para. 13-202.2, 1991.

Johnson v. Johnson, 701 F. Supp. 1363, 1367 (N.D. Ill. 1988).

Johnson v. Johnson, 766 F. Supp. 662 (N.D. Ill. 1991).

Layton, J. (1993). When the abused child fatally says "No More!" Can Parricide be self-defense in Ohio? *University of Dayton Law Review*, 18(2), 447-474.

Lofthus, E. (1994). The suggestibility of memory for childhood trauma. *Consciousness and Cognition* (Special Issue). Jan.

Mary D. v. John D., 216 Cal. App. 3d 285, 264 Cal. Rptr. 633 (1989).

Mitchell, J. (1993). Memories of a disputed past. *Sunday Oregonian*, Aug. 8, p. L1.

Mones, P. (1985). The relationship between child abuse and parricide: An overview. In E. Neuberger and R. Borne (Eds.), *Unhappy Families: Clinical and Research Perspectives on Family Violence*. Littletown, MA: PSG.

Mones, P. (1991). *When a Child Kills: Abused Children Who Kill Their Parents*. New York: Pocket Books.

Moreno, J. A. (1989). Killing daddy: Developing a self-defense strategy for the abused child. *University of Pennsylvania Law Review*, 137, 1281-1307.

People v. Franklin, Superior Court of San Mateo, 1992.

Pezdek, K., and Banks, W. (1994). The recovery of lost childhood memories for traumatic events. *Consciousness and Cognition* (Special issue), Jan.

Rodgers, K. E. (1993). Child abuse cases should have extended statutes of limitations. In *How Should the Legal System Respond to Child Abuse?* San Diego, CA.: Greenhaven Press.

Schneider, E. (1986). Describing and changing: Women's self-defense work and the problem of expert testimony on battering. *Women's Rights Law Reporter*, 195, 202.

Scobey, J. N. (1992). Self-defense parricide: Expert testimony on battered child syndrome. *Hamline Journal of Public Law and Policy*, 13, 181-198.

State v. Holden (Ohio Ct. App. Sept. 26, 1985).

State of Washington v. Janes, 822 P. 2d 1234, 64 Wash. App. 134 (1992).

Wakefield, H., and Underwager, R. (1993). *Accusations of Child Sexual Abuse*. Springfield, IL: Charles C. Thomas.

Walker, L. (1979). *The Battered Woman*. New York: Harper and Row.

Williams, L. M. (1994). Recovered memories of abuse in women with documented child sexual victimization histories. *Consciousness and Cognition* (Special issue), Jan.

Wilson, M. and Daly, M. (1993). Let's get serious about victim-killer relationships in homicide research. Paper presented at the American Society of Criminology annual meeting, Phoenix, AZ, Oct. 29.

Wright, L. (1993a). Remembering Satan: Part I. *New Yorker*, May 17, pp. 60-81.

Wright, L. (1993b). Remembering Satan: Part II. *New Yorker*, May 24, pp. 54-76.

Appendix

Harmon, R. (1989). *How to Find the Law: Introductory Syllabus*. San Jose, CA: San Jose State University, Clark Library.

American Psychological Association. (1990). *Publication Manual*. (3rd ed.). Washington, DC: APA.

Stein, T. (1991). *Child Welfare and the Law*. New York: Longman.

INDEX OF CASES

Note: Cases with asterisks (*) are discussed in some depth in the text.

INDEX

About the Authors

Inger J. Sagatun is the chair of the Administration of Justice Department at San Jose State University, San Jose, California. She received her Ph.D. from Stanford University in sociology and taught at the University of Bergen, Norway, and the University of California, Riverside, before coming to San Jose State University. She is serving a second four-year term as executive counselor of the Western Society of Criminology. Her main areas of interest include child abuse, family violence and juvenile delinquency, and she has written many journal articles on these subjects. She is the principal investigator on a longitudinal study of the treatment of drug-exposed infants in the social welfare and dependency system, which is funded by the California Office of Criminal Justice Planning (OCJP). She is currently a co-investigator with the American Bar Association's center on Children and the Law on a three-year study of risk factors associated with parental and family child abductions, funded by the Office of Juvenile Justice and Delinquency Prevention, Washington, D.C.

Leonard P. Edwards is a judge of the Santa Clara County Superior Court. In that capacity he has served as supervising judge of the Family Court and presiding judge of the Superior Court. He is now serving his eighth year as presiding judge of the Juvenile Court. Judge Edwards has been active locally and nationally in juvenile and family law. He is chair of the Juvenile Court Judges of California and a member of the Board of Trustees of the National Council of Juvenile and Family Court Judges. He has taught juvenile and family law at the University of Santa Clara Law School, Stanford Law School, and the California Judicial College. Judge Edwards has also written widely in both juvenile and family law. Judge Edwards served in the U. S. Peace Corps in Malaysia as a teacher and was a civil rights worker in Mississippi during the 1960s. He has been given many awards both locally and nationally. He recently was named Juvenile Court Judge of the Year by the national Court Appointed Special Advocates (CASA) Association.